ADVANCES IN PORTFOLIO CONSTRUCTION AND IMPLEMENTATION

Butterworth-Heinemann Finance

aims and objectives

- books based on the work of financial market practitioners, and academics
- presenting cutting edge research to the professional/practitioner market
- combining intellectual rigour and practical application
- covering the interaction between mathematical theory and financial practice
- to improve portfolio performance, risk management and trading book performance
- covering quantitative techniques

market

Brokers/Traders; Actuaries; Consultants; Asset Managers; Fund Managers; Regulators; Central Bankers; Treasury Officials; Technical Analysts; and Academics for Masters in Finance and MBA market.

series titles

Return Distributions in Finance
Derivative Instruments: theory, valuation, analysis
Managing Downside Risk in Financial Markets: theory, practice & implementation
Economics for Financial Markets
Performance Measurement in Finance: firms, funds and managers
Real R&D Options
Forecasting Volatility in the Financial Markets
Advanced Trading Rules
Advances in Portfolio Construction and Implementation

series editor

Dr Stephen Satchell

Dr Satchell is the Reader in Financial Econometrics at Trinity College, Cambridge; Visiting Professor at Birkbeck College, City University Business School and University of Technology, Sydney. He also works in a consultative capacity to many firms, and edits the journal *Derivatives: use, trading and regulations* and the *Journal of Asset Management*.

ADVANCES IN PORTFOLIO CONSTRUCTION AND IMPLEMENTATION

Edited by

Stephen Satchell

Alan Scowcroft

AMSTERDAM BOSTON HEIDELBERG LONDON NEW YORK OXFORD
PARIS SAN DIEGO SAN FRANCISCO SINGAPORE SYDNEY TOKYO

Butterworth-Heinemann
An imprint of Elsevier
Linacre House, Jordan Hill, Oxford OX2 8DP
200 Wheeler Road, Burlington MA 01803

First published 2003

British Library Cataloguing in Publication Data

Advances in portfolio construction and implementation
   1.   Portfolio management   2.   Risk management
   I.   Satchell, Stephen E.   II.   Scowcroft, A.
   332.6

ISBN 0 7506 5448 1

Library of Congress Cataloguing in Publication Data

A catalogue record for this book is available from the Library of Congress

ISBN 0 7506 5448 1

For information on all Butterworth-Heinemann finance publications
visit our website at www.bh.com/finance

Typeset by Laserwords Private Limited, Chennai, India
Printed and bound in Great Britain by Biddles Ltd. www.biddles.co.uk

Contents

Contributors

Emmanuel Acar is a Principal and Manager of Risk Management Advisory, London, at the Bank of America. He has previously worked at Citibank as a Vice-President in the FX Engineering Group. He was a proprietary trader for almost 10 years at Dresdner Kleinwort Benson, BNZ, and the London branch of Banque Nationale de Paris. He has experience in quantitative strategies, as an actuary, and having completed his PhD on the stochastic properties of trading rules.

Chris J Adcock is Professor of Financial Econometrics at the University of Sheffield, one of the UK's leading universities. Previously he was Reader in Finance and Financial Economics at the University of Bath. Before becoming an academic, he worked in quantitative portfolio management in the City in London, and, earlier in his career, in management science consultancy. His research interests are in the successful development and application of quantitative techniques to problems in portfolio management. He has acted as a consultant to several quantitative asset management firms. He is the founding editor of the *European Journal of Finance* and an associate editor of several other finance journals. He may be contacted at Dept of Economics, University of Sheffield, Mappin Street, Sheffield S1 4DT, UK; tel: +44 (0)114 222 3402; email c.j.adcock@shef.ac.uk

Gustavo M de Athayde is Senior Quantitative Manager at Banco Itaú. He has a PhD I Economics from the Escola de Pós-Gradução em Economia, Fundação Getúlio Vargas, Rio de Janeiro. He has a practical knowledge of the Brazilian financial markets and his present research interests include portfolio design in static and dynamic settings, the econometrics of risk management models, exotic derivatives, and derivatives pricing with non-normal distributions. He may be contacted at Banco Itaú SA, Rua Boa Vista, 9 andar, corpo 3, São Paulo, 01014-919 SP, Brazil; email: gustavo.athayde@itau.com.br

Sid Browne is currently Professor of Risk Management at the Graduate School of Business at Columbia University, where he received tenure in 1996, and a Senior Risk Consultant to Goldman Sachs. From June 1998 to January 2002, he was Head of the Quantitative Modelling Group in the Firmwide Risk Management department at Goldman Sachs. While there, he was directly responsible for all issues related to risk methodology, portfolio analytics and risk-based performance measurement for all trading portfolios, and is the co-inventor on two patents on risk methodologies held by Goldman Sachs. He has published widely in premier academic and practitioner journals on quantitative approaches to portfolio theory, asset allocation and mathematical figures. He may be contacted at: Graduate School of Business, Columbia University, 402 Uris Hall, New York, NY 10027, USA; email: sb30@columbia.edu

Dr Julian Coutts obtained a first-class Honours degree in Physics in 1983, and a Doctorate in Laser Physics in 1986, both from Oxford University. He also obtained an MBA from Warwick University. He has 16 years' post-doctoral experience in mathematical modelling, including research in the USA (at the Joint Institute for Laboratory Astrophysics, Boulder, Colorado). He has worked in the oil industry for BP, and as a quantitative analyst and fund manager at Morgan Grenfell Asset Management. He was appointed Investment Risk Director at Standard Life Investments in 1997.

Richard Dawson was born in 1969 and graduated from the University of Sheffield with an Honours degree in Physics in 1990. After postgraduate research in optoelectronics, he began a career as a software engineer. He has worked on a variety of military projects, including naval command software and novel radar systems. Recently he has worked in the City in London, primarily on Quantec's portfolio risk analysis software, before developing the core algorithms for their Policy Guidelines Simulator.

Dan diBartolomeo is President and founder of Northfield Information Services, Inc. He is an active member of the Financial Management Association, the Chicago Quantitative Alliance, QWAFAFEW, the Society of Quantitative Analysts, the Southern Finance Association, and is a former member of the Board of Directors of the Boston Computer Society. He teaches a continuing education course sponsored by the Boston Security Analysts' Society entitled 'Advanced Quantitative Techniques'. He has been published in the *Journal of Investing*, the *Journal of Performance Measurement*, and the *Financial Analysts*

Journal. Other writings include chapters in *The Handbook of Municipal Bonds*, and AIMR's *Equity Specialization Program Readings.*

Renato G Flores Jr is Professor and Research Director at the Escola de Pós-Gradução em Economia, Fundação Getúlio Vargas, Rio de Janeiro. His fields of interest are dynamic econometrics and international finance and trade, on which he publishes regularly.

Alla Gil is a Managing Director and the Head of the Strategic Risk Analytics and Modelling Group in Citigroup's Capital Markets division. In this role she is responsible for the development of the new methodology for advising the senior management of major Citigroup clients on currency and interest rate risk management and optimization, asset/liability management policies, evaluation of credit risk in clients' portfolios, and credit portfolio optimization. Prior to Citigroup, she spent three years at Goldman Sachs doing interest rate derivatives modelling and two years at CIBC developing credit derivatives models.

Grant Hillier is Professor of Econometrics at the University of Southampton. He has published extensively in top econometrics journals and is acknowledged as one of the world leaders in finite sample econometrics.

Soosung Hwang is a Senior Lecturer in Finance in the Faculty of Finance and the Deputy Director of the Financial Econometrics Research Centre, Cass Business School, London. He is also an Honorary Research Associate of the Department of Applied Economics, Cambridge University. He received his PhD from Cambridge University, and his research interests include finance, financial econometrics and forecasting.

Professor Gautam Mitra is an internationally renowned research scientist in the field of operational research in general and computational optimization and modelling in particular. He has developed a world-class research group in his area of specialization, with researchers from Europe, the UK and the USA. He has published three books and over 80 refereed research articles. He was Head of the Department of Mathematical Science at Brunel University between August 1990 and July 2001 and is currently director of the Centre for the Analysis of Risk and Optimization Modelling Applications: CARISMA. Professor Mitra is also a Director of UNICOM Seminars and UNICOM Consultants (trading as OptiRisk Systems Ltd). Many of the research results are exploited through these companies. (Contact: +44 1895 203304, gautam.mitra@brunel.ac.uk http://www.carisma.brunel.ac.uk)

Yuri Polyakov is a senior member of the Strategic Risk Advisory Group in Citigroup's Capital Markets division. In this role he is responsible for implementation and delivery of new methodologies for assessing and mitigating interest rate, currency and credit risks; addressing the issues of capital determination and risk budgeting. Prior to Citigroup, he spent four years at CIBC's Financial Products division managing the derivatives analytics group. His background is in applied mathematics and computer science.

Professor Stephen Satchell is an academic advisor to many financial institutions; a fellow of Trinity College, Cambridge; the Reader in Financial Econometrics at Cambridge University; and a visiting Professor at Birkbeck College and City University Business School in London. He is one of the most highly regarded academics within the UK investment industry. He specializes in econometrics and finance, and has published over 80 articles in refereed journals. He has PhDs from both Cambridge University and the LSE.

Alan Scowcroft was educated at Ruskin College, Oxford and Wolfson College, Cambridge, where he was awarded the Jennings Prize for academic achievement. He taught econometrics at Clare College, Cambridge before joining Phillips & Drew as an econometrician in 1984. There he worked with the leading macro research group at UBS and since that time he has worked on every aspect of quantitative modelling from stock selection to asset allocation. He has been closely associated with pioneering work on equity style and portfolio analysis developed by UBS Warburg. His research interests include practical applications of Bayesian econometrics and portfolio optimization. He is currently the global Head of the II top ranked equities quantitative research team at UBS Warburg. He may be contacted at: UBS Warburg, 1 Finsbury Avenue, London EC2M 2PP; tel: +44 20 7568 1871; e-mail: alan.scowcroft@ubsw.com

Professor James Sefton is a Director of UBS Warburg's Equities Quantitative Group, Professor of Economics at Imperial College's Management School and a Visiting Fellow at the National Institute of Economic and Social Research. His first book was a set of Reconciled National Accounts for the UK and more recently he constructed the first set of Generational Accounts for HM Treasury. He has published widely in academic journals in areas as diverse as mathematical analysis, control feedback theory, econometrics, economics and finance. He was educated at Christ's College, Cambridge from where he received a PhD in Systems Theory. He may be contacted at: UBS Warburg, 1 Finsbury Avenue, London EC2M 2PP; tel: +44 20 7568 1873; e-mail: james.sefton@ubsw.com

Michael Stutzer earned a PhD in Economics at the University of Minnesota, USA. He has worked for the Federal Reserve System and the University of Minnesota, and has served on the Board of Advisors to the Minnesota State Board of Investment, a US$40bn long term investment fund. He is currently Professor of Finance at the University of Iowa, USA. He has applied information-theoretic statistics to develop a unified approach to option pricing, asset pricing model parameter estimation and error diagnostics, and portfolio choice. His contribution to this volume is an extension of an earlier portfolio choice criterion he devised, which was the basis for Morningstar Inc's Global Star Ratings of mutual funds. He may be contacted at Dept of Finance, University of Iowa, Iowa City, IA 52242, USA: tel: 319 3351239; email: michael-stutzer@uiowa.edu

Dr Niklas Wagner is a lecturer in Finance at Munich University of Technology, Germany. He holds a PhD in finance from Augsburg University had visiting appointments at the Haas School of Business, U.C. Berkeley, and at Stanford GSB. He is a former faculty member of Dresden University of Technology's Business and Economics Department. His industry background is in portfolio management with HypoVereinsbank. He may be contacted at: Munich University of Technology, 80333 Munich, Germany; email niklas.wagner@wi.tum.de

Dr Tim Wilding is the Head of Research and Development at EM Applications, where he has specialized in factor modelling and optimization techniques. Dr Wilding has a PhD from the Department of Physics at Cambridge University. His work has been published in eminent journals. He is very experienced in modelling stochastic processes, model-fitting techniques, and handling large datasets. He has spent the last 10 years applying these skills working for investment risk analysis firms. He has designed and built models of equity returns and volatility for several different markets. At EM Applications, Dr Wilding has developed general-purpose estimation routines to fit any type of factor model to a large dataset while accounting for missing data. He has also developed proprietary extensions to factor models that allow them to be used with different asset classes. (EM Applications Ltd, 75 Cannon Street, London EC4N 5BN, UK. Tel: +44 (020) 7556 7102; email: tim.wilding@emapplications.com)

Dr Stephen M Wright is a quantitative analyst specializing in providing computer tools and advice to support the investment decision-taking process. He joined UBS in 1994 to develop an economic sector model of the UK equity market. More recently, he has developed a toolkit to assist CEOs and fund managers in allocating assets between different asset types, markets and sectors around the world. Prior to working in the financial services industry, Stephen worked at British Aerospace in future projects and flight control, working on mathematical modelling of all aspects of aircraft dynamic behaviour. This led to senior research and operations management roles in a career with BAe spanning nearly 20 years. Stephen has an Honours degree in Control Engineering from Leeds University and a PhD in Computer Vision from Cambridge University. He is a chartered electrical engineer. He may be contacted at: UBS Warburg, 1 Finsbury Avenue, London EC2M 2PP; tel: +44 20 7568 1874; e-mail: stephen-m.wright@ubsw.com

Richard Young graduated in Electrical Engineering with a Masters in Software Engineering, and has worked for the last six years in equities risk modelling and Monte Carlo simulation. He was the head of Research and Product Development at Quantec Ltd, a leading risk modelling software house in the City in London. He is currently a consultant to Thomson Financial Ltd in practical uses of Monte Carlo simulation and applications of quantitative methodologies. As Chairman of Metacraft Ltd, a venture software firm that specializes in creating solutions for non-software start-ups, he has a number of computer-modelling interests outside finance. He is also Chief Technology Officer for Alpha Strategies LLC, a quantitative consultancy group.

Introduction

This volume on portfolio optimization and construction originated from conversations between a number of the contributors and the editors. We were inspired to write by the common realization that a lot of exciting unrecognized new work is being done by both academics and practitioners.

Initial concerns that we would not find enough contributors to fill a volume changed rapidly to wondering whether this book, should be in one, two, or n volumes.

This selection of papers presents an excellent overview of a wide variety of new developments in portfolio construction methods. Everybody, but particularly newcomers to the field, can profitably read Chapter 1, an overview by Professor Gautam Mitra. The next eight chapters present practitioners approaches to portfolio issues. Topics covered include how to build portfolios robustly, how to simulate, how to account for tax issues, how to use sophisticated mathematical tools, how to include multiple asset classes, such as fixed income and hedge funds, and how to address index issues. The order in which they appear having no necessary relationship with intrinsic merit.

The academic contributions occur in Chapters 10 to 17; the theory covered here is demanding in places, covering advanced mathematical statistics and subtleties of optimization. The topics covered in this section address absolute and relative optimization, higher moment portfolio efficient frontiers, exact distributions, reverse optimization, robust optimization and some advances based on different choices of gain and loss. This volume comprehensively addresses a wide range of portfolio construction issues and it will be profitably added to both practitioner and academic book collections.

Chapter 1

A review of portfolio planning: models and systems

GAUTAM MITRA (CO-AUTHORS: TRIPHONAS KYRIAKIS, CORMAC LUCAS, MEHNDI PIRBHAI)

ABSTRACT

In this chapter, we first provide an overview of a number of portfolio planning models which have been proposed and investigated over the last fifty years. We revisit the mean-variance (MV) model of Markowitz and the construction of the risk-return efficient frontier. A piecewise linear approximation of the problem through a reformulation involving diagonalization of the quadratic form into a variable separable function is also considered. A few other models, such as, the Mean Absolute Deviation (MAD), the Weighted Goal Programming (WGP) and the Minimax (MM) model which use alternative metrics for risk are also introduced, compared and contrasted. Recently asymmetric measures of risk have gained in importance; we consider a generic representation and a number of alternative symmetric and asymmetric measures of risk which find use in the evaluation of portfolios. There are a number of modelling and computational considerations which have been introduced into practical portfolio planning problems. These include: (a) buy-in thresholds for assets, (b) restriction on the number of assets (cardinality constraints), (c) transaction roundlot restrictions. Practical portfolio models may also include: (d) dedication of cash-flow streams, and (e) immunization which involves duration matching and convexity constraints. The modelling issues in respect of these features are discussed. Many of these features lead to discrete restrictions involving zero-one and general integer variables which make the resulting model a quadratic mixed-integer programming model (QMIP). The QMIP is a NP-hard problem; the algorithms and solution methods for this class of problem are also discussed. The issues

Continued on page 2

__ *Continued from page 1* _____

of preparing the analytic data (financial datamarts) for this family of portfolio planning problems are examined. We finally present computational results which provide some indication of the state-of-the-art in the solution of portfolio optimization problems.

1.1 INTRODUCTION AND OVERVIEW

The mean-variance (MV) model of Markowitz is a single period static portfolio planning model and, in recent times, it has become the core decision engine of many portfolio analytics and planning systems in the construction of the risk-return efficient frontier.

Markowitz shows that for a rational investor maximizing expected utility, a chosen portfolio is optimal with respect to both expected return and variance of return. He defines such a non-dominated portfolio as *efficient*, that is, it offers the highest level of expected return for a given level of risk and the lowest level of risk for a given level of return. His normative MV rule for investor behaviour both implies and justifies the observable phenomenon of diversification in investment. Determining the efficient set from the investment opportunity set, the set of all possible portfolios, requires the formulation and solution of a parametric quadratic program (QP). Plotted in risk-return space the *efficient* set traces out the *efficient frontier*.

Hanoch and Levy (1969) show that the MV criterion is a valid efficiency criterion, for any individual's utility function, when the distributions considered are Gaussian normal. A study comparing alternative utility functions appears in Kallberg and Ziemba (1983). They show that portfolios with 'similar' absolute risk-aversion indices have 'similar' optimal compositions, regardless of the functional form and parameters of the utility function. Hence, MV analysis is justified for any general concave utility function of the Von Neumann–Morgenstern type (Von Neumann and Morgenstern, 1944).

The estimation of the underlying parameters (returns, variances and covariances) which are required as the input to MV analysis is an important modelling step. Small changes in the input can have a large impact on the optimal asset weights. Chopra and Ziemba (1993) found that, for a typical investor's risk tolerance level, errors in the forecast means are more than ten times as important as errors in the variance and about twenty times as important as errors in covariances. For practical aspects of portfolio analysis see Perold (1984), Hensel and Turner (1998) and Grinold and Kahn (1995). The modern portfolio theory has developed in tandem with simplifications to the QP required by MV analysis; these simplifications centre around linearizing the quadratic objective function or reducing the number of parameters to be estimated. Both approaches involve either an approximation or a decomposition of the covariance matrix.

Tobin (1958) developed the separation theorem which states that, in the presence of a risk-free asset, the optimal risky portfolio can be determined without any knowledge of investor preferences. Ziemba et al. (1974) show that the solution to the portfolio problem involving a risk-free asset can be obtained by a two-stage process: first solving a deterministic linear complementarity problem and then solving a univariate stochastic nonlinear program.

Sharpe (1963) proposed that the single index, or 'market', model was a sufficient model of covariance. Subsequently, Sharpe (1964), Lintner (1965) and Mossin (1966) independently developed the capital asset pricing model. This linear model of equilibrium asset prices explains the covariance of asset returns solely through their covariance with the market. King (1966) presented evidence of the influence of industry factors that the market model did not take into account. Rosenberg (1974) proposed a multifactor model that incorporated industry and other factors. Ross (1976), using factor analysis, developed the arbitrage pricing theory, which is a multi-index equilibrium model.

Since Markowitz's seminal paper (1952), a number of alternative models have been proposed for portfolio planning. The main underlying motivations for these alternative models are (a) such models are easier to process from a computational point of view compared to Markowitz's quadratic programming approach; and (b) they take into consideration alternative risk metrics. In Section 1.2 of this chapter we describe a number of alternative models taking into consideration the motivations discussed above. In Section 1.3 we introduce alternative risk measures for financial planning problems. Although not all of them are used as such in a single period planning model, they play an important role in defining measures which can be used in a 'portfolio analytics' tool. In Section 1.4 we present a number of extensions of the original Markowitz model. Some, if not all, of these extensions are used in many modern portfolio planning systems. Preparation of asset data in a financial data mart is an important aspect of portfolio systems. The method of preparation of this analytic information is discussed in Section 1.5. Real world portfolio planning problems include various practical restrictions which reflect financial industry realisms in respect of threshold constraints, cardinality of assets held and transaction roundlots. These translate to discrete optimization problems with a convex quadratic objective function. The resulting problems are NP-hard. In Section 1.6 we discuss solution methods for processing such QP and quadratic mixed integer programming (QMIP) problems. In Section 1.7 we consider computational results based on our experience of a current state-of-the-art portfolio optimization system. We conclude the chapter with a discussion of the leading issues. In Appendix 1 we set out the method of linearizing and also approximating the QP. In Appendix 2 we provide a comparative analysis of alternative portfolio selection models and their relative performance in respect of a small yet representative dataset of assets.

1.2 ALTERNATIVE COMPUTATIONAL MODELS

In this section, we present five different portfolio planning models: (1) Markowitz's MV model presented as two quadratic programs (QP1 and QP2); (2) reformulation of QP as diagonal models (DIAG1, DIAG2, DIAG3), the piecewise linear approximations of which are given in Appendix 1; (3) the mean-absolute deviation model (MAD); (4) the weighted goal programming (WGP) model and (5) the minimax (MM) model. These five models are presented within a unified framework. The basic set of notations common to all these models is defined below as Indices, Parameters and Decision variables.

Indices:
Let
$i, j = 1, \ldots N$: denote the different risky assets
$t = 1, \ldots, T$:... the time periods of past historical data

Parameters:
Let
r_{it}: denote the return of asset i at time t
μ_i:... the expected return of asset i
σ_{ij}:... the coefficients of the $(N \times N)$ variance-covariance matrix V defined for asset i and asset j
$(\sigma_{ii} = \sigma_i$ the diagonal coefficients for the asset i)
ρ:... the desired level of return for the portfolio

Decision variables:
Let
x_i: denote the fraction of the portfolio value invested in asset i $(0 \leq x_i \leq 1)$
x:... the $N \times 1$ vector of portfolio weights x_i

1.2.1 The markowitz mean-variance model and the risk-return frontier

The portfolio selection model of Markowitz (1952, 1959) laid the basis of Modern Portfolio Theory. The Markowitz model, put forward in 1952, is a multi-(two) objective optimization model which is used to balance the expected return and variance of a portfolio. Markowitz (1952) shows how rational investors can construct optimal portfolios under conditions of uncertainty. For an investor, the returns (for a given portfolio) and the stability or its absence (volatility) of the returns are the crucial aspects in the choice of portfolio. Markowitz uses the statistical measurements of expectation and variance of return to describe, respectively, the benefit and risk associated with an investment. The objective is either to minimize the risk of the portfolio for a given level of return, or to maximize the expected level of return for a given level of risk. The mean-variance (MV) approach still underpins much of the quantitative analysis of portfolio selection as carried out by the financial industry today.

The classical MV model (Markowitz, 1952, 1959) and an alternative approach towards computing the Markowitz Efficient Frontier (MEF) are set out below.

QP 1:

$$\text{Min } Z_{QP1} = \sum_{i=1}^{N} \sum_{j=1}^{N} x_i x_j \sigma_{ij} \tag{1.1}$$

subject to

$$\sum_{i=1}^{N} x_i \mu_i = \rho \tag{1.2}$$

$$\sum_{i=1}^{N} x_i = 1 \tag{1.3}$$

$$x_i \geq 0 \qquad i = 1, \ldots, N \tag{1.4}$$

Varying the desired level of return, ρ, in QP1 and repeatedly solving the quadratic program identifies the minimum variance portfolio for each value of ρ. These are the efficient portfolios that compose the efficient set. By plotting the corresponding values of the objective function (the variance) and ρ (the return) respectively, we trace out the MEF in the MV plane. Markowitz (1956) describes a 'critical line' solution algorithm tracing out the efficient frontier by identifying 'corner' portfolios–points at which a stock either enters or leaves the current portfolio. It is typical practice to use standard deviation rather than variance as the risk measure because the σ versus ρ frontier is linear if a risk-free asset exists, see Tobin (1958) and Ziemba et al. (1974).

An alternative formulation of QP1 explicitly trades risk against return in the objective function using the Arrow–Pratt absolute risk-aversion index R_A (see Kallberg and Ziemba, 1983). R_A is defined as

$$R_A = \frac{-u''(w)}{u'(w)} \tag{1.5}$$

where w is portfolio wealth and u', u'' are the first and second derivatives of a Von Neumann–Morgenstern utility function u.

QP2:

$$\text{Max } Z_{QP2} = \sum_{i=1}^{N} x_i \mu_i - \frac{R_A}{2} \sum_{i=1}^{N} \sum_{j=1}^{N} x_i x_j \sigma_{ij} \tag{1.6}$$

subject to

$$\sum_{i=1}^{N} x_i = 1 \tag{1.7}$$

$$x_i \geq 0 \qquad i = 1, \ldots, N \tag{1.8}$$

By increasing R_A from zero and solving the different instances of QPs, we trace out the efficient frontier. Empirical results by Kallberg and Ziemba (1983) show that $R_A \geq 6$ leads to very risk-averse portfolios, $2 \leq R_A \leq 4$ represents moderate absolute risk aversion and $R_A \leq 2$ leads to risky portfolios. $R_A = 4$ corresponds approximately to pension fund management (typically, holdings of 60% stocks and 40% bonds). In practice, it is common to model the risk-return trade-off using a parameter λ, $0 \leq \lambda \leq 1$, with the following objective function:

$$\text{Min } Z = \lambda \sum_{i=1}^{N} \sum_{j=1}^{N} x_i x_j \sigma_{ij} - (1 - \lambda) \sum_{i=1}^{N} x_i \mu_i \tag{1.9}$$

Setting

$$\frac{R_A}{2} = \frac{\lambda}{(1 - \lambda)} \tag{1.10}$$

shows equivalence with the objective function in QP2. The same efficient frontier generated by QP1 can be traced out by varying the value of λ and repeatedly solving QP2. This is the most frequently used way of generating the efficient frontier, the parameter λ is systematically varied between 0 and 1, which correspond to the maximum return and minimum variance portfolios respectively.

1.2.2   Models with diagonal quadratic form as objectives

Diagonal models are of interest as the corresponding quadratic forms can then be expressed as variable separable functions which in turn are approximated as piecewise linear functions (see Appendix). Since these are convex programming problems, piecewise linear approximations lead to a linear programming (LP) reformulation of the given problem; the solution of the LP guarantees global optimum solution of the given approximated QP. A detailed description of diagonalization methods (based on Cholesky decomposition, an approach that exploits the decomposition of the covariance matrix (see also Vanderbei and Carpenter, 1993) and diagonal QPs (based on index or factor models for describing asset returns) can be found in Horniman et al. (2000).

Diagonal model 1

By applying Cholesky decomposition the given covariance matrix, V, can be re-expressed as

$$V = L^T L$$

where $L(N \times N)$ is a lower triangular matrix. The objective function of model QP1, in matrix form is $Z_{QP1} = x^T V x$ which can be expressed as $Z_{QP1} = x^T L^T L x$. Defining a new vector $y(N \times 1)$ such that $y = Lx$ with elements

$$y_i = \sum_{j=1}^{i} l_{ij} x_j \qquad i = 1, \ldots, N \tag{1.11}$$

leads to the equivalent formulation of the portfolio selection problem, model DIAG1. The number of terms in the objective function of model QP1 is reduced from N^2 to below N at the cost of N additional constraints (1.11) and N additional variables (1.11).

DIAG1:

$$\text{Min } Z_{DIAG1} = \sum_{i=1}^{N} y_i^2 \tag{1.12}$$

subject to

$$y_i = \sum_{j=1}^{i} l_{ij} x_j \qquad i = 1, \ldots, N \tag{1.13}$$

$$\sum_{i=1}^{N} x_i \mu_i = \rho \tag{1.14}$$

$$\sum_{i=1}^{N} x_i = 1 \tag{1.15}$$

$$x_i \geq 0 \qquad i = 1, \ldots, N \tag{1.16}$$

$$g_i^y \leq y_i \leq h_i^y \qquad i = 1, \ldots, N \tag{1.17}$$

For a general quadratic form, y_i would be a free variable $(-\infty < y_i < +\infty)$. However, with constraints (1.14), (1.15) and (1.16), there are finite upper and lower bounds on x_i for $i = 1, \ldots, N$. As a consequence, there exist finite upper (h_i^y) and lower (g_i^y) bounds on y_i, $i = 1, \ldots, N$ (see Brearley et al., 1975). These bounds are a necessity for the piecewise linear approximations of the quadratic terms.

Diagonal model 2

A similar approach (see Vanderbei and Carpenter, 1993) exploits the composition of the covariance matrix V given that it has been calculated from returns R observed over T periods. Given that the matrix of mean returns is $\overline{R}$, the covariance matrix V is calculated as

$$V = \frac{1}{N-1}(R - \overline{R})^T (R - \overline{R})$$

defining S $(T \times N)$ as

$$S = \frac{1}{\sqrt{N-1}}(R - \overline{R})$$

the covariance matrix can be expressed as

$$V = S^T S$$

This leads to a model similar to DIAG1 with T (instead of N) new decision variables y_t and T (instead of N) additional constraints compared to model QP1. We refer to it as DIAG2.

DIAG2:

$$\text{Min } Z_{DIAG2} = \sum_{t=1}^{T} y_t^2 \tag{1.18}$$

subject to

$$y_t = \sum_{i=1}^{N} s_{it} x_i \qquad t = 1, \ldots, T \tag{1.19}$$

$$\sum_{i=1}^{N} x_i \mu_i = \rho \tag{1.20}$$

$$\sum_{i=1}^{N} x_i = 1 \tag{1.21}$$

$$x_i \geq 0 \qquad i = 1, \ldots, N \tag{1.22}$$

$$g_t^y \leq y_t \leq h_t^y \qquad t = 1, \ldots, T \tag{1.23}$$

In this instance, the number of terms in the objective function (1.19) is reduced to T, with the addition of T variables (1.23) and T constraints (1.19). Again, there are finite upper (h_t^y) and lower (g_t^y) bounds on y_t, $t = 1, \ldots, T$.

Diagonal model 3

The use of factor models to describe asset returns can also lead to a diagonal form provided the composition of the covariance matrix is appropriately exploited. Sharpe (1971) introduced this feature for the single index model and the technique can be extended to any number of factors or indices (see Rosenberg, 1974 and Perold, 1984). For a model with K factors, let f_k denote the level of the kth factor, β_{ik} the sensitivity of asset i to factor k, α_i the mean return of asset i and e_i the random component of return of asset i; then asset returns r_i can be expressed as a linear form by

$$r_i = \alpha_i + \sum_{k=1}^{K} \beta_{ik} f_k + e_i$$

If the factors are constructed (or transformed) so that there is no correlation between the factors and specific returns, and it is further assumed that the specific returns are uncorrelated, the covariance matrix, V, can be decomposed as

$$V = B^T Q B + D$$

where B is the $K \times N$ matrix of factor sensitivities, Q is the $K \times K$ diagonal matrix of factor variances $\sigma_{f_k}^2$, and D is the $N \times N$ diagonal matrix of specific variances, $\sigma_{\varepsilon_i}^2$. (If the factors are constructed to be orthonormal, then Q reduces to the $K \times K$ identity matrix).

Having decomposed the covariance matrix in this fashion, model DIAG3 can be stated as follows:

DIAG3:

$$\text{Min } Z_{DIAG} = \sum_{k=1}^{K} y_{P,k}^2 + \sum_{i=1}^{N} x_i^2 \sigma_{\varepsilon_i}^2 \tag{1.24}$$

subject to

$$y_{P,k} = \sum_{i=1}^{N} x_i \beta_{ik} \sigma_{f_k} \qquad k = 1, \ldots, K \tag{1.25}$$

$$\sum_{i=1}^{N} x_i \mu_i = \rho \tag{1.26}$$

$$\sum_{i=1}^{N} x_i = 1 \tag{1.27}$$

$$x_i \geq 0 \qquad i = 1, \ldots, N \tag{1.28}$$

$$l_k^y \leq y_{P,k} \leq u_k^y \qquad k = 1, \ldots, K \tag{1.29}$$

In this approach, the objective function of QP1 is reduced to a sum of squares in $N + K$ terms with an additional K variables $y_{P,k}$ (expressed as linear forms of x_i) (1.25) with finite upper (u_k^y) and lower (l_k^y) bounds (see (1.29)).

1.2.3   The mean-absolute deviation (MAD) model

Konno (1988) proposed a portfolio optimization model using a piecewise linear risk function. The MAD model, a special case of the piecewise linear risk model, has been shown to be equivalent to the Markowitz model under the assumption that returns are multivariate normally distributed (Konno and Yamazaki, 1991). That is, under this assumption, the minimization of the L_1 measure (the sum of absolute deviations of portfolio returns about the mean) is equivalent to the minimization of the L_2 measure (the variance). Let m_t denote the absolute deviation of the portfolio return (from the mean) at time t, then the MAD model is stated as:

MAD:

$$\text{Min } Z_{MAD} = \frac{1}{T} \sum_{t=1}^{T} m_t \tag{1.30}$$

subject to

$$\sum_{i=1}^{N} (r_{it} - \mu_i) x_i \leq m_t \qquad t = 1, \ldots, T \tag{1.31}$$

$$\sum_{i=1}^{N} (r_{it} - \mu_i) x_i \geq -m_t \qquad t = 1, \ldots, T \tag{1.32}$$

$$\sum_{i=1}^{N} x_i \mu_i = \rho \tag{1.33}$$

$$\sum_{i=1}^{N} x_i = 1 \tag{1.34}$$

$$m_t \geq 0 \qquad t = 1, \ldots, T \tag{1.35}$$

$$x_i \geq 0 \qquad i = 1, \ldots, N \tag{1.36}$$

The objective function (1.30) minimizes the mean of the absolute deviation calculated using constraints (1.31) and (1.32), with m_t restricted to be non-negative (1.35).

A comparison of the MV model and the mad model

Konno and Yamazaki claim that the MAD model credibly replaces the MV model as it incorporates all its positive features. They present the following three arguments in support of their claim:

a) In the formulation of the MAD model, there is no requirement for the covariance matrix of asset returns;

b) the relative ease with which a linear program can be solved compared to a quadratic one–thus large scale problems can be solved faster and more efficiently;

c) mean absolute deviation portfolios have fewer assets–this fact implies lower transaction costs in portfolio revisions.

Simaan (1997) discusses the advantages and disadvantages of the MAD model. He puts forward a contrary viewpoint and shows that ignoring the covariance matrix results in greater estimation risk that outweighs the benefits. In both models, estimation risk is more severe in small samples (small observations relative to the number of assets) and for investors with high risk tolerance. The MV model's lower estimation risk is most striking in small samples and for investors with low risk tolerance.

1.2.4   The goal programming model

Goal programming is a branch of multi-objective decision-making and is based on the concept of finding feasible points as close as possible to a number of goals. A set of targets/goals is chosen by the decision maker. Any (unwanted) deviations from these targets are penalized in order to get a satisfactory solution. How these penalties are implemented depends on the type of goal program.

Weighted Goal Programming (WGP) attaches weights according to the relative importance of each objective as perceived by the decision maker and minimizes the sum of the weights. Zero weights are attached to deviations that do not have to be minimized (for example, positive deviations from the expected portfolio return goal). Lexicographic Goal Programming (LGP) separates the objectives into a number of priority levels where the satisfaction of goals with higher priority is regarded as infinitely more important than the satisfaction of lower level goals. A practical LGP model, first introduced by Lee and Chesser (1980), and a WGP formulation of Lee's model can be found in Tamiz et al. (1996).

Tamiz et al. (1996), using a factor model of stock returns, measure the risk of a portfolio as the sum of absolute deviations of the portfolio's factor sensitivities from those of a specified target. Unsystematic risk receives no direct treatment. To force diversification of the stock specific risks, they apply a constraint on the total holdings allowed in each industry sector.

We present a simplified version of such a WGP model; the objective of the model is to minimize the risk associated with the portfolio and maximize the expected return. We do not specify a particular measure of risk. The only limit on the risk measure is that the portfolio risk is a linear combination of the risks associated with the component stocks.

We also introduce a few additional parameters and variables for this model.

Parameters:
Let

W_1: denote the positive penalty weight associated with shortfalls in portfolio return below the target
W_2: denote the positive penalty weight associated with excess portfolio risk in relation to the target
$Risk_P$: denote risk associated with the portfolio
$Risk_i$: ...risk associated with the asset i

Decision variables:
Let

n_1: denote the negative deviation from the target level of portfolio return
p_1: ...the positive deviation from the target level of portfolio return
n_2: ...the negative deviation from the target risk level
p_2: ...the positive deviation from the target risk level

WGP:

$$\text{Min } Z_{WGP} = W_1 n_1 + W_2 p_2 \tag{1.37}$$

subject to

$$\sum_{i=1}^{N} x_i \mu_i + n_1 - p_1 = \rho \tag{1.38}$$

$$\sum_{i=1}^{N} Risk_i x_i + n_2 - p_2 = Risk_P \tag{1.39}$$

$$\sum_{i=1}^{N} x_i = 1 \tag{1.40}$$

$$n_1, n_2, p_1, p_2 \geq 0 \tag{1.41}$$

$$x_i \geq 0 \qquad i = 1, \ldots, N \tag{1.42}$$

The objective function (1.37) seeks to minimize risk and maximize return by penalizing excess risk and shortfalls in return, relative to the respective targets. Lower levels of risk and higher levels of return are not penalized. The shortfalls in return and excesses in risk are determined by constraints (1.38) and (1.39) respectively.

The MAD model can be formulated as a weighted goal program. By replacing inequalities (1.31) and (1.32) with the constraints

$$\sum_{i=1}^{N} (r_{it} - \mu_i)x_i = p_t - n_t \tag{1.43}$$

$$p_t \geq 0 \tag{1.44}$$

$$n_t \geq 0 \tag{1.45}$$

and replacing m_t in the objective function by $p_t + n_t$. This results in a weighted goal program that penalizes absolute deviations from the portfolio mean. Not penalizing deviations above the mean, using a zero penalty weight on p_t, leads to a weighted goal program version of a negative semi-MAD model, such as employed by Speranza (1996).

1.2.5 The minimax model (MM)

The principle underlying this model (Young, 1998) can be described as choosing a portfolio based directly on how it would have performed in the past, over the historical observations $t = 1, \ldots, T$. The minimum return that could have occurred in the past is employed as the measure of risk. The model seeks to maximize this value while achieving a specified level of expected return. An alternative, and perhaps more appropriate, statement of the minimax portfolio selection rule is the minimization of the maximum loss that would have occurred over the observation period. The minimax model uses the L_∞ norm to measure risk which implies a strong absolute aversion to downside risk (Gonin and Money, 1989). The solution can be strongly affected by only one outlying value in the data.

We introduce a variable M_P which represents the minimum return achieved by the portfolio over all observation periods. That is, $M_P = \min_t \sum_{i=1}^{N} x_i r_{it}$.

The Minimax model (MM) is then stated as

MM:

$$\text{Max } Z_{MM} = M_P \tag{1.46}$$

subject to

$$\sum_{i=1}^{N} x_i r_{it} \geq M_P \qquad t = 1, \ldots, T \tag{1.47}$$

$$\sum_{i=1}^{N} x_i \mu_i = \rho \tag{1.48}$$

$$\sum_{i=1}^{N} x_i = 1 \tag{1.49}$$

$$l^{M_P} \leq M_P \leq u^{M_P} \tag{1.50}$$

It is easily seen that finite upper bound (u^{M_P}) and finite lower bound (l^{M_P}) apply to the variable M_P. Young (1998) also suggests an alternative formulation of the model that maximizes the expected portfolio return subject to a given lower bound on the portfolio return for every observation period.

1.3   SYMMETRIC AND ASYMMETRIC MEASURES OF RISK

1.3.1   Sources of risk and choice of appropriate measures: risk dilemmas

The introduction of Markowitz's MV framework provided financial institutions and portfolio managers with a powerful tool that allowed them, for the first time, to utilize the concepts of risk and return in a combined paradigm. Despite the progressive acceptance and wide-spread use of the MV framework, and its numerous extensions, in practice there has been a considerable debate among academics and practitioners on the validity of variance as a representative measure of risk. The notion of risk has found practical application within the science of risk management, or risk control. Risk control deals with limiting or eliminating specific types of risk, in as much as this is possible by taking an active position in one or more types of risk. Deciding which types of risk to mitigate is the *first dilemma* of a financial institution and demands considerable attention, since focusing on one particular risk category may lead to a hedged portfolio for a particular source of risk but may result in exposure to other sources of risk. This issue becomes more challenging when optimization models are used. For instance, optimization may result in minimization of the risk (measure) included in the model, but the solution may be sensitive to other sources of risks that were not considered and better measured by another metric.

In general, risk measures can be divided into two groups depending on the perception of risk. The first group contains the so-called dispersion risk measures that quantify risk in terms of probability-weighted dispersion of results around a specific reference point, usually the expected value, and are otherwise classified as *symmetric measures of risk*. Measures in this category penalize negative as well as positive deviations from a pre-specified target. Two of the most well-known and widely applied risk measures, in this group, are Markowitz's (1952, 1959) 'variance' or 'standard deviation' and the 'expected' or 'mean absolute deviation' (MAD) of Atkinson (1970) and Konno and Yamasaki (1991). The second group comprises measures which quantify risk according to results and probabilities below reference points, selected either subjectively or objectively, and are otherwise classified as *asymmetric measures of risk*. Such risk measures include the 'expected value of loss' from Domar and Musgrave (1944), Roy's (1952) 'safety first', the 'semi-variance' proposed by Markowitz (1959), Value at Risk–VaR–(Morgan, 1993) and its extension Conditional VaR–CVaR– (Uryasev and Rockafellar, 1999), and Fishburn's $\alpha-t$ criterion (1977). The latter not only constitutes the generalized case for the above 'below-target' risk measures, but it is also capable of representing the symmetric risk measures. Set against this background, a financial institution faces a *second dilemma* of deciding which of the two main risk metric categories symmetric or asymmetric measures of risk – represent its attitude towards risk and, therefore, should be utilized.

The incorporation of risk in the investment decision process should also reflect the benchmark relative to which a financial institution or an individual assesses its portfolio performance. The simplest approach is that of comparing the performance relative to the portfolio's past history. This is achieved by computing the risk measure as a function of the portfolio composition and the random returns of the assets. Typically, the standard deviation would then reflect the deviation of the asset returns from the expected portfolio return. On the other hand, the portfolio performance can be measured relative to a benchmark index or an alternative investment opportunity. In this case, the risk measure is also a function of a target level of return. The standard deviation in this case would then reflect the deviation of the asset returns from the expected target return (e.g. FTSE100). Utilizing the two alternative approaches – portfolio return and target return–implies tackling different planning problems. In particular, the portfolio return approach is mostly suitable for maximum return strategies, whereas the target return framework is suitable for 'index tracking' or 'goal achievement' strategies. Furthermore, the two approaches lead to different portfolio asset mix decisions and, therefore, for financial institutions choosing the appropriate framework, becomes the *third dilemma*.

1.3.2 A generic approach to risk representation and quantification

Bawa (1975) and Fishburn (1977) consolidated the existing research on risk measures up to that time, and developed the $\alpha-t$ *model*, and introduced a general definition of 'below target' risk in the form of lower partial moments (LPM).

Let α be a parameter specifying the moment of the return distribution. In some cases α may be taken as indicating different attitudes towards risk. Let τ be a predefined target level of the investment return, and $F(x)$ the cumulative probability distribution function of the investment with return x. The LPM of order α for a given τ defines the $\alpha-t$ *model* and has the following form:

$$F_\alpha(\tau) \equiv LPM_\alpha(\tau;x) = \int_{-\infty}^{\tau} (\tau - x)^\alpha f(x)\mathrm{d}x = E\{(\max[0, \tau - x])^\alpha\}, \alpha > 0$$

(1.51)

The introduction of the LPM is a major advance in the field of risk, as it provides the most generic representation of risk. Within this framework both symmetric and asymmetric measures of risk are encapsulated. Alternative formulations of well-known symmetric and asymmetric risk measures are shown below as special cases of the generic approach of LPM.

Symmetric measures of risk

The main difference in the symmetric measures of risk, when compared with the asymmetric, is that returns above the pre-specified target are also included. In that case, the returns used to calculate the risk measures can take values between $[-\infty, +\infty]$. The two symmetric risk metrics we consider are variance and MAD.

Variance: the classical representation of variance deals with measuring the spread of the expected returns relative to the average expected portfolio return. Therefore, $\tau = \bar{x}$ and $\alpha = 2$.

$$\sigma^2 \equiv LPM_2(\bar{x};x) = \int_{-\infty}^{+\infty} (\bar{x} - x)^2 f(x)\mathrm{d}x = E\{(\bar{x} - x)^2\}$$

(1.52)

In the case that the target level of return is not equal to the average expected portfolio return, the representation of the variance from target τ is given by:

$$\sigma^2 \equiv LPM_2(\tau;x) = \int_{-\infty}^{+\infty} (\tau - x)^2 f(x)\mathrm{d}x = E\{(\tau - x)^2\}$$

(1.53)

Mean Absolute Deviation: by setting $\alpha = 1$, the MAD measure of risk can be represented as:

$$MAD \equiv LPM_1(\bar{x};x) = \int_{-\infty}^{+\infty} |\bar{x} - x|^1 f(x)\mathrm{d}x = E\{(|\bar{x} - x|)^1\}$$

(1.54)

Asymmetric measures of risk

It is easily seen that all asymmetric risk measures for different levels of τ and α are special cases of the $a - t$ risk. Adopting the general $a - t$ risk measure, we provide the formulations of a set of (interesting) below-target risk measures.

Safety First: The 'Safety First Criterion' is a special case of the α–t risk when $\alpha \rightarrow 0$.

$$SF \equiv LPM_{\alpha \rightarrow 0}(\tau; x) = F_{\alpha \rightarrow 0}(\tau) = \int_{-\infty}^{\tau} (\tau - x)^{\theta \rightarrow 0} f(x) dx$$

$$= E\{(\max[0, \tau - x])^{\alpha \rightarrow 0}\} \qquad (1.55)$$

Expected Downside Risk: When $\alpha = 1$ the $a - t$ model equals the expected downside risk.

$$\overline{D} \equiv LPM_1(\tau; x) = F_1(\tau) = \int_{-\infty}^{\tau} (\tau - x)^1 f(x) dx = E\{(\max[0, \tau - x])^1\}$$

$$(1.56)$$

If the target is set equal to the expected portfolio return then the measure can be viewed as a special case of the MAD risk measure where only the negative deviations from the target are considered, thus leading to the Semi-MAD measure:

$$MAD^- \equiv LPM_1(\overline{x}; x) = F_1(\overline{x}) = \int_{-\infty}^{\overline{x}} (\overline{x} - x)^1 f(x) dx$$

$$= E\{(\max[0, \overline{x} - x])^1\} \qquad (1.57)$$

Semi-Variance: as shown by Fishburn in his seminal paper, the semi-variance is a special case of the $a - t$ model, for $\alpha = 2$.

$$\sigma^{-2} \equiv LPM_2(\tau; x) = F_2(\tau) = \int_{-\infty}^{\tau} (\tau - x)^2 f(x) dx = E\{(\max[0, \tau - x])^2\}$$

$$(1.58)$$

Worst Case Scenario: For $\alpha \rightarrow +\infty$ the $a - t$ model defines the worst-case scenario as considered by Boudoukh et al. (1995).

$$WCS \equiv F_{\alpha \rightarrow +\infty}(\tau) = LPM_{\alpha \rightarrow +\infty}(\tau; x) = \int_{-\infty}^{\tau} (\tau - x)^{\alpha \rightarrow +\infty} f(x) dx$$

$$= E\{(\max[0, \tau - x])^{\alpha \rightarrow +\infty}\} \qquad (1.59)$$

Value-at-Risk (VaR): the VaR of a portfolio at the β probability level is the left quantile of the losses of the portfolio, i.e., the lowest possible value such that the probability of losses less than VaR exceeds $\beta \times 100\%$. The VaR is given as

$$VaR(x, \beta) = \theta \qquad (1.60)$$

where the corresponding LPM is

$$LPM_0(\theta; x) = F_0(\theta) = \int_{-\infty}^{\theta} (\theta - x)^0 f(x) dx = 1 - \beta$$

1.4 COMPUTATIONAL MODELS IN PRACTICE

The MV model as described in Section 1.2.1 and the alternative models described in the rest of Section 1.2 provide adequate mathematical description of the investment decision problem in its general form. In real life situations, to apply such models it is necessary to consider the trading requirements and other aspects of portfolio performance. For instance, it is meaningful (a) not to have very small holdings, (b) to restrict the total number of holdings and (c) to take into consideration the roundlot of assets that can be bought or sold in a bunch. These requirements can be modelled as threshold constraints (Section 1.4.1), cardinality constraints (Section 1.4.2) and roundlot constraints (Section 1.4.3); in general they all lead to sets of discrete variables and constraints.

The original perspective (which is also a restrictive and narrow view) of portfolio planning is that of asset management, namely buying, selling and rebalancing of assets. In this approach no explicit attention is paid to the investor's liabilities. Yet if the assets are bonds/fixed income securities, then coupon payments, reinvestment of cash and the fund's liabilities immediately call for cash flow matching. This is formally known as portfolio dedication and is discussed in Section 1.4.4. The prices of fixed income securities are dependent on the term structure of interest rates and hence exposed to interest rate risk. Thus, measurement and modelling of such risks using duration and convexity and the corresponding restrictions also known as immunization are described in Section 1.4.5.

1.4.1 Buy-in thresholds for assets

Buy-in thresholds and cardinality constraints are formulated using a discrete programming modelling structure which is well-known as variable upper and lower bounds or semi-continuous variables (Beale and Forrest, 1976). For discrete programming solution systems which do not support semi-continuous variables, such threshold restrictions may be specified using a binary variable and a pair of bounding restrictions. Using finite upper and lower bounds l_i, u_i for the stock weight x_i and the binary variable δ_i, the corresponding threshold restriction is represented by the constraint pair

$$l_i \delta_i \leq x_i \leq u_i \delta_i \qquad \text{and} \qquad \delta_i = 0, 1 \qquad i = 1, \ldots, N$$

The introduction of the binary variables transforms the QP to a quadratic mixed-integer program (QMIP) which becomes larger in size and computationally more complex. These constraints and the binary variable δ_i are also used to represent cardinality constraints which specify the number of stocks in a given portfolio. Imposing constraints that restrict stock holdings to integer multiples of specified roundlots increases the complexity of the model yet further.

The reformulation of model QP1 with buy-in thresholds is set out below.

BUY-IN:

$$\text{Min } Z_{BUY-IN} = \sum_{i=1}^{N} \sum_{j=1}^{N} x_i x_j \sigma_{ij} \qquad (1.61)$$

subject to

$$\sum_{i=1}^{N} x_i \mu_i = \rho \qquad (1.62)$$

$$\sum_{i=1}^{N} x_i = 1 \qquad (1.63)$$

$$l_i \delta_i \leq x_i \leq u_i \delta_i \qquad i = 1, \ldots, N \qquad (1.64)$$

$$\delta_i = 0 \text{ or } 1 \qquad i = 1, \ldots, N \qquad (1.65)$$

$$x_i \geq 0 \qquad i = 1, \ldots, N \qquad (1.66)$$

Constraints (1.64) and (1.65) ensure that if $\delta_i = 1$, then $l_i \leq x_i \leq u_i$ otherwise $\delta_i = 0$ which imposes $x_i = 0$.

1.4.2 Cardinality constraints

In order to control transaction costs or for other monitoring and control issues, some investors may wish to limit the number of assets held in their portfolios. By counting the binary variables introduced in model BUY-IN we can construct the cardinality constraint which limits the portfolio to a fixed number of assets k. Thus, by adding the restriction

$$\sum_{i=1}^{N} \delta_i = k \qquad (1.67)$$

to the model BUY-IN above we extend it to model CARD.

It may be worthwhile to point out that buy-in thresholds and cardinality constraints are implicitly linked. For example, a buy-in threshold of 10% of the value of a portfolio implies that up to 10 stocks can be bought.

1.4.3 Roundlot transactions

In the transaction roundlot model, we introduce the requirement that we can purchase stocks in set 'blocks'. Each block, or roundlot, can be described as a cash value or a number of stocks. For each asset i, a block is defined as a fraction f_i of the total portfolio wealth. Introducing integer number of blocks y_i, we re-express x_i as

$$x_i = y_i f_i, \qquad i = 1, \ldots, N$$

which is the fraction of portfolio wealth to be invested in stock i. The roundlot model can be stated as follows.

LOT:

$$\text{Min } Z_{LOT} = \sum_{i=1}^{N} \sum_{j=1}^{N} y_i f_i y_j f_j \sigma_{ij} + \gamma \varepsilon^- + \gamma \varepsilon^+ \tag{1.68}$$

subject to

$$\sum_{i=1}^{N} y_i f_i \mu_i = \rho \tag{1.69}$$

$$\sum_{i=1}^{N} y_i f_i + \varepsilon^- - \varepsilon^+ = 1 \tag{1.70}$$

$$l_i \leq y_i f_i \leq u_i \qquad i = 1, \ldots, N \tag{1.71}$$

$$y_i \text{ integer} \qquad i = 1, \ldots, N \tag{1.72}$$

$$\varepsilon^-, \varepsilon^+ \geq 0 \tag{1.73}$$

Using discrete lot sizes of share purchases, it may not be possible to satisfy exactly the requirement $\sum_{i=1}^{N} x_i = 1$. Hence, this restriction is made 'elastic' as in goal programming. Thus (1.70) includes undershoot and overshoot variables $\varepsilon^-, \varepsilon^+$ respectively which are in turn penalized in the objective function with a high cost γ. As a consequence, in an optimum solution $\varepsilon^-, \varepsilon^+$ are made as small as possible and the fractional stock holdings x_i sum to a value 'as close as possible' to 1.

1.4.4 Portfolio dedication

Given that the investment process is in general dynamic and that there are liabilities or obligations to be taken into account, the fund managers need to:

- match cash flows for known obligations arising out of, say, general investment contracts (GICs); and
- plan borrowing of shortfall and reinvestment of surplus;

both considered over future time periods.

Let

F_{it} denote the positive cash flows from asset i in time period t,
$L_t \ldots$ liability in time period t,
$\rho_t \ldots$ a reinvestment rate,
$\rho_t + \Delta \ldots$ the borrowing rate with Δ as the difference between this rate and the reinvestment rate.

We introduce two variables, v_t^+, v_t^- as cash surplus and shortfall respectively in time period t.
Then the restrictions set out below

$$\sum_{i=1}^{N} F_{i0} x_i + v_0 + v_0^- = v_0^+$$

$$\sum_{i=1}^{N} F_{it} x_i + (1 + \rho_t)v_{t-1}^+ + v_t^- = L_t + v_t^+$$

$$+ (1 + \rho_t + \Delta)v_{t-1}^-, \quad \text{for all } t = 1, \ldots, T$$

capture portfolio dedication as cashflows matching with borrowing and reinvestment. For a detailed discussion of this and related topics, see Zenios (2002).

1.4.5 Portfolio immunization

Bond prices are affected by yields which in turn depend on market interest rates; also, short bonds and long bonds are affected non-uniformly by the interest rate movement. The interest rate sensitivity or risk is traditionally measured by 'bond duration'. Duration of a bond is generally defined as the weighted average of the present values of the cash flows (the coupon payments). There are alternative definitions of duration (see Douglas, 1990 and Luenberger, 1998) but in general duration is a first order condition and provides a measure of the interest rate sensitivity or risk of a given fixed income security. A portfolio which is made up of only bonds can also have a duration measure.

Let D_i denote the duration of the ith bond
Then the duration of the portfolio is computed as

$$D_P = x_1 D_1 + x_2 D_2 + \cdots + x_N D_N$$

If we also compute the duration of all the liabilities, then by balancing the portfolio duration and liability duration

$$D_P = x_i D_1 + \cdots + x_N D_N = D_L$$

we immunize the portfolio against interest rate risk.

Convexity restrictions

The price-yield relationship of a fixed income security is a non-linear function for which the second order condition (differential) is called convexity. Whereas duration matching ensures that for small changes in term structure of interest rates, asset and liabilities move together, it is necessary also to put a restriction on convexity in order to have comparable shape for larger changes.

Let

Q_i denote the first derivative of duration (with respect to the interest rate) for the asset $i, i = 1, \ldots, N$; then Q_i is defined as the convexity of asset i; and let Q_L denote the convexity of the liabilities.

Then

$$Q_1 x_1 + Q_2 x_2 + \cdots + Q_N x_N \geq Q_L$$

is a constraint which in some sense restricts the sensitivity to the shape of the term structure or the 'shape risk' of the portfolio.

Factor immunization

Factor models are well established in most modern portfolio systems since they play an important role:

- in analysing and discovering information within the market data; and
- in defining the quadratic objective function of the risk.

By using a linear factor model (typically, principal component analysis) one may choose to include k factors to represent return variability. The first order and second order measures can be now redefined in this light as:

- factor modified duration; and
- factor modified convexity.

Further immunization restrictions can be written in terms of these parameters and the corresponding model then includes factor immunization conditions. For a fuller treatment of this topic the readers are referred to Zenios (2002).

1.5   PREPARATION OF DATA: FINANCIAL DATA MARTS

Deciding on the portfolio asset mix for a given planning horizon is a core task in the operations of a financial institution. The adoption of portfolio models underpins such a task, and in particular these models are used to make robust hedged decisions. Yet the effective use of the portfolio planning models, described above, in practice requires their inclusion in an integrated decision support framework. In this framework it is necessary to consider the roles of data, information and decision models (see Figure 1.1). This integrated framework is also underpinned by the concept of translating transactional data into analytical data and the integration of information analysis models together with portfolio optimization models through the combined use of a common data mart.

Within information systems methodology, there is a clear awareness in respect of data stored in transactional/production databases and information stored in analytical databases. Transactional data refer to historical market data and internal (institution specific) data: existing portfolio positions, client orders, cash flows. Information analysis models filter transactional data and synthesize them into information that is then stored into the analytical database. The information is subsequently used to instantiate decision models and in turn the optimal solutions are stored in the decision database. The integration of the analytical database and the decision database is better known as *data mart* (Koutsoukis et al., 1999). For industry standard portfolio analysis systems such as Northfield Systems and UBS Warburg PAS (see Chapter 4), the use of analytical databases is pivotal, and the underlying information model is illustrated in Figure 1.1.

In respect of our portfolio applications, the information analysis models themselves can be broken down further into sub-categories taking into consideration the analysis stage in which they are utilized (see Table 1.1).

Our overall view of the transactional data, information models, analytic database and decision models is set out in Figure 1.2. This view can be explained in the following way.

The transactional data are collected on a day-to-day basis and stored in the production database which the information analysis models filter into information and generate an analytical database. We refer to this as the *pre-analytical database* because the information is generated before any optimization takes place. The pre-analytical database comprises:

- **Pre-analysis data:** information that provides insight on the portfolio performance to date and assist the decision maker to identify market trends to select an appropriate investment style and asset universe. The pre-analysis data includes styles, financial ratios, asset and portfolio statistics, and performance comparisons.

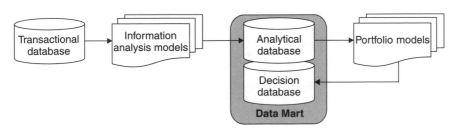

Figure 1.1   *Data information and decision models*

Table 1.1   *A breakdown of information analysis models*

Information analysis models			
Pre-analysis	Model data parameters	Solution analysis	Post-analysis
Performance indicators	Historical data	What if analysis	Performance indicators
Style analysis	Weighted moving	Scenario analysis	Risk statistics and
Financial ratios	average	Simulation	indices
CAPM	Factor models	Backtesting	Financial ratios
APT	Time series models	Internal company	CAPM
Simulation models	ARCH, GARCH,...	models	APT
Internal company	Neural networks		Simulation models
models	Genetic algorithms		Risk metrics
	Kalman filters		Internal company
	Chaos		models
	Internal company		
	models		

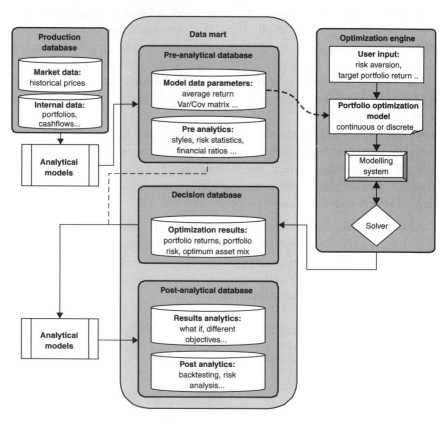

Figure 1.2   *Integrated decision support framework*

- **Model data parameters:** the data input for the portfolio planning model. The model data parameters typically include the asset universe, the expected return of the assets over the given planning horizon, and the expected risk of the assets (variance–covariance matrix). The remaining data parameters are application specific and depend on the constraints that the organization wishes to satisfy. The quality of the data parameters is essential for the quality of the solution that the optimization model provides and therefore information models for generation of the model parameters can be highly sophisticated (for a review see Grinold and Kahn, 1995).

The optimization decision engine processes the portfolio optimization model which is instantiated by data/information taken from the pre-analytical database. Subsequently the optimization results (optimum solution) are stored in the *decision database*. The output is model specific and mainly comprises the optimum asset mix, the expected portfolio return(s), and the expected portfolio risk(s). The information within the decision database can be further filtered to obtain additional information utilizing once again the information analysis models. The contents and the processing leading to the *post-analytical database* is described below:

- Results analysis data: information on the efficacy and the robustness of the optimal solution. The analyst may carry out 'what-if' analyses, where the decision-maker changes the input values, that is, using different model data instances. This technique examines the changes of the optimal solution and the optimal objective value with respect to variations of some parameters that are considered to be important. It is usually done by varying one parameter at a time. Another technique that varies uncertain parameters is scenario analysis. In this approach different scenarios, that is certain combinations of possible values of the uncertain parameters, are considered. Thereafter, the problem is solved for each of these scenarios. Thus, by solving the problem repeatedly for different scenarios and studying the solutions obtained, the decision-maker observes the sensitivities and decides on an appropriate solution by following a heuristic approach.
- Post-analysis data: information that provides insight on the expected performance of the optimum portfolios. The decision maker can calculate the risk exposure in the form of VaR or expected shortfall of the portfolio and compare its expected return with that of a benchmark index or a chosen portfolio.

1.6 SOLUTION METHODS

Whereas quadratic programs (QPs) can be solved rapidly using solution algorithms with a low order polynomial complexity, the solutions to quadratic mixed integer programs are difficult (NP-hard) and challenging. For instance consider the problem of accurately computing the discrete constraint efficient frontier (DCEF). Each point of the DCEF curve represents the global optimum solution of a 'discrete non-convex' optimization problem. Given that the quadratic form for the minimization problem is positive semidefinite, relaxing the discreteness restriction on the variables leads to a convex programming problem. This continuous variable QP relaxation of the problem provides a lower bound and is easily embedded (see Mitra, 1976 and Lawler and Wood, 1966) in a branch-and-bound tree search paradigm.

The FortQP system implemented within the FortMP solver (Ellison et al., 1999) has both interior point method (IPM) and sparse simplex (SSX) solution capabilities. The system is extensively tested using QLIB test data (Maros and Meszaros, 1997) and models from the Finance industry. For the given family of QMIP problems at hand the branch-and-bound algorithm has been specially constructed taking into consideration the following design issues:

SSX versus IPM. In medium-to-large test problems IPM performs better than SSX. Yet as an embedded solver of subproblems within branch-and-bound, IPM is not well suited since the 'warm start' property is relatively poor. We have therefore chosen SSX as our embedded 'optimization engine' for solving subproblems. The dual algorithm is used to solve these subproblems efficiently.

Information sharing and algorithm choice. In solving the sub-problems in the child node we share (re-use) the optimum basis information (basis list and the basis factors) of the parent node. We also apply the dual algorithm which reduces the total number of pivotal steps for reoptimization. These features also justify our choice of algorithm and vindicate the useful 'warm start' properties of the SSX.

Integer restart heuristic. In the construction of the DCEF involving, say, 500 points we are unlikely to solve all these models to QMIP optimality. As a consequence, we are likely to lose the 'pareto efficient' property of the frontier and our experiments confirm this. We do, however, adopt a scheme of computing the DCEF from the highest return, and its corresponding risk, to lower return and reduced risk. We use the previous integer solution in this sequence as the 'first feasible and upper bounding QP value' for the next point (problem). Given the previous solution is feasible (or optimal), this solution is automatically a feasible solution for the current optimization problem, as we decrease the desired level of return from its highest value to the smallest and hence relax the constraint. This has the effect that we obtain an 'efficient' DCEF which is optimal (if all problems are solved to optimality) or sub-optimal (if the algorithm is terminated at a feasible solution). However, the frontier we generate cannot contain inefficient points as we either stay at the previous solution or we improve on it. We believe, and our experimental results vindicate, that this approach is preferable to applying modern heuristics to this discrete non-convex programming problem.

1.7 COMPUTATIONAL EXPERIENCE

In this section, we first describe the software system architecture and the computational platform that we use for the investigation of this class of portfolio problems. We also describe our computational experience in respect of the discrete constraint efficient frontier (DCEF) model with threshold (BUY-IN) and cardinality (CARD) constraints using five data sets drawn from the Hang Seng, DAX, FTSE, S&P and Nikkei indices with 31, 85, 89, 98 and 225 stocks respectively, see Chang et al. (2000). Recently we have further enhanced our discrete QMIP solver to process a range of models supplied by the UBS Warburg PAS system; these computational results are also discussed in this section.

1.7.1 Modelling and the solution tools

We have adopted a modular component based approach whereby we are able to mix and match modelling and solver tools to process different portfolio problems. The overall computational platform is shown in Figure 1.3. Data from the data mart (see Section 1.5) is stored and transmitted through EXCEL datasheets. Using the MPL or AMPL algebraic modelling systems (see MAXIMAL, LUCENT), the QP or QMIP as appropriate is generated. The model is then processed by FortMP (QP) or FortMP (QMIP) and the results/solution files are again stored in the decision database. The system runs under Windows NT and Windows 2000. In the experiments reported in Sections 1.7.2 and 1.7.3,

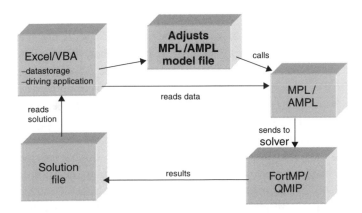

Figure 1.3 *Data, modelling and solver architecture*

we have used a Pentium III, 500 MHZ processor with 128 MB of RAM. This system is also available as a web application; see (OSP-CRAFT, 2001).

1.7.2   DCEF study for five stock indices

We have developed an integer restart heuristic which allows us to rapidly compute points on the DCEF. We investigate our heuristic approach using model CARD for the five data sets drawn from the Hang Seng, DAX, FTSE, S&P and Nikkei indices. We set $l_i = 0.01$, $i = 1, \ldots, N$ and use the cardinality constraint $k = 10$. To analyse the experimental results we follow the metric used in Chang et al. (2000). The deviations of the points on the heuristically obtained DCEF are measured as the minimum absolute distance (vertical or horizontal) from the MEF. Since they do not calculate the exact DCEF but need to measure the usefulness of the heuristically computed frontier points, this deviation measure which they call 'error' provides a reasonable metric for comparison. These reported 'errors' mainly reflect the systematic deviations due to the discrete constraints. Using the same metric allows a comparison with the modern heuristic results of Chang et al. (2000). For each data set and solution method, we generate the frontiers by solving 500 optimization problems. This number is chosen arbitrarily and the points are equally spaced with respect to the decrease in the desired level of return, ρ.

The QMIP problems are solved to the second, improving, feasible integer solution subject to a limit of 500 nodes in the branch-and-bound algorithm. Table 1.2 presents the results for the integer restart method applied to the five data sets. The table includes the mean and median percentage errors, the total number of DCEF points computed, the number of integer optimal points and the total solution time in seconds. The number of optimal points obtained does not appear to influence the size of the errors observed, suggesting that when optimality is not reached, the second integer solution is a good approximation of the optimal solution.

For each data set the mean error is below 0.02% with the median error below 0.015%. In all instances, the mean is greater than the median indicating positively skewed error distributions. The size of the errors reported indicate that the DCEFs obtained are very close to the corresponding MEFs. This is borne out by a mean error of 0.008% (median error 0.006%) for the DCEF solved to optimality (3000) points for the Hang Seng.

In order to establish the computational advantage of the integer restart heuristic, we also calculate the DCEF without starting with the previous solution vector. The integer restart heuristic finds more non-dominated points and more optimal points with a smaller mean deviation in less time. To achieve similar error and optimality results, the number of nodes to be searched in the branch-and-bound (B&B) algorithm needs to be increased. For example, for the S&P

Table 1.2 *Results for the integer restart heuristic*

Index	Number of stocks	Total number of DCEF points	Number of integer optimal points	Solution time	Mean error	Median error
Hang Seng	31	500	492	57.55	0.014 15	0.009 97
DAX	85	500	228	8 405.33	0.013 99	0.011 59
FTSE	89	500	244	10 978.12	0.011 41	0.008 60
S & P	98	500	192	15 831.97	0.015 86	0.013 25
Nikkei	225	500	486	18 345.56	0.006 18	0.002 52
Hang Seng	31	3000	3000	382.21	0.008 26	0.006 28

data set, the number of nodes has to be increased from 500 to 2500 but the solution time also increases five fold.

Comparison with modern heuristic methods

The integer restart and reoptimization heuristics outperform the modern heuristic methods of Chang et al. (2000) who report average mean and median deviations in excess of 1% (see Table 1.3). Clearly this makes both of our heuristic schemes very attractive, from the point of view of the quality of the discrete solution. The computational times are difficult to compare. Unfortunately, it is not possible to further compare the results since their full DCEFs are not available (Chang et al., 2000).

1.7.3 Experience with UBSW-PAS models

The 'optimization' requirements of the UBSW-PAS system in respect of the average as well as the largest instance of their application pose an even greater challenge in respect of processing such portfolio planning applications. Typically the total universe of assets can be as large as 8000 and cardinality constraints (CARD) may have values $k = 100$; we have tested the system for cardinality of $k = 500$ to $k = 800$. Since the solver must be part of a portfolio analytics and solution tool, a good discrete feasible solution must be obtained within a 'reasonable' time frame.

To process these models we have introduced an 'enhanced' depth first tree search heuristic to include multiple variable fixing. The heuristic operates in two stages. In the first stage multiple number of discrete variables are fixed in one step; some 'down' ($\delta_i = 0$) and others 'up' ($\delta_i = 1$); fixes are carried out (the number is controlled by a parameter). As a result

1 a number of assets are excluded completely ('down' fixes), and
2 a number of assets are brought into the portfolio ('up' fixes).

This sequence is followed through a number of depths in the tree search until the criteria for invoking stage 2 is realized. In stage 2 only 'up' fixes are undertaken

Table 1.3   *Comparison with modern heuristic approaches*

Index	Number of stocks	Solution method	Number of efficient points	Mean error	Median error
Hang Seng	31	Integer restart heuristic	500	0.014 15	0.009 97
			3000	0.008 26	0.006 28
		GA heuristic	1317	0.945 70	1.181 90
		TS heuristic	1268	0.990 80	1.199 20
		SA heuristic	1003	0.989 20	1.208 20
		Pooled (GA, TS, SA)	2491	0.933 20	1.189 90
DAX	85	Integer restart heuristic	500	0.013 99	0.011 59
		GA heuristic	1270	1.951 50	2.126 20
		TS heuristic	1467	3.063 50	2.538 30
		SA heuristic	1135	2.429 90	2.467 50
		Pooled (GA, TS, SA)	2703	2.192 70	2.462 60
FTSE	89	Integer restart heuristic	500	0.011 41	0.008 60
		GA heuristic	1482	0.878 40	0.596 00
		TS heuristic	1301	1.390 80	0.713 70
		SA heuristic	1183	1.134 10	0.636 10
		Pooled (GA, TS, SA)	2538	0.779 00	0.593 80
S & P	98	Integer restart heuristic	500	0.015 86	0.013 25
		GA heuristic	1560	1.715 70	1.144 70
		TS heuristic	1587	3.167 89	1.148 70
		SA heuristic	1284	2.697 00	1.128 80
		Pooled (GA, TS, SA)	2759	1.310 60	1.068 60
Nikkei	225	Integer restart heuristic	500	0.006 18	0.002 52
		GA heuristic	1823	0.643 1	0.606 2
		TS heuristic	1701	0.989 1	0.591 4
		SA heuristic	1655	0.637	0.629 2
		Pooled (GA, TS, SA)	3648	0.569	0.584 4

GA: Genetic Algorithm; SA: Simulated Annealing; TS: Tabu Search

Table 1.4   *Parameter of a typical UBSW-PAS example*

	Model 1	Model 2	Model 3	Model 4	Model 5
Stock universe	757	1304	1305	1305	1305
Initial portfolio size	332	251	251	251	251
Target for maximum assets	400	250	250	250	250
Risk acceptance parameter	0.6	0.6	0.6	0.6	0.6

one by one until a full discrete optimum solution is reached. Sub-problems in stage 1 and stage 2 are always solved using the dual algorithm.

Computational results for a set of five models (see Table 1.4) are summarized in Table 1.5. These were portfolio rebalancing problems in which portfolios with a given cardinality of holdings were moved to that with an improved new maximum number of holdings.

Table 1.5   *Test results for a typical UBSW-PAS example*

	Model 1	
Relaxed QP	Objective Value	0.18882922E-13
	Time to optimum (secs)	32.42
FortMP (QMIP)	IP Nodes	400
	IP processing time	1903.94
	IP Objective	0.28018533E-07
Two-stage heuristics	IP Nodes	129
	Time (secs)	121.48
	Objective function	0.28437663E-07
	Model 2	
Relaxed QP	Objective Value	0.41097040E-01
	Time to optimum (secs)	10.92
FortMP (QMIP)	IP Nodes	250
	IP processing time	163.98
	IP Objective	0.41098065E-01
Two-stage heuristics	IP Nodes	84
	Time (secs)	62.86
	Objective function	0.41098065E-01
	Model 3	
Relaxed QP	Objective Value	0.32291911E-15
	Time to optimum (secs)	172.32
FortMP (QMIP)	IP Nodes	250
	IP processing time	2943.12
	IP Objective	0.17839276E-05
Two-stage heuristics	IP Nodes	84
	Time (secs)	235.45
	Objective function	0.15851747E-05
	Model 4	
Relaxed QP	Objective Value	0.24351583E-16
	Time to optimum (secs)	130.89
FortMP (QMIP)	IP Nodes	250
	IP processing time	2992.06
	IP Objective	0.17895076E-5
Two-stage heuristics	IP Nodes	85
	Time (secs)	228.00
	Objective function	0.159762557E-5
	Model 5	
Relaxed QP	Objective Value	0.24748111E-17
	Time to optimum (secs)	121.89
FortMP (QMIP)	IP Nodes	250
	IP processing time	2936.82
	IP Objective	0.17780700E-5
Two-stage heuristics	IP Nodes	85
	Time (secs)	235.05
	Objective function	0.15851747E-05

The processing of these models using the built-in QMIP search and the enhanced two-stage heuristic is shown in Table 1.5 which also includes the objective value of the quadratic function indicating the quality of these discrete solutions. Since this two-stage heuristic is parameter-dependent, we have supplied the average values in respect of nine runs carried out for each model.

It is easily seen that the 'two-stage heuristic' performs extremely well and reduces the processing time substantially; the quality of the solution is sometimes marginally worse but more often it is better than the straight branch-and-bound approach labelled as FortMP (QMIP).

1.8   DISCUSSIONS AND CONCLUSIONS

Over the last 20 years there have been considerable acceptance and deployment of analytical/quantitative models for portfolio planning, asset management and asset and liability management. The evolving Basle accord (BIS 1988, 2001) and its impact on the finance industry with respect to measurement and control of risk is already considerable. These regulatory requirements of risk also continue to determine the finance industry's need for models and software systems. Set against this growing recognition and requirements of such tools, we have reviewed and presented in a consolidated form major developments in this field. In conclusion we would like to observe how development of portfolio planning and asset/liability management systems require a convergence of different skill sets. Thus in addition to:

1)   financial engineering and quantitative modelling,

it is necessary to introduce

2)   information engineering to create analytical databases.

Finally these models must be processed efficiently which requires

3)   algorithmic and software engineering skills.

Only by bringing together all these skill sets is it possible to create a new generation of financial planning systems.

1.9   APPENDIX 1: PIECEWISE LINEAR APPROXIMATION OF THE QUADRATIC FORM

The advantage of transforming the original quadratic form into a diagonal form which is a variable separable function is that the quadratic objective function can be approximated by a piecewise linear function of line segments. In practice, the choice of the number of line segments is critical if accurate function values are to be computed. Increasing the discrete points by which the function is approximated not only increases the accuracy of the approximation but also increases the model size. An alternative way of increasing the quality of the approximation is to apply standard bound analysis to the linear forms in order to derive a lower and upper bound on each variable appearing in the quadratic function and discretize the function only within this range. Hence, for a given number P, the density of discretizing points might now be increased as only the area of interest is taken into consideration. More details about piecewise linear polynomial approximations can be found in Darby-Dowman et al. (1988).

For a set of P points on the function $f(y_i) = y_i^2$, express these as $y_i = a_{ip}$, $y_i^2 = b_{ip}$, $p = 1, \ldots, P$. It is easily seen that $a_{i1} = g_i^y$, $a_{iP} = h_i^y$.

Model LA, the linear approximation to QP1, based on the diagonalization DIAG1 is now presented.

LA:

$$\text{Min } Z_{LA} = \sum_{i=1}^{N} \sum_{p=1}^{P} \lambda_{ip} b_{ip} \tag{1.74}$$

subject to

$$\sum_{p=1}^{P} a_{ip} \lambda_{ip} = \sum_{j=1}^{N} l_{ij} x_j \qquad i = 1, \ldots, N \tag{1.75}$$

$$\sum_{p=1}^{P} \lambda_{ip} = 1 \qquad i = 1, \ldots, N \tag{1.76}$$

$$\sum_{i=1}^{N} x_i \mu_i = \rho \tag{1.77}$$

$$\sum_{i=1}^{N} x_i = 1 \tag{1.78}$$

$$x_i \geq 0 \qquad i = 1, \ldots, N \tag{1.79}$$

$$0 \leq \lambda_{ip} \leq 1 \qquad i = 1, \ldots, N; \qquad p = 1, \ldots, P \tag{1.80}$$

This linear programming problem is easier to solve than the associated quadratic program. As a result, additional discrete constraints (such as described in the introduction) can be imposed on the model more easily. For LA to be a valid approximation of DIAG1, it is necessary that either only adjacent λ_{ip}'s for a given i are positive or any one λ_{ip} is positive or taking the value unity. These restrictions are known as special ordered set of type 2 (SOS2) restrictions and they are automatically satisfied in a convex programming problem. Hence LA is a valid approximation of DIAG1.

1.10   APPENDIX 2: COMPARATIVE COMPUTATIONAL VIEWS OF THE ALTERNATIVE MODELS

In this appendix we consider a few alternative models: mean absolute deviation (MAD), minimax (MM) and the discrete constraint efficient frontier (DCEF), and study their computational results after applying them to a small illustrative dataset of stocks (equity assets). The respective efficient frontiers of these models are juxtaposed with the MV model and its frontier; the role of the latter is that of a benchmark (taking standard deviation as the accepted risk measure) against which the performance of the other models are evaluated.

Dataset

The historical prices of a set of 30 stocks chosen out of the FTSE 100 shares are considered. The four-year price history of these 30 stocks is first downloaded from Datastream feed as a table of 208 weekly prices. In order to create the financial datamart for this small universe of 30 stocks the returns are first analysed and filtered against historical facts (typically no extraordinary events, new issues, or administration have occurred). The return on stocks are computed on a logarithmic scale and the 208 price values per stock are used as historical observations (these make up columns of the observation matrix) and are used in turn to calculate:

1) the estimate (average); and
2) the variance and covariance,

of return.

All these calculations are carried out in Excel.

The model results

We first compute for the model QP1, that is the MV model, the entire risk–return frontier without imposing any other restrictions. The software system outlined in Section 1.7 is used and by varying the return ρ discretely over a range of ρ_{min} return corresponding to min value of risk (variance of the portfolio) and ρ_{max} the max value of return (solved as an LP). In this range, $j = 1, \ldots, P$; $P = 100$ points were used corresponding to returns. $\rho_1 = \rho_{max}$, $\rho_2 = \rho_1 - \Delta, \ldots \ldots \rho_{100} = \rho_{min}$. It is easily seen that

$$\Delta = \frac{\rho_{max} - \rho_{min}}{P - 1}$$

QP1 and QP2

We first use the model QP2 Equations (1.9) and (1.10) and solve it (a) for $\lambda = 1$ which gives us ρ_{min} and then solve (b) for $\lambda = 0$ which gives us ρ_{max}. We then

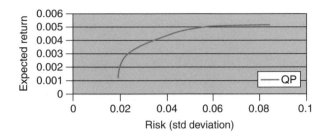

Figure 1.4 *Quadratic programming model*

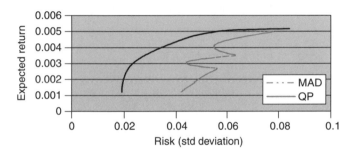

Figure 1.5 *Quadratic programming and MAD model*

compute the MV efficient frontier for a discretization of $P = 100$ points. The frontier is illustrated in Figure 1.4.

MAD

In this model we vary the rhs ρ of Equation (1.33) over the same range of values and points $\{(\rho_{max}, \rho_{min}), P = 100\}$. For each of these expected returns, the standard deviations of the portfolios (of assets) are computed. The corresponding frontier with the same range of return $\rho_{min} \leq \rho \leq \rho_{max}$ but the risk recomputed as standard deviation is illustrated in Figure 1.5.

According to Konno and Yamazaki (1991), the fact that the standard deviation efficient frontier of the MAD model does not coincide with the MEF is largely attributable to the non-normality of the returns data.

MM

The results of the minimax model are obtained and the corresponding risk figures are recomputed as standard deviation; in this we follow a procedure which is analogous to MAD procedure discussed above. The corresponding efficient frontier is displayed in Figure 1.6.

The comparison of the MM frontier with the MEF (Figure 1.5) is not especially meaningful since the minimax rule is not directly related to the quadratic risk term.

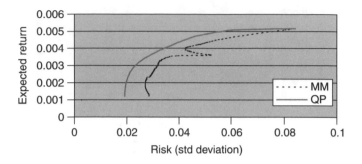

Figure 1.6   *Quadratic programming and MM model*

Discrete constraints efficient frontier (DCEF)

Discrete constraints (see Sections 1.4.1, 1.4.2) represent practical trading requirements and introduce discontinuities in the otherwise continuous efficient
frontier. To illustrate the relationship of the DCEF in respect of the original efficient frontier, we consider the given dataset of the same 30 stocks and introduce
a threshold of 0.1 and a cardinality constraint of $k = 2$ and $k = 4$ (thus only
two and four stocks at a level of 0.1 or more may be included in the portfolio).
Figure 1.7 displays the discrete efficient frontiers for model CARD. The two
discrete frontiers were constructed by solving 100 optimization problems with
varying levels of return ρ and in each instance the optimal solution was found.
Each of the two DCEFs contain discontinuities; also these discrete frontiers are
completely dominated by the continuous MV efficient frontier.

In Jobst et al. (2001), we also discuss the missing portion of the DCEF and
provide a fuller discussion of these and related issues.

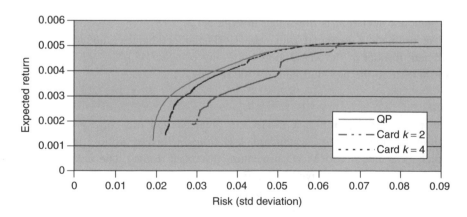

Figure 1.7   *Quadratic programming model and DCEF*

REFERENCES

Atkinson, A.B. (1970) On the measurement of inequality, *Journal of Economic Theory*, **2**, 244–63.

Basle Committee on Banking Supervision (1988) International Convergence of Capital Measurement and Capital Standards. Basle, Switzerland, Basle Committee on Banking Supervision, 1988.

Basle, The New Basle Capital Accord (2001) Dec, http://www.bis.org/publ/bcbsca.htm

Bawa, V.S. (1975) Optimal Rules for Ordering Uncertain Prospects, *Journal of Financial Economics*, **2**, 95–121.

Beale, E.M.L. and Forrest, J.J.H. (1976) Global Optimization using special ordered sets, *Mathematical Programming*, **10**, 52–69.

Brearley, A.L., Mitra, G. and Williams, H.P. (1975) Analysis of mathematical programming problems prior to applying the simplex algorithm, *Mathematical Programming*, **8**, 54–83.

Chang, T.-J., Meade, N., Beasley, J.E. and Sharaiha, Y.M. (2000) Heuristics for cardinality constrained portfolio optimisation, *Comp.& Opns Res*, **27**, 1271–302.

Chopra, V.K. and Ziemba, W.T. (1993) The effect of errors in means, variances and covariances on optimal portfolio choice, *Journal of Portfolio Management*, 6–11.

Darby-Dowman, K., Lucas, C., Mitra, G. and Yadegar, J. (1988) Linear, Integer, Separable and Fuzzy Programming Problems: A Unified Approach Towards Reformulation, *The Journal of the Operational Research Society*, **39**, 161–71.

DiBartolomeo, D. (2000) Recent Advances in Management of Taxable Portfolios, Northfield information services, [www.northinfo.com].

Domar, E. and Musgrave, R.A. (1944) Proportional Income Taxation and Risk Taking, *Quarterly Journal of Economics*, **57**, 388–422.

Douglas, L.G. (1990) *Bond Risk Analysis: A guide to duration and convexity*, NYIF Corp.

Ellison, E.D.F., Hajian, M., Levkovitz, R., Maros, I. and Mitra, G. (1999) *A Fortran Based Mathematical Programming System*, FortMP, Brunel University, Uxbridge, UK, and NAG Ltd, Oxford, UK.

Fishburn, P.C. (1977) Mean-Risk Analysis with Risk Associated with Below-Target Returns, *American Economic Review*, **67**, 116–26.

Gonin, R. and Money, J. (1989) *Non-linear L_p-Norm Estimation*, Wiley, New York, NY.

Grinold, R.C. and Kahn, R.N. (1995) *Active Portfolio Management: Quantitative Theory and Applications*, McGraw-Hill.

Hanoch, G. and Levy, H. (1969): The efficiency analysis of choices involving risk, *Rev. Econ. Stud.*, **36**, 335–46.

Hensel, C.R. and Turner, A.L. (1998) Making superior asset allocation decisions: a practitioner's guide. In *Worldwide Asset and Liability Modelling* (ed. W.T. Ziemba and J.M. Mulvey) Cambridge University Press.

Horniman, M.D., Jobst, N.J., Lucas, C.A. and Mitra, G. (2000) Constructing efficient portfolios with discrete constraints – a computational study, Technical Report TR/06/00, Department of Mathematical Sciences, Brunel University, Uxbridge.

Jobst, N.J., Horniman, M.D., Lucas, C.A. and Mitra, G. (2001) Computational aspects of alternative portfolio selection models in the presence of discrete asset choice constraints, *Quantitative Finance*, **I**, 1–13.

Kallberg, J.G. and Ziemba, W.T. (1983) Comparison of alternative utility functions in portfolio selection problems, *Management Science*, **29**, 1257–76.

King, B.F. (1966) Market and industry factors in stock price behaviour, *Journal of Business*, **39**, 139–90.

Konno, H. (1988): Portfolio Optimization using L_1 Risk Function, IHSS Report, 88–9, Institute of Human and Social Sciences, Tokyo Institute of Technology.

Konno, H. and Yamasaki, H. (1991) Mean-Absolute Deviation Portfolio Optimization Model and Its Applications to Tokyo Stock Market, *Management Science*, **37**, 519–31.

Koutsoukis, N.S., Mitra, G. and Lucas, C. (1999) Adapting Online Analytical Processing for Decision Modelling: The role of Information and Decision Technologies, *Decision Support Systems*, **26**, 1–30.

Lawler, E.L. and Wood, D.E. (1966) Branch-and-bound methods: a survey. *Operations Research*, **14**, 699–719.

Lee, S.M. and Chesser, D.L. (1980) Goal Programming for Portfolio Selection, *Journal of Portfolio Management*, **7**, 23–25.

Lintner, J. (1965) The valuation of risk assets and the selection of risky investments in stock portfolios and capital budgets, *Rev. Economics Statistics* 13–37.

Luenberger, D.G. (1998) *Investment Science*, Oxford University Press, New York.

Maros, I. and Meszaros, C. (1997) A repository of convex quadratic programming problems. Department Technical Report, DOC 97/6 Department of Computing, Imperial College, London.

Markowitz, H.M. (1952) Portfolio Selection, *Journal of Finance*, **7**, 77–91.

Markowitz, H.M. (1956) The optimisation of a quadratic function subject to linear constraints, *Naval Research Logistics Quarterly*, **3**, 111–33.

Markowitz, H.M. (1959) *Portfolio Selection: Efficient Diversification of Investments*, Wiley, New York, NY.

Mitra, G. (1976), *Theory and Application of Mathematical Programming*. Academic Press, New York.

Morgan, J.P. (1996) RiskMetrics™, Technical Document, 4 edn.

Mossin, J. (1966) Equilibrium in a capital asset market, *Econometrica*, **34**, 768–83.

Optimisation Service Provider: OSP (2001), EU CRAFT Project IST-1999-56410; www.osp-craft.com

Perold, A.F. (1984) Large-Scale Portfolio Optimization, *Management Science*, **30**, 1143–60.

Rosenberg, B. (1974) Extra-market components of covariance in security returns, *Journal of Financial and Quantitative Analysis*, **9**, 263–73.

Ross, S.A. (1976) The arbitrage theory of capital asset pricing, *Journal of Economic Theory*, **13**, 341–60.

Roy, A.D. (1952) Safety first and the holding of assets, *Econometrica*, **20**, 431–449.

Sharpe, W.F. (1963) A simplified model for portfolio analysis, *Management Science*, **9**, 277–93.

Sharpe, W.F. (1964) Capital asset prices: a theory of market equilibrium under conditions of risk, *Journal of Finance*, **19**, 425–42.

Sharpe, W.F. (1971) A Linear Programming Approximation for the General Portfolio Analysis Problem, *Journal of Financial and Quantitative Analysis*, **6**, 1263–75.

Simaan, Y. (1997) Estimation Risk in Portfolio Selection: The Mean Variance Model Versus the Mean Absolute Deviation Model, *Management Science*, **43**, 1437–46.

Speranza, M.G. (1996) A heuristic algorithm for a portfolio optimisation model applied to the Milan stock market, *Computers and Operations Research*, **23**, 433–41.

Tamiz, M., Hasham, R., Jones, D.F., Hesni, B. and Fargher, E.K. (1996) A Two-Staged Goal Programming Model for Portfolio Selection. In *Multi-Objective Programming and Goal Programming: Theories and Applications* (ed. M. Tamiz), Springer-Verlag, Berlin, 286–99.

Tobin, J. (1958) Liquidity preference as behaviour towards risk, *The Review of Economic Studies*, **25**, 2, 65–86.

Uryasev, S. and Rockafellar, R.T. (1999) Optimization of conditional Value-at-Risk, Research Report 99-4, ISE Dept., University of Florida.

Vanderbei, R.J. and Carpenter, T.J. (1993) Symmetric indefinite systems for interior point methods, *Mathematical Programming*, **58**, 1–32.

Von Neumann, J. and Morgenstern, O. (1944) *Theory of Games and Economic Behaviour*, Princeton, NJ, Princeton University Press.

Young, M.R. (1998) A Minimax Portfolio Selection Rule with Linear Programming Solution, *Management Science*, **44**, 673–83.

Zenios, S.A. (2002) Practical Financial Optimization: Decision making for financial engineers, Manuscript, HERMES Centre on Computational Finance and Economics, University of Cyprus, Nicosia, CY.

Ziemba, W.T., Parkan, C. and Brooks-Hill, R. (1974) Calculation of investment portfolios with risk-free borrowing and lending, *Management Science*, **21**, 209–222.

WEB REFERENCES

http://www.bis.org/publ/bcbsca.htm
www.osp-craft.com
www.optirisk-systems.com
carisma.brunel.ac.uk

ACKNOWLEDGEMENTS

The authors would like to thank INQUIRE (UK) for supporting and funding part of this research; thanks are also due to UBS Warburg Research for their close collaboration in the development of our heuristic for large scale QMIP problems.

Chapter 2

Generalized mean-variance analysis and robust portfolio diversification

STEPHEN M WRIGHT AND S E SATCHELL

ABSTRACT

This paper presents a new approach to portfolio optimization, which we call generalized mean-variance (GMV) analysis. We consider this to be, in effect, the rank (or quantile) equivalent of conventional Markowitz mean-variance analysis. The first stage of this process is to generate rank probability statistics using historic data, Monte Carlo analysis or direct user input. The second stage is optimization based on those rank statistics to calculate recommended portfolio weights.

The approach we take to optimization uses state preference theory to derive an objective function that can be minimized using standard quadratic programming techniques. The paper outlines a number of advantages of this method which include a more intuitive fully diversified (or minimum risk) position on the efficient frontier with all the portfolio holdings equally weighted. It also results in more stable portfolios due to reduced sensitivity to the perfect substitute problem, as well as the well-known robustness of rank statistics to the presence of outliers in the data.

The disadvantage of the approach is that if we use ranked mean and ranked variance in the search for robustness, it throws away some of the information available in the conventional analysis. However our GMV approach allows use of a mix of a ranked mean and a conventional variance to construct portfolios, or indeed other combinations,

_Continued on page 41 _

__ Continued from page 40 __

so that the trade off between efficiency and robustness can be varied to fit the circumstances.

2.1 INTRODUCTION

Mean-variance (MV) analysis is widely accepted as the best way of analysing and explaining the benefits of diversification of holdings across a portfolio of assets at least in principal. In addition the MV framework is tractable and allows us to incorporate constraints, tilts, inequalities, and indeed all the features of linear and quadratic programming. Together these benefits make MV analysis popular both with teachers of financial market theory and with system implementers within the investment technology industry.

At the same time, among practitioners and specialists in financial market theory, MV analysis and the portfolios that result from MV optimization continue to attract a steady flow of detailed criticism. To quote R.O. Michaud (1998), 'the basic problem is that MV portfolio efficiency has fundamental investment limitations as a practical tool of asset management'. Four major problems that occur in practice are discussed next.

Firstly, it is often difficult for practitioners to produce forecasts in the form required for MV optimization. They will often prefer to forecast relative return between assets, or wish to restrict their forecasts to those assets currently impacted by 'big picture' issues. Also many fund managers prefer to forecast rank rather than linear return. Turning these alternative forms back into the format required by standard mean-variance analysis can be an inelegant and error prone compromise.

Secondly, our MV optimal portfolio can be highly sensitive to the exact value of the return forecasts. This problem is magnified by the fact that the forecasting process is known to usually produce results which are highly inaccurate and noisy. This leads to undesirable instability in recommended portfolio holdings (see Merton (1981) among many others). This instability is then further compounded by the fact that the correlation coefficients used in standard mean variance analysis can themselves be worryingly unstable over time.

Thirdly, many investors feel uneasy about the use of variance as a risk measure. The most counter-intuitive feature is its equal penalization of gains and losses, see Sortino and Forsey (1996). However, it is also possible for returns on a minimum variance portfolio to be dominated by a nominally riskier portfolio which, while more volatile, still always produces a higher return. Also, depending on the choice of asset set, if one of the assets has much less volatile returns than the others, then a minimum risk portfolio in a mean-variance sense will be heavily concentrated in this one asset rather than diversified across a wide range of holdings.

Finally, it is usual when using MV optimization to exclude assets with a highly non-normal distribution of return (e.g. options, or some of the dynamic trading strategies executed by hedge funds) as the conventional summary statistics do not fully capture the distribution of the return on these assets and hence the portfolio statistics could conceal undesirable concentrations of risk. Similarly less liquid assets such as property or private equity show artificially low volatilities which lead to an over allocation in mean-variance analysis.

Given these problems, it is not clear which aspects of MV analysis to retain and which one should jettison. It is desirable to use the linear quadratic framework of the MV world without limiting ourselves to the specific choice of mean return and variance or tracking error of return as the parameters which drive the investor decision function. This approach has already been adopted in the literature. Wang (1999) uses a MV model to solve multiple benchmark problems. Chow and Kritzman (2001) convert MV analysis into value at risk-based capital allocations. We plan to take this further by putting all these cases into a general framework. In particular, we show how non-parametric statistics can be incorporated into this framework. The approach we use is based on state preference theory, see Copeland and Weston (1988), we derive an objective function which can be minimized using standard quadratic programming techniques.

We will then show how this generalization of the mean variance framework allows a more robust portfolio construction process that is less sensitive to noise in the input parameters and we will introduce an innovative set of summary statistics that provide a very intuitive representation of downside risk.

At the heart of the investment management process is a simple question: 'In what proportion should I hold this range of assets given my expectations about future risk and return on each one'. In principle, the process for arriving at this optimal set of portfolio weights has been firmly established since Markowitz introduced mean-variance analysis, see Markowitz (1959).

As one might expect, this deceptively simple question hides a vast range of complications. In practice, in order to apply classical mean-variance analysis you have to make a number of simplifying assumptions. Many of these assumptions are routinely violated in practice.

The first assumption is that risk and standard deviation of expected return are synonymous. In reality, investors' appetites for upside and downside risk are very different! If the forecast return on all your assets can be adequately modelled by a normal distribution then upside and downside risk are equal and this is merely a semantic quibble. However, investors are becoming increasingly concerned about the asymmetric behaviour of return on many asset types, hence alternative approaches have been developed to address this problem, see Sortino and Forsey (1996). Usually these approaches require accurate modelling of the higher moments of the return distribution hence they are extremely sensitive to limitations in the next assumption.

The next problem is that estimating the parameters used in mean-variance optimization (expected return, standard deviation and correlation of return on all assets) is a process which is plagued by data problems. In particular, correlation estimates can be quite unstable with the diversification effect calculated in normal times reducing dramatically when most needed as the markets go through a turbulent period. Suggested improvements involve separately modelling normal and abnormal market behaviour and mixing the results in some way, see Chow et al. (1999), or employing less summarized risk statistics, see Embrechts et al. (1999), or Gardener et al. (2000). Equally, the return forecasts used will typically be subject to estimation error. This can lead to further instability in the recommended holdings; in fact the process of optimization has been referred to as one of error maximization! (See Jorion, 1992).

The final problem is that providing an excess return forecast for each asset is not a very effective format for capturing the insight of professional investors into likely market movements. Usually investors will feel more confidence in some forecasts than others. Typically, they will feel more confident about relative return forecasts than absolute return forecasts, and they would prefer to only forecast return for that limited range of assets currently being affected by 'the big picture' while leaving the remainder to set to a neutral value. This has led to the use of Bayesian approaches to building up a forecast from multiple partial views; see Black and Litterman (1992). While this can be very effective, the mathematics involved can be intimidating, and the detailed implementation decisions made are critical to achieving well-behaved intuitive results.

From an investment practitioner's perspective, our initial simple question has turned into a vast specialist subject where the best approach is highly dependent on the detailed circumstances in which the optimization is done. In the many investment organizations who can afford to develop (or commission) the correct level of specialist expertise, this is not a problem. For many others, a two-culture situation develops. Practical fund managers distrust and dislike the black box characteristics of the usual diversification approaches. Specialist quantitative analysts dislike and distrust the apparently 'ad hoc' nature of many investment decisions. For a final group, the value added by formal risk management is so outweighed by the costs and complexities of implementation that they adopt one of a range of alternative heuristic approaches to diversification.

Most attempts to date to make the assumptions inherent in mean-variance analysis more closely reflect day-to-day realities of the investment world have usually involved ever more sophisticated mathematics. Unfortunately, for many people the complexity of the mathematics is a barrier to acceptance in its own right. An alternative is to use a diversification technique which is based on mathematics which is inherently less sensitive to noise in the data, less dependent on the assumed form of the forecast return distributions, and with built in assumptions which are essentially simple to understand. Robust statistics addresses all of these issues with the potential penalty of not being able to use all available information. In addition this approach builds on and formalizes the established practice among an important subset of fund managers who actively use ranking approaches in their forecasting and portfolio construction processes.

In Section 2.2, we present a discussion on what we call generalized mean-variance analysis which attempts to put the above problems and approaches into a general framework. The procedure we advocate to replace expected returns is m-tile membership. The concept of m-tile membership means what m-tile does the stock belong to when ranked over the universe of stocks. If $m = 10$, for example, we are asking what decile the stock belongs to.

In Section 2.3 we detail our 'mean-variance' approach whilst in Section 2.4 we present details of more Monte Carlo investigations and empirical implementations. Conclusions follow in Section 2.5

2.2   GENERALIZED MEAN-VARIANCE ANALYSIS

In modelling decision making for an organization, we can afford to be a little more hazy than in modelling the decision making of an individual, where the accepted wisdom is to use a variant or generalization of expected utility theory. The reason for this laxity is the fact that we have very few clear guidelines as to how to aggregate the preferences of individual stakeholders into the decision function of the organization. To take a simple example of a company with an employee pension plan, the interest of the average shareholder typically conflicts with the interests of the pension plan members. Conflicting interests may be resolved via the use of game-theoretic notions, but such resolutions usually depend upon a set of auxiliary assumptions describing the behaviour of the individuals playing the game.

The preliminary remarks above justify, in our view, presenting a firm's decision function in terms of an $(n \times 1)$ vector of positive attributes a associated with the n investible assets in the universe, together with a positive definite matrix $C(n \times n)$. Then, for a given set of portfolio weights $\underset{\sim}{\omega}(n \times 1)$, the firm maximizes

$$\underset{\sim}{\omega}'\underset{\sim}{a} - \lambda\underset{\sim}{\omega}'\underset{\sim}{C}\underset{\sim}{\omega} \qquad (2.1)$$

where λ represents the trade off between the attribute of the portfolio $(\underset{\sim}{\omega}'\underset{\sim}{a})$ versus the risk of the portfolio $(\underset{\sim}{\omega}'\underset{\sim}{C}\underset{\sim}{\omega})$. For obvious reasons, we call such an analysis generalized mean-variance analysis. Together with some additional constraints, such as $\omega'e = 1$ or 0, where $e = (1,1,1,1,1,1)'$, or $\omega_i \geq 0$ (long-only positions) we have a conventional quadratic programming problem.

We next turn to the choice of attribute and the choice of $n \times n$ measure $\underset{\sim}{C}$. Necessary features for $\underset{\sim}{a}$ would be that more $\underset{\sim}{\omega}'\underset{\sim}{a}$ is desirable for the firm and that $\underset{\sim}{a}$ is approximately linear so that if $r_p = \frac{1}{2}r_1 + \frac{1}{2}r_2$, then $a_p \approx \frac{1}{2}a_1 + \frac{1}{2}a_2$. We say approximately linear because an attribute that is almost linear but reasonably easy to measure and/or forecast should lead to better portfolios than an attribute, such as the expected rate of return, which is exactly linear and very difficult to forecast.

One attribute of considerable interest is m-tile membership where m is a divisor of n, the number of stocks in the universe. If $m = 10$, for example, this tells us what decile of the universe of stocks we expect the stock to lie in. If $m = n$, then the attribute is the expected rank. At first glance, it might seem that the theory of order statistics might help us advance our analysis. Sadly, that theory is based on the assumptions that the n returns are a random sample, i.e. independent identically distributed (i.i.d.) random variables. Equity returns are anything but iid. To illustrate the type of mathematical issues set $m = 2$ and $n = 4$, then for stock 1 we can compute the probability stock 1 is in the top two of the four stocks. Denoting R_i as the return of stock i, call this event A, then denoting Probabilities by $P()$,

$$P(A_1) = P(R_1 > R_2 \text{ and } R_1 > R_3) + P(R_1 > R_3 \text{ and } R_1 > R_4)$$
$$+ P(R_1 > R_2 \text{ and } R_1 > R_4)$$

Now analogously, we calculate $P(A_i)$, $i = 1, 4$, and retain the two stocks with the largest $P(A_i)$'s then, in the population rather than the sample, we would have defined what we mean by top-half stocks. If we took many samples from our universe we could construct sample estimators of $P(A_i)$, thus we could identify and estimate top-half membership. Of course with real data the changing time varying nature of return distributions inhibits this.

In the population, decile (or m-tile) membership will be partly linear. For weights ω_i, $\Sigma\omega_i = 1$, if assets $(1, \ldots, k)$ belong to m-tile j, then, $\max(R_i) = \Sigma\omega_i\max_{i\in1,\ldots k}(R_i) \geq R_p \geq \Sigma\omega_i \min_{it}(R_i) = \min(R_i)$ so that R_p also lies in m-tile j. By the same argument if $(1, \ldots, k)$ lie between m-tiles j, and k so will

$R_p = \Sigma\omega_i R_i$ also lie between m-tiles j and k. It should also be clear that m-tile membership is not fully linear as the following example demonstrates.

Consider stocks 1 to 6 with returns 10, 9, 8, 7.5, 7.4 and 0 and $m = 3$, thus stocks 1 and 2 are in the top ter-tile, stocks 3 and 4 are in the second ter-tile and stocks 5 and 6 are in the third ter-tile. Suppose we construct a portfolio of 0.8 stock 2 (rank 1) plus 0.2 stock 6 (rank 3), the portfolio rank is $0.8 \times 1 + 0.2 \times 3 = 1.4$, thus the portfolio is a rank 2 asset according to linearity. However, its return is $0.8 \times 9 + 0.2 \times 0 = 7.2$ which is in the third ter-tile, since assets 5 and 6 have returns 0 and 7.4

2.3   THE STATE PREFERENCE THEORY APPROACH TO PORTFOLIO CONSTRUCTION

In conventional mean-variance analysis, we use correlation matrices as a key intermediate variable when calculating the optimum. When we do this, we are assuming that knowing the mean, standard deviation, and correlation of the return on all the constituents of the portfolio is all that is needed to fully describe the risk characteristics of any portfolio built from these constituents. In practice, the real distribution of return may often be fat-tailed, skewed, and/or discontinuous as will the multivariate probability distributions.

Unfortunately it is not obvious that the mean-variance results derived for conventional correlation apply equally to rank correlation statistics. Even worse, there are alternative non-parametric statistics that we might think of using (i.e. Spearman's rank order correlation or Kendall's Tau). Hence the need to go back to first principles in order to prove our method.

In the state preference model, uncertainty takes the form of not knowing what the state of nature will be at some future date. To the investor, each security is a set of possible payoffs, each one associated with a mutually exclusive state. Once the uncertain state of the world is revealed, the payoff on each security is determined exactly. This is a very flexible way of modelling complex valuation and decision-taking processes. This very flexibility is also its main problem. There are usually an infinite number of states (high/low) hence the usual assumption of normal distribution of return in order to make the mathematics tractable.

When considering m-tiles, we can consider all cases from $m = 2$ to $m = n$ (rank). We shall investigate the rank case next. If we assume that the states of nature are adequately represented by the rank order of the portfolio, then for an 'n' asset problem the number of states of nature has reduced from infinite to 'n' factorial. This total falls even further as we reduce the resolution of the calculation from rank to m-tile. If we then further assume that the actual probabilities observed are a sample drawn from a distribution which is continuous and with limited magnitude of first derivative then we do not need to exhaustively evaluate all 'n' factorial states in order to optimize our weights. However, by sampling repeatedly, the probability that stock i belongs to m-tile j can easily be determined with any degree of accuracy.

In effect this generates a time series for which we can find a formula for the 'mean' and 'variance'.

For values of m that are reasonably large, it is clear that conventional historic data cannot be simply applied to compute rank probabilities as there are not enough degrees of freedom. However, as mentioned above, given assumptions about the data-generating process (DGP), for example, that returns $\underset{\sim}{r}$ are multivariate normal with mean vector μ and covariance matrix $\underset{\sim}{\Sigma}$,

$$\underset{\sim}{r} \sim N(\underset{\sim}{\mu}, \underset{\sim}{\Sigma}) \tag{2.2}$$

we can employ Monte Carlo methods to compute rank probabilities by simulation. The benefit of the above approach is that we can replace (2.2) by more complex assumptions, i.e. we can model non-normality, extreme returns, conditional volatility etc. without complicating matters unduly; all we need to be able to do is to simulate the DGP.

Once we have evaluated the p_k, we can set up our quadratic optimization. x_k is the return (i.e. rank) of the portfolio on each of 'm' possible states. p_k is the probability) of each of the 'm' possible states. ω_i is the weight of each of the 'n' asscts. r_{ik} is the rank of each asset in each state.

$$x_k = \sum_{i=1...n} \omega_i r_{ik} \qquad \text{(m-tile value)}$$

$$\ast = \sum_{k=1...m} \left(\sum_{i=1...n} (\omega_i r_{ik} p_k / m) \right) \qquad \text{(average m-tile value)}$$

$$\ast^2 = \left(\sum_{k=1...m} \left(\sum_{i=1...n} (\omega_i r_{ik} p_k / m) \right) \right)^2 \qquad \text{(squared m-tile value)}$$

$$x_k{}^2 = \sum_{i=1...n} \left(\sum_{j=1...n} (\omega_i r_{ik} \omega_j r_{jk}) \right) \qquad \text{(squared root value)}$$

$$v = \left(\sum_{k=1...m} (x_k{}^2 p_k) - m \ast^2 \right) / (m-1) \qquad \text{(rank variance)}$$

$$\theta = \ast - \lambda v \qquad \text{(objective function)}$$

$$\theta = \ast - \lambda \left(\sum_{k=1...m} (x_k^2 p_k) - m \ast^2 \right) / (m-1) \qquad \text{(substituted for variance)}$$

$$\theta = \sum_{k=1...m} \left(\sum_{i=1...n} (\omega_i r_{ik} p_k / m) \right) - \lambda \left(\sum_{k=1...m} (x_k^2 p_k)/(m-1) \right)$$

$$+ m\lambda \left(\sum_{k=1...m} \left(\sum_{i=1...n} (\omega_i r_{ik} p_k / m) \right) \right)^2 / (m-1)$$

$$\theta = \sum_{k=1...m} \left(\sum_{i=1...n} (\omega_i r_{ik} p_k / m) \right) - \lambda \left(\sum_{k=1...m} \left(\sum_{i=1...n} \left(\sum_{j=1...n} (\omega_i r_{ik} \omega_j r_{jk}) \right) \right. \right.$$

$$\left. \left. \times p_k \right) \right) \Big/ (m-1) + m\lambda \left(\sum_{k=1...m} \left(\sum_{i=1...n} (\omega_i r_{ik} p_k / m) \right) \right)^2 / (m-1)$$

As this is a standard quadratic objective function, it can be minimized using all the conventional quadratic programming algorithms.

In the above we consider m-tile rank as our 'return' and rank variance as our 'risk'. Actually, hybrid procedures could be used. For example, if we thought that tracking error/conventional variance was a sensible risk measure, then we could use this in conjunction with a ranked return. In mixing different characteristics, care needs to be taken in the determination of λ. This is not, however, an insurmountable problem as we can take the λ of the market portfolio based on the mix assumed much as is done in conventional mean-variance analysis where you choose the λ which makes the FT All-Share optimal. Then by varying λ we can assume that we are more or less risk tolerant than the market representative agent.

2.4   IMPLEMENTATION AND SIMULATION

In order to test the properties of the ranking approach to mean-variance analysis, a number of simulations were run to demonstrate different aspects of the approach. The first test was to look at the 'perfect substitute' problem. This occurs where some assets in a portfolio have such similar forecast risk characteristics that the optimizer sees little extra risk in moving a holding from fully in one of the pair into fully in the other as the relative forecast return for the pair of assets changes sign. Unconstrained, this results in large long–short bets for such asset pairs, and sharp changes in recommendation over small change in forecast return.

To demonstrate this, we chose a three asset portfolio containing French equity, and French and German bonds. Historically, the latter two assets have been closely correlated. The first plot below (Figure 2.1a) shows the changing holdings recommended by conventional mean-variance analysis (at a constant tracking error) as the forecast return varies over half a percentage point. The second chart

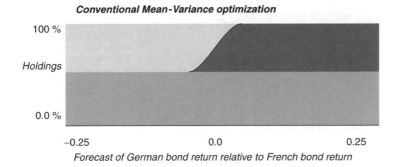

Figure 2.1a *Conventional mean-variance optimization*

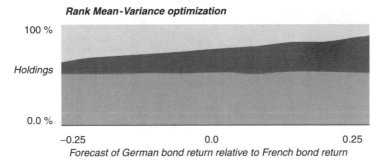

Figure 2.1b *Rank mean-variance optimization*

(Figure 2.1b) shows the same test done with rank optimization demonstrating the desired reduction in sensitivity to small changes in the user's input forecast. (Tracking error in this case is only approximately constant hence the slight 'wobble' in the lines.)

The second issue with mean-variance analysis is the problem of defining risk. Taking a typical global asset allocation portfolio of European, Asian and American equities and bonds looked at from a US dollar perspective, the efficient frontier calculated using five years of return history from 1986 to 2001 shows recommended holdings which vary along the efficient frontier as shown in Figure 2.2a. The minimum risk portfolio is in reality not very well diversified, consisting as it does largely of US bonds. This represents a very concentrated exposure to forecasting errors.

The same exercise undertaken using rank optimization (Figure 2.2b) results in a minimum risk portfolio with equally weighted holdings as by definition placing the same bet on every asset must result in zero volatility of average rank return. This is intuitively a much more diversified position than the standard mean-variance analysis above.

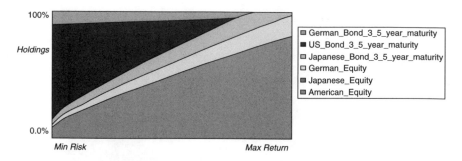

Figure 2.2a   *Conventional efficient frontier*

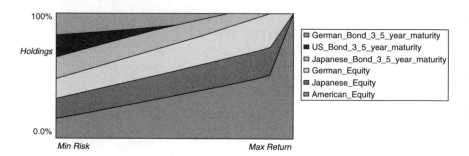

Figure 2.2b   *Rank efficient frontier*

The third issue is volatility of recommended holdings caused by noise in the correlation matrix over a period of time. Figure 2.3 shows the same set of assets with constant forecast returns but now at a fixed tracking error position recalculated monthly over the period 1998 to 2001. This was calculated using three years of monthly data, exponentially weighted with a weighting half-life of one year) This can be seen to routinely produce substantial short-term movements in recommended holdings that are highly undesirable from a practical investment perspective.

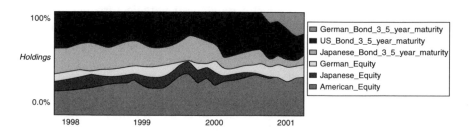

Figure 2.3   *Volatility of optimum portfolio due to correlation matrix changes over time*

Volatility of coefficients in the calculated correlation matrix is an inevitable consequence of the stochastic nature of the time series being compared. In an ideal world, where there is an underlying 'true' value of correlation, the distribution of the estimated values around that 'true' value can itself be estimated using a knowledge of the method used to calculate the correlation coefficients. The width of this distribution is then usually taken as a measure of the significance of the estimated coefficient.

In linear correlation, occasional large values of return (fat tails) and uncertainty about the form of the joint probability distribution create uncertainty as to the formula to use to calculate the significance of the correlation estimate. In rank correlation, there is no uncertainty over the distribution of returns from which any given sample is drawn (it is always drawn from the set of integers 1 to n). Hence the correct formula to calculate the significance of the correlation is known. As the joint probability distribution of the underlying variables approaches a bivariate normal distribution, the significance of the linear estimates becomes as good as those produced from the rank correlation. In fact the significance formula becomes the same, viz: $T = r * \mathrm{sqrt}((N - 2)/(1 - r^2))$.

Another way of putting this is that for any given level of underlying real correlation, and sample size, as the underlying distribution deviates more and more from bivariate normal, the volatility of the estimated linear correlation coefficient increases relative to the volatility of the rank correlation. Given that these deviations from normality are unknown and potentially large and time varying, the implicit use of rank correlation rather than linear correlation must reduce this source of volatility in recommended holdings. Given a hypothetical sample size of a hundred data points and historic distribution of return for the above asset set, this could reduce the volatility of correlation coefficients very significantly.

The final problem with traditional mean-variance analysis is forecasting return in a way that is intuitive to a typical fund manager. Capturing this insight into likely market movements is an art not a science. In due course, a range of alternative methods are likely to be developed to capture this information. However all of these methods need to convert the manager's input, in whatever form it is most conveniently entered, into a standard set of summary statistics used for analysis. In mean-variance analysis these summary statistics are the means, and covariance of return. The equivalent summary statistics in our approach is the rank (or m-tile) probability matrix illustrated below.

This m-tile probability matrix is a very simple way of describing intuitively the likely rank of each asset. There is one column per asset and in each column the probability of that asset being in each quantile is indicated in the relevant row. In the rank case the matrix is a matrix of probabilities, hence all the rows and all the columns must sum to 100%. Such a matrix is called bi-stochastic.

We give an example below.

Rank probability matrix

USB	CVB	EAFE	R1000	R2000
16.47	23.96	5.94	17.19	36.44
16.65	23.18	11.44	29.99	18.74
16.23	23.41	26.66	20.14	13.56
19.74	19.64	27.24	19.88	13.50
30.91	9.81	28.72	12.80	17.76

The above matrix, which details an $m = n = s$ case, tells us for example, the probabilities that R2000 is ranked first is 36.44%. The row sum adding to one simply means that the sum of probabilities that different stocks could be first should add to 1. Likewise the second row is the sum of probabilities that different stocks could be second, which again adds to 1. The column numbers, say the second column, CVB, tells us the rank probabilities of CVB, which again add to 1. One can deduce immediately from such a column the expected rank of CVB. An alternative graphical representation is shown in Figure 2.4 where the height of each band of grey is proportional to the probability of that asset being in that quantile.

As with covariance matrices, these m-tile probability matrices provide summary statistics that give a valuable insight into likely investment out-turn. They implicitly contain joint probability information. They are straightforward to calculate from the state probability values, and are easily interpreted.

Any optimization process, inherently optimizes an average expected value. Given that return is frequently highly non-normal (even if we choose to ignore

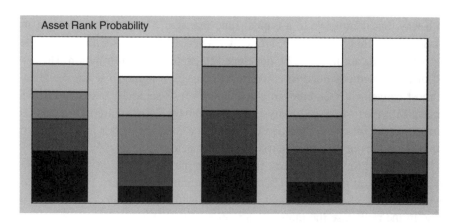

Figure 2.4   *Rank asset probability*

this fact in the interests of tractable computation), this average could hide concentrations of downside risk which are highly undesirable. The m-tile probability matrix allows this downside probability to be observed in a very direct way.

When combined with the fact that the significance of rank correlation is much more robust to non-normality in the return distributions, the presence of this safeguard makes it practical to include assets in a portfolio being diversified which have a very non-normal distribution of forecast return. This considerably extends the range of asset types and forecasting methods which can be reliably employed in this type of diversification exercise.

In particular, scenario forecasts are more naturally handled in this environment, unlike standard mean-variance analysis which requires that you forecast a single vector of mean returns. This approach allows you to postulate a range of alternative scenarios and allocate probabilities to each. Monte Carlo simulation enables you to combine these scenarios to generate a forecast of the probability of different assets outperforming each other.

2.5   CONCLUSIONS AND SUGGESTED FURTHER WORK

It can be seen from the preceding section that the recommended holdings produced using GMV analysis are more stable than those calculated using standard mean-variance analysis.

Choosing an appropriate definition of risk is ultimately a matter of your particular circumstances and preferences. Defining the minimum risk portfolio such that it is the equally weighted set of holdings has the attraction that it is more consistent with our intuitive ideas of full diversification than are portfolios produced using the minimum volatility criteria.

In addition, this approach is much less sensitive to problems caused by non-normal forecast return distributions than classical mean-variance analysis. The ability to display the rank (or m-tile) probability matrix provides an easily interpreted safeguard against hidden concentrations of risk. The fact that the significance level of the rank correlation is independent of the return distribution, avoids the problem with classical mean-variance which can lead to unreliable recommended portfolios if the significance of the calculated linear correlation coefficient proves to be particularly low.

As we have retained the linear quadratic framework of the MV world, we can incorporate constraints, tilts, inequalities, and indeed all the other operationally convenient features of linear and quadratic programming. However, we have also retained the simplifying assumption that the return distribution is adequately represent by its (rank) mean and standard deviation. Hence if users have marked preferences for the shape of the probability distribution of forecast portfolio rank return as well as for its mean and standard deviation, they should compare this GMV approach to those based on optimizing downside deviation, value at risk, or stochastic dominance. Simple extensions of our approach can allow optimization based on the m-tile equivalent of these criteria.

The main problem using this approach is the other side of the robustness coin. The standard mean variance model has beatified excess return and tracking error as measures of performance and risk. It will take considerable effort to establish alternative non-parametric risk and return measures in general use. However, in practice this may not be the major problem that it first appears. While the holdings are optimized on the basis of the m-tile (or rank) statistics, the results can still be reported in terms of tracking error, excess return etc., hence achieving the best of both worlds.

REFERENCES

Black, F. and Litterman, R. (1990) Global Portfolio Optimisation, *Financial Analysts Journal Robust Diversification* (September/October).

Chow, G. and Kritzman, M. (2001) Risk Budgets, *Journal of Portfolio Management*, Winter, 56–61.

Chow, G., Jacquier, E., Kritzman, M. and Lowry, K. (1999) Optimal Portfolios in Good Times and Bad, *Financial Analysts Journal* (May/June).

Copeland and Weston (1988) Financial Theory and Corporate Policy, *State Preference Theory* (3rd Edition, Ch. 5). Addison Wesley Publishing (ISBN 0-201-10).

Embrechts, P., McNeil, A.J. and Straumann, D. (1999) *Correlation: Pitfalls and Alternatives*, *RISK* **12**(5), 69–71.

Gardener, D., Bowie, D., Brooks, M. and Cumberworth, M. (2000) Predicted Tracking Errors Fact or Fantasy? Faculty and Institute of Actuaries Investment Conference, Hatfield Heath, 25–27 June.

Jorion, P. (1992) Portfolio Optimisation in Practice, *Financial Analysts' Journal* (January/February).

Markowitz, H.M. (1959) *Portfolio Selection: Efficient Diversification of Investments*, John Wiley, New York.

Sortino, F.A. and Forsey, H.A. (1996) On the Use and Misuse of Downside Risk, *Journal of Portfolio Management*.

Chapter 3

Portfolio construction from mandate to stock weight: a practitioner's perspective

DR JULIAN COUTTS

ABSTRACT

Whereas risk analysis is all about the risks run in a predefined portfolio, portfolio construction is about the general shape a portfolio should take to assume predefined risks. The risk analysis problem is fairly well defined. Portfolio construction, on the other hand, has been largely treated heuristically by the investment community.

This work has been undertaken to provide a more objective framework for designing funds. This framework leads to a 'flight envelope' for the fund – a term specifically chosen to evoke images of how test pilots assess the safe regimes for flying aircraft, which can then be used by other pilots responsible for the safety of hundreds of passengers.

How should risk be allocated to the various risk-taking activities in the fund?

The result of a non-linear optimization can be used to allocate tracking error optimally to the various teams, bearing in mind their abilities and other constraints.

How should we set appropriate bet sizes within a stock level portfolio?

We present an approximation to the covariance matrix that introduces a Euclidean distance measure as a suitable proxy. We find expressions for the tracking errors of arbitrary portfolios. We consider inserting industry bets into portfolios. We make use of the distance measure not only for setting fund specifications but for other purposes too, e.g. fund turnover limit setting.

How far should ideas be supported within a portfolio?

Continued on page 56

Continued from page 55

By re-deriving the core CAPM results in an active fund context, and making use of our approximation to the covariance matrix, we derive simple formulae, which make intuitive sense. The formulae should provide a useful starting point for setting stock weightings, when tradability of stocks is not a major issue. The output of this investigation is a methodology – a smooth way to mutate a portfolio from on-index to progressively more aggressive stances. The key is the algorithm used to treat the no-short-selling constraint.

3.1   INTRODUCTION

This document is a summary of a large body of research and development work aimed at portfolio construction. This work was delivered by the Risk Management Team, at Standard Life Investments, during the period January 1998 to May 2001. This is a rich vein of research, and intensive work continues on this subject.

Whereas risk analysis is all about the risks run in a predefined portfolio, portfolio construction is about the general shape a portfolio should take to assume predefined risks. The risk analysis problem is fairly well defined. Software packages are continually being built to dissect portfolios in novel ways and the debate about risk analysis has moved on from whether the job can be done, to whether it can be done better using different algorithms.

Portfolio construction, on the other hand, has been largely treated heuristically by the investment community. Experienced fund managers write specifications for funds by considering the competition and use their combined years of wisdom to set how aggressive a portfolio needs to be and how to implement that aggression.

This work has been undertaken to provide a more objective framework for designing funds, from benchmark setting through to position taking. This framework leads to a 'flight envelope' for the fund – a term specifically chosen to evoke images of how test pilots assess the safe regimes for flying aircraft, which can then be used by other pilots responsible for the safety of hundreds of passengers.

It is difficult to 'explode' the fund risk into how it can be forecast from other parameters. Time is too limited to explore all the funds that could be drawn from all the assets in all the asset classes throughout the possible universe. Rather, we have made approximations to cut to the principal decisions made by fund managers.

These are the questions we seek to answer in this chapter:

How Should Risk be Allocated to the Various Risk Taking Activities in the Fund?

This is addressed in Section 3.2. The competition defines the tracking error taken at asset allocation level, which must then be married to the abilities of the various decision-taking groups to turn risk into return. The result of a non-linear optimization can be used to allocate tracking error optimally to the various teams.

How Should We Set Appropriate Bet Sizes within a Stock Level Portfolio?

In Section 3.3 we present an approximation to the covariance matrix that introduces a Euclidean distance measure as a suitable proxy. This can be shown to work well empirically within asset classes. We also take this consequence of the covariance matrix approximation further to find expressions for the tracking errors of arbitrary portfolios (from the highly aggressive 10 stock portfolios through intermediate strength portfolios through to the index fund). The tail of uninvested small stocks is of particular importance. The core result can be extended to suggest the numbers and extents of overweighted stocks for any particular portfolio risk requirement.

Market practice can be shown to reduce the overweightings for large funds (an empirical fact that is not reflected in any analysis package and justifies the use of load ratios as risk control tools). We consider the effect on tracking error of inserting industry bets into portfolios. Finally, we bring all the analysis together to set up a flight envelope for a variety of funds. We make use of the distance measure not only for the standard application in setting fund specifications – here we show how to do this for the emerging market equity class – but for others too, such as for fund turnover constraint setting.

How Far Should Ideas be Supported within a Portfolio?

In Section 3.4 we begin by re-deriving the core CAPM results but in an active fund context. We find expressions for the optimal portfolio and information ratio. We make use of our new approximation to the covariance matrix, which allows simple expressions for portfolio weightings to be derived. The shapes of the formulae make intuitive sense: for example, the efficient frontier is a straight line through the origin. The formulae should provide a useful starting point for setting stock weightings, when tradability of stocks is not a major issue.

The output of this investigation is a methodology described in Section 3.5 – a smooth way to mutate a portfolio from on-index to progressively more aggressive stances, by taking a predefined level of risk producing results in close agreement with a commercial optimizer, when fed with the same preferences. The key is the algorithm used to treat the no-short-selling constraint.

3.2   ALLOCATING TRACKING ERROR FOR MULTIPLE PORTFOLIO FUNDS

3.2.1   Introduction

As part of the effort to gather best practice in portfolio construction, we consider how a fund director might allocate the ability to take risk among the reporting asset class managers. This Section presents two tools, a simple rule of thumb and a more sophisticated non-linear allocator. Examples using two types of product (UK pension fund and global equity) are presented.

3.2.2   Rationale and approach

When deciding on how much risk asset class managers should be allowed to take, it is a useful check to ensure that no one manager is shouldering more than a fair allocation of fund risk.

We can develop a simple rule of thumb which equalizes the potential for downside between asset allocation and stock selection. This rule of thumb assumes that managers have no skill.

Conversely, those who are skilful managers should be given more opportunity. The ability to perform should be spread between asset allocation and stock selection. However, there are some practical limitations resulting from the fact that tracking error can never be negative and is bounded on the upper side by some fraction of index volatility.

We can use Lagrangian techniques to define a set of rules where tracking error is allocated optimally.

3.2.3   Mathematics

The rule of thumb equalizes the tracking error taken on in one asset class, assuming that all others are on index, and also taking an asset allocation bet in that asset class.

Consider a benchmark of two assets: Y in asset A and $1 - Y$ in asset B. Consider a fund of X in asset A and $1 - X$ in asset B. The fund has the B component on index. The A component is run with stock selection tracking error. The monthly outperformance will be

$$
\begin{aligned}
r_{fund} - r_{bm} &= X(r_a + \delta r_a) + (1 - X)r_b - (Yr_a + (1 - Y)r_b) \\
&= (X - Y)(r_a - r_b) + X\delta r_a
\end{aligned}
\tag{3.1}
$$

Note that the first term is what contributes to asset allocation tracking error, and the second is the stock selection tracking error. The first term is of the order of the volatility of asset A, but may be less, depending on the decorrelation between A and B. If the assets A and B are fully uncorrelated and of equal volatility, then the standard deviation of the asset allocation term will be the volatility of A divided by the square root of 2.

$$(Bet)_i * (Volatilty)_i \sim (Weight)_i * (Tracking\ Error)_i * \sqrt{2} \qquad (3.2)$$

This shows the start of a theme that will emerge more fully, that the tracking error that should be taken in asset class i is roughly inversely proportional to weight of that asset class in the fund. Simple back of the envelope calculations show that this rule produces sensible numbers for asset weights around 50% and bet sizes around 5%. Equally, it is important to notice that a smaller asset class weight in the fund leads to the ability to take higher tracking errors within asset class.

However, there is a problem. If the weight gets very small, the tracking error can become unfeasibly high. In practical terms, it is difficult to find a single stock (the ultimate portfolio) with a tracking error much more than a few times the volatility of the index. Babcock versus the FT Allshare has a tracking error of 3 * (volatility) of the FT Allshare. Glaxo or BP both have individual tracking errors close to 1.5 * (volatility). These, however, are somewhat impractical limits. By the time we have moved to four stocks, the tracking error is 0.7 * (volatility of index). So for practical portfolios, it is sensible to limit the tracking error taken to (at the very most) the volatility.

The most sophisticated analysis comprises two equations, one for the value added by the managers and the other for the risk taken on by the fund. The first equation is

$$\langle Value\ Added \rangle = IR_{AA} + \sum_{i=1,n} w_i IR_i \sigma_{TE,I} \qquad (3.3)$$

and the second is

$$\sigma_{TE}{}^2 = \sigma_{AA}{}^2 + \sum_{i=1,n} w_i^2 \sigma_{TE,i}{}^2 \qquad (3.4)$$

In these equations, the Information Ratio for asset class i is IR_i ($IRAA$ for asset allocation), w_i is the weight of the fund in asset class i, and the tracking errors for the asset classes are $\sigma_{TE,I}$, combining to a total tracking error of σ_{TE}.

We want to maximize the value added for the risk we are taking into the fund, so we optimize this equation set using Lagrange multipliers. Writing down the Lagrangian and setting the first derivatives of the Lagrangian with respect to the variables to zero, leads to several conditions that must be met for the value obtained by the risk taken to be maximal. They are

$$\sigma_{AA} = (\lambda/2) * IR_{AA} \tag{3.5}$$

$$\sigma_{TE,i} = (\lambda/2) * (IR_i/w_i) \tag{3.6}$$

$$\langle Value\ Added \rangle = (\lambda/2) * \left[IR_{AA}^2 + \sum_{i=1,n} IR_i^2 \right] \tag{3.7}$$

In Equations (3.5–3.7), λ is the Lagrange multiplier. If the managers are skilful in their markets, they should be allowed to take more risk. The benefits and objections outlined above still hold. Lower weight leads to higher tracking error allowances but only up to a limit. There is an additional problem. Information ratios can be negative, which may invalidate this analysis. The practical consequence is to limit those asset classes which consistently lose money to index performance, bounding the tracking error at zero. The money would be passivated in this case anyway.

This in fact makes the problem non-optimal. We can improve, however, on the bounded solution. The ratio of the value added by the bounded solution to the value added by the ideal solution can be used to amplify the risks taken by the asset classes whose risk allocation upper limit is still not biting until the value added converges on that of the ideal solution. Thus, the risk limited funds stay risk limited, but the others take progressively more risk until the return objective is met.

One way to think about this analysis simply is to think of the team of managers who all contribute to fund performance. To a first approximation, it would seem sensible to force each portfolio manager to shoulder an equal amount of responsibility for outperformance. This prevents the whole fund from being unduly dependent on the fortunes of the manager of the largest asset class. However, this may force some asset classes to take unreasonably high risks. The funds have to stand by themselves as rational, well diversified portfolios, largely clipping their ability to add equal value and the strain has to be borne by the largest asset classes.

3.2.4 Prototype implementation

The mathematics of the non-linear optimization does, unfortunately, converge slowly. An Excel spreadsheet designed as an example of this approach has been written which takes some 10 iterations to approach the ideal value-added target.

The prototypes for UK pension types and for a global (but country-based) equity type fund can be requested from the author. Both of these, of course, just have sample data in place. In particular, the information ratios achieved by the asset classes are completely made up; we have not yet done the exercise to measure the information ratios achieved by asset classes over meaningful time periods.

On these spreadsheets, we begin from the observation that we can calculate the theoretical information ratio for the whole fund (everyone contributes to the added value in the optimal proportions). The Lagrange multiplier then takes on the role of scaling the House capability (measured by the theoretical whole fund information ratio) to the value-added target set by the client. We also know the theoretical tracking error taken by the fund, therefore. Having established the size of the multiplier, we then apply the optimality conditions above to set the theoretical tracking errors for the components of the whole fund, bearing in mind the component information ratios. Several clamps then need to be applied. Firstly, an information ratio that is negative should result in an indexed fund for this component, so the ratio should be lower bounded by zero. Secondly, the ideal tracking errors for components to take will, in some cases, be higher than sensible upper bounds. Other parts of the spreadsheet are a simple iteration scheme designed to amplify the risk taken by those parts of the fund that can, until the return target is met.

3.2.5 Examples

As simple examples of this prototype, see Tables 3.1 and 3.2. These are a UK pension fund type and a (country-based) global equity type. Plausible but imaginary information ratios are inserted. The weights in the funds are inserted. The upper bounds on the tracking error have been set as plausible values for the spectrum of product we have at Standard Life Investments. The typical concentrated portfolios of some global clients have tracking errors close to 8%, but these are less risk-seeking for the UK type. It is interesting to note that the small components nearly always have their ideal tracking errors clipped, with additional risk being taken in the larger classes. Lower skill classes are permitted less tracking error, as are classes present at large weights in the benchmark. Sector-based work is withheld.

3.2.6 Conclusions

Even at the level of allocating sensible tracking errors to component parts of funds, compromises and trade-offs must be made. Negative information ratios are bounded to zero and upper limits on tracking error are fixed ultimately by the 'no gearing' rule, although there are other reasons why tracking error may be upper bounded for component portfolios in a fund. However, by adjusting the tracking error taken by the larger classes in the fund, the binding upper limits on the tracking error need not prevent a return target being met.

Table 3.1 *UK Pension prototype*

Creating the tracking error targets for portfolios imposing constraints
(UK pension prototype)

Fund weight	Information ratios	Asset classes	Ideal te to take	Final te to take	Ideal risk	Actual risk	Ideal value	Actual value	Min TE	Max TE
55%	0.5	UK	0.6%	1.2%	9.61E-06	4.05E-05	0.16%	0.32%	0%	2%
5%	-0.1	US	-1.2%	0.0%	3.85E-07	0	0.01%	0.00%	0%	4%
6%	0.5	Japan	5.2%	4.0%	9.61E-06	5.79E-06	0.16%	0.12%	0%	4%
6%	0.5	Pac x J	5.2%	5.0%	9.61E-06	9.04E-06	0.16%	0.15%	0%	5%
6%	0.7	Eur x UK	7.2%	5.0%	1.88E-05	9.04E-06	0.30%	0.21%	0%	5%
1%	0.1	Lat Am	6.2%	6.0%	3.85E-07	3.62E-07	0.01%	0.01%	0%	6%
10%	0.2	UK Bonds	1.2%	2.0%	1.54E-06	4.02E-06	0.02%	0.04%	0%	2%
5%	0.5	Int Bonds	6.2%	3.0%	9.61E-06	2.26E-06	0.16%	0.08%	0%	3%
6%	0	Cash	0.0%	0.0%	0	0	0.00%	0.00%	0%	0%
	0.25	AA	0.16%	0.3%	2.4E-06	1.01E-05	0.04%	0.08%	0%	1%
							Max achievable value add			1.38%
					0.79%	0.90%	1.00%	1.00%		

100% chksum

Value to be added	Theory TE	Lambda			
1.00%	0.79%	0.012			

Ideal whole fund IR
1.27

Actual IR achieved
1.09

Table 3.2 *Global regional type*

Creating the tracking error targets for portfolios
imposing constraints
global regional type

Fund weight	Information ratios	Asset classes	Ideal te to take	Final te to take	Ideal risk	Actual risk	Ideal value	Actual value	Min TE	Max TE
10%	0.5	UK	10.0%	8.0%	0.0001	6.4E-05	0.50%	0.40%	0%	8%
45%	0.5	US	2.2%	2.5%	0.0001	0.000135	0.50%	0.58%	0%	8%
15%	0.5	Japan	6.7%	7.7%	0.0001	0.000135	0.50%	0.58%	0%	8%
7%	0.5	Pac x J	14.3%	8.0%	0.0001	3.14E-05	0.50%	0.28%	0%	8%
23%	0.5	Eur x UK	4.3%	5.0%	0.0001	0.000135	0.50%	0.58%	0%	8%
	0.5	AA	1.00%	1.2%	0.0001	0.000135	0.50%	0.58%	0%	2%

Max achievable value add 5.00%

| 100% chksum | | | | | 2.45% | 2.52% | 3.00% | 3.00% | | |

Value to be added 3.00%

Theory TE 2.45%   Lambda 0.040

Ideal whole fund IR 1.22

Actual IR achieved 1.19

3.3   TRACKING ERRORS FOR ARBITRARY PORTFOLIOS

3.3.1   Introduction

In this Section, we begin by deriving an approximation for the covariance matrix, which will allow us to derive estimates for the tracking error found in arbitrary portfolios. This leads to insights into portfolio construction, both in terms of the number of stocks in a portfolio, but also how the tracking error depends on the size of the fund. The analysis works at both the 10 stock portfolio aggressive end and the index fund end. Trading practice can be shown to limit the tracking error obtainable with larger funds.

3.3.2   Deriving the distance measure

We begin by stating the tracking error

$$TE^2 = (\underline{h}_p - \underline{h}_{bm})^T \cdot \underline{\underline{\sigma}} \cdot (\underline{h}_p - \underline{h}_{bm}) = \underline{b}^T \cdot \underline{\underline{\sigma}} \cdot \underline{b}$$
$$= \sum_i \sigma_i^2 b_i^2 + \sum_i \sum_{j \neq i} b_i b_j \sigma_i \sigma_j \rho_{ij} \tag{3.8}$$

In this formula $\underline{h}_p$ and $\underline{h}_{bm}$ are the vectors of the percentage weights in the portfolio and benchmark respectively, and define the bet, $\underline{b}$. Note the space of the vectors is the union of the sets of benchmark and portfolio holdings.

Let us assume that the stock variances are all comparable and thus we can define

$$\sigma_i = \sigma_j = \langle \sigma \rangle, \forall i, j \tag{3.9}$$

$$TE^2 = \langle \sigma \rangle^2 * \left(\sum_i b_i^2 + \sum_i \sum_{j \neq i} b_i b_j \rho_{ij} \right) \tag{3.10}$$

Further, we assume that the correlation between the assets can also be represented by the average value

$$\rho_{ij} = \langle \rho \rangle, \forall i, j \tag{3.11}$$

$$TE^2 = \langle \sigma \rangle^2 * \left(\sum_i b_i^2 + \langle \rho \rangle \sum_i \sum_{j \neq i} b_i b_j \right) \tag{3.12}$$

We can simplify this expression further, using the nature of bets

$$b_i + \sum_{j \neq i} b_j = 0, \text{ so } \sum_{j \neq i} b_j = -b_I \tag{3.13}$$

and substitute this.

Then,

$$TE^2 = \langle\sigma\rangle^2 * (1 - \langle\rho\rangle) * \sum_i b_i^2 \tag{3.14}$$

$$TE^2 = \langle\sigma\rangle^2 * (1 - \langle\rho\rangle) * D^2 \tag{3.15}$$

In Equation (3.15), we have introduced D, the Euclidean distance. This makes the tracking error approximately related to the norm of the vector of bets. This is intuitively correct. Portfolios that are 'further away' from the benchmark have higher tracking error. The distance is modified by average values of volatility for assets and the correlation between them. In fact the key result that carries forward into system design is that D is easy to calculate from accounting systems and the covariance matrix is not. The fractional change in TE is the same as the fractional change in D.

We can use this approximation to make a number of portfolio construction problems simple.

3.3.3 Initial empirical tests

Consider two funds. Both are based on a 20 stock benchmark. Both funds contain all the stocks in the benchmark. The first fund contains 10 off +1% stock bets and 10 off −1% stock bets. The second fund contains two off +5% stock bets and two off −5% stock bets. Both funds have equal active monies but the second fund is clearly more aggressive. The second fund is quite a 'long way from the benchmark' and it will have the higher tracking error.

It is worth exploring the link between distance and tracking error empirically in more realistic cases. The first trial is to consider the link between TE and D for typical asset allocation stances. This is effectively a 10 stock (index) portfolio but the correlations and volatilities are distinctly different from the ideal above.

The result of creating possible asset allocation mixes and comparing the D and TE measures leads to the result that

$$TE = 14\% * D \tag{3.16}$$

A more realistic test is to take the FTSE and compare the TE and D measures arising from taking 1% and 2% bets, both positive and negative. The experiments were to measure TE and Excel to measure D. The results are shown in Figure 3.1. This appears to suggest that the D and TE measures are broadly proportional to each other.

A better test still is to take the top 50 stocks in the FTSE and equally weight them. This portfolio was set up as a benchmark, and + or −2% bets were taken at

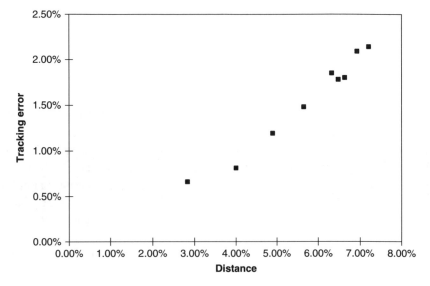

Figure 3.1   *Tracking error v distance for FTSE100 stock bets*

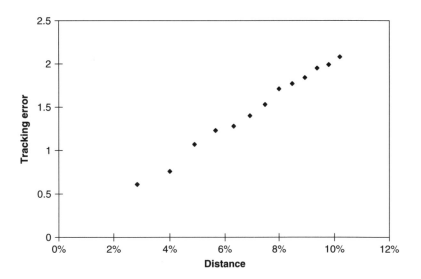

Figure 3.2   *Tracking error v distance for the top 50 FTSE stocks, equally weighted*

the stock level with respect to this benchmark. The results are shown in Figure 3.2. This is an even more convincing proportionality.

This suggests that the D measure can be used as a tool. A regression of TE on D would give good statistics but even this is not required to estimate the impact of a proposed change on a current tracking error. The relevant marginal formula is

$$\Delta TE/TE = \Delta D/D \qquad (3.17)$$

Thus we have empirically explored a rule of thumb that operates at the stock level for assessing the tracking error impact of changing the stock bets. It has the advantage that, for broad portfolios, it does not require a covariance matrix and can thus be driven from in-house systems simply. The statistics appear quite good at the stock level and at the asset class level, so we may infer that sector level data would also support this measure.

3.3.4 The 10 stock portfolio

For this aggressive portfolio, we have 10 good ideas, broadly equally weighted, with no further restrictions. In general, the weight of the stocks in the benchmark is sufficiently low that the equal weighting is broadly similar to equal overweighting. In this case, as described below:

$$D^2 \approx \sum N^{-2} \approx N^{-1} \qquad (3.18)$$

How do we treat such a portfolio? Where is such a portfolio to be found?

If we start from a crude approximation to pension fund thinking, we begin with a scheme with equities representing the cohorts who are still working and bonds representing the cohorts who have retired. The currency of the assets and liabilities is sterling for a UK pension fund. Into this bonds and equities portfolio is admixed various other asset classes for risk reduction, with the aim of adding value too. The portfolio gets closer to some efficient frontier.

The important point to note at this stage is that the 'admixtures for diversification' argument in pension fund design relies on indices. It is assumed that the portfolios that would operate in practice in the admixtures are index funds. This is a sub-optimization over asset classes, ignoring the stock selection element.

The smaller the admixture, the higher the tracking error that should be run, if all members of the team are expected to contribute equally to the performance of the fund. The converse also holds true. That is why, for a typical scheme, the UK equity component is run with a lower risk than the Latin American component.

In Table 3.3, we show the results of a non-linear optimizer that allocates the tracking error taking capability among the asset classes. This shows the tracking error implications of outperforming a UK Pension class of funds by a target of 1%. The UK element takes an ideal tracking error that is low but the Latin American part takes a far higher tracking error. Now we apply constraints. Most funds buy into sensibly constructed portfolios, by which we mean funds with a lower tracking error than ideal. Thus the smaller asset classes 'have their (tracking error) wings clipped' and the net result is that the larger asset classes have to make up the difference, from a risk perspective. Thus we arrive at the final construction seen in the industry, with 2% tracking error taken in the UK and 4–5% tracking error taken in the admixtures.

There is an interesting further point that is not so obvious. The fact that the admixture funds are sensibly constructed makes for funds that do generally follow the index, with some value added. Thus the funds hold true to the original aim of the international diversification, as defined by indices. Thus for the UK institutional market, it is natural to find admixture funds of a well defined construction and the only difference is that the larger funds can afford to be segregated and the smaller funds make use of pooled funds.

Compare these results to Table 3.4, where the target is now plus 2%. Now the tracking errors taken in the asset classes are pretty dramatic. Even the core UK equities takes nearly 4% tracking error and the admixtures could take 10% tracking error at the least. These admixture funds are fairly aggressive. To what extent is a 10% tracking error consistent with a 10 stock portfolio?

Tracking error	Number of stocks
5	32
6	22
7	16
8	13
9	10
10	8
11	7
12	6
13	5
14	4
15	4

This shows that the number of stocks declines rapidly as the tracking error demands rise. Indeed this provides strong backing to the concept that a 10 stock, equally weighted portfolio is a suitable vehicle for a 10% tracking error fund.

However, this may be close to the limit of rational portfolio construction, since the number of stocks is very small. Consider the CAPM result

$$\sigma_P^2 = \beta^2 \sigma_M^2 + \sigma_{SS}^2 \tag{3.19}$$

where we relate the portfolio variance (σ_P) to the market variance (σ_M) together with specific risk (σ_{SS}). If we say that the stocks are broadly uncorrelated, then the component of portfolio variance that is not Beta dependent becomes equal

Table 3.3 *Risk budget for a standard UK Pension Fund*

Creating the tracking error targets for portfolios
imposing constraints
UK pension fund type, WM local authority ex property end 2Q 1998

Fund weight	Information ratios	Asset classes	Ideal te to take	Final te to take	Actual value	Min TE	Max TE
56.0%	0.4	UK	0.8%	2.1%	0.48%	0%	3%
4.0%	0.3	US	8.3%	5.0%	0.06%	0%	5%
3.0%	0.3	Japan	11.1%	5.0%	0.05%	0%	5%
3.0%	0.3	Pac x J	11.1%	5.0%	0.05%	0%	5%
12.0%	0.3	Eur x UK	2.8%	5.0%	0.18%	0%	5%
1.0%	0.3	Lat Am	33.3%	6.0%	0.02%	0%	6%
12.0%	0.4	UK Bonds	3.7%	1.0%	0.05%	0%	1%
4.0%	0.3	Int Bonds	8.3%	2.0%	0.02%	0%	2%
5.0%	0	Cash	0.0%	0.0%	0.00%	0%	0%
	0.2	AA	0.22%	0.5%	0.10%	0%	0.5%

100% chksum

Actual value total: 1.00%

Max TE total: 1.19%

Value to be added	Ideal TE	Lambda	Actual IR achieved	Actual TE
1.00%	1.05%	0.022	0.68	1.47%

Table 3.4 *Risk budget for an aggressive UK Pension Fund*

Creating the tracking error targets for portfolios
imposing constraints
UK pension fund type, WM local authority ex property end 2Q 1998

Fund weight	Information ratios	Asset classes	Ideal te to take	Final te to take	Actual value	Min TE	Max TE
56.0%	0.4	UK	1.6%	4.4%	0.98%	0%	5%
4.0%	0.3	US	16.7%	10.0%	0.12%	0%	10%
3.0%	0.3	Japan	22.2%	10.0%	0.09%	0%	10%
3.0%	0.3	Pac x J	22.2%	10.0%	0.09%	0%	10%
12.0%	0.3	Eur x UK	5.6%	10.0%	0.36%	0%	10%
1.0%	0.3	Lat Am	66.7%	10.0%	0.03%	0%	10%
12.0%	0.4	UK Bonds	7.4%	2.0%	0.10%	0%	2%
4.0%	0.3	Int Bonds	16.7%	3.0%	0.04%	0%	3%
5.0%	0	Cash	0.0%	0.0%	0.00%	0%	0%
	0.2	AA	0.44%	1.0%	0.20%	0%	1.0%
					2.00%		2.14%

100% chksum

Value to be added	Ideal TE	Lambda	Actual IR achieved	Actual TE
2.00%	2.11%	0.044	0.67	2.97%

to the market component at roughly four stocks. This result is in full accord with fund manager intuition that a four stock portfolio cannot be said to be following a market. The diversification benefits established using index level analyses have been lost. All that is left is a few good stock ideas, wherever in the world they may be. There may of course be an argument for currency diversification according to a predefined asset allocation.

The view on 10 stock portfolios is that they are indeed appropriate for higher risk funds. They do correspond to a refinement on other model funds, and so are a different process, and the information ratio may not be the same for the 10 stock portfolio as it is for the 30 stock portfolio. Whether these portfolios are appropriate, depends on the marketing of the funds as a whole. If the clients are expecting a high risk, high value-added portfolio, then the 10 stock portfolio is what is required. The 10 stock portfolio is at the very limit of portfolio construction, in the sense that anything with fewer stocks cannot be said to be market related and so the original fund construction with diversifying elements fails.

3.3.5   The other extreme: the index fund

One approach to indexing is to fully replicate the index, to a level close to the full number of stocks in the benchmark – say we will hold N stocks out of an index of M. This means that the bet structure is

$$(\underline{h}_p - \underline{h}_{bm})^T = (0, 0, 0, \ldots, 0, 0, -\underline{h}_{bm,N+1}, -\underline{h}_{bm,N+2},$$
$$- \underline{h}_{bm,N+3}, \ldots, -\underline{h}_{bm,M}) + \underline{\varepsilon} \qquad (3.20)$$

Here we need to add in an error vector ε such that the active portfolio has zero net weight. This error is spread over all M stocks, and is small compared to $\underline{h}_{bm,N+1}$. So D^2 is the sum of the benchmark weights squared, from the $(N + 1)$th stock through to the Mth stock. This can only be handled empirically, given that the shape of the index weights as a function of rank is only very approximately a power law. (A plot of ln(Index weight) against ln(rank) is currently comprised of two straight line segments, one for the FTSE250 and beyond and one for the FTSE100. See Figure 3.3.) We have calculated the distance measure using the above approximation (Figure 3.4). We have also calculated the tracking errors for optimizations to the index, with constraints on the number of stocks (Figure 3.5).

The result of the empirical comparison is that both the distance measure for the above bet structure and the optimized portfolio tracking errors are both fitted very well by the empirical law

$$D^2 = (a * (\ln N/N) + b)^2 \qquad (3.21)$$

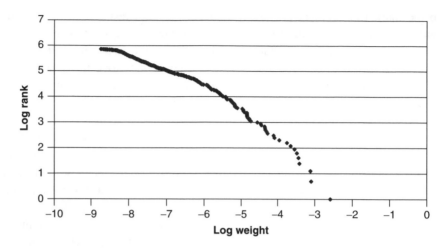

Figure 3.3 *Log rank as a function of log weight for the FTSE350*

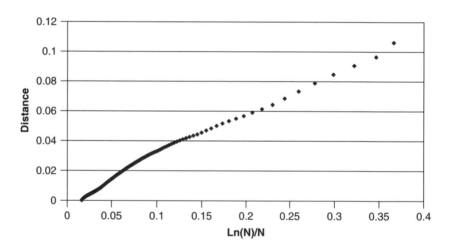

Figure 3.4 *Square root of cumulative weight squared v Ln(N)/N for the FTSE350*

The shape of the index defines the functional form. There is no particular *ab initio* reason as to why this particular function works well. Note that all we are checking here is that the distance measure operates just as well at the nearly full replication end of fund design, as it does at the few stock portfolio end.

3.3.6 Intermediate portfolios

If the approximation works well at both extremes, it ought to work as an interpolation for intermediate portfolios. The key to this is to recognize that there are two distinct sets of positions in an intermediate portfolio. The positions actively

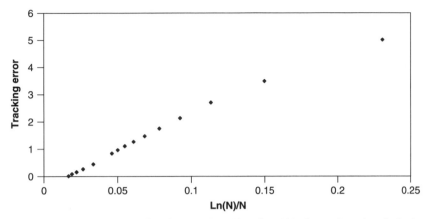

Figure 3.5 *Tracking errors plotted against Ln(N)/N, where N is the number of stocks in the portfolio*

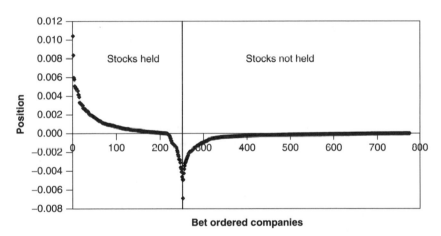

Figure 3.6 *Portfolio positions*

chosen and the positions passively ignored. Figure 3.6 shows the situation for a 200 stock portfolio. To the left is the explicit 200 stock overweights and underweights. To the right is the remaining 'tail' of 600 stocks that are passively ignored, leading to many small negative bets. As a more obvious example, take a 50 stock active portfolio. The way to calculate the distance for such portfolios is to consider the 50 stocks directly and then add a correction for the passive ignored stocks. Thus:

$$D^2 = \sum_{i=1,N} s_i^2 + (a * (\ln N/N) + b)^2 \qquad (3.22)$$

In this formula, N is the number of stocks in the portfolio, a and b are found from the fit of the index fund to the passive benchmark and s is an explicit active bet. We note that the distance calculated at the stock level correctly takes account of the true distance in the portfolios. Sector neutral structures show low risk levels at the industry level, although a lot of stock specific risk is inserted by choosing the 'best' stock to represent the sector.

Some examples:

For 10 stocks, $\sigma = 0.4$, $\rho = 0.5$, $D^2 = 0.1$, $D = 0.316$ and TE is close to 9%.

Using actual FTSE350 data, a is 0.412 661, and b is -0.006 39. A typical 70 stock portfolio has a bet structure with 10 @ +2%, 10 @ +1%, 10 @ -1% and 40 @ 0. In this case the 'passive ignored' correction is $0.018\,656^2$, D calculates to be 0.074 7, implying that the tracking error is 2.1%.

A 36 stock portfolio has equal weights at nearly 3% bets, typically. The correction is calculated as above, and $D = 0.169$, implying a tracking error of 4.7%.

A practical example: turnover limits in funds: an underpinning

This example addresses how limits on stock turnover should be set.

The basic way to approach this problem is to recognize that, if all funds are following commonality of views, and those views change, then a concentrated fund must turn over more stock to keep in line than a diversified fund. Thus turnover should scale with tracking error.

Estimating this, we assume that there are roughly 20 good ideas in a fund. The rest of the stocks are there for risk control. The ideas change roughly twice per year, implying that the 20 positions are reversed halfway through the year. If the bets are at the 1% level, then the turnover in the fund will be at the 80% level. If the bets are at the 2% level, the turnover will be 160%.

Formalizing this, we make use of our link between the distance measure and the tracking error in the fund. The distance is a simple function of the turnover.

$$TE^2 = \sigma^2(1 - \rho) * (1/(4^2 n_b)) * (Turnover)^2$$

If we use $n_b = 20$, volatility $= 40\%$, correlation $= 0.5$, then we have

$$(Turnover) \sim (63) * (Tracking\ Error)$$

A diversified UK fund with tracking error 2% should have a limit at roughly 125%. A narrow Japanese fund with tracking error 5% should have a limit of roughly 300%.

Continued on page 75

Continued from page 74

UK Equities	Diversified	150%
	Concentrated	250%
	Aggressive	400%
US Equities	Diversified	250%
	Concentrated	400%
Europe ex UK Equities	Diversified	250%
	Concentrated	400%
Japan Equities	Diversified	300%
	Concentrated	500%
Pacific Basin Equities	Diversified	300%
	Concentrated	500%
Lat Am Equities	Diversified	300%

3.3.7   A typical distribution of bet sizes

If we look at portfolios in regions where the benchmarks are very dispersed, with low weightings and many stocks (like the TOPIX) we tend to find portfolios with (effectively) zero weighted stocks, singly weighted stocks and doubly weighted stocks. For example, a 40 stock portfolio with 0%, 2%, and 4% weightings. It is not so easy to see, but similar structures appear in portfolios closer to benchmark. A good idea gets 2%, a very good idea gets 4% and a not very good idea is similar to a bad idea and gets zero.

To come to a view on a reasonable spectrum of bet sizes, we assume that the strength of view is approximately normally distributed. Kinetic theory can be used to derive the fact that $\langle b^2 \rangle$ can be described with a parameter σ_b^2 (provided the average bet size is zero). This is a standard deviation of bet sizes. Then

$$TE^2 = \langle \sigma \rangle^2 (1 - \langle \rho \rangle) * (N\sigma_b^2 + (a * (\ln N/N) + b)^2) \quad (3.23)$$

If we know that a 30 stock strong portfolio has a tracking error of 5%, then we can calculate that σ_b is about 3.2%. We would then expect a spectrum of bets with 1/5th of them greater than +3%, 1/5th of them below −3%, and 3/5th within these boundaries.

3.3.8   Very large funds

It is well known that funds above a certain size, dependent on the market, begin to get unwieldy. More diversification creeps in and the tracking error reduces. There is nothing in a risk analysis, or indeed in the approximations above, that suggests that fund size is an important parameter. Empirically, however, it is. The reason lies in the nature of the way that positions are taken. Fund managers are nervous that they cannot get out of positions quickly, should something go wrong with a stock story. They might not be able to 'cut their losers'. Obviously enough, with a very large fund, as with a small fund, it is the arithmetical difference in portfolio and benchmark weights that gives rise to a contribution to fund performance. For a large fund, though, the number of shares this position amounts to can be much larger than the typical buffers of stock that the market making community keep as market lubricant. Large positions liquidated quickly create market impact.

We can get a handle on the almost social science of what size of trade leads to market impact from a SEC rule (Section 3.22(e) of the Investment Company Act, 1940) which requires a fund to be able to redeem its shares in five working days, in the normal course of business. Also, no more than 15% of the fund should be invested in illiquid securities, where illiquidity means *not* being able to dispose of the shares in five working days. Dealers have interpreted this rule to mean that '85% of a fund should be able to be dumped within five working days, trading at 30% of the median daily trading volume'.

We may apply this argument to the overweights in a very large fund. For example, if 2 000 000 shares of a particular stock are traded in a day, then the maximum overweight should be 3 600 000 shares. Now consider fund structure. A 100 stock portfolio might have 1% overweights, for a tracking error close to 2%. If the average share price is £5, then the fund size cannot be larger than £2 bn. If the fund gets larger than this, then the overweights have to be reduced accordingly and the tracking error reduces linearly with fund size.

Empirically it is possible to obtain the average trading volume over 30 days for the FT Allshare and fit that to market cap (Figure 3.7). The fit is not perfect, but it is plausible that the fit of ln(market cap) to ln(cap traded) is close to one (Figure 3.8). This shows that a load ratio is a proxy for the time it would take to trade a position. Thus, for very large funds, load ratios are sensible control mechanisms, even though it inevitably means that larger bets can be entertained in the FTSE than in the FT Small Cap. Figure 3.9 shows the bet structure for a typically large fund, in percentage over weights. Figure 3.10 shows the same fund, oriented with the portfolio at the left, with the positions expressed in days trading. The load ratio concept has ensured that the fund is close to a few days trade away from neutralizing an idea that goes wrong.

3.3.9   Bets at the industry level and their influence on tracking error

It will be noted that the above work has treated the portfolio of stocks as undifferentiated. Of course the correlation matrix for the UK splits into industrial and style groupings as well. If one insurance company is bid for, and marked up, others will be marked up too. We have done significant work to assess the effect

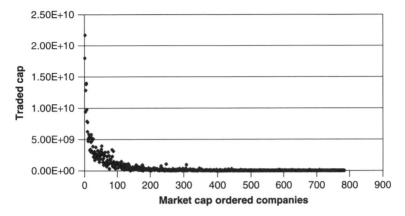

Figure 3.7 *Trading volume*

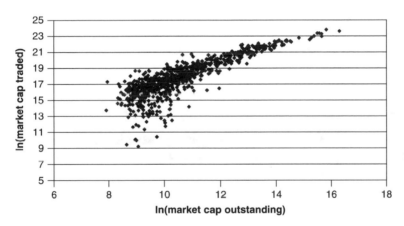

Figure 3.8 *Market cap and trading volume*

of industries on tracking error within portfolios. This work has started from optimizing portfolios to different numbers of stocks with particular industry bets inserted as constraints in the optimizations. In the UK market, this has largely involved positions in oil, telecoms, banks and pharmaceuticals. We thus collect a data set comprised of a broad set of portfolios with different bet structures, different stock numbers and different tracking errors. It is a straightforward job to find a suitable best fit functions for the data – it turns out to be (for the FT Allshare).

$$TE = [(a' * (\ln N)/N + b')^2 + c' * D_{ind}^2]^{(1/2)} \tag{3.24}$$

With $a' = 24.5$, $b' = -0.164$ and $c' = 0.02473$. The error in this fitting function is described with a standard deviation of 7.5bp (Figure 3.11). This is very low and implies that the tracking error in real portfolios is well described by

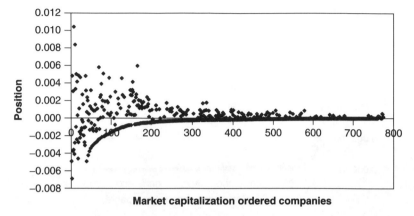

Figure 3.9   *Portfolio positions*

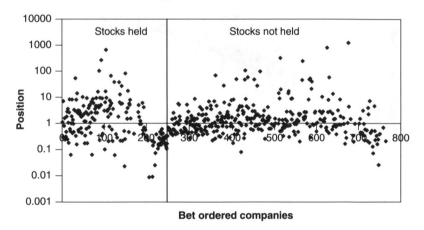

Figure 3.10   *Positions in days trading*

functions of this form, that perhaps vary by market. Real portfolios exhibit more risk than this. This is because an optimized portfolio will try to move to equalize the constrained portfolio and constrained benchmark sector weights. If the number of stocks permits and close to equal stock weighting is possible, the optimized solution will choose several (for example) banks, to provide a low risk bank basket. Real managers will, in contrast, perhaps choose one bank, at a weight to represent the sector as a whole, thus shoe-horning more stock selection risk into the portfolio than the optimization would suggest. It is for this stock specific reason that we would prefer to use the stock level analysis above and use the industry level analysis here to provide additional constraints for portfolio engineering.

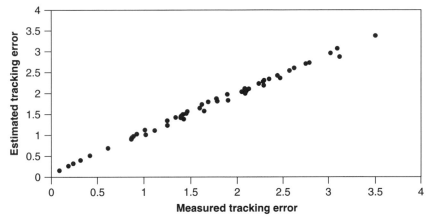

Figure 3.11 *Comparison of fitted tracking error and measured tracking error for industry positions*

3.3.10 A portfolio flight envelope

As an additional equity example, we consider the construction of a practical flight envelope, based on the above tracking error analysis.

The portfolio has an outperformance target of 3%. If we assume a top quartile information ratio of 0.5, then this would imply a tracking error of 5–7%. What number of stocks should we have?

Starting from the intermediate portfolio case above, $(a * (\ln N)/N + b) + (1/N) = D^2$, for an equally weighted portfolio. (This is an approximation to the equally overweighted portfolio, if the stock numbers are low, and the benchmark broad. At $TE = 5\%$, we can solve for N, by relating D to TE, finding $D = 0.197$, and $N = 30$. Similarly at $TE = 7\%$, $N = 15$). Thus this portfolio could have 15 to 30 stocks with individual stock bet sizes of up to 7%.

At the industry level, we set the $TE = 6\%$, $N = 22$, and use the empirical results above to solve for a D_{ind}.

$$TE = 6\% = [(24.5 * (\ln 22)/22 - 0.164)^2 + 0.02473 * D_{ind}{}^2]^{(1/2)}$$

To find that $D_{ind} = 32$, or roughly 10% bets in 8 industry sectors.

3.3.11 Flight envelopes for correlated regional equity markets, with particular reference to emerging markets

The starting point is the expressions for value-added and risk taken.

$$VA = IR_{AA}\sigma_{AA} + IR_{SS}\sigma_{SS} \tag{3.25}$$

$$\sigma_{TE}{}^2 = \sigma_{AA}{}^2 + \sigma_{SS}{}^2 \tag{3.26}$$

In these formulae, σ_{AA} is the tracking error taken at the asset allocation level, and σ_{SS} is the tracking error taken at stock selection level. The value added is linearly related to the risk taken at asset allocation (between countries) and stock selection. The constants are information ratios. The total risk taken is the root mean square of the risks taken at asset allocation and stock selection. Here we assume the tracking errors for the two processes are decorrelated. This is reasonable, since in emerging markets, the country risks are still partially influenced by PEST analyses and the currencies are not all perfectly tied to the US$.

The risk equation is the equation of an ellipse in risk space, and the value added equation is a straight line. The optimal point can be found as the point of tangent of the value added lines and the risk ellipse. We use Lagrange multipliers to find the point of tangency. We find that the optimal condition is

$$\sigma_{SS}/\sigma_{AA} = IR_{SS}/IR_{AA} \tag{3.27}$$

The emerging markets team spend equal amounts of time on both stock selection and country selection, so we should assume in the first instance that the information ratios will be comparable. Thus, the tracking errors run at country selection level and stock selection level should be comparable. If the total value added target is 3%, and the information ratios are 0.4 (typical of just below top quartile), then 1.5% is expected for each dimension. The tracking errors run on each dimension should be 4%.

We now have to express how the tracking errors within countries cumulate. If the correlation between tracking error generating processes within countries is zero, then the in country stock selection tracking errors add in quadrature. If the correlation between tracking error generating processes is correlated, then the tracking errors add linearly.

$$\sigma_{TE}^2 = \sum w_i^2 \sigma_{TEi}^2 \quad (uncorrelated) \tag{3.28}$$

$$\sigma_{TE}^2 = \left[\sum w_i \sigma_{TEi}\right]^2 \quad (correlated) \tag{3.29}$$

In the case of the emerging markets, it is felt that stock selection would be driven by global themes, and thus the tracking error generating processes will be correlated.

Consider the asset allocation dimension. We have built a full covariance matrix built on MSCI indices for the region. We have used this to probe how the tracking error varies with bet sizes. This gives a way of examining individual bet structures and allows us to rank markets by their impact on tracking error. However, for control purposes, we would prefer a simpler method. We have an approximation to the covariance matrix, in terms of the distance measure. The distance measure is the square root of the sum of the squares of the bets, and is related to the tracking error via the average volatility of the markets and the typical correlation coefficient. We have used the covariance matrix to check the results, which agree satisfactorily.

$$TE^2 = \langle\sigma\rangle^2 * (1 - \langle\rho\rangle) * D^2 \tag{3.30}$$

Here, we use 0.4 for the factor between TE and D. If the tracking error is 4%, then $D^2 = 100$, and the matrix proposed by the emerging markets team is indeed appropriate. If 'core' markets have 1VH@5%, 1VL@5%, 1H@3% and 1L@3%; 'secondary' markets have 1VH@3%, 1VL@3%, 2H@1% and 2L@1%; and 'satellite' markets have 1VH@1%, 1VL@1%, 1H@1% and 1L@1%: then $D^2 = 94$.

It should be remembered that this analysis would allow bets to be shuffled around such that the D measure is satisfied without regard to the tradability of the markets. The matrix proposed by the emerging markets team takes account of the liquidity in the markets and should be adopted, in our view.

For risk allocation between countries, we note that ideally we should have equal contributions to value-added from every country. This would allocate risk in inverse relation to the weight in the country. However, this would make the risk taken in tiny countries unreasonably high. Jordan would have to run a tracking error of 125%! This is hardly pragmatic. In reality, even two large cap stocks in a country tracks the country index to a tracking error of the order of 10%–20%.

In order to address these issues, we have built an optimizer which limits the tracking error taken to 10% in the satellite countries and reallocates the risk to the larger countries such that the total value added remains on target. This sets the in country tracking errors to the values shown in the accompanying table.

For stock selection bets within country, we make use of our work to relate stock bets to tracking error in country. Tracking error at this level comes from two sources – the bets put on deliberately and the stocks not held. To address these issues, to set the stock number levels and the bets sizes, we have analysed the following markets: Mexico, Brazil, South Africa, Argentina (as an example of a secondary market) and Venezuela (as an example of a satellite market). Where possible, we fit to an equation of the form:

$$\sigma_{TE}{}^2 = \langle\sigma\rangle^2(1 - \langle\rho\rangle)\sigma_b{}^2 N + (a \ln (N)/N + b)^2 \tag{3.31}$$

in which σ_b is the standard deviation of the bets taken, N is the number of stocks, and the factor depending on $\ln(N)$ is a statistical fit to the tracking errors found from optimizing to a country benchmark with a set of stocks limited to N, which represents the influence of the stocks not held. Clearly this is an empirical fit which depends on country index structure, but seems to have a wide applicability of functional form. This set of analyses leads to the following matrix for stock bets (we close the problem by assessing the variance contributions from the two elements – bets, and tail not held).

Country	Weight %	Tracking error %	Stock numbers	Stock bets std deviation %
Mexico	20.2	2.0	10–20	1.5
South Africa	15.9	2.5	15–30	1.5
Brazil	15.7	2.5	15–30	1.5
Greece	9.2	4.0	10–20	1.5
Israel	9.1	4.0	5–10	10.0
Turkey	7.1	5.0	5–10	10.0
Chile	5.6	5.0	5–10	10.0
Argentina	3.8	7.0	5–10	10.0
Russia	4.3	7.0	5–10	10.0
Poland	2.4	10.0	0–5	Equally wtd
Hungary	2.3	10.0	0–5	Equally wtd
Czech Rep	1.4	10.0	0–5	Equally wtd
Peru	1.3	10.0	0–5	Equally wtd
Venezuela	1.1	10.0	0–5	Equally wtd
Colombia	0.5	10.0	0–5	Equally wtd
Jordan	0.2	10.1	0–5	Equally wtd

3.4   ACTIVE CAPM, OR HOW FAR SHOULD A BET BE TAKEN?

In this Section, we rework the classic CAPM covariance minimization using Kuhn Tucker conditions to derive the equivalent to CAPM when there is no risk free asset – i.e. the competitive asset is not cash, but an index fund. This is necessary pre work to find expressions for optimal bets, which make use of the approximation to the covariance matrix found above. Along the way we find the limitations to the CAPM approach.

An active portfolio is formed via

$$\underline{h}_{portfolio} - \underline{h}_{benchmark} = \underline{h} \tag{3.32}$$

in which $\underline{h}$ refers to the vector of weights in the space of possible investments.

Prudent active management is concerned with minimizing risk while capitalizing on the added value form our return estimates.

This implies that we minimize the tracking error

$$\min\{\underline{h}\}(1/2)\underline{h}^T.\underline{\underline{V}}.\underline{h}$$

such that

$$\underline{h}^T.\underline{e} = E$$
$$\underline{h}^T.\underline{1} = 0 \qquad\qquad (3.33)$$

In these constraints we are stating the conditions that the added value E on the portfolio will be the sum of relative contributions from the positions and that the sum of active weights is zero. The vector $\underline{e}$ is the vector of next period returns for the assets that are entries in $\underline{h}$.

Using the Lagrange multiplier approach:

$$\min\{\underline{h}, \lambda, \gamma\}L = (1/2).\underline{h}^T.\underline{\underline{V}}.\underline{h} + \lambda(E - \underline{h}^T.\underline{e}) + \gamma(0 - \underline{h}^T.\underline{1}) \qquad (3.34)$$

Forming the Kuhn Tucker conditions:

$$\partial L/\partial\underline{h} = \underline{\underline{V}}.\underline{h} - \lambda\underline{e} - \gamma\underline{1} = 0 \qquad\qquad (3.35)$$
$$\partial L/\partial\lambda - E - \underline{h}^T\underline{e} - 0 \qquad\qquad (3.36)$$
$$\partial L/\partial\gamma = -\underline{h}^T.\underline{1} = 0 \qquad\qquad (3.37)$$

Note that the third of these conditions is compatible with the second constraint. We can invert the first condition to find a solution for $\underline{h}$.

$$\underline{h} = \lambda\underline{\underline{V}}^{-1}.\underline{e} + \gamma\underline{\underline{V}}^{-1}.\underline{1} \qquad\qquad (3.38)$$

Now we premultiply this solution by $\underline{e}^T$ and use the second of the conditions:

$$E = \lambda\underline{e}^T.\underline{\underline{V}}^{-1}.\underline{e} + \gamma\underline{e}^T.\underline{\underline{V}}^{-1}.\underline{1} \qquad\qquad (3.39)$$

Similarly, we can premultiply by $\underline{1}^T$ and use the third condition:

$$0 = \lambda\underline{1}^T.\underline{\underline{V}}^{-1}.\underline{e} + \gamma\underline{1}^T.\underline{\underline{V}}^{-1}.\underline{1} \qquad\qquad (3.40)$$

Now, these last two equations are simultaneous and we may solve them to recover a more useful form of solution.

Defining:

$$A = \underline{1}^T.\underline{\underline{V}}^{-1}.\underline{e} \tag{3.41}$$

$$B = e^T.V^{-1}.e \tag{3.42}$$

$$C = \underline{1}^T.\underline{\underline{V}}^{-1}.\underline{1} \tag{3.43}$$

The simultaneous equations become:

$$E = \lambda B + \gamma A \tag{3.44}$$

$$0 = \lambda A + \gamma C \tag{3.45}$$

Which leads to:

$$\gamma = -AE/D \tag{3.46}$$

$$\lambda = CE/D \tag{3.47}$$

where $D = CB - A^2$

Leading to the solution

$$\underline{h} = (E/D) * (C.\underline{\underline{V}}^{-1}.\underline{e} - A.\underline{\underline{V}}^{-1}.\underline{1}) \tag{3.48}$$

Now we consider the active variance, which we have set up (in this analysis) to be the tracking error squared:

$$\sigma^2 = \underline{h}^T.\underline{\underline{V}}.\underline{h} = (C/D)E^2 \tag{3.49}$$

This is a fascinating result. An 'information ratio', or E/σ, can be calculated, which is a function both of the covariance matrix, i.e. history, and the vector of next period returns, namely a projected portfolio return. There is only one optimal portfolio, whose added value depends on how well we predict the returns for the stocks over the next period, and we also see the correct result that the tracking error is proportional to the added value. More risk, more return – but the equivalent to the efficient frontier is a straight line. Gratifyingly, this line goes through the origin, as it must, given that full replication index funds should have no active positions and thus no added value over the benchmark.

This solution is pretty abstract as it stands and would only be amenable to numerical calculation in its full detail. Fortunately, we have derived (at the start of Section 3.3) an approximation for the covariance matrix which allows us to simplify the above solution and its consequences considerably. This leads to better insights into portfolio construction.

Given that tracking error squared is given in the approximation by:

$$\sigma^2 = \underline{h}^T.\underline{\underline{V}}.\underline{h} = \langle\sigma\rangle^2(1 - \langle\rho\rangle)\underline{h}^T.\underline{h} \tag{3.50}$$

We can identify

$$\underline{\underline{V}} = \langle\sigma\rangle^2(1 - \langle\rho\rangle)\underline{\underline{I}} \tag{3.51}$$

in which $\langle\sigma\rangle$ is the average volatility for the stocks in the benchmark (individually) and $\langle\rho\rangle$ is the average correlation between the stocks. Using this approximate expression, we can evaluate the quadratic forms A, B, C and D.

$$A = \underline{I}^T.\underline{\underline{V}}^{-1}.\underline{e} = N\langle e\rangle/((1 - \langle\rho\rangle)\langle\sigma\rangle^2) \tag{3.52}$$

$$B = e^T.V^{-1}.e = N\langle e^2\rangle/((1 - \langle\rho\rangle)\langle\sigma\rangle^2) \tag{3.53}$$

$$C = \underline{I}^T.\underline{\underline{V}}^{-1}.\underline{1} = N/((I - \langle\rho\rangle)\langle\sigma\rangle^2) \tag{3.54}$$

In these expressions, $\langle e\rangle$ represents the arithmetic average of the estimates for returns for all the stocks, and $\langle e^2\rangle$ represents the average of the squares of the returns. N is the total number of assets in the universe (the union of the sets of the benchmark holdings and the portfolio holdings).

Using these estimates

$$\underline{h} = (E/N) * (\underline{e} - \langle e\rangle\underline{1})/\text{Var}\{e\} \tag{3.55}$$

In this expression, E is the expected relative return of the portfolio over the benchmark. Note that this expression has an appealing structure. The portfolio is made more intense as the return target is raised, in a linear fashion (at small perturbations on the benchmark – see Section 3.5 for the treatment with respect to the non-linear constraints arising from the no-short-selling constraint). If the added value is zero, the active portfolio is zero and the fund is on index. If the expected return for a stock is above average, the active portfolio is upweight of the benchmark. Similarly, a portfolio is underweight a stock which returns less than the average. If all the stocks return close to the same amount, the variance of the returns is close to zero and the fund bets are large to win added value. If the variance is very high, only small positions are required. All stocks are potentially equally attractive as money-making opportunities, provided they can be traded in a meaningful size for the fund in question.

Consider an example: There are three assets in the universe. One will return $+20\%$, one will return 0 and one will return -20%. Thus $\underline{e} = (+20\%, 0, -20\%)$. We find that $\langle e\rangle = 0$, and $\text{Var}\{e\} = 0.0267$. We want to add 1% relative to the benchmark. Using the expression for the optimal portfolio above, we find that

Table 3.5 *CAPM optimal portfolios*

Stocks	Benchmark	Stock return	First guess active	First guess portfolio	Contribn	Suggested optimal	Suggested portfolio	Contribn	Return less than market	uwt?	Contribution positive
a	15%	−5.0%	−1%	14%	0.0500%	−0.85%	14.15%	0.0427%	yes	yes	yes
b	10%	−5.0%	−1%	9%	0.0500%	−0.85%	9.15%	0.0427%	yes	yes	yes
c	9%	−5.0%	−1%	8%	0.0500%	−0.85%	8.15%	0.0427%	yes	yes	yes
d	8%	−5.0%	−1%	7%	0.0500%	−0.85%	7.15%	0.0427%	yes	yes	yes
e	7%	−4.0%	−1%	6%	0.0400%	−0.65%	6.35%	0.0262%	yes	yes	yes
f	7%	−4.0%	−1%	6%	0.0400%	−0.65%	6.35%	0.0262%	yes	yes	yes
g	6%	−4.0%	−1%	5%	0.0400%	−0.65%	5.35%	0.0262%	yes	yes	yes
h	5%	−4.0%	−1%	4%	0.0400%	−0.65%	4.35%	0.0262%	yes	yes	yes
i	5%	−3.0%	−1%	4%	0.0300%	−0.45%	4.55%	0.0136%	**no**	**yes**	**yes**
j	4%	−3.0%	−1%	4%	0.0000%	−0.45%	3.55%	0.0136%	**no**	**yes**	**yes**
k	3%	−1.0%	0%	3%	0.0000%	−0.05%	2.95%	0.0005%	**no**	**yes**	**yes**
l	3%	−0.5%	0%	3%	0.0000%	0.05%	3.05%	−0.0002%	no	no	no
m	2%	−0.5%	0%	2%	0.0000%	0.05%	2.05%	−0.0002%	no	no	no
n	2%	−0.5%	0%	2%	0.0000%	0.05%	2.05%	−0.0002%	no	no	no
o	2%	0.0%	0%	2%	0.0000%	0.15%	2.15%	0.0000%	no	no	no
p	2%	0.0%	0%	2%	0.0000%	0.15%	2.15%	0.0000%	no	no	no
q	1%	0.0%	0%	1%	0.0000%	0.15%	1.15%	0.0000%	no	no	no
r	1%	0.5%	1%	2%	0.0050%	0.25%	1.25%	0.0012%	no	no	yes
s	1%	0.5%	1%	2%	0.0050%	0.25%	1.25%	0.0012%	no	no	yes
t	1%	0.5%	1%	2%	0.0050%	0.25%	1.25%	0.0012%	no	no	yes
u	1%	1.0%	1%	2%	0.0100%	0.35%	1.35%	0.0035%	no	no	yes
v	1%	4.0%	1%	2%	0.0400%	0.95%	1.95%	0.0378%	no	no	yes
w	1%	4.0%	1%	2%	0.0400%	0.95%	1.95%	0.0378%	no	no	yes
x	1%	5.0%	1%	2%	0.0500%	1.15%	2.15%	0.0573%	no	no	yes
y	1%	5.0%	1%	2%	0.0500%	1.15%	2.15%	0.0573%	no	no	yes
z	1%	5.0%	1%	2%	0.0500%	1.15%	2.15%	0.0573%	no	no	yes
checksum	100%		0.0%	100%		0.0%	100%				
weighted sum retn		−3.18%									
av retn		−0.73%		value add	0.65%		value add	0.56%			
				risk	0.0424		risk	0.0334			
				IR	0.15		IR	0.17			

$\underline{h} = (+2.5\%, 0, -2.5\%)$, which can be checked to give the right result, of $+1\%$ value added.

However, one oddity is that the market return is a weighted average return and the relevant average referred to above is unweighted. This flies in the face of the market adage 'overweight the stocks you think will outperform the market'. A spreadsheet was written to examine this in closer detail (Table 3.5). This shows a small market portfolio with the small cap stocks providing the return and the large cap stocks showing negative price action. The market return is -3.18%. A first guess portfolio is shown, with a typical fund manager response, with nine overweights and nine underweights. We calculate the value added, the risk taken (in our approximate form of 'distance') and a ratio which behaves like an information ratio. We then show the suggested optimal portfolio driven by the unweighted average process shown above. The particular point we wish to make here is that there are situations where the stocks are returning less than the unweighted average, but more than the market. If these stocks are underweighted, the portfolio receives a positive contribution. Note also that the information ratio has improved using the weightings driven from the formula above. It is possible to play with the weightings in this spreadsheet by hand but overweighting the highlighted stocks as market outperformers has, in all the cases run to date, led to a reduction in the value added. These overweights have to be paid for from somewhere else in the portfolio, thus reducing the optimality.

Consider the tracking error:

$$\sigma^2 = \underline{h}^T . \underline{\underline{V}} . \underline{h} = \langle \sigma \rangle^2 (1 - \langle \rho \rangle) \underline{h}^T . \underline{h}$$
$$= \langle \sigma \rangle^2 (1 - \langle \rho \rangle) * E^2 / (N * \mathrm{Var}\{e\}) \tag{3.56}$$

and the information ratio:

$$IR = E/\sigma = [(N * \mathrm{Var}\{e\}) / (\langle \sigma \rangle^2 (1 - \langle \rho \rangle))]^{1/2} \tag{3.57}$$

Note that the tracking error reduces like the inverse of root N. The higher the number of assets, the smaller the bets need to be to meet the target. The smaller the bets, the smaller the tracking error. Note that the information ratio rises with the number of assets in the portfolio. Note also that this whole analysis is based on portfolio construction for the optimal portfolio where the return in the following period is known for all the stocks in the universe. Of course, this is where the whole CAPM methodology has nothing to say! If we know the returns, we can calculate a cute portfolio. However, we have to estimate the returns and we get this wrong. The interesting point is how wrong the estimates of return are.

Consider the above example: Using $\langle\sigma\rangle = 0.4$, $\langle\rho\rangle = 0.5$, then the tracking error calculates to be 1%, and the information ratio is 1.

Consider another example: $N = 10$ assets in the universe. $\text{Var}\{e\} = 0.02$, $\langle\sigma\rangle = 0.4$, $\langle\rho\rangle = 0.5$, then the information ratio calculates to be 1.58. This is for perfect foresight.

Top quartile managers seem to be able to achieve information ratios of 0.5. For a FTSE portfolio, the theoretical information ratio calculates to be 5! This is such an outrageously high number that we can only square this with reality by suggesting that fund managers only really have strong views on 10 or so holdings. The rest become (broadly) tracking error reduction tools to keep the fund performance within a pre-agreed tolerance, should the predictions of return prove wrong. If true, this analysis provides a strong support for highly active satellite portfolios, with index core portfolios, providing the dilution.

The above analysis relies on being able to short securities, if required. Of course this is not permitted in many cases, leading to a non-linear constraint. It is not possible to be more underweight than zero weight. This is a trivially small bet size compared to the typical upweighting bet and leads to the view that the main bets in a portfolio are positive ones. The way this could be thought about is as the adding back of a 'no-short-selling' (NSS) portfolio back onto the ideal portfolio. The NSS portfolio is in the opposite direction when compared to the ideal portfolio for, typically, half the stocks. Thus, to the extent that the positive bet sizes are large compared to the typical benchmark holding, the NSS portfolio deoptimizes the ideal portfolio and likely reduces the information ratio by a factor of two. The information ratio for 10 strong ideas, with perfect foresight, could be 0.8. More ideas raise the information ratio, lack of perfect foresight reduces it.

A practical implementation – an optimizer for buy-side asset allocation
An optimizer was required that would find the optimum portfolio for adding a certain number of basis points with the House View, around an arbitrary benchmark. This is not an absolute risk/return efficient frontier generator. We need to add value and minimize tracking error, in the hedge fund that is the set of positive and negative positions within the Standard Life House View.

There are sophisticated, highly engineered systems that will accommodate constraints. A simple device was built in Excel based on some maths done above, in particular implementing the equation:

$$\underline{h} = (E/D) * (C.\underline{\underline{V}}^{-1}.\underline{e} - A.\underline{\underline{V}}^{-1}.\underline{1})$$

Continued on page 89

___ *Continued from page 88* ___

This device is unconstrained, so should only be used to give a guide to small overweights and underweights. This device is based on an analytical solution to the problem of minimizing tracking error subject to a defined value to be added. This is like CAPM, but instead of referencing everything to a risk free rate (the absolute investor concept) we are referring to a benchmark. This shift in formalism has a number of consequences. The value added and tracking error are linear in bet size, but, more fundamentally, there is only one optimal portfolio, and an analytical expression can be written for it, in terms of operations on the inverse of the covariance matrix.

The advantages of this approach are that the results of the optimization are available in real time (as the returns vector is altered) and the maths is not buried inside a numerical scheme. The disadvantages are similar to all optimizers. The results depend critically on the return estimates. Small increases in expected returns can move the optimal portfolio around quite dramatically. Also, the results are dependent on the covariance matrix, which depends on historical data. Another criticism of optimizers does not apply here, in that the number of assets is small, allowing us to estimate the covariance matrix sensibly from five years of historical data. Our covariance matrix has a well-defined inverse.

One oddity that has appeared in other areas before, is that property is a bizarre asset class. Because the assets are valued infrequently, and on a rolling basis, the volatility of the property asset class is artificially reduced. This has the effect of making property the low volatility asset of choice, perhaps prompting a short cash, long property position. When a truer volatility is reinserted into the covariance matrix, property ceases to dominate stochastically to quite the same extent. The ability to influence the calculation is an advantage of having access to the formulae directly.

3.5   IMPLEMENTING IDEAS IN REAL STOCK PORTFOLIOS

3.5.1   Introduction

This Section investigates a way of implementing buys, sells and holds in a portfolio. The output of this investigation is a methodology – a smooth way to mutate a portfolio from on-index to progressively more aggressive stances, by taking a predefined level of risk. Key to the methodology is the algorithm, or recipe, used to accommodate the 'no-short-selling' constraint.

Results that are in tune with fund manager instinct can be found with a program which sells underweights to buy overweights as far as possible, then when no short selling becomes a binding constraint, neutral stocks have to be sold down. The method has been coded in Excel.

3.5.2   Rationale and approach

The object of this exercise is to find a way of implementing stock level bets to come up with an advisory fund profile of a predefined risk level, that can vary from on-index to highly aggressive. An advantage would be a heightened visibility of the connection between stock preferences, portfolio shape and portfolio risk. This would reduce the opacity of commercial optimization software. The output of this methodology, while being self-consistent, would only provide advice. There will inevitably be hard issues (like transactions costs) and soft issues (some buys are more equal than others) that dictate final portfolio structure.

Preferences are first converted into an ideal over- or under-weighting. The ideal fund is the benchmark plus this satellite hedge fund. However, the combination of the hedge fund and the benchmark will end up with underweights that imply short positions, which are not permitted by the no-short-selling rule. The problem becomes one of finding a suitable way of implementing the bets as far as possible consistent with these constraints. Initially, small positions can be self-funded – the buys are funded by the sells. Eventually, this process can no longer fund the buys directly. Some other stocks must be raided. The question is how? One way of doing this is to sell down the benchmark pro-rata to fund the buys. However, this program has a pathology. If the risk becomes truly extreme, the buys have to be extensively funded by selling down the benchmark and we can end up with large cap stocks going underweight, even though they are buys! Unsurprisingly, fund managers object to this. A buy on Glaxo is the same as a buy on Photo-me International, it is just that the companies are many orders of magnitude different in size.

An alternative program has been followed in this document, which is more in tune with fund manager instinct. Effectively, underweights are sold down even further to fund overweights, and once the under-weights are all sold out, then the neutral stocks are sold out. This program ends, at very high risk, with all overweights being equally overweight, and there being no presence in the neutral or underweight stocks at all.

It will be noted that the risk profile of the fund has changed during this process. Large cap underweights and neutrals are progressively more heavily bet against than the overweights are bet for. Thus most high risk funds, (although they contain very positive statements, implemented as fully as possible) have an asymmetric risk profile, being over-exposed to outperformance in a few large cap stocks not represented. Conversely, small cap stocks in the fund are over exposed to underperformance in the stocks chosen, and less prone to unrepresented stocks outperforming.

One way out of this dilemma may be to think of the overweighting percentage as a trigger level. Stocks in the fund below this weighting in the index are exposed to underperformance, stocks above this weighting in the index are exposed to non-representation in the fund. The aim should be to diversify adequately among the stocks held for small stocks and diversify out the stocks not held for large stocks.

Another outcome is that equally overweighted funds (with only a few stocks) are so overweight in the few stocks that they appear almost equally weighted. Most portfolios would then just be constructed on an equally weighted basis to short circuit the intermediate steps.

3.5.3   Mathematics and implementation: model problem

The model problem has been constructed within Excel. The spreadsheet consists of a simple imaginary benchmark, broadly exponentially weighted. A full covariance matrix has been created by symmetrizing a triangular array of random numbers between -1 and 1 (adding the lower triangular block to its transpose, 1 has then been inserted on the diagonal). The purpose of this covariance matrix is to be able to calculate the tracking error inherent in the implementation of varying degrees of aggressiveness (as measured by the ideal active portfolio inserted on top of the benchmark).

The ideal active portfolio perhaps conflicts with the no-short-selling rule as well as any other constraints that can be inserted on the spreadsheet. If this happens then the active portfolio becomes unbalanced and has a borrowing or lending requirement. Rather than accommodating this from the benchmark, the active portfolio is scaled to zero weight. This, in all practical cases, forces the neutrals to assume slight negative bets – since the desired overweighting is large compared to the natural stock weighting in the benchmark. This rescaled active portfolio is applied to the benchmark. This will in turn lead to slight conflict with the constraints and a simple iteration scheme leads to a converged solution.

The tracking error of the final portfolio is calculated and compared to a target. A goal-seeking algorithm can be used to drive the portfolio to a desired riskiness or aggressiveness in the fund. Finally, the stocks in the fund and the benchmark are compared as a histogram.

3.5.4   Results: model problem

Three sets of results are presented here. Figure 3.12. shows the fund and the benchmark where the preferences are only implemented to a small level of risk.

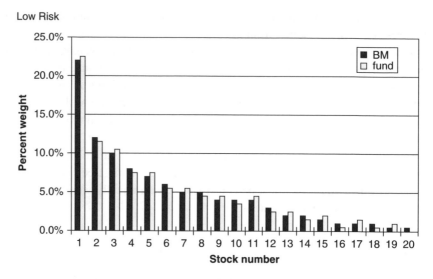

Figure 3.12   *Effect of constraints on implementing preferences – result 1*

Unsurprisingly, the index structure is left nearly intact, with small overweights and underweights visible.

The next set of results are shown in Figure 3.13. The risk level has been driven up. We begin to see large load ratios applied to small stocks. Many stocks have sold out. Underweights larger in absolute size than the overweights begin to be seen. However, the risk inherent in the portfolio is not so high that disliked stocks are sold out altogether – risk control presences can be seen.

The next set of results are shown in Figure 3.14. The risk level has been driven very high. The disliked stocks have been sold out completely. The over-weighted stocks are equally overweighted. The system is now stable. No further risk can be taken into the portfolio on this basis of preferences. Any further risk must come from a re-examination of the preferences – some further refinement to the very best ideas is required.

3.6   CONCLUSIONS

The codes described here are intended to describe how a portfolio construction methodology can be built that takes the output of a stock selection process and applies the stock preferences at various levels of aggressiveness to come up with portfolios either close or less close to the index.

The nature of the constraint on no-short-selling becomes apparent in the compromises that need to be made to fund overweight positions. If the purchases come from the fund as a whole, then the main contributor to the purchases comes from the large cap stocks, which can even end up underweight, even though they

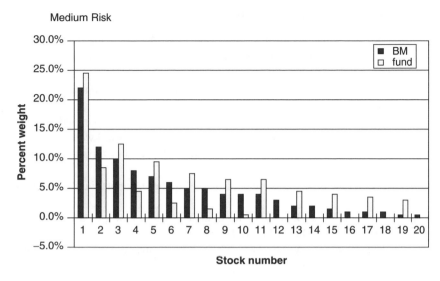

Figure 3.13 *Effect of constraints on implementing preferences – result 2*

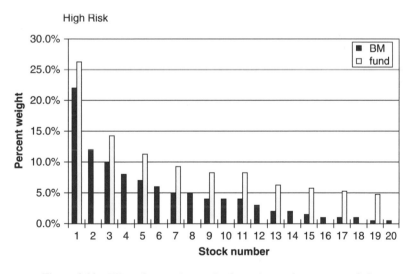

Figure 3.14 *Effect of constraints on implementing preferences – result 3*

are liked. Another way to fund the buys is to rob the underweights and neutrals. This has the advantage that buys stay as overweight but the underweight stocks go very underweight, implying a stronger view than may really be present. Further work is necessary to understand the asymmetrical large and small cap risk statements in a broad portfolio.

REFERENCES AND FURTHER READING

Hartmann, S., Wesselius, P., Steel, D. and Aldred, N. (2001) Laying the foundations: exploring the pitfalls of portfolio construction and optimisation, *ABN Amro Global Quantitative Analysis*.

Huang, C.F. and Litzenberger, R.H. (1988) *Foundations for Financial Economics*, Prentice Hall.

Ingersoll, J.E. (1987) *Theory of Financial Decision Making*, Rowman and Littlefield.

Markowitz, H.M. (1991, after 1959 edn) *Portfolio Selection*, Blackwell.

Mathews, J. and Walker, R.L. (1970) *Mathematical Methods of Physics*, 2nd edition, Benjamin Cummings.

Scowcroft, A. (1999) *Tracking Errors*, UBS AG Equities Quantitative Research, London.

Scowcroft, A. and Sefton, J. (2001) Understanding risk: a new global country-sector model, UBS Warburg Global Equity Research, London.

Sefton, J. and Scowcroft, A. (2001) Portfolio risk sensitivity, UBS Warburg Global Equity Research, London.

Chapter 4

Enhanced indexation

ALAN SCOWCROFT AND JAMES SEFTON

ABSTRACT

Over the past twenty years, index funds have gained tremendous popularity among both retail and institutional equity investors. In part, this must be due to disillusionment with the performance of active funds, but predominantly it reflects attempts by fund managers to minimize their costs. Managers adopt strategies that allocate capital to both passive index and active management funds. A large proportion of their fund is therefore run at the reduced costs of a passive fund, allowing the managers to concentrate their resources on the smaller active component.

Enhanced index funds have evolved as a synthesis between the pure active fund, and this more recent combined fund or fund of funds approach. These enhanced index funds are benchmarked tightly to a recognized index, thus maintaining the substance of a passive fund. However, at the same time the fund manager actively 'tilts' the index in line with his forecasts so as to earn a slightly better return. As diBartolomeo (2000) says, 'Enhanced index funds generally involve a quantitatively defined strategy that "tilts" the portfolio composition away from strict adherence to some popular market index to a slightly different composition that is expected to produce more return for similar levels of risk'.

The aim of this chapter is to outline, in some detail, the UBS Warburg approach to designing enhanced index funds. Firstly, though, we shall briefly summarize the arguments in favour of enhanced indexation. This summary draws heavily on the work of diBartolomeo (2000) and to a much lesser extent Riepe and Werner (1998).

4.1   INTRODUCTION

4.1.1   Enhanced index funds

We shall define enhanced index funds as equity funds with less than 2.5% ex ante tracking error to their benchmark, which are designed using quantitative strategies to increase their expected returns. We therefore do not include in our definition any funds that use a derivative overlay, or any form of cross-asset alpha portability to increase returns. Riepe and Werner (1998) investigate these types of funds, which are sometimes called enhanced index funds too.

As diBartolomeo (2000) argues, the principle motivation for enhanced index funds is that they are designed to be mean-variance efficient. The information available to the fund manager is efficiently incorporated into the portfolio so as to maximize the return to risk ratio of the fund. It is this feature which distinguishes them from funds made up of a combination of an active and passive fund.

In fact, the design strategy of combining passive and active funds to achieve in aggregate a moderately 'tilted' fund is likely to be far from efficient. The active component of these combined funds tends to be a fund that takes relatively large positions vis-à-vis the market, as opposed to being mildly tilted. This is in part so that the combined portfolio has moderate size position, in part to recoup the dead-weight costs of running active funds, and in part because it is seen as a better use of the active fund manager – if you are paying a skilled manager, let him use his skill, don't over constrain him. Now Grinold and Kahn (2000) have argued that it is far harder for the fund managers of these very active funds to use their information efficiently because of the 'long-only' constraint that is imposed on almost all equity funds. The 'long-only' constraint does not allow these funds to ever be significantly underweight small cap stocks, and hence by implication overweight large cap stocks. Grinold and Kahn (2000) show that this capitalization bias can significantly reduce the performance of these funds. Broadie (1993) argues that, in addition, these active funds can also often underperform because they must rely heavily on information that is inherently more difficult to estimate or collate. These funds are forced to hold stocks that will generate a high return to reward the investor for taking on the higher risk of the fund. However, identifying stocks that give a high return, as opposed to those that simply give a better than average return, is a hard task. Picking the exceptional performers means choosing companies that are innovating and often dramatically changing. Clearly estimating the returns of such companies can be a hazardous task at the best of times.

Finally, the original motivation for the combined fund strategy was to reduce costs. However, it is somewhat ironic that an approach designed to reduce costs can end up paying the costs of a passive fund, and a number of active fund managers. As diBartolomeo (2000) notes, a number of active managers are often employed so as to reduce the reliance on one particular manager outperforming, and as a means of pursuing a more involved investment strategy. At some level, these managers can be seen to be trading between themselves, therefore increasing costs with absolutely no benefit to the aggregate portfolio.

Enhanced index funds suggest a way around nearly all these problems. They are only mildly 'tilted' and so their efficiency is unlikely to be effected by 'long-only' constraints; they do not try and pick the super performers and so avoid problems of spotting outliers and they provide a quantitatively rigorous way of combining a number of strategies in a single portfolio. In addition, because of their close adherence to an index, the degree of trading can be kept to a minimum.

4.1.2   A summary of the chapter

In this chapter we aim to describe the UBS Warburg approach to the design of enhanced index funds. The next Section starts by arguing that a fund manager's or a strategist's forecasts are best described as a return to a chosen portfolio. Thus if the strategist has a sector view, then this can be described as a return to the global sector portfolio; or if a fund manager has style view then this can be captured as a return to a portfolio of all companies that satisfy a set of accounting ratio constraints.

Following this discussion, we will then introduce the Theil–Goldberger mixed estimator. This estimator provides a consistent and rigorous way to combine these forecasts with the unconditional return and risk matrix of stock returns, so as to derive a distribution of stock returns next period.

The enhanced portfolio is constructed from these 'tilted' estimates of the mean and variance of next period returns using the UBS Warburg optimizer. We then show that if the default estimate of the unconditional expected returns are the reversed optimized returns, we ensure 'strict adherence' to the benchmark index. For in the absence of any forecasts, the optimizer returns the index as the optimal enhanced portfolio.

In the final Section we illustrate this design process by working through an example. One issue, which we explore in this Section, is a comparison of our 'bottom up' or stock level approach to portfolio design, with a 'top down' or asset allocation approach. The two are directly comparable in our illustrative example, as all the strategists' views are expressed at the sector or country level. We also discuss how modifying or reducing the number of strategists' forecasts effects the final stock selection.

4.2   CONSTRUCTING A CONSISTENT VIEW

There are broadly two types of fund manger: the stock selectors and the asset allocators. In this Section, we shall argue that the forecasts or views of both these types of managers can be best described as the return to a chosen portfolio.

Stock selectors often 'cherry pick' stocks on the basis of fundamental valuation information. The 'screening process' aims to identify a basket of stocks, all of which possess various characteristics. These are the characteristics that the manager believes are going to put the underlying company in a relatively better position to take advantage of the current prevailing economic conditions. Thus the manager might screen for growth or value stocks using simple accounting ratios, or stocks with a low debt to asset ratio or stocks that have performed well recently, so-called momentum stocks. From this basket, the fund manager will pick his favoured stocks possibly with some eye to the overall risk characteristics of the final portfolio.

This very process of screening is a process of constructing portfolios of stocks. As all the stocks in these portfolios possess a factor, which the manager believes is likely to indicate out-performance, then the manager's view can be captured by ascribing an above average return to this portfolio. Therefore, the information available to the manager can be described as the return to a set of chosen portfolios. Further, it is also possible to assign a confidence to each of these views as a range within which the return of the portfolio is likely to lie. Thus if the fund manager is confident that this portfolio is likely to outperform then the range is likely to be small around his central estimate. Conversely, if the particular view has only a marginal impact on his complete picture the confidence is likely to be much lower.

An alternative approach adopted by stock selectors is to rank stocks according to their expected returns. This information can again be captured in a similar manner. The universe of stocks may be broken down into quantiles in accordance with the rankings. Each quantile would constitute a portfolio, and the portfolios of higher ranking stocks would be ascribed a higher expected return. Some judgement must be applied here as to the 'optimal' number of quantiles or portfolios; the trade-off being between maximizing resolution and minimizing the transmission of estimation error, a type of signal to noise ratio.

In contrast, asset allocators usually make top down or aggregate level forecasts concerning sector, country or global style performance. Clearly, these views can be very naturally described as the return to a sector, country or style portfolio. Again, it is also possible to describe the confidence the fund manager or strategist has in these views, as a confidence interval around the central return prediction.

Asset allocators and stock selectors alike must eventually pick a set of stocks based on their views. Though this can be done in a structured fashion, with attention paid throughout to the risk characteristics of the final portfolio, the process, ultimately, must rely on an ad-hoc set of rules. It is therefore at this final stage where we shall use quantitative methods to systematically arrive at the final portfolio selection.

4.2.1 Theil–Goldberger mixed estimator

We have argued that strategists' and analysts' views are most easily captured in terms of views on, or as a forecast of returns to, a given set of portfolios. The problem now is how to integrate these views into consistent quantitative framework. The UBS Warburg approach to this problem is based on Theil and Goldberger's (1961) mixed estimator. Later Theil (1971) rephrased his derivation in a Bayesian probabilistic framework; this exposition will draw heavily on the terminology in this latter presentation.

Assume that there are n stocks in our investable universe, and denote next period's returns on these assets by the n by 1 vector r_t. These returns can be considered to be a sum of the long run equilibrium return of the assets, denoted μ, and the stochastic return, ε_t. We shall assume ε_t is distributed as a multi-variate normal with zero mean and variance of Σ, thus

$$r_t \sim N(\mu, \Sigma) \tag{4.1}$$

The covariance matrix Σ is often called the risk matrix, and is the information at the core of any risk model of stock returns.

Under the semi-strong efficient market hypothesis, the hypothesis that all publicly available information is already incorporated into asset prices, the expected return in the next period to holding these assets, $E(r_t)$, is simply the corresponding element of the mean vector μ. Now there are two reasons why strategists might believe they could improve on this estimate:

- That they have an insight or information into the stocks' future performance not yet in the public domain. This information therefore is not yet reflected in prices and could be used to construct an estimate of the stochastic returns, ε_t, and a portfolio with the likelihood of earning superior returns in the short run to the market portfolio.
- That asset returns are partly forecastable. Indeed there is a growing body of evidence, summarized in Cochrane (1999), to this effect. If this is the case, then the strategist could improve on the initial estimate $E(\varepsilon_t) = 0$ and further would want to tilt his portfolio to reflect this knowledge.

We shall now quantify the distribution of the strategist's forecasts of future stock returns. We have argued that the strategist's views are best expressed as a view on the likely future returns of a set of Portfolios.[1] Let these portfolios be represented by the m by n matrix P, where the rows of the matrix P are the stock holdings in each of these m portfolios.[2] Now the strategist's forecasts, f_t, are assumed to be distributed around the final realized vector of returns with an error, v_t. The error has multivariate normal distribution with variance Ω. Thus

$$f_t = P(r_t - \mu) + v_t \quad \text{where } v_t \sim N(0, \Omega) \tag{4.2}$$

For reasons we will discuss later, we have assumed that the strategist forecasts returns relative to the long run equilibrium (that is they forecast ε_t) rather than absolute returns.

In addition to Equation (4.2), we also assume that the forecast error, v_t, is uncorrelated with the realized returns

$$E(v_t'\varepsilon_t) = 0 \tag{4.3}$$

Now, though these two formulae look relatively innocuous, they need discussing in some detail. We need to make the following observations:

(1) We have assumed that there is no consistent bias in the strategist's forecast; the expected value of the forecast equals the expected returns on the portfolios.

(2) The forecast is rational in the sense that there is no information in the errors, Equation (4.3). Another way of the saying the same thing is that the strategists do not consistently make systematic errors. For example they will not consistently forecast that the industry group Basic Materials will outperform its long run average whilst the industry group Energy will underperform it; for we know the performance of these two sectors is very highly correlated.

(3) We have phrased the strategist's forecasts as the return of his portfolios relative to the long run equilibrium portfolio return. Though in this framework we have assumed that the long run average stock returns are known, and relative returns can be converted to absolute and vice-versa with ease, this in practice is obviously not the case. We have therefore phrased the problem in this manner so that it is consistent with any approach to estimating these equilibrium rates of return.

(4) The volatility of the strategist's forecasts is strictly greater that the volatility of the returns he is forecasting. This is because the volatility of the forecasts is equal to the inherent volatility of the portfolio returns plus the volatility of his errors.

$$\text{Var}(f_t) = P\Sigma P' + \Omega \tag{4.4}$$

However, this does not imply there is no information in these forecasts, simply that the strategist does make errors.

(5) We can also write down the conditional probability density function of the strategist's forecasts given that we know stock returns in period t,

$$f_t|r_t \sim N(P(r_t - \mu), \Omega) \tag{4.5}$$

This answers the question: if we knew what the stock returns in period t were, how well could we have predicted what the strategist would have forecast (given of course that he does not know these actual realized returns). It does not answer the question: what would the strategist have forecasted if he knew what actual realized returns are. This latter question, of course, has the rather trivial answer that he would have forecasted perfectly.

Within this framework, it is now possible to construct an estimate of next period's stock returns given the strategist's forecasts, $r_t|f_t$. The derivation here uses a straightforward application of Bayes' theorem, that

$$\Pr(r_t|f_t) \propto \Pr(f_t|r_t) \Pr(r_t) \tag{4.6}$$

Substituting in our assumptions about the distributions, and after some simple algebraic manipulations (details are given in Appendix A) gives,

$$r_t|f_t \sim N(\mu + (\Sigma^{-1} + P'\Omega^{-1}P)^{-1}P\Omega^{-1}f_t, (\Sigma^{-1} + P'\Omega^{-1}P)^{-1}) \tag{4.7}$$

Hence we have derived an optimal estimate of the distribution of next period's stock returns by 'mixing' the strategist's views on some key portfolios with the estimated risk matrix of stock returns. Again, we need to make some observations:

(1) The expected value, or central estimate, of next period stock returns is

$$E(r_t|f_t) - \mu = (\Sigma^{-1} + P'\Omega^{-1}P)^{-1}P\Omega^{-1}f_t \tag{4.8}$$

where we have expressed these returns as relative to the long run equilibrium level of returns. Therefore, in this sense, the inference of the strategist's forecasts for the estimates of this period stock returns is independent of the estimates of the long run equilibrium rates of returns and depends only on the strategist's forecasts and the risk matrix. This is desirable for as both Merton (1980) and Jorion (1986) have pointed out, the risk matrix can be estimated with a great deal more confidence that the equilibrium levels of returns.

(2) To understand the construction of the central estimate of next period stock returns, rewrite Equation (4.8) as

$$E(r_t|f_t) - \mu = \Sigma P'(P\Sigma P' + \Omega)^{-1} f_t \qquad (4.9)$$

using an application of the matrix inversion theorem and some algebraic manipulation.[3] The central estimates are constructed by first weighting the strategist's forecasts in inverse proportion to their variance, see Equation (4.4), or equivalently in proportion to the confidence one can have in these forecasts. Then these scaled forecasts are multiplied by the covariance matrix between the stock's stochastic return, ε_t, and the stochastic return of the strategist's portfolios, $P\varepsilon_t$. Thus if a stock's returns vary, or are highly correlated with, the portfolios' returns, then its expected return will be modified in line with the forecasts. In contrast, if there is little correlation between the stock's returns and the portfolios' returns, then there will be little change made to the expected value of the stock's return next period.

An alternative way to explain Equation (4.9) for the special case when $\Omega = 0$, is as a solution to a minimum least squares problem. The problem is minimize the error

$$(E(r_t|f_t) - \mu)' \Sigma^{-1} (E(r_t|f) - \mu) \qquad (4.10)$$

subject to the condition $P(E(r_t|f) - \mu) = f_t$. In words, find the minimal adjustment to expected returns from their long run equilibrium levels such that the expected return to the strategist's portfolios equal their forecasts.

(3) The revised risk matrix, which could be used when we construct our enhanced index portfolio, is

$$\text{Var}(r_t|f_t) = (\Sigma^{-1} + P'\Omega^{-1}P)^{-1} \qquad (4.11)$$

(4) The mixed estimator weights together the strategist's forecast with the information in the risk matrix. To understand better how this weighting works, we shall focus on the estimated expected returns on the strategist's key portfolios, that is

$$P(E(r_t|f_t) - \mu) = P(\Sigma^{-1} + P'\Omega^{-1}P)^{-1}P\Omega^{-1}f_t$$
$$= P\Sigma P'(P\Sigma P' + \Omega)^{-1} f_t \qquad (4.12)$$

The second line comes, in an identical way to Equation (4.9), from an application of the matrix inversion formula and some straightforward manipulation (these steps are detailed in Appendix A). From this second line, it is clear that if the strategist is confident in his views, $\Omega \to 0$, then the mixed estimator forecasts equals the strategist's forecasts. Conversely if the strategist is guessing, $\Omega \to \infty$, then no weight is put on the forecasts and expected relative returns are equal to zero.

4.2.2 The difference between forecasting absolute performance or performance relative to the market

In this section, we discuss a few issues concerned with the construction or encapsulation of the strategist's views into this framework. In particular, we shall concentrate on the difference in phrasing these views in terms of absolute performance or performance relative to the market.

The difference is best illustrated with reference to an example. Suppose the strategist holds the view that the Financial Sector is likely to perform well over the next year and this view is expressed simply that the Financial Sector will give a return next period in excess of its equilibrium level of returns.[4] Now the Financial Sector portfolio has a market beta very close to 1 with the market able to account for about 50% of the sector's return volatility, see for example Scowcroft and Sefton (2002). Therefore, the model, in the absence of any other information, will deduce that about half of the above average sector performance can be accounted for by the above average performance of the market. Hence the model, when inferring the implication of this forecast for other sectors, will assign an above average performance to all other sectors too, and in particular those sectors with high market betas, such as Technology.

In contrast to this scenario, assume that the strategist's view is expressed in relative terms that the Financial Sector will outperform the market in the coming year.[5] In this scenario, the model must attribute all of the above average performance to the sector. Therefore, it will assign an above average performance to those sectors whose performance, ex the market, is highly correlated with the financial sector's and a below average performance to those that have historically been inversely correlated. In this case, it is likely that the model will deduce that Technology will underperform, as historically its performance ex the market has been inversely correlated with the Financial sector.

4.3   ENHANCED INDEXING

So far we have deferred any discussion of how to calculate the long run equilibrium returns. This was deliberate, as the mixed estimator problem can be phrased in terms of returns relative to these long run equilibrium returns, enabling us to remain agnostic as to what approach to use to estimate them. However, if we are to build investable portfolios, then we must finally address this issue.

There are three fundamental approaches in the literature, all others being basic variations on these three. They are:

- historical mean or average returns;
- the equilibrium returns as defined by the Capital Asset Pricing Model (CAPM);
- the reversed optimized rates of return.

As many authors have pointed out, Frankfurter et al. (1971), Merton (1980) and Jorion (1986) being good examples, it is almost impossible to estimate equilibrium returns by averaging past returns. To illustrate, assume a stock's return has an average annual volatility of 30% (this is on the low side), then the mean return can be expected to be estimated with an accuracy of $\pm 30/\sqrt{n}$ where n is the number of data observations. Therefore, even with a 100 years of data (and assuming there has been no structural change in the market!), one could only hope to estimate the mean return to within $\pm 3\%$. Increasing the frequency of the data observations does not help, as the volatility rises at the same rate as the number of observations.[6] Though Jorion (1986) suggested using a Stein estimator to improve the accuracy a little, the approach remains impractical.

Given the difficulty with this first approach, some authors have suggested using the structural CAPM model to help inform the estimation process. This approach has been popularized by Black and Litterman (1992). Under the assumptions of CAPM,[7] an asset's equilibrium return is equal to the risk free rate plus its market beta times the average market return. The market betas, as they are correlation coefficients, can be estimated with more accuracy than mean returns and, as every stock's equilibrium return is proportional to the average market return, errors in the estimate of the market return do little to affect relative rates of return. Though this solution is theoretically attractive, using it to build portfolios quantitatively is fraught with difficulties.

The principal difficulty is that portfolio optimizers, in the words of Michaud (1999), are 'error maximizers'. To illustrate what he means by this phrase, assume it is estimated that the equilibrium return of an asset is particularly good relative to other assets, simply because its market beta was erroneously estimated to be large. Now any optimizer assumes that these model parameters are estimated without error, and therefore if one asset gives a good return relative to other assets, it will want to heavily overweight this asset. If short selling is allowed, this tendency will be even more extreme. Therefore, small estimation errors can cause large changes in optimal asset holdings. As Michaud argues, the errors do not have to be very large before this effect drives entirely the optimal asset allocation.

The final approach, and the one adopted by UBS Warburg, is to estimate the equilibrium returns using reverse optimization. The idea underlying this approach is that in the absence of any views about next period's return, an investor should hold the benchmark portfolio or equivalently the index. In line with this idea, the equilibrium returns are estimated to be those returns such that, in the absence of any further information, the portfolio optimizer returns the benchmark portfolio as the optimal portfolio. Therefore, the equilibrium returns are reverse engineered. In practice, this implies that the equilibrium returns are a simple function of the risk matrix, Σ, and the benchmark weights. In a mean-variance framework, the function is particularly straightforward:

$$\mu = s^{Mkt}\Sigma w \quad \text{where } s^{Mkt} = \frac{\mu^{Mkt}}{w'\Sigma w} \tag{4.13}$$

where w is the n-vector of the benchmark portfolio weights (normalized so as to sum to 1), μ^{Mkt} is the long run equilibrium benchmark return and s^{Mkt} is the Sharpe ratio of the benchmark portfolio. As the reverse optimization process only estimates the relative returns of the assets, we have normalized the level of these equilibrium returns so that the long run equilibrium return of the benchmark portfolio equals the historical average return of the benchmark.

4.3.1   Our definition of enhanced indexing

We are now in a position to describe precisely what we understand by enhanced indexing. It makes explicit the terms, 'quantitatively defined strategy', 'strict adherence' and 'tilts' in Dan diBartolomeo's original definition of enhanced index funds:

> *Enhanced Index funds generally involve a quantitatively defined strategy that 'tilts' the portfolio composition away from strict adherence to some popular market index.*

Our enhanced index funds are built using the latest version of the UBS Warburg mean-variance optimizer. The functionality of this optimizer is described in detail in Appendix B, but fundamentally it constructs an optimal portfolio that minimizes a mean-variance criterion subject to a set of linear and integer constraints. The principal inputs to this optimizer are the expected returns and variance of next period's returns. It is in this sense that we understand a 'quantitatively defined strategy'.

The default estimates of the expected returns and variance of next period's returns are the reversed optimized returns and the covariance matrix calculated using the UBS Warburg global country sector model. We therefore ensure that in the absence of any further information, the optimizer will return the benchmark or index portfolio as the optimal fund. In this way we guarantee 'strict adherence' to the benchmark index. The funds are then 'tilted' by shifting the estimates of the distribution of next period expected returns from the default estimates to a distribution whose mean and variance is a mixture of these default estimates and the views of the strategists. The synthesis is performed by codifying the strategist's views as a set of predictions, with confidence bounds, on the returns to a chosen set of portfolios; and then combining these views with the reversed optimized returns and risk matrix using the Theil–Goldberger mixed estimator.

The enhanced portfolio is finally constructed from these 'tilted' estimates of the mean and variance of next period returns using the UBS Warburg optimizer. This final portfolio will therefore be 'tilted' towards or slightly overweight those stocks whose returns are highly correlated to those portfolios favoured by the strategist, and underweight those stocks highly correlated to those portfolios unfavoured by the strategist.

The final enhanced portfolio will be mean-variance efficient with respect to the 'tilted' distribution of next period's returns. By this we mean, that given our updated view on the distribution of next periods returns, there is no other portfolio that will offer a higher expected return for the same level of risk, or lower risk for the same level of expected return. At this point, it is of course worth reminding ourselves that even though we have used the strategist's views in an efficient and rational manner to construct a portfolio, the performance of this enhanced portfolio will succeed or fail based on the quality of the strategist's forecasts.

4.4   AN ILLUSTRATIVE EXAMPLE: TOP-DOWN OR BOTTOM-UP?

In this Section we will illustrate the design process of a 100 stock 'enhanced index fund' that reflects the current[8] views of both UBS Warburg global sector analysts' and country desks. The emphasis of the discussion will be on the design process, rather than on the final portfolio though we include a short discussion of this portfolio.

One issue, which we will explore first, is comparing a 'bottom up' or stock level approach to portfolio design, with a 'top down' or asset allocation approach. The two are directly comparable in this illustrative example, as all the strategists' views are expressed at the sector or country level. Clearly, if some of these views could not have been phrased in terms of the returns to broad asset classes, no direct comparisons would have been possible. Now assuming linearity is observed, then as Haitovsky (1973) and Johnston (1984) prove under some quite restrictive conditions, the two approaches can deliver identical results at the aggregate asset level. However, in practice, there are some strong non-linearities in any portfolio design approach. The most important of these being the introduction of no-short constraints and the inclusion of integer constraints on the number of stocks in the portfolio. Therefore, this exercise can be thought of as a quantitative investigation into the importance of accounting for these non-linearities in the portfolio design process.

The 'bottom up' or stock level approach is implemented on the UBS Warburg Portfolio Analysis System (PAS). It is therefore worth describing briefly the approach underlying this model, precise details of its functions are described in the two UBS Quantitative Research publications 'Understanding Risk: A new country-sector model' and 'Where the numbers come from'. The PAS system uses a time-series or factor approach to construct the risk matrix. The advantage of this approach is that it enables the risk characteristics of a portfolio to be allocated precisely to a selection of risk factors; that is market, sector, country and style risks. One by one, the returns of each stock are regressed on the time-series returns of these risk factors. The risk factor returns are the returns to the market index, the returns to the 10 Dow Jones industry group indices (adjusted so that they are market neutral[9]), the returns to eight regional Dow Jones indices (adjusted so that they are sector neutral), and the returns to the UBS Warburg global growth and value indices. Two-step Bayesian consistency regression checks are performed on the regression coefficients or factor betas; these amount to setting any factor betas to zero that are statistically insignificant and shrinking the estimates of the market betas back to towards general means. The risk matrix is then constructed directly from these regression results using the imposed factor structure.

Next the PAS system uses the Theil–Goldberger mixed estimator to construct estimates of next period expected returns in the manner described earlier in this article. Finally, the optimal portfolio is constructed so as to minimize a mean-variance criterion subject to both no-short constraints and a limit to the maximum number of stocks in the portfolio.

In contrast to the PAS system, the asset allocation model (AAM) built for this article is more streamlined.[10] This was deliberate as we wished the differences between the results of the two models to be directly attributable to the sophistication of the PAS system rather than the asset allocation model (AAM). The 80 assets included in the AAM were each of the local sector indices in the 10 sectors in the eight equity regions. The risk matrix for this model was, like PAS, built by a time series approach using the identical market, sector and country risk factors as used in the PAS model. However, the style risk factors were omitted from the AAM model, and no consistency or robustness checked performed.[11] In an identical manner to the PAS system, a Theil–Goldberger mixed estimator was used to construct the estimates of next period's expected returns, and mean-variance analysis used to build the optimal asset allocation portfolio. However, in the case of AAM, the portfolio was built without imposing any short constraints, though at the index level these constraints are obviously likely to be less binding. Further, in an AAM model it is obviously not possible to impose any constraints on the maximum number of stocks in a portfolio.

Though there are some minor differences between the PAS and AAM models in the procedure used to estimate the risk matrix, the principal difference between the two models lies in the imposition in the PAS system of both no-short constraints and a limit to the number of stocks in the portfolio.

4.4.1 The strategists' forecasts

In this illustrative example we will use the views of the UBS Warburg global sector strategists and the UBS Warburg regional economic desks on likely equity returns over the six months from February 2002 to each of the 10 global industry groups and to the seven main economic regions. Unless otherwise stated, the universe of stocks is assumed to be the Dow Jones Global Universe, with all classifications into Industries and Countries based on the Dow Jones Classifications. All figures quoted are calculated on monthly returns over the previous five years.

In Table 4.1 we have summarized the views of the global sector strategists. These views are expressed as returns relative to the market, thus it is expected that the Energy Sector will underperform the market over the six months beginning February 2002 by an annualized rate of 2%. Further, we have assigned a confidence to these forecasts equal to 50% of the average volatility of the corresponding index relative returns.[12] These forecasts are based on the view that:

> '*Over the next 12 months, the issue of which sectors will participate strongly in an environment of rising global equity markets depends on the combination of two main forces: sector sensitivity to a cyclical upturn and the extent of over-investment over the past few years. While we think the typically cyclical sectors are liable to rise along with the broader market in anticipation of a global economic recovery, their performances may be compromised by pockets of over-investment, low capacity utilization rates and minimal pricing power. Sectors with favourable industry conditions, where there are strong product cycles, high capital efficiencies, strong branding and market concentration should do well in this environment. Based upon the outlook for those industry conditions, we believe technology should remain the highest secular growth sector over the next few years, driven primarily by favourable product cycles. Utilities, basic materials and industrials are weighed down by their mature product cycles, heavy capital intensity, lack of branding and pockets of fragmentation, and are expected to record inferior secular returns over the next few years.'*
> *UBS Warburg Global Analyser, 1 February 2002.*

Table 4.1 *Global sector strategists' forecast of returns to the 10 Dow Jones global industry groups*

Dow Jones group classification	Forecasted return Feb 2002–Aug 2002 (annualized)	Confidence in forecast (annualized standard error)	% by market cap of the global Dow Jones universe
Basic Materials	0.32	6.36	3.69
Consumer Cyclical	0.45	4.00	13.95
Energy	−2.02	6.00	6.65
Financial	−0.14	4.95	21.96
Healthcare	−0.15	5.86	11.63
Industrial	0.47	4.04	11.13
Consumer Non-Cyclical	−0.29	4.26	7.70
Technology	1.98	6.79	13.65
Telecommunications	−0.32	7.67	6.06
Utilities	−2.93	3.61	3.58

The forecasts are returns relative to the market.
Source: UBS Warburg.

In Table 4.2, we have recorded the corresponding numbers of the UBS Warburg forecasts for the seven principal global equity regions. These are based on the numbers reported in the UBS Warburg publication 'Tactical Asset Allocation' by Larry Hatheway and Jeffrey Palma in February 2002. Similarly, these numbers are the forecasts for returns in these regions over the next six months, though the figures are all quoted at an annualized rate. The forecasts are based on the view that:

> *'The world economy is staging a recovery from the recessionary vice that took hold toward the back end of last year. Business confidence indicators in nearly every major economy have stabilized or picked up a little. . . . The second estimate of US GDP for the final quarter of last year suggests an annualized expansion of 1.4% over the quarter. With purchasing managers' surveys close to the expansion mark of 50, new orders showing a tentative recovery and the deterioration in the labour market beginning to slow, the US recession, that was formally estimated to have begun last March, may prove to be one of the mildest in recent memory. . . . (In contrast) Japan, the world's third largest economy, has managed to disappoint once again with its latest government package. As a result, we believe that the only path open to policy makers is greater monetization by the BoJ'. Global Economic Perspectives, 28 February 2002.*

4.4.2 A comparison of asset allocation v stock selection

We shall now use the strategists' forecasts of next period's returns to a chosen set of portfolios or indices to update our estimates of the returns to all stocks or asset

Table 4.2   *Global sector strategists' forecast of returns by region*

Country	Forecasted return Feb 2002–Aug 2002 (annualized)	Confidence in forecast (annualized standard error)	% by market cap of the global Dow Jones universe
Canada	−1.66	6.37	2.16
United Kingdom	−0.46	4.07	9.64
Japan	−11.66	8.87	8.06
United States	2.54	4.27	57.91
EMU Region	0.74	5.70	12.08
Europe ex EMU and UK	−4.26	4.35	3.84
Pacific ex Japan	−1.26	8.69	5.06
Latin America	N/A	N/A	1.25

The forecasts are returns relative to the market.
Source: UBS Warburg.

classes within our universe. In the section entitled the Theil–Goldberger Mixed Estimator, we described in detail how to perform this update. This estimator updates the returns to all assets in the universe on the basis of the historical correlation between the returns of these assets and each of the strategists' chosen portfolios. If an asset's returns have been historically highly correlated with a given portfolio's returns, then its expected return next period will be updated in line with the strategists' forecast for this portfolio. The greater the confidence in the forecast, the more the asset's returns will be moved into line with the forecast. Using the Theil–Goldberger estimator this whole process can be done consistently for all assets and all forecasts, to derive the most likely or optimal forecast for all assets.

In Table 4.3 and Table 4.4 we give the details of the constructed forecasts of next period's returns update for each of the local sector indices. The forecasts in Table 4.3 were calculated by the UBS Warburg Portfolio Analysis System (PAS) at the stock level; those in Table 4.4 were done at the index level by a basic asset allocation model (AAM). The first observation is that the numbers from the two approaches agree very closely, save perhaps in Latin America. However, this region is the smallest regional equity market and is notoriously volatile and marked by dramatic structural economic changes. We shall therefore conclude that the differences between the two approaches at this stage are minimal.

The row and column totals give the market cap weighted averages of the expected returns across all regions for a given industry and the expected returns across all industries for a given region respectively. These totals concord closely with the views of the strategists, though in every case the totals are a margin smaller than the forecasts of the analysts. This is because the final forecast from the Theil–Goldberger mixed estimator will be a matrix weighted average

Table 4.3   *Annualized relative expected returns next period by industry and region after combining strategists' forecasts with the Default Risk Matrix at the stock level using the UBS Warburg Optimizer*

	Canada	United Kingdom	Japan	United States	EMU Region	Europe Ex EMU and UK	Pacific Ex Japan	Latin America	Industry Totals
Basic Materials	0.51	−0.25	−9.68	2.68	1.96	−0.55	−0.97	0.68	−0.02
Consumer Cyclical	−1.02	0.95	−6.84	2.96	1.73	−1.20	−1.36	1.80	0.84
Energy	−1.92	−1.23	−14.10	−2.64	−0.70	−2.17	−1.96	0.27	−1.98
Financial	0.66	−0.19	−13.28	2.76	−0.36	−2.78	−1.44	−0.03	0.27
Healthcare	−0.81	−0.79	−10.82	0.97	−2.56	−4.92	−2.55	0.00	−0.39
Industrial	−0.34	−1.05	−10.04	2.07	0.10	−2.09	−1.16	0.28	−0.43
Consumer Non-Cyclical	−1.08	−0.49	−11.19	1.11	−1.27	−3.67	−1.82	1.00	−0.49
Technology	−1.06	0.59	−9.14	2.09	0.85	−3.86	2.90	0.00	1.26
Telecommunications	−1.97	−1.54	−17.39	2.76	−0.33	−2.24	−2.34	1.24	−0.02
Utilities	−1.76	−2.53	−8.89	−1.05	−1.51	0.00	−3.38	0.88	−2.36
Regional totals	−0.40	−0.59	−9.94	1.78	−0.06	−3.17	−0.88	0.80	0

Source: UBS Warburg. The industry and regional totals are the market cap weighted average of the respective row and columns.

Table 4.4   *Annualized relative expected returns next period by industry and region after combining strategists' forecasts with Default Risk Matrix at the index level*

	Canada	United Kingdom	Japan	United States	EMU Region	Europe Ex EMU and UK	Pacific Ex Japan	Latin America	Industry Totals
Basic Materials	1.25	−1.07	−10.40	4.38	2.47	−3.44	−1.68	2.70	0.10
Consumer Cyclical	−1.49	1.74	−5.43	2.50	1.62	−0.67	−0.51	3.22	0.71
Energy	−2.98	−2.08	−14.54	−1.22	−0.90	−7.75	−3.60	−4.68	−1.69
Financial	0.62	−0.18	−14.47	3.11	−0.68	−4.71	−1.13	1.63	−0.20
Healthcare	−1.19	−1.93	−9.98	1.35	−1.48	−2.63	−0.87	−1.73	−0.11
Industrial	3.03	2.31	−8.74	2.02	0.77	−1.26	−1.07	2.57	−0.23
Consumer Non-Cyclical	2.91	−1.52	−9.29	1.76	−0.63	−1.68	−0.09	1.62	0.01
Technology	−3.52	1.47	−8.29	2.62	1.13	−0.25	−2.58	0.00	1.41
Telecommunications	−1.44	1.81	−11.27	0.61	2.43	−0.21	−0.45	1.44	0.30
Utilities	0.50	−0.29	−8.98	−0.62	−1.56	−2.17	−1.16	1.12	−1.99
Regional totals	−0.20	−0.25	−9.42	1.94	0.18	−2.78	−1.17	1.26	0

Source: UBS Warburg. The industry and regional totals are the market cap weighted average of the respective row and columns.

of the strategists' forecasts and the long run equilibrium levels. As all the results have been expressed as relative to the long run equilibrium returns, these final numbers are therefore a weighted average of strategists' forecasts and zero. If we reduced our confidence in the strategists' forecasts by increasing the bounds in Table 4.1 and Table 4.2, this shrinking effect would become more and more pronounced.

Table 4.5   *Optimized Portfolio Tilt by industry and region after combining strategists' forecasts with the Default Risk Matrix at the stock level using the UBS Warburg Optimizer*

	Canada	United Kingdom	Japan	United States	EMU Region	Europe Ex EMU and UK	Pacific Ex Japan	Latin America	Industry Totals
Basic Materials	−0.11	0.01	0.01	1.06	0.66	0.26	−0.05	0.12	1.96
Consumer Cyclical	−0.11	−0.20	−1.50	−0.22	0.13	0.05	−0.35	0.11	−2.10
Energy	−0.17	0.18	−0.06	−0.66	0.39	−0.07	−0.06	0.02	−0.43
Financial	−0.45	−0.32	−0.70	−0.81	−0.47	−0.79	−0.97	−0.02	−4.53
Healthcare	−0.04	0.59	−0.39	3.09	0.15	−0.74	−0.06	0.00	2.61
Industrial	−0.19	−0.20	−0.24	3.88	0.04	0.05	0.03	0.07	3.43
Consumer Non-Cyclical	0.02	0.10	−0.15	1.97	0.00	−0.47	−0.12	0.01	1.36
Technology	−0.18	0.01	−0.65	0.97	0.43	−0.15	−0.13	0.00	0.29
Telecommunications	−0.10	−0.01	−0.27	−0.10	0.14	−0.07	−0.20	0.00	−0.61
Utilities	0.23	−0.36	−0.07	−1.42	−0.59	0.00	−0.13	0.37	−1.98
Regional totals	−1.08	−0.21	−4.03	7.75	0.88	−1.92	−2.06	0.67	0

Source: UBS Warburg. The industry and regional totals are the sum of the respective row and columns.

Table 4.6   *Optimized Portfolio Tilt next period by industry and region after combining strategists' forecasts with the Default Risk Matrix at the Index Level*

	Canada	United Kingdom	Japan	United States	EMU Region	Europe Ex EMU and UK	Pacific Ex Japan	Latin America	Industry Totals
Basic Materials	−0.18	0.08	0.04	0.61	0.30	−0.08	0.15	0.07	0.98
Consumer Cyclical	−0.09	0.10	−0.70	0.61	0.33	−0.13	0.04	0.00	0.15
Energy	−0.37	0.01	−0.04	0.32	0.21	−0.02	0.02	−0.05	0.09
Financial	−0.64	0.23	−0.63	1.25	0.72	−1.17	0.10	−0.01	−0.16
Healthcare	−0.07	0.24	−0.12	1.50	0.28	−0.70	0.03	0.03	1.19
Industrial	−0.13	0.25	−0.15	2.05	0.30	−0.31	0.18	0.03	2.22
Consumer Non-Cyclical	0.10	0.09	−0.20	0.49	0.19	−0.50	0.03	−0.06	0.14
Technology	−0.13	−0.02	−0.29	0.46	0.19	−0.21	0.02	0.00	0.02
Telecommunications	−0.17	−0.02	−0.17	−0.03	0.16	−0.11	−0.05	−0.15	−0.54
Utilities	−0.08	−0.41	−0.88	−1.87	−0.68	0.11	−0.18	−0.13	−4.10
Regional totals	−1.76	0.56	−3.14	5.39	1.99	−3.11	0.35	−0.28	0

Source: UBS Warburg. The industry and regional totals are the sum of the respective row and columns.

We now shall compare the optimal asset allocations calculated using the different approaches. To try and understand what is driving the differences in the results between the two models, we shall do this in two steps. In the first stage, there is no constraint imposed on the PAS system as to maximum number of stocks that it can include in the portfolio. Only at the second stage do we re-optimize the PAS portfolio under the constraint that there must be only 100 stocks in the portfolio.

In Table 4.5 and Table 4.6, we report the optimal asset allocations from PAS and AAM respectively. There are now more substantial differences between the recommendations of two models, in particular in the allocations to the Financial and Consumer Cyclical sectors. However, these sectors apart, the numbers are again remarkably close. It is of considerable interest as to why the optimal allocations to these sectors are markedly different between the two models.

To this end, we have reproduced a table from our publication, 'Understanding Risk: A new country sector model'. In Table 4.7, we have broken down the variance of each of the 80 local sector indices into the component that can be attributed to the global market factor, the component that can be attributed to the 10 global sector factors, the component that can be attributed to the eight country factors and the residual component, the stock specific risk. We have also recorded in the top square the average annual standard deviation of the returns of each of these local sector indices.

The important observation from this table is that if the sectors are ranked by the degree to which the local market factors can explain the co-movement in index returns, the Consumer Cyclical and Financial sectors are ranked at the top.

Consumer Cyclicals is made up of a very diverse set of industries, automobile, media, construction and entertainment services being the major constituents. Though some of the firms in this sector are undeniably global businesses, there is little coherence in the performance of these firms over and above their dependence on the global market. Therefore, the performance of these firms is predominantly a function of the markets in which their businesses are located. Therefore, the asset allocation to this sector will be driven by the strategist's forecasts for the local market and not by his sector forecast.

The Financial sector is very different. It is predominantly comprised of two very distinct but internally coherent groups: the retail and investment banks. The performance of the retail banks is cyclical and therefore very much a function of the local markets in which they operate. On the other hand, the investment banks conduct their business globally and there is a marked coherence in their performance across the group. In terms of the asset allocation, the allocation to the retail banks will be very much a function of the strategists' forecasts for the local market, whereas the allocation to investment banks is more a function of the strategists' forecasts for the global sector. The PAS system is able to pick up this distinction as its allocation is done at the stock level, whereas the AAM can not. We shall discuss these sectors as an illustrative example in the next section.

In the final stage, we restrict, in the PAS system, the number of stocks in the optimal portfolio to 100. In Table 4.8, we have recorded the asset allocation of this portfolio by sector and country. In Table 4.9, we have noted in which of the local sectors the 100 stocks are held. By comparing Table 4.5

Table 4.7   *Variance breakdown of local market sector returns using the method described in the UBS Warburg publication, 'Understanding Risk: a new country-sector model' (2002)*

	United States	United Kingdom	Canada	Euro-Bloc	Europe ex Euro-Bloc & ex UK	Pacific ex Japan	Japan	Latin America
			Annual standard deviations of return					
Energy	17.2	20.1	21.6	16.5	26.8	22.8	30.4	43.3
Basic Materials	20.0	20.8	26.0	16.4	19.7	23.2	24.3	27.9
Industrial	16.2	16.0	19.1	16.6	17.0	25.1	20.4	30.2
Technology	32.1	43.2	46.3	30.2	38.5	37.2	27.8	40.5
Telecommunications	18.9	24.6	25.5	27.2	24.0	28.2	33.4	33.0
Utilities	14.5	13.1	15.3	14.3	13.4	19.5	17.1	34.9
Healthcare	15.2	16.6	30.0	13.4	13.4	19.8	18.9	31.2
Consumer Non Cyclical	14.3	13.0	14.7	13.9	13.8	24.2	21.0	23.7
Consumer Cyclical	15.4	15.5	18.3	17.5	16.3	19.8	17.5	30.8
Financial	18.9	15.8	19.9	17.3	21.3	26.2	26.6	32.4
			% of Variance explained by Global Market Factor					
Energy	23.8%	26.9%	15.0%	36.8%	15.4%	36.4%	6.3%	29.4%
Basic Materials	35.7%	34.0%	24.9%	39.3%	31.6%	37.1%	15.7%	47.1%
Industrial	86.3%	43.2%	61.0%	53.8%	54.1%	45.5%	41.5%	36.4%
Technology	53.4%	29.6%	25.7%	44.4%	37.2%	37.1%	46.4%	
Telecommunications	41.2%	28.8%	53.4%	35.9%	37.1%	54.7%	30.7%	50.6%
Utilities	5.4%	6.5%	14.5%	25.0%	14.3%	23.1%	4.6%	25.8%
Healthcare	23.4%	9.4%	36.2%	13.6%	20.9%	40.1%	11.7%	16.7%
Consumer Non Cyclical	48.4%	9.9%	11.4%	35.7%	28.0%	40.2%	20.1%	52.3%
Consumer Cyclical	75.5%	40.5%	48.6%	50.2%	53.5%	53.7%	48.7%	44.3%
Financial	43.5%	40.1%	45.9%	55.9%	52.4%	48.1%	29.4%	31.8%
			% of Variance explained by Global Sector Factors					
Energy	61.5%	52.7%	62.2%	35.4%	51.4%	32.9%	14.9%	3.0%
Basic Materials	53.5%	48.7%	54.0%	24.7%	37.7%	33.8%	16.2%	9.3%
Industrial	6.9%	29.9%	19.9%	20.8%	26.1%	7.9%	7.1%	5.8%
Technology	23.0%	24.8%	26.1%	24.2%	22.0%	11.1%	20.4%	
Telecommunications	27.7%	37.9%	15.2%	38.7%	20.0%	21.4%	16.6%	3.6%
Utilities	68.6%	32.0%	44.1%	13.3%	33.4%	29.5%	26.2%	4.9%
Healthcare	68.1%	38.8%	20.4%	23.9%	31.4%	24.2%	20.7%	10.6%
Consumer Non Cyclical	38.2%	45.1%	44.6%	26.3%	31.4%	14.2%	12.5%	9.5%
Consumer Cyclical	12.1%	26.9%	15.0%	18.1%	13.6%	13.3%	10.0%	16.5%
Financial	29.5%	14.2%	24.3%	10.5%	17.0%	5.8%	19.0%	4.6%
			% of Variance explained by Local Market Factors					
Energy	6.8%	11.9%	15.6%	23.1%	14.5%	19.8%	50.9%	49.2%
Basic Materials	6.4%	11.9%	6.1%	30.1%	25.4%	23.9%	50.0%	34.9%
Industrial	3.9%	18.2%	12.8%	21.6%	15.1%	45.2%	47.0%	43.2%
Technology	9.1%	9.0%	5.5%	23.3%	9.1%	22.0%	27.7%	
Telecommunications	16.3%	15.9%	18.3%	19.9%	30.9%	13.6%	28.4%	25.5%
Utilities	10.7%	33.5%	21.0%	51.1%	33.0%	38.1%	46.3%	59.7%
Healthcare	5.7%	29.0%	19.2%	36.8%	32.8%	22.9%	51.6%	35.9%
Consumer Non Cyclical	6.9%	34.2%	32.2%	37.9%	28.0%	35.5%	53.4%	30.6%
Consumer Cyclical	6.4%	24.4%	31.1%	27.6%	20.1%	30.1%	34.2%	24.6%
Financial	20.9%	31.6%	25.8%	29.2%	28.5%	40.0%	39.7%	54.6%

Source: UBS Warburg estimates.

Table 4.8 *Optimized Portfolio Tilt by industry and region after combining strategists' forecasts with the Default Risk Matrix at the stock level using the UBS Warburg Optimizer and limiting stock selection to 100 stocks*

	Canada	United Kingdom	Japan	United States	EMU Region	Europe Ex EMU and UK	Pacific Ex Japan	Latin America	Industry Totals
Basic Materials	−0.28	1.22	−0.47	1.09	2.24	−0.19	−0.38	−0.09	3.14
Consumer Cyclical	−0.15	−1.07	−2.18	−1.62	1.82	−0.20	−0.55	−0.09	−4.03
Energy	−0.33	2.10	−0.06	0.28	2.00	−0.08	−0.09	−0.09	3.74
Financial	−0.69	1.21	−1.35	−0.32	0.71	−1.14	−1.65	−0.24	−3.46
Healthcare	−0.06	0.77	−0.50	2.52	0.20	−0.90	−0.07	0.00	1.97
Industrial	−0.24	−0.64	−1.63	3.49	−0.66	−0.47	−0.63	−0.09	−0.88
Consumer Non-Cyclical	−0.07	−0.27	−0.44	3.52	0.11	−0.54	−0.24	−0.13	1.95
Technology	−0.18	−0.12	−0.72	2.83	0.45	−0.24	−0.79	0.00	1.22
Telecommunications	−0.11	0.03	−0.27	0.69	0.58	−0.10	−0.45	−0.41	−0.07
Utilities	−0.03	−0.36	−0.45	−1.72	−0.70	0.00	−0.20	−0.11	−3.58
Regional totals	−2.16	2.86	−8.06	10.77	6.74	−3.84	−5.06	−1.25	0

Source: UBS Warburg. The industry and regional totals are the sum of the respective rows and columns.

Table 4.9 *Number of stocks selected in each industry and region after combining strategists' forecasts with the Default Risk Matrix at the stock level using the UBS Warburg Optimizer and limiting stock selection to 100 stocks*

	Canada	United Kingdom	Japan	United States	EMU Region	Europe Ex EMU and UK	Pacific Ex Japan	Latin America	Industry Totals
Basic Materials	0	1	0	4	2	0	0	0	7
Consumer Cyclical	0	0	0	6	3	0	0	0	9
Energy	0	2	0	2	3	0	0	0	7
Financial	0	5	0	12	5	0	0	0	22
Healthcare	0	2	0	12	1	0	0	0	15
Industrial	0	0	0	9	0	0	0	0	9
Consumer Non-Cyclical	0	1	0	8	1	0	0	0	10
Technology	0	0	0	11	3	0	0	0	14
Telecommunications	0	1	0	4	2	0	0	0	7
Utilities	0	0	0	0	0	0	0	0	0
Regional totals	0	12	0	68	20	0	0	0	100

Source: UBS Warburg. The industry and regional totals are the sum of the respective rows and columns.

and Table 4.8, it is clear that the addition of this constraint effects, unsurprisingly, the asset allocation dramatically. Now stocks are only held in the UK, EMU or US. Stocks are still held in all global sectors, save Utilities. Excluding the Financial and Consumer Cyclical sectors again, the tilts directly reflect the strategists' forecasts. The ex ante tracking error of the fund rises from 1.91 to 2.55 after introducing this stock constraint. As this is on the upper bound of the acceptable range for enhanced index funds, this could be reduced slightly by either increasing the number of stocks in the portfolio, reducing the confidence levels of the strategists' forecasts or increasing the risk aversion parameter in the mean-variance analysis.

4.4.3   Simplifying the design process

The portfolios were constructed in the previous section using a comprehensive set of strategists' forecasts for all of the 10 global sectors and eight economic regions. However, it would be a mistake to conclude that it is always necessary to have such a comprehensive set of views. Amassing a consistent set of views is both time-consuming and demanding, and as we show in the next example, often unnecessary.

From the quotes given in Section 4.4.1, it is apparent that the key themes in the strategists' view centre on the Technology and Utilities industries and focus on the US and Japanese regions. In Table 4.10, we have restated these key ideas.

We designed a 100 stock portfolio or enhanced index on the basis of these four forecasts. The portfolio tilt and stock allocation are recorded in Table 4.11 and Table 4.12 respectively. The principal difference between this portfolio and the one designed earlier, on the basis of a comprehensive set of forecasts, is that this portfolio has significantly greater tilts in the Financial and Consumer Cyclical sectors and a smaller allocation of stocks in the European Ex EMU region.

We noted earlier that the Financial sector comprises stocks that are sensitive to both the local market performance and to the global sector performance. Therefore, the optimal holdings in this sector are particularly sensitive to relative changes in the sector performance against the regional performance. In moving from the comprehensive to the condensed set of strategy views, we have become more positive towards the US relative to the EMU and more positive on global financial stocks. Table 4.13 records the changes in the holdings and alphas of the stocks in the Financial sector during the move from the comprehensive to the condensed set of views. Concentrating on the stocks entering the portfolio,

Table 4.10   *Summary table of strategists' strong views*

Dow Jones group classification	Forecasted return Feb 2002–Aug 2002 (annualized)	Confidence in forecast (annualized standard error)	% by Market cap of the global Dow Jones universe
Japan	−11.66	8.87	8.06
United States	2.54	4.27	57.91
Technology	1.98	6.79	13.65
Utilities	−2.93	3.61	3.58

Source: UBS Warburg.

Table 4.11 *Optimized Portfolio Tilt by industry and region after combining strategists' strong views with the Default Risk Matrix at the stock level using the UBS Warburg Optimizer and limiting stock selection to 100 Stocks*

	Canada	United Kingdom	Japan	United States	EMU Region	Europe Ex EMU and UK	Pacific Ex Japan	Latin America	Industry Totals
Basic Materials	−0.28	−0.34	−0.47	1.54	−0.59	−0.19	−0.38	−0.09	−0.80
Consumer Cyclical	−0.15	−1.07	−2.18	2.03	1.35	−0.20	−0.55	−0.09	−0.86
Energy	−0.33	2.01	−0.06	1.45	1.70	−0.08	−0.09	−0.09	4.52
Financial	−0.69	1.43	−1.35	1.73	1.74	−0.41	−1.65	−0.24	0.56
Healthcare	−0.06	−0.12	−0.50	0.14	0.15	0.97	−0.07	0.00	0.51
Industrial	−0.24	−0.64	−1.63	1.25	−0.66	−0.47	−0.63	−0.09	−3.12
Consumer Non-Cyclical	−0.07	0.17	−0.44	2.39	−0.84	1.16	−0.24	−0.13	2.00
Technology	−0.18	−0.12	−0.72	2.84	−0.17	−0.24	−0.79	0.00	0.61
Telecommunications	−0.11	0.03	−0.27	1.35	0.12	−0.10	−0.45	−0.41	0.15
Utilities	−0.03	−0.36	−0.45	−1.72	−0.70	0.00	−0.20	−0.11	−3.58
Regional totals	−2.16	1.00	−8.06	12.99	2.09	0.45	−5.06	−1.25	0

Source: UBS Warburg. The industry and regional totals are the sum of the respective row and columns.

Table 4.12 *Number of stocks selected in each industry and region after combining strategists' strong views with the Default Risk Matrix at the stock level using the UBS Warburg Optimizer and limiting stock selection to 100 stocks*

	Canada	United Kingdom	Japan	United States	EMU Region	Europe Ex EMU and UK	Pacific Ex Japan	Latin America	Industry Totals
Basic Materials	0	0	0	2	0	0	0	0	2
Consumer Cyclical	0	0	0	10	3	0	0	0	13
Energy	0	2	0	3	2	0	0	0	7
Financial	0	5	0	15	5	1	0	0	26
Healthcare	0	2	0	11	1	2	0	0	16
Industrial	0	0	0	7	0	0	0	0	7
Consumer Non-Cyclical	0	1	0	6	0	1	0	0	8
Technology	0	0	0	11	2	0	0	0	13
Telecommunications	0	1	0	4	1	0	0	0	6
Utilities	0	0	0	0	0	0	0	0	0
Regional totals	0	11	0	69	14	4	0	0	98

Source: UBS Warburg. The industry and regional totals are sum of the respective row and columns.

they fall into two categories: large US retail banks, that is Bank of New York, FleetBoston and Wells Fargo, and large global investment banks, that is UBS and Merrill Lynch. The alphas also reflect this change with the alphas of the US retail banks remaining largely unchanged but the alphas of the global investment banks increasing significantly. Hence, the shift in the portfolio tilts is entirely consistent with shift in views.

Table 4.13   *A comparison of the portfolio holdings and alphas in the Financial sector moving from the comprehensive to the condensed set of strategists' forecasts*

Stock	Country	Benchmark weight	Condensed set of strategy views Portfolio weight	Alpha	Comprehensive set of strategy views Portfolio weight	Alpha	Difference in portfolio weights
American Express Company	United States	0.22	1.70	3.2	1.52	3.2	0.17
American International Group	United States	0.99	2.16	0.7	2.16	0.4	0.00
Banco Bilbao Vizcaya Argenta	Spain	0.19	0.93	2.5	0.75	0.4	0.18
Banco Santander Central	Spain	0.19	1.07	2.2	0.90	0.2	0.18
Bank of America Corp	United States	0.51	0.98	4.7	1.13	1.4	−0.15
Bank of New York Co Inc	United States	0.16	0.62	4.0		4.2	0.62
Bank One Corp	United States	0.22	0.62	5.0	0.58	4.5	0.04
Barclays	United Kingdom	0.27	0.65	2.0	0.65	0.5	−0.01
BNP Paribas	France	0.20	0.82	2.0	0.69	0.0	0.13
Citigroup Inc	United States	1.26	1.73	3.7	1.64	1.2	0.08
Deutsche Bank	Germany	0.20	0.79	2.1	0.65	0.2	0.14
Fannie Mae	United States	0.42	0.72	2.4	0.67	2.9	0.04
FleetBoston Financial Corp	United States	0.18	0.53	4.5		4.4	0.53
Freddie Mac	United States	0.24	0.48	3.0	0.47	3.6	0.01
HBOS	United Kingdom	0.22	0.53	1.0	0.47	−0.1	0.06
HSBC Holdings	United Kingdom	0.54	1.55	1.6	1.43	−0.4	0.12
ING Groep N.v.-Cva	Netherlands	0.21	1.39	1.4	0.99	−0.5	0.40
JP Morgan Chase	United States	0.35	0.68	3.2	0.73	0.5	−0.05
Lloyds TSB Group	United Kingdom	0.30	0.71	1.4	0.68	0.3	0.04
Merrill Lynch & Co	United States	0.21	0.87	1.1		−2.2	0.87
Morgan Stanley Dean Witter	United States	0.28	0.94	3.9	0.86	1.4	0.08
Royal Bank of Scotland Group	United Kingdom	0.33	0.57	1.3	0.55	0.3	0.02
UBS AG	Switzerland	0.30	0.72	2.0		−2.3	0.72
US Bancorp	United States	0.21	0.13	4.9	0.21	5.0	−0.08
Wachovia Corp	United States	0.23	0.20	5.8	0.30	3.8	−0.10
Wells Fargo & Company	United States	0.41	0.43	4.7		4.9	0.43

Source: UBS Warburg.

In Table 4.14 we have reported the same statistics for the Consumer Cyclicals sector. This sector is very diverse, with most of its volatility being explained by global and local markets. Again the shifts in portfolio tilt are towards the US and away from EMU with the big US retailers Comcast, Lowe's, McDonald's and Walgreen entering the portfolio, and a reduction in the holdings of Phillips, the Dutch electrical goods manufacturer.

The risk characteristics of the portfolio changed little during this simplification process with the tracking error falling slightly from 2.55 to 2.45 with the reduction being due to a slightly lower exposure to region equity risk.

Therefore to summarize, reducing the set of forecasts or concentrating on the strongly held views only slightly modifies the asset allocation of the optimal portfolio. We were able to trace and explain the large shifts in the portfolio allocations in terms of the changes to the slightly modified set of forecasts.

Table 4.14   *A comparison of the portfolio holdings and alphas in the Consumer Cyclical sector moving from the comprehensive to the condensed set of strategists' forecasts*

	Country	Benchmark weight	Condensed set of strategy views		Comprehensive set of strategy views		Difference in portfolio weights
			Portfolio weight	Alpha	Portfolio weight	Alpha	
Aol Time Warner	United States	0.58	0.89	5.5	0.78	5.5	0.12
Comcast Corp-Special	United States	0.17	0.52	−0.3		−0.3	0.52
Daimlerchrysler AG	Germany	0.17	1.66	4.3	1.57	4.3	0.09
Home Depot Inc	United States	0.60	1.61	1.0	1.40	1.0	0.21
Lowe's Companies	United States	0.16	1.14	4.3		4.3	1.14
McDonald's Corporation	United States	0.18	0.64	1.4		1.4	0.64
Philips Electronics NV	Netherlands	0.18	0.63	3.7	1.19	3.7	−0.55
Target Corp	United States	0.20	1.20	4.8	1.08	4.8	0.12
The Walt Disney Co	United States	0.22	0.95	2.6	0.93	2.6	0.02
Viacom Inc-Cl B	United States	0.33	1.26	0.5	1.11	0.5	0.15
Vivendi Universal SA	France	0.22	0.79	1.0	0.80	1.0	−0.01
Wal-Mart Stores Inc	United States	0.85	1.24	2.5	1.07	2.5	0.17
Walgreen Co	United States	0.19	0.55	−0.1		−0.1	0.55

Source: UBS Warburg.

4.5   CONCLUSIONS

In this chapter, we have argued that, given some market information,[13] the UBS Warburg approach to constructing enhanced index funds produces portfolios that are superior in a mean-variance sense to passive indexation. Further, the approach will capture alpha more efficiently than a mixture of an index fund and an actively managed portfolio. The focus of our approach lies in the recognition that it is easier to forecast alpha for portfolios of stocks that share a common characteristic, such as industry or style, than it is to produce forecasts for individual stocks. Moreover, we demonstrate that it is a straightforward matter to translate the distribution of stock alphas implied by these forecasts into consistent inputs for a stock level optimization.

In the illustrative example we show that in the absence of stock level constraints there is a high degree of correspondence between the optimal country and sector weights of portfolios constructed using a simple asset allocation model and the same weights derived from a stock level optimization, when the conditional alphas are computed using the Theil–Goldberger formula. However, not all industries are homogenous. The stock level optimization is better able to distinguish stocks which have a greater loading on the global factors from those which are more local in character using the betas from the global country sector model. The difference between the two approaches becomes more marked when we introduce integer restrictions to limit the number of stocks in the final optimal portfolio.

It is also interesting to note that the nature of the optimal portfolio does not change substantially when we construct the prior distribution using only the key or central forecasts of the strategists' as opposed to using a full set of forecasts for all countries and sectors. We believe therefore that this is a practical method for constructing enhanced index portfolios. In the absence of any prior view, the method will result in holding the benchmark. However, given a set of key forecasts for some portfolios, the method will generate a consistent set of stock alphas which can be used with an optimizer to generate efficiently tilted portfolios. Such portfolios will be optimally tilted in favour of the strategists' macro views yet still be subject to a set of tight risk controls.

4.6 APPENDIX 1: DERIVATION OF THE THEIL–GOLDBERGER MIXED ESTIMATOR

We shall start the analysis from Bayes' relation in Equation (4.6), which we rewrite below:

$$\Pr(r_t|f_t) \propto \Pr(f_t|r_t)\Pr(r_t) \tag{4.14}$$

Now substituting in the parameterization of the distributions given in Equations (4.1) and (4.5) we have

$$\Pr(r_t|f_t) \propto \frac{1}{\sqrt[M]{2\pi|\Omega|}} e^{-\frac{1}{2}(Pr_t - f_t)'\Omega^{-1}(Pr_t - f_t)} \frac{1}{\sqrt[N]{2\pi|\Sigma|}} e^{-\frac{1}{2}r_t'\Sigma^{-1}r_t} \tag{4.15}$$

We have ignored the μ as these cancel out in the long run and only serve therefore to complicate the analysis. Now we shall rearrange the sum of the two exponents so as to complete the square. This gives

$$-\frac{1}{2}(Pr_t - f_t)'\Omega^{-1}(Pr_t - f_t) + -\frac{1}{2}r_t'\Sigma^{-1}r_t = -\frac{1}{2}r_t'(P'\Omega^{-1}P + \Sigma^{-1})r_t$$

$$+ r_t'(P'\Omega^{-1}f_t) - \frac{1}{2}f_t'\Omega^{-1}f_t = -\frac{1}{2}(r_t - (P'\Omega^{-1}P + \Sigma^{-1})^{-1}P'\Omega^{-1}f_t)'$$

$$\times (P'\Omega^{-1}P + \Sigma^{-1})(r_t - (P'\Omega^{-1}P + \Sigma^{-1})^{-1}P'\Omega^{-1}f_t) - \frac{1}{2}f_t'\Omega^{-1}f_t$$

$$+ \frac{1}{2}f_t'\Omega^{-1}P(P'\Omega^{-1}P + \Sigma^{-1})^{-1}P'\Omega^{-1}f_t$$

Of the two expressions on the right hand side the second is independent of r_t and can be ignored (it is part of the constant of integration). The first term is now expressed in terms of the square of r_t. Therefore the distribution of $\Pr(r_t|f_t)$ is also normal with mean $(P'\Omega^{-1}P + \Sigma^{-1})^{-1}P'\Omega^{-1}f_t$ and variance $(P'\Omega^{-1}P + \Sigma^{-1})$. This is the result given in Equation (4.7).

We shall now derive the alternative expression for the mean of this distribution quoted in the text. By the matrix inversion lemma,

$$(P'\Omega^{-1}P + \Sigma^{-1})^{-1} = \Sigma - \Sigma P'(P\Sigma P' + \Omega)^{-1}P\Sigma \qquad (4.16)$$

and so

$$(P'\Omega^{-1}P + \Sigma^{-1})^{-1}P'\Omega^{-1}f_t$$
$$= \Sigma P'\Omega^{-1}f_t - \Sigma P'(P\Sigma P' + \Omega)^{-1}P\Sigma P'\Omega^{-1}f_t$$
$$= \Sigma P'(P\Sigma P' + \Omega)^{-1}((P\Sigma P' + \Omega) - P\Sigma P')\Omega^{-1}f_t$$
$$= \Sigma P'(P\Sigma P' + \Omega)^{-1}f_t$$

This is the alternative expression given in the text.

4.7 APPENDIX 2: OPTIMIZATION

The illustrative example contrasts two approaches to constructing optimal portfolios using forecasts for country and sector indices. A 'top down' or asset allocation level approach and a 'bottom up' or stock level approach. In practice, both approaches are often useful since working with aggregate indices at the asset allocation level permits the use of powerful graphical simulation techniques to analyse the sensitivity of portfolio weights to changes in the prior distribution. Whilst stock level optimization is ultimately necessary to impose the wide range of restrictions often required for particular mandates.

The stock level optimizer maximizes a quadratic utility function using the forecast alphas from the Theil–Goldberger formula and the covariance matrix from the UBS Warburg global risk model, subject to a comprehensive set of bounds, linear and integer restrictions. The latter are required to implement two sets of constraints: holding thresholds and cardinality constraints imposed on the number of assets held. Formally, the enhanced index problem may be stated as:

Maximize:

$$U(\mathbf{x}) = \alpha'(\mathbf{x} - \mathbf{b}) - \lambda(\mathbf{x} - \mathbf{b})'\Sigma(\mathbf{x} - \mathbf{b}) - \mathbf{p}'\mathbf{x}^+ - \mathbf{s}'\mathbf{x}^- \qquad (4.17)$$

Subject to:

$$\sum_{i=1}^{N} x_i = 1 \qquad (4.18)$$

$$L \leq \mathbf{Ax} \leq U \qquad (4.19)$$

$$l\delta_i \leq x_i \leq u\delta_i \quad i = 1, \ldots, N \tag{4.20}$$

$$\sum_{i=1}^{N} \delta_i = K \quad \delta_i \in \{0, 1\} \tag{4.21}$$

Where $\boldsymbol{\alpha}$, $\mathbf{x}$, and $\mathbf{b}$ denote the vectors of alpha, portfolio and benchmark weights. $\boldsymbol{\Sigma}$ is the forecast covariance matrix, λ a risk aversion coefficient and $\mathbf{p}$ and $\mathbf{s}$ denote the transaction cost vectors. L and U are the row wise lower and upper bounds on the linear constraints. Equation (4.17) is maximized subject to the constraints (4.18) to (4.21). The integer constraints (4.20) and (4.21) are clearly related, the parameters l and u represent thresholds forcing the portfolios weights to act as semicontinuous variables. Equation (4.21) is often referred to as the cardinality constraint, in the illustration $K = 100$.

Solving this optimization problem is non-trivial since the presence of the integer restrictions makes the resulting quadratic mixed-integer (QMIP) problem NP-hard. A good discussion of the difficulties encountered is presented in Horniman et al. (2000) and the chapters by Gautam Mitra et al. and Tim Wilding in this book. A major consideration is that in the presence of discrete constraints not only is the efficient frontier discontinuous but simple heuristic approaches like dropping algorithms can converge on a sub-optimal solution (see e.g. Jobst et al., 2001).

The first issue to be addressed in computing the solution is the potential size of the required arrays. Fortunately, since the covariance matrix $\boldsymbol{\Sigma}$ is computed using the UBS Warburg global risk model, we can exploit the factor structure to greatly reduce the storage requirements. The solution algorithm first computes the continuous solution using the FortMP[14] Sparse Simplex Solver for Quadratic Programs (SSX-QP) ignoring any discrete constraints. The choice of the powerful SSX-QP solver is particularly important, since in the tree search stage, the sub-problems are rapidly processed using the optimum basis of the parent and a dual algorithm. The discrete solver then searches for the best K stock portfolio in the neighbourhood of the initial continuous solution using a customized variant of the integer restart heuristic described in Jobst et al. (2001).

The integer programming heuristic operates in two stages. In the first stage the problem size is reduced by multiply-fixing the most obvious choices either forcing stocks out of or into the solution set. This stage is repeated and the resulting problem is re-solved each time until by default 30% of the desired number of stocks is reached. The stocks are then fixed singly, the sub problem re-solved at each step, until the target number of assets is reached. At this stage all remaining assets are forced out by the cardinality constraint and the resulting sub-problem (if feasible) is a valid integer solution to this problem.[15]

REFERENCES

Black, F. and Litterman, R. (1992) Global Portfolio Optimization, *Financial Analysts' Journal*, **48**(5), Sept–Oct, 28–43.

Broadie, M. (1993) Portfolio Optimisation with estimated Parameters, *Annals of Operations Research*, **45**, 21–45.

Bulsing, M., Sefton, J., Jones, A. and Kothari, M. (2000) *Global Style Returns*, Global Equities, UBS Warburg, May.

Cochrane, J. (1999) Cochrane, J.H. (1999a) New Facts in Finance, Economic Perspectives XXIII (3) Third quarter, Federal Reserve Bank of Chicago.

diBartolomeo, D. (2000) The Enhanced Index Fund as an Alternative to Indexed Equity Management, Northfield Information Services, Boston.

Frankfurter, G., Phillips, H. and Seagle, J. (1971) Portfolio Selection: the Effects of Uncertain Means, Variances and Covariances, *The Journal of Financial and Quantitative Analysis*, Sept, **6**, 1251–62.

Grinold, R. and Kahn, R. (2000) *Active Portfolio Management: A Quantitative Approach for Providing Superior Returns and Controlling Risk, 2nd edn.* McGraw-Hill.

Haitovsky, Y. (1973) *Regression Estimation from Grouped Observations*, Hafner Publishing, New York.

Horniman, M.D., Jobst, N.J., Lucas, C.A. and Mitra, G. (2000) Constructing Efficient Portfolios: Alternative Models and Discrete Constraints – A Computational Study March, Dept. of Mathematical Sciences, Brunel University.

Jobst, N.J., Horniman, M.D., Lucas, C.A. and Mitra, G. (2001) Computational aspects of alternative portfolio selection models in the presence of discrete asset choice constraints, *Quantitative Finance* Volume 1, 1–13.

Johnston, J. (1984) *Econometric Methods*, Third Edition, McGraw-Hill Publishing Co., New York.

Jorion, P. (1986) Bayes-Stein Estimation for Portfolio Analysis, *The Journal of Financial and Quantitative Analysis*, Sept, **21**(3), 279–92.

Merton, R. (1980) On Estimating the Expected Return on the Market, *Journal of Financial Economics*, **8**(Dec.), 321–61.

Michaud, R. (1999) *Efficient Asset Management: A Practical Guide to Stock Portfolio Optimization and Asset Allocation*, Financial Management Association Survey and Synthesis Series, Harvard Business School Press.

Riepe, M. and Werner, M. (1998) Are Enhanced Index Mutual Funds Worthy of their Name? *Journal of Investing*, **7**(2), 6–15.

Scowcroft, A. and Sefton, J. (2002) Understanding Risk: A new country sector risk model, January, UBS Warburg Quantitative Research Paper.

Stoye, S. and Ashton, R. (2000) Where the numbers come from: WDR Portfolio Analysis System, February, UBS Warburg Quantitative Research Paper.

Theil, H. (1971) *Principles of Econometrics*, John Wiley and Sons, New York and North-Holland Publishing Company, Amsterdam.

Theil, H. and Goldberger, A.S. (1961) On pure and mixed statistical estimation ineconomics, *International Economic Review*, **2**, 65–78.

NOTES

1. Clearly, these portfolios could be single stock portfolios and thus this approach can encompass views on single stocks.
2. The rows of the matrix P therefore sum to 1 if the strategist is taking a view on long only portfolio, or zero if the strategist is taking a view on a portfolio's performance relative to the market, a market hedged portfolio.
3. Note that unlike Equation (4.8) which requires the inversion of N by N matrices, Equation (4.9) only needs to invert one M by M matrix, this is an important practical consideration when N is very large. Exploiting the factor structure of the covariance matrix Σ further simplifies the calculation, which can be most efficiently computed using for example the BLAS routines from the NAG Fortran SMP library.
4. The corresponding row in the matrix P will have positive entries corresponding to stocks in the Financial sector (probably proportional to the stocks' market capitalization) and zeros elsewhere, with the weights scaled so that they sum to 1.
5. In this case the relevant row in the matrix P will be the vector of the market cap weights of the stocks in the Financial sector (if the stock is not in the sector the corresponding entry will be zero) minus the vector of the market cap weights. As the weights of both of these separate vectors sum to 1, the weights in the final vector sum to zero. It is important that the scale is maintained, so that the resultant portfolio is long the financial sector and short the rest of market.
6. Assuming the returns in each period are independent.
7. The strongest of these being that markets are complete, there are no taxes or transaction costs, no short constraints and that all expectations are homogeneous.
8. Current is as of the end of February 2002.
9. This adjustment is far from straightforward and is described in detail in the publication 'Understanding Risk', January 2002.
10. This asset allocation model is not related to the UBS Warburg Asset Allocation Toolbox (AAT). The AAT is a far more sophisticated asset allocation model than the one built here and, like PAS, is designed to be an investment tool for fund managers.
11. This latter omission is important, as it is a source of non-linearity between the PAS and AAM model.
12. These were calculated using the methodology described in the UBS Warburg publication 'Understanding Risk: A new global country sector model' by Alan Scowcroft and James Sefton (2002).
13. This market information may be as simple as the choice of benchmarking the fund to one index rather than another.
14. http://www.optirisk-systems.com/docs/FortMP/PDF/fortmp-manual.pdf contains a full description of the system.
15. We would like to thank Frank Ellison and Gautam Mitra of CARISMA based in the Department of Mathematical Sciences, Brunel University for their contribution in the development and testing of this algorithm.

Chapter 5

Portfolio management under taxes

DAN DIBARTOLOMEO

ABSTRACT

Taxable portfolios represent a special challenge to the investment manager. To active managers, the imposition of capital gains taxes makes many strategies that they believe will be profitable on a pre-tax basis into certain losers on an after-tax basis. In many jurisdictions such as the USA, Japan and the UK, both active and passive managers must deal with the imposition of capital gains taxes when portfolio positions are liquidated to meet cash withdrawal require ments. Many alternatives such as index funds, ETFs and simple loss harvesting strategies have been considered with respect to tax efficiency, but most active managers faced with running large numbers of taxable accounts are choosing to pursue optimal loss/gain matching procedures through portfolio optimization.

5.1 INTRODUCTION

Taxable portfolios represent a special challenge to the investment manager. To active managers, the imposition of capital gains taxes makes many strategies that they believe will be profitable on a pre-tax basis into certain losers on an after-tax basis. In many jurisdictions such as the USA, Japan and the UK, both active and passive managers must deal with the imposition of capital gains taxes when portfolio positions are liquidated to meet cash withdrawal requirements. Due to the additional complications associated with taxes, managers of taxable accounts have been largely unable to achieve the decreases in labour intensity associated with quantitative strategies and automated portfolio rebalancing, both of which are very common in the pension fund arena.

In recent years, changes in the relative importance of different classes of investors have spurred the development of technological solutions for the problems of managing taxable equity accounts. The long bull market of the 1980s and 1990s has lead to unprecedented levels of household wealth being concentrated in the taxable stock market accounts. In addition, the rising popularity of separately managed accounts for non-institutional investors such as 'wrap' programs offered to retail investors in the USA and Europe have vastly increased the number of taxable accounts that investment managers must deal with.

Insurance company investment portfolios are also taxable in most countries and have the additional complexity that under the accounting standards of those nations, realized capital gains (losses) can be counted for the computation of the company's profit (or loss), while unrealized gains and losses are not marked to market for corporate income calculation.

A relatively new innovation in the USA is the nuclear decommissioning trust (NDT). NDTs are taxable entities but otherwise have the asset/liability characteristics of non-taxable investors such as pension funds. With the advent of NDTs, institutional investment firms were faced with incorporating taxes into their frequently automated portfolio decision processes.

5.2   DO TAXES REALLY MATTER TO INVESTORS AND MANAGERS?

The most obvious indication that taxes are of considerable interest to investors is that the pricing of many financial instruments is very dependent on the tax circumstances of the investors likely to be interested in that instrument. For example, in the USA, the income from municipal government bonds is free from federal government taxation, while income from federal bonds is taxable. As such, US Treasury bonds must offer higher yields to investors than municipal bonds of similar maturity, despite the obvious superior creditworthiness of the federal bonds. While there is a rich literature in this area, a mathematically rigorous general treatment is provided in Dermody and Rockafellar (1995). Kim et al. (2000) provide an econometric analysis of potential tax arbitrages. Tax effects appear to have differing levels of influence at different bond maturity levels. This issue is examined in Harwood and Manzon (2000) and Jordan (1997). Derivative pricing is also seen as highly dependent on tax circumstances. Lui and Wu (2000) study the impact of taxation on credit risk derivatives, while Laatsch (2000) studies pricing of total return swaps under taxes.

For the retail investors of many nations such as the USA, the dramatic impact of taxes on investment returns has been amply demonstrated. Most prominent are the studies of Dickson and Shoven (1993) and Dickson et al. (2000). This work showed that performance rankings of mutual funds on a pre-tax and post-tax basis yield nearly unrelated results. The international accounting firm KPMG has distributed an extensive white paper edited by Wolfson (2000) detailing the dramatic effects of taxation on mutual fund investors.

The dramatic impact of taxation on active equity portfolio management strategies in the USA was first described by Arnott and Jeffrey (1993), who found that even most successful alpha prediction strategies do not produce a net gain after taxes. Two papers by Arnott et al. (2000, 2001) review the relationship of pre-tax to after-tax returns among institutional investment managers.

Elliman (1989) presented a computer simulation study of the impact of taxation on the implementation of value oriented equity selection strategies for managers with different levels of information coefficients for their forecasts. It found that a single stock, considered in isolation, must be extremely undervalued or overvalued to make trading worthwhile for the taxable investor.

A rigorous mathematical analysis of active management under taxes is presented in Apelfeld et al. (1996). This paper illustrated the key insight that within any actively managed equity portfolio the cross-sectional volatility of security returns over short time intervals is larger than the mean return of all the assets. As such, managers could mitigate the impact of taxes by offsetting realized gains on profitable positions by realizing losses on losing positions on a regular basis. This approach is the basis of most tax sensitive active equity portfolio strategies in use today.

In Garland (1997), the issues of tax-management of index funds are explored. This paper argues that investors who think they are minimizing tax effects by virtue of the minimum of portfolio turnover associated with passive index investing are still far from an optimal solution. Meziani, Seddick and Yang (2001) consider the tax benefits associated with Exchange-Traded-Funds (ETFs) in the USA. It should be noted that some equity indices are far more suitable than others from a tax perspective. For example, the Russell 2000 index of small capitalization US equities is reconstituted every 30 June. To the extent that many stocks are removed from this particular index because they have risen in market capitalization through share price increase, an investor would have no choice but to realize a substantial amount of capital gains in order to keep their portfolio in conformity with the revised index membership.

Several theoretical studies of portfolio rebalancing with tax considerations have appeared in the literature such as Talmor (1985), Fedenia and Grammatikos (1991) and Fisher et al. (1992).

5.3 THE CORE PROBLEMS

Taken to a ridiculous extreme, one can minimize capital gain tax effects simply by never selling anything. This approach of simply minimizing turnover can work for an index fund if you are confident that cash flows will always be into, rather than out of, the fund. Since dividend flows are very stable for a large fund, the impact of taxes on the dividend stream may easily be incorporated into security return expectations. In the event of net cash outflows, even the index fund case becomes quite problematic. We must have a mechanism to optimally trade-off our desire to minimize taxes with our desire to keep the index fund portfolio as close as possible in composition to the underlying index.

Unfortunately, the idea of avoiding selling securities to defer taxes had been the standard approach for many years. Bank trust departments and other invest-ment advisers that handled taxable accounts routinely continued to charge active management fees, while justifying a lack of any portfolio activity to add return or reduce risk by citing the inhibitions to trading posed by tax considerations. Obviously, charging active management fees for 'closet' passive accounts led to significant long-term underperformance even on a pre-tax basis, net of fees. Interestingly, Smolira (1999) argues that the level of turnover in mutual fund portfolio (as defined by regulations of the US Securities and Exchange Com-mission) is not a powerful explanatory variable for taxable distributions from US funds.

The complexity of the problem is considerable. Managers of taxable accounts must simultaneously consider not only the return and risk aspects of each portfolio but also the tax circumstances of the investor and the tax consid-erations of the existing portfolio. In some countries such as the USA, cost basis must be considered on a tax lot-by-tax lot basis. The UK uses a sliding scale scheme. When faced with handling large numbers of accounts, portfolio man-agers are simply unable to respond promptly to new information about market conditions while concurrently considering the myriad tax issues of proposed portfolio changes.

Strategies to address tax efficiency in portfolio management must have three key properties. First, they must reduce the cost of taxes, the spread between pre-tax and after-tax returns to investors. Second, they must provide minimum inhibition (i.e. not limiting turnover) to the portfolio management process, so as to allow active management strategies to be effectively pursued. Third, tax efficient strategies must be able to be implemented in an automated fashion so that separate account managers can keep up with what otherwise would be the hopeless burden of handling hundreds or thousands of accounts.

5.4   THE STATE OF THE ART

Apelfeld et al. (1996) presented a practical approach for active managers. In this paper, a traditional mean-variance portfolio optimization procedure is used. Capital gains taxes are treated as additional transaction costs which occur on sales only and the magnitude of which are specific to the tax lot of the security that is being sold. To mechanically implement this approach, they make each tax lot (different tax cost basis) of a security, a separate stock for the purposes of the optimization algorithm (i.e. IBM stock lot 1 is a different stock from IBM stock lot 2). During the portfolio rebalancing process, the optimizer harvests capital losses on some stocks to offset the realized capital gains on other stocks. As is currently customary, they used a factor risk model to measure the risk of the portfolio for optimization purposes. A particularly high level of computational care must be exercised with this combination of methods, as factor models assume that the stock specific risk of each stock in a portfolio is uncorrelated with the stock specific risk of all other stocks. Clearly, this assumption is faulty when we treat different tax lots of the same stock as though they were shares in different companies.

In 1997, Northfield commercially introduced an approach that is similar but does not treat different tax lots as different securities. We specify capital gains taxes as a selling only transaction cost which is linear piecewise. That is, different percentage transaction costs may result from selling different amounts of a security. As long as the amount to be sold is equal to or less than the size of a given tax lot, the tax effect is treated in the same fashion as a regular transaction cost. Given the gradient method used in our portfolio optimization algorithm, the same security may be 'traded' multiple times in a given rebalancing. In order to implement taxes as linear piecewise transaction costs, we need only constrain the size of each trade such that only the shares contained in the highest basis cost tax lot can be traded in a single iteration of the algorithm. Other shares of the same stock in other tax lots can be traded in subsequent transactions with their appropriate tax costs attached.

The key to understanding the benefit of tax-awareness for active management is that we are not trying to reduce turnover. Instead, our goal is to actively offset realized capital gains with realized capital losses. In many cases, the turnover of the portfolio actually increases relative to turnover that would occur ignoring taxes. For example, the process may find that a particular stock is an 'average' contributor to a portfolio's return and risk characteristics. If this position was held in multiple lots, some of which had unrealized capital gains while other lots had unrealized capital losses, the algorithm might choose to sell the lots with unrealized losses, which could then be offset against the realization of capital gains elsewhere in the portfolio. In this fashion, active management strategies with considerable turnover can be accommodated in taxable accounts, without worry that the tax bite will exceed the benefit of a successful active strategy.

Many managers are reluctant to use portfolio optimization techniques. This reluctance often arises from the incorrect belief that for portfolio optimization to be effective, managers must make explicit and accurate forecasts of the expected return from each stock. Jobson and Korkie (1981) advocate for presuming the expected return of each stock to be equal. Bernstein and Tew

(1994) demonstrate the effectiveness of this simple assumption. Miller et al. (1998) provide a mechanism for traditional 'stock picking' managers to convert their historical 'rightness' percentage into expected average return values suitable for optimization use under taxes.

One simple way to deal with the large numbers of taxable portfolios is to maintain a 'model' account that is managed without any attention to taxes at all. The optimization algorithm then has the reduced task of maintaining each actual account to have as close as possible expected behaviour to the model account, while minimizing the amount of taxes required to maintain an acceptable level of similarity.

5.5   THE MULTI-PERIOD ASPECT

One tricky aspect of the taxable account problem is that in reality it is a multi-period problem, when traditional mean-variance optimization looks at the future as a single long period. These time sensitive aspects of the problem specification can arise from a variety of sources. In most cases, deferring the sale of a stock with an unrealized capital gain results in just deferring payment of taxes. Eventually, the stock is likely to be sold and the capital gains taxes paid. In such a case, the only financial benefit is the time value of the tax payment, not a savings in taxes. However, if a US shareholder dies (or donates the shares to charity) before selling the stock, the capital gains taxes may be escaped entirely. Perhaps, the level of capital gains taxes themselves will be raised or lowered in the future.

Market expectations can also introduce this multi-period aspect. Imagine a case where a portfolio has a large number of stocks with unrealized capital gains, but none with capital losses. Such portfolios are common today given the strong stock market performance over the last decade. Given our forecasts of future stock returns and risks, it may be optimal to sell some stocks with unrealized gains and pay the required taxes. If we believe that the stock market is going to go through a very volatile period in the near future, we might believe that our portfolio would soon contain some securities with capital losses. It might then be optimal to wait, so that the capital gains might be offset with capital losses and the portfolio rebalanced without incurring any immediate taxes.

Another example is a passively managed portfolio that starts with a concentration in a single stock with a large unrealized gain. By selling the stock, we would incur a large tax, but the risk of the portfolio (tracking error) to its index might be dramatically reduced for many years. How much tax we should be willing to pay to reduce risk is tied to over how long a time period we expect such reductions in risk to persist.

To help deal with the multi-period aspect of the problem, we introduce a transaction amortization factor, which is merely a percentage value multiplied by all taxes and transaction costs. Put simply, the investment manager is able to control how much of the tax burden of possible current transactions is to be charged against portfolio objectives (increased return or reduced risk) on an annual basis. What is a reasonable value for this factor will depend on the tax situation, expectations of portfolio turnover and market outlook of the parties. One can also use this amortization feature to vary the level of tax-sensitivity through the calendar year. Some firms basically ignore taxes in the early part of the year and gradually increase the sensitivity to tax concerns as we move toward the end of the tax year.

One way to think of the tax amortization process is to pretend that when we incur taxes that must be paid, we borrow the funds to make the tax payments using our investment assets as collateral for the loan. We can infinitely defer the payment of the principal of the tax loan as long as your collateral is sufficient. As such, the after-tax cost of loan interest becomes the true cost of the taxation. If portfolio trades will improve return or reduce risk sufficiently to justify this interest cost, the transactions are a net improvement to the portfolio. Of course, in the real world, cash flow needs and estate transfers make the idea of infinitely deferring the repayment of tax loan principal somewhat unrealistic in most cases.

Investor risk preferences also play an important consideration structuring of taxable portfolios. To the extent that the imposition of taxes, truncates the distribution of after-tax returns as compared to pre-tax returns, taxable investors prefer to take on greater levels of risk than even those same investors would care to do in a tax-exempt account. Finally, capital gain taxes are levied on absolute returns, while active managers are generally measured on benchmark-relative returns. To the extent that investors have different willingness to bear absolute risk and benchmark relative risks, the economic tradeoffs become more complex. Wilcox (2000) argues that investors ought have the same willingness to bear absolute and relative risk.

The problem of taxation also tends to produce style biases in portfolios. If our expectations are that future stock returns will be completely random, we could maximize our tax position by holding onto stocks that had risen in value and selling those that had fallen. As such, price momentum strategies may be redundant in taxable portfolios, which are implicitly biased toward high price momentum stocks. A value approach may offset this natural bias, but is the most likely to generate unfavourable tax consequences. As such, value oriented active managers may have the most to benefit from tax-awareness in portfolio construction and rebalancing. Sundar et al. (2000) document investor preferences for equity 'growth' or 'value' portfolios based on tax considerations.

5.6 LOSS HARVESTING

One approach to taxable active management that can be accomplished with a minimum of analytical effort is simple 'tax loss' harvesting. In these strategies, a stock is sold automatically whenever it has gone down in price a prescribed percentage from the purchase cost. In essence, the investor seeks to 'bank' a cushion of tax losses even in advance of having any capital gains to offset. Arnott (2001) evaluates such strategies and provides suggestions on their implementation. Brunel (1997) suggests a portfolio bias toward high volatility securities, as providing a greater opportunity for tax loss harvesting. Samuelson (1998) argues that loss harvesting can be done too aggressively, leaving the portfolio with nothing but positions with gains left, a condition known as 'lock up'. Chay et al. (1999) evaluate the tax timing issue in an explicit option framework.

There are a number of important considerations with respect to simple loss harvesting strategies. The first is that in many jurisdictions, tax losses cannot be carried forward indefinitely, so having an excess of losses over the amount needed to offset realized may not be useful. Another is that transaction costs are always incurred, so the time value of the tax deferral must be carefully considered in markets where transaction costs are not very small. Finally, many nations have 'wash sale' rules that will nullify an investor's tax loss if the investor repurchases the same stock within a prescribed period (e.g. 30 days in the USA). Unless a manager has strategies that have very long holding periods, it is likely that the timing of an investment purchase is sensitive to particular new information or market conditions. Loss harvesting may create circumstances where attractive investment opportunities must be passed up, in order to not nullify previously realized tax losses.

5.7 AFTER-TAX BENCHMARKS

Another issue for taxable investors is that of benchmark indices. In the USA, the AIMR performance presentation standards simply provide for inclusion of realized tax costs in computation of after-tax performance. When these after-tax returns are compared to pre-tax returns for popular benchmark indices, managed accounts obviously look like they are broadly disadvantageous. Poterba (1997) outlines the difficulties with trying to take the economic value of the unrealized gains (losses) into account for measurement of investment performance.

At the surface, the simple answer would be to create after-tax benchmark indices. As discussed in Stein (1998), this is much more complex than it seems. It would seem that we could simply measure the taxes arising from a hypothetical index fund on the particular index in question and then compute the after-tax return. However, the cost basis of the index fund in question would depend on when shares were purchased and at what prices. As such, the after-tax return of the index fund for a given period would be dependent on the starting date of the index fund. The after-tax return on the index for 1999 would be different if had started the fund in 1990 as compared to 1985 or 1995. Gulko (1999) proposes a time-weighting scheme to deal with this issue. In addition, the existence of taxes reduces the volatility of after-tax returns, relative to pre-tax returns. As such, the investor's choice of benchmarks may be different, even for the same investment objective, in a taxable setting. This issue is explored in Stein, Siegel, Narasimhan and Appeadu (2000).

5.8 CONCLUSIONS

Over the past few years our understanding of the managing investment portfolios under taxes has increased markedly. The technology necessary to implement appropriate new techniques is readily available and is being rapidly adopted by sophisticated investment firms. Measuring the performance and evaluating the performance of taxable accounts remains problematic.

REFERENCES

Apelfeld, R., Fowler, G. and Gordon, J. (1996) Tax Aware Equity Investing, *Journal of Portfolio Management*, 1996, **22**(2,Winter), 18–28.

Apelfeld, R., Granito, M. and Psarris, A. (1996) Active Management of Taxable Assets: A Dynamic Analysis of Manager Alpha, *Journal of Financial Engineering*, 1996, **5**(2,Jun), 117–146.

Arnott, R.D. (2001) Loss Harvesting: What Its Worth to the Taxable Investor? *Journal of Wealth Management*, Spring, 10–18.

Arnott, R. and Jeffrey, R. (1993) Is Your Alpha Big Enough to Cover its Taxes, *Journal of Portfolio Management*, 1993, **19**(3,Spring), 15–26.

Arnott, R.D., Berkin, A.L. and Jia Ye. (2000) How Well Have Taxable Investors Been Served in the 1980s and 1990s?, *Journal of Portfolio Management*, **26**(4,Summer), 84–93.

Arnott, R.D., Berkin, A.L. and Jia Ye. (2001) The Management and Mismanagement of Taxable Assets, *Journal of Investing*, **19**(1,Spring), 15–21.

Bernstein, R. and Tew, B. (1994) Improving Quantitative Models through Optimization, *Journal of Investing*, **3**(4), 24–31.

Brunel, J. (1997) The Upside-Down World of Tax Aware Investing, *Trusts and Estates*, February, **5**(2), 34–42.

Chay, J.B., Dosoung Choi and Pontiff, J. (1999) Market Valuation of Tax Timing Options: Evidence from Capital Gains Distributions, University of Auckland Working Paper, September.

Dermody, J.C. and Rockafellar, R.T. (1995) Tax Basis and Nonlinearity in Cash Stream Valuation, *Mathematical Finance*, **5**(2), 97–119.

Dickson, J.M. and Shoven, J. (1993) Ranking Mutual Funds on an After-Tax Basis, Working Paper 4393, National Bureau of Economic Research.

Dickson, J.M., Shoven, J.B. and Sialm, C. (2000) Tax Externalities of Equity Mutual Funds, *National Tax Journal*, **53**(3,Sep), 607–28.

Elliman, D. (1989) Traditional Investing in the Computer Age, *Proceedings of Computers in Global Investment*, Northfield Client Conference Series.

Fedenia, M. and Grammatikos, T. (1991) Portfolio Rebalancing and The Effective Taxation of Dividends and Capital Gains Following the Tax Reform Act of 1986, *Journal of Banking and Finance*, 1991, **15**(3), 501–520.

Fisher, D., O'Bryan, D., Schmidt, T. and Parker, J. (1992) Portfolio Optimization Subject to Tax Bracket Constraints: A Linear Programming Approach, *Journal of the American Taxation Association*, 1992, **14**(2), 112–122.

Garland, J. (1997) The Advantages of Tax-Managed Index Funds, *Journal of Investing*, 1997, **6**(1,Spring), 13–20.

Gulko, L. (1998) An After-Tax Equity Benchmark, General Re Working Paper.

Harwood, E. and Manzon, Jr. G.B. (2000) Tax Clienteles and Debt Maturity, *Journal of the American Taxation Association*, **22**(2,Fall), 22–39.

Jobson, J.D. and Korkie, B. (1981) Putting Markowitz Theory to Work, *Journal of Portfolio Management*, 1981, **7**(4), 70–74.

Jordan, B. (1997) On the Relative Yields of Taxable and Municipal Bonds: A Theory of the Tax Structure of Interest Rates, University of Missouri Working Paper.

Kim, H.Y., Junsoolee, L., Lile, S.E. and Ramsey, J.R. (2000) Municipal Bonds And Tax Arbitrage: A Cointegration Analysis, *Public Finance Review*, **28**(4,Jul), 372–89.

Laatsch, F.E. (2000) Tax Clienteles, Arbitrage, and the Pricing of Total Return Equity Swaps, *Journal of Derivatives*, **8**(2,Winter), 37–46.

Lui, Sheen and Chunchi Wu (2000) Taxes and the Prices of Credit Risk Derivatives, Syracuse University Working Paper, July.

Meziani, S. and Yang, J. (2001) Fresh Alternative to Mutual Funds Offers Tax Benefit, *Practical Tax Strategies*, **67**(2,Aug), 100–8.

Miller, K., Samak, V. and Sorensen, E. (1998) Allocating Between Active and Passive Management, *Financial Analysts Journal*, 1998, **54**(5,Sep/Oct), 18–31.

Poterba, J.M. (1997) Issues in Setting After-Tax Benchmarks & Reporting Portfolio Performance, *AIMR Conference Proceedings*, February.

Samuelson, P.R. (1998) Taxable Investing in the Long Run: Using a Simulation Environment to Quantify the Impacts of Investor Preferences and Investment Strategies, *Northfield Conference Proceedings*, November.

Smolira, J. (1999) Turnover and Taxable Distributions in Mutual Funds, Belmont University Working Paper, September.

Stein, D. (1998) Measuring and Evaluating Portfolio Performance After Taxes, *Journal of Portfolio Management*, 1998, **24**(2,Winter), 117–121.

Stein, D.M., Siegel, A.F., Narasimhan, P. and Appeadu, C.E. (2000) Diversification in the Presence of Taxes, *Journal of Portfolio Management*, **27**(1,Fall), 61–71.

Sundar, Cuddalore S., Hill, J.M. and Lajaunie, J.P. (2000) Tax Incentives and Individual Investor Behaviour, *Applied Economics Letters*, **7**(2,Feb), 91–4.

Talmor, E. (1985) Personal Tax Considerations in Portfolio Construction: Tilting the Optimal Portfolio Selection, *Quarterly Review of Economics and Business*.

Wilcox, J.W. (2000) Better Risk Management, *Journal of Portfolio Management*, **26**(4,Summer), 53–64.

Wolfson, N. (Ed). (2000) Tax Managed Mutual Fund and the Taxable Investor, KPMG Working Paper, New York.

Chapter 6

Using genetic algorithms to construct portfolios

DR T WILDING

ABSTRACT

Markowitz's (1952) mean-variance optimization framework was an excellent development in pushing portfolio construction towards a science and away from being an art. However, there are a number of drawbacks one faces when using quadratic programming in practice. This chapter will focus on the practical need to restrict the number of securities held or traded to construct the final portfolio. This constraint is often known as the cardinality constraint. When the problem incorporates this constraint, the resultant optimization becomes part of a class of problems that can be very difficult to solve using traditional optimization methods such as branch-and-bound. In this chapter, we review alternative methods and investigate the use of genetic algorithms for efficiently selecting a subset of stocks to trade, while satisfying other optimization objectives.

6.1 LIMITATIONS OF TRADITIONAL MEAN-VARIANCE PORTFOLIO OPTIMIZATION

Fund managers, building on the work of Markowitz (1952), are increasingly using quantitative techniques to build their final portfolios. Markowitz formulated the portfolio construction problem as a utility maximization problem and used this to develop a framework for assembling portfolios. Markowitz made several additional assumptions that further simplified the portfolio selection to a quadratic programming problem, developing a technique known as mean-variance portfolio optimization.

Several drawbacks with mean-variance portfolio optimization have meant that very few investors use plain quadratic programming as formulated by Markowitz to build portfolios. In practice, fund managers often want to place other constraints on the final portfolio such as turnover constraints, limits on the holding in individual securities, limits on the holdings in a particular category of securities and, finally, limits on the number of securities traded or held in the final portfolio.

The following is a practical version of the portfolio optimization function that fund managers might use to construct their portfolios. Assuming there are n securities in the investable universe, we can formulate the actual portfolio optimization problem in the following way:

Maximize the quadratic objective function:

Quadratic utility function $f(x) = c'x - \lambda x'Vx - p'x_p - s'x_s$ (6.1)

subject to:

Budget constraint $\displaystyle\sum_{1}^{n} x_i = 1$ (6.2)

Additional linear constraints $A'x = b$ (6.3)

Variable bounds $l_i \leq x_i \leq u_i$ (6.4)

where c is a $n \times 1$ vector of expected returns for each security, x is the $n \times 1$ vector of portfolio weights in each security, λ is the risk-aversion coefficient, V is the $n \times n$ covariance matrix, p is the $n \times 1$ vector of purchase costs for each security, x_p is the $n \times 1$ vector of purchases in each security (or 0 if the position in the security was not increased), s is the $n \times 1$ vector of sales costs for each security, and x_s is the $n \times 1$ vector of sales in each security (or 0 if the position in the security was not decreased).

Equation (6.3) shows additional linear constraints that are often designed to constrain portfolio exposure to a particular sector or industry. Equation (6.4) shows additional bounds on the holdings in any particular security. These variable bounds serve to prevent the portfolio becoming concentrated in any particular security. This problem can be further modified to incorporate long-short portfolios.

This practical optimization model is still limited by several of the assumptions that it contains:

- the investment decision is a single period;
- either the investor's utility function is quadratic, or returns are normally distributed and the shape of the investor's utility function is irrelevant;
- assets are infinitely divisible;

- the variance and average of returns over the period is known exactly (see Michaud (1998) for a full discussion of some of the consequences of this);
- all costs, returns and constraints can be summarized using a linear component and are known exactly.

Most of these assumptions have been discussed widely in the literature. For instance, there is much discussion of the shape of the investor's utility function (e.g. Konno and Yamazaki, 1991). In this chapter we will focus on the final issue and, in particular, how to build a portfolio containing a limited number of securities and/or a limited number of trades using genetic algorithms. The constraint on the number of securities is often known as the cardinality constraint.

The cardinality constraint is motivated by portfolio construction costs that are not taken into account by the mean-variance framework above. For example, the costs could be:

- Settlement costs: the administrative cost of settling trades is a function of the number of trades and not their value.
- Custody costs: custodial services usually make some of their charges on a per ticket basis.
- Due diligence: except in the rare cases of exclusively quantitative management, it is usual for portfolio construction, even if quantitatively aided, to be subject to (human) judgmental overlay. This requires the portfolio manager to accept responsibility for trades undertaken and necessitates his review of a trade list before final execution. Given the value of a portfolio manager's time a limited number of trades is to be preferred.
- Efficient dealing: except where reliance on automated dealing is total, a shorter list of trades is more likely to facilitate working of an order to get the best execution price.
- Compliance costs: checks on the regulatory compliance of a portfolio would increase costs in proportion to the number of trades and securities in the final portfolio.

These costs cannot be incorporated in a Quadratic Program, since they are not simple linear or non-linear functions of the trade size or position in the final portfolio. Figure 6.1 shows a chart comparing three different transaction cost models. Model 1 is a simple linear transaction cost model typically encountered in the enhanced form of Markowitz optimization detailed above. In the linear model there is no barrier to purchasing a position in any security no matter how small that position is. The marginal cost of purchasing each additional security is the same no matter how much of the security has been purchased. Model 2 shows a fixed cost of purchase combined with a linear transaction cost. There is a fixed 'hurdle' cost associated with deciding to purchase the security and

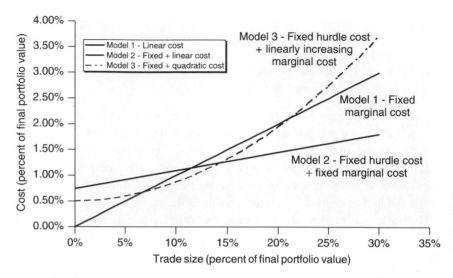

Figure 6.1 *Alternative transaction cost models. Model 1 shows a linear cost model with a fixed marginal cost (or fixed cost per incremental trade). Model 2 shows a model in which there is a fixed hurdle cost incurred for making the purchase followed by a fixed marginal cost per incremental trade that is made in the security. Model 3 shows a quadratic cost model with a fixed hurdle cost, a fixed marginal cost and a linearly increasing cost per incremental trade (which makes the total trade cost a quadratic function of the volume traded)*

a fixed marginal cost for purchasing each additional amount of the security. The second model is probably a more realistic model of transaction costs even though it is possible to imagine various practical additions to this model. For example, one could consider a marginal cost for purchasing additional amounts of the security that increases linearly with the amount purchased (resulting in quadratic transaction costs, Model 3) or piecewise linear transaction costs (e.g. Perold, 1984). These costs are, in general, a function of the number of securities in the final portfolio and/or the number of trades required to construct the final portfolio (Figure 6.2). Since these costs are fixed costs, the value of the final portfolio can be a determining factor in considering them. For example, fixed costs may be very significant if your assets under management are US$10m, but would be less significant if the assets under management are US$100m.

Figure 6.2 shows the effect a fixed cost has on the trading costs incurred in building or rebalancing a portfolio. The chart shows the costs of different numbers of trades given a fixed level of turnover. The figure shows that the fixed cost forces a fund manager to lower the number of trades and/or the number of securities in the final portfolio. Lowering the number of trades and/or securities in the final portfolio will lower the total costs involved in constructing the portfolio.

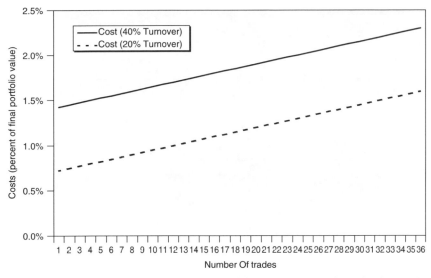

Figure 6.2   *The effect a fixed hurdle cost has on portfolio construction. It shows that for any given level of turnover a fixed base cost forces a fund manager to lower the number of trades made in constructing the final portfolio. It assumes that transaction costs are composed of a fixed hurdle cost and a linear cost (Model 2 in Figure 6.1). The graph shows the effect of a fixed hurdle cost with a portfolio that is being traded with two levels of turnover. Each line corresponds to a different level of turnover. For each level of turnover, we are assuming that the trades are distributed evenly between the securities. This shows that the best way to reduce costs given a set level of turnover is to reduce the number of securities traded*

There are other motivations for limiting the number of trades besides direct trading costs. For example, the duration of an estimated alpha might be an issue. If a fund manager is working with short-term alphas, then he may need to consider the efficiency with which he can execute a particular trade. The shorter the duration the more desirable it would be to limit the trades to a list that can be executed as soon as possible.

Since we are modifying the problem to incorporate additional costs, we might expect the objective function (Equation (6.1)) to be modified to account for the costs. For example, we could add costs to the equation that are linear functions of the number of securities and number of trades required to construct the final portfolio. However, there are a couple of reasons why we do not formulate the problem this way: lack of information and efficiency of solving the problem. In a practical scenario, a fund manager typically does not have full information about his costs. The fund manager resolves this by examining the trade-off between the number of securities traded and the final objective without accounting for the fixed hurdle costs. For example, see Figure 6.3 for a chart showing the trade-off between tracking error and number of securities in the final portfolio. The fund manager would then use Figure 6.3 to select the portfolio that has the

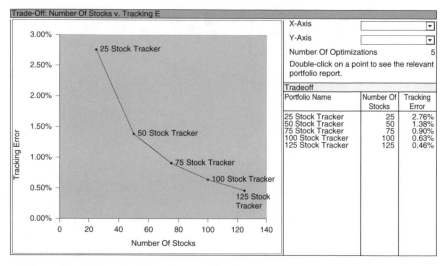

Figure 6.3   *Trade-off made as the optimal solution is allowed to contain more stocks. As expected, the marginal improvement of tracking error with number of stocks decreases as the number of securities in the final portfolio increases*

best combination of tracking error and number of securities. This is similar to using the level of turnover in the portfolio to control transaction costs. Although models of transaction costs exist, a fund manager often models transaction costs as a linear function of the turnover of the final portfolio and then examines the trade-off between the objective function and the level of turnover. It is more efficient to treat the number of securities as a constraint because this makes evaluation of the objective function faster. By constraining the number of securities, the evaluation of the objective function can be transformed into a quadratic programming problem for a subset of securities that is relatively easy to solve. There exists a vast amount of literature about quadratic programming and there are various efficient models for the solution of a quadratic program.

Incorporating the limit on the number of securities in the final portfolio leads to the following enhanced portfolio optimization problem:

Maximize the quadratic objective function subject to:

$$\text{The cardinality constraint} \quad \sum_{1}^{n} \delta_i = K \tag{6.5}$$

the budget constraint, additional linear constraints, and a modified form of the original variable bounds (shown in Equation (6.4)):

$$\text{Modified variable bounds} \quad l_i \delta_i \leq x_i \leq u_i \delta_i \tag{6.6}$$

In Equations (6.5) and (6.6), δ_i is a variable that can take only integer values 0 or 1 and represents a decision to purchase a particular security, and K is the number of different securities in the final portfolio.

In practice, this modification is only the start. Since the motivation for adding the cardinality constraint was trading costs, a user is likely to require an additional constraint on the number of trades required to construct the final portfolio. In other words, the problem formulation would require the following additions:

Constraint on number of trades
$$\sum_{1}^{n} \gamma_i = T \tag{6.7}$$

Modified trading bounds
$$\gamma_i (u_i - x_{0,i}) \geq x_{p,i}$$
$$\gamma_i (x_{0,i} - l_i) \geq x_{s,i} \tag{6.8}$$

where γ_i is 0–1 integer variable that represents a decision to trade in a particular security, $x_{0,i}$ is the holding in the original portfolio, and T is the number of different trades required to construct the final portfolio. The addition of these constraints to the portfolio optimization problem alters various practical aspects of the solution. For example, the efficient frontier is no longer continuous when the cardinality constraint is added (Chang et al., 2000).

Various other modifications to the portfolio optimization problem exist, but this chapter will only deal with an algorithm designed to handle the additional constraints on the number of holdings and the number of trades.

6.2   SELECTING A METHOD TO LIMIT THE NUMBER OF SECURITIES IN THE FINAL PORTFOLIO

Limiting the number of securities in the final portfolio changes the nature of the optimization problem from a quadratic programming problem to a quadratic mixed integer-programming problem. In traditional optimization literature, a method such as branch-and-bound (BB) would be used to solve this problem. BB starts off with the entire universe of securities. The algorithm then 'branches' on each security by deciding whether to incorporate the security in the final problem. The algorithm proceeds to branch at another security until the algorithm has generated a feasible solution. The algorithm then examines alternate branches until it has determined the optimal solution. For a full description of the BB method see standard optimization texts (e.g. Nemhauser and Wolsey, 1998). Often BB methods are combined with a method of generating cutting planes to reduce the search area (see Bienstock, 1996).

BB algorithms guarantee a convergence to the true optimal solution. However, there is one drawback–this class of problems is NP-complete (Mansini and Speranza, 1999). A BB solution may take an exponentially long time to complete as the algorithm goes through all possible subsets of securities that contain the right number of securities in the final portfolio. Optimization systems do not currently use the full BB solution because it would be beyond a current PC's capability to generate a full solution. One would have to terminate a BB algorithm early and generate a solution that could possibly be no better than a solution generated using a heuristic.

There have been two approaches to solving this problem. The first approach is to modify the form of the portfolio optimization problem. The modified form would be designed to be easy to solve with current algorithms and to generate a solution that only contains a limited number of securities. The portfolio optimization problem is usually modified by converting it into some form of linear programming problem that only has solutions with the correct number of securities (e.g. Konno and Yamazaki, 1991).

The second approach has been to develop a heuristic that solves the resultant problem. Commercially available optimizers typically use heuristics to determine the effect of the cardinality constraint on the final portfolio. This decision has been motivated by a couple of factors. First, algorithms that guarantee convergence to the optimal solution can be computationally expensive and may only generate a marginally better portfolio than a heuristic. Second, since the inputs to the optimization process are merely estimates of the actual variance matrix, the optimal portfolio generated using a particular model may not be any closer to the 'true' optimal portfolio than the portfolio generated by the heuristic. Michaud (1998) contains a full discussion of the consequences of the lack of precision in the model of the variance matrix.

A number of heuristics have been used to solve the problem in practice and to overcome the limits on processor time. Early heuristics were often very simple and could generate solutions that were far from optimal. More recently, effort has been directed towards developing more optimal solutions to the problem. Here are brief descriptions of some of the heuristics that have been tried:

- Paring Heuristics – most commercially available optimizers use a form of paring heuristic. This is an algorithm that starts off with a solution to the full problem with no constraint on the number of securities. The algorithm then gradually removes the smallest securities by weight until a portfolio with the required number of securities is created. Discarding more than one security at a time could accelerate this algorithm. In other variants, multiple baskets of securities are created. Securities are removed from each of these baskets and the baskets are combined until the algorithm is left with the required number of securities.
- Incrementing Heuristics – This was a popular early method for limiting the number of securities. Incrementing heuristics would add securities

to the current set of securities one at a time and solve the optimization problem derived from the current set of securities. Securities were usually added to the current set on the basis of their marginal contributions to utility at the final solution. The algorithm was terminated when the current set contained the correct number of securities. This method had the advantage that it was very fast to reach a solution since solutions started from very small problems, but the final solutions would often be far from optimal.

- Tabu Search (TS) – TS follows the method of Glover and Laguna (1997). TS starts from a randomly generated solution. This solution is then used to generate solutions that are close to the current solution. The best solution is found from these nearby solutions and is then used as the seed point to look for more nearby solutions. The transition from the previous solution to the current best solution is stored. It is known as TS because the algorithm prevents cycling by using the list of transitions that have already been made.

- Simulated Annealing (SA) – SA is similar to TS in that it generates transitions from one solution to the next. SA derives its name from its origin as a simulation of the cooling of material in a heat bath and was first applied as an optimization technique by Kirkpatrick et al. (1983). SA differs from TS in that there is a probability that the algorithm will accept a worse solution than the currently stored maximum. SA uses a parameter known as the 'temperature' to determine this probability. As the algorithm progresses, the 'temperature' is lowered and the algorithm converges to a solution. The ability of the algorithm to move to a potentially worse solution prevents the algorithm from getting trapped in local maxima.

- Genetic Algorithm (GA) – GAs are very popular optimization algorithms developed by Holland (1975) and reviewed very thoroughly by Goldberg (1989). A GA represents a particular subset of securities as an 'individual'. The GA starts with a population of these individuals. For each individual the GA optimizes the portfolio using the subset of securities that corresponds to the individual. The GA then examines the population and selects new subsets using the more successful members of the population.

We wanted to select an algorithm that would allow us to solve problems that had constraints on the number of trades and/or the number of securities. Each one of the above algorithms requires modifications so that they can solve such problems. Additionally, we also wanted to allow a user to be able to force or deny inclusion of certain securities in the final portfolio. For example, if a fund manager wants IBM to be in the final portfolio then the fund manager must be able to express that wish. Again, all of these heuristics would have to be expanded to accommodate this new problem.

There are very few papers that review the use of these algorithms to solve the cardinality-constrained problem. Chang et al. (2000) present three algorithms designed to solve the problem – tabu search, simulated annealing, and genetic algorithms. Chang et al. conclude that some combination of GA and SA would provide the best solution to the problem. Horniman et al. (2000) have presented a comparison of these three algorithms with the full branch-and-bound solution. Horniman et al. also review the effect of the cardinality constraint on the efficient frontier. They conclude that the branch-and-bound algorithm produces the best results but do not include information on timing and efficiency of the algorithm. Shapcott (1992) reviews the use of GAs as a method for selecting index-tracking portfolios. Grinold and Kahn (1994) briefly mention that BARRA had compared their heuristic approach to a genetic algorithm but dismissed the genetic algorithm because it took '48 hours of CPU time' on a typical 1998 PC to generate a solution similar to BARRA's existing heuristic. Unfortunately, Grinold and Kahn do not provide significant details about the GA code that was used for the comparison.

Although Chang et al. (2000) suggest that the choice of algorithm comes down to a choice between a GA and an SA, we found that distinction is somewhat artificial. In the literature, the term GA can be used to cover a wide variety of algorithms depending on the choice of problem representation and population breeding methods. Chang et al. only implement a limited form of a GA. They only use crossover techniques for breeding new members of the population while typical GAs use a combination of crossover and mutation methods. Chang et al. suggest that the ideal solution would be to implement a combination of the GA and SA approach. In fact, GAs approach their description of an algorithm that uses a combination of GA and SA techniques for generating new solutions. Implementing a GA left us free to incorporate a population breeding method that is equivalent to the operator used to generate neighbouring random portfolios in simulated annealing. We might therefore reasonably expect that a well-designed genetic algorithm with its mix of operators should perform better than a SA algorithm with its single operator. For that reason, we chose and implemented a GA as the best available heuristic for solving the problem. Once we have implemented the GA, we can further test to determine what the optimal mix of breeding methods should be to determine the final solution (see the later section on refinement of GA parameters). In fact, a well-designed GA can incorporate many of the best features of other heuristic search techniques. In addition, we believe GAs have a number of advantages:

1. Easy to implement – the wide availability of source code and libraries for GAs helps with the design and implementation of GAs in practice (for example, see http://lancet.mit.edu/ga/ for a publicly available library of codes).

2. Quick to generate a reasonable solution – GAs work only with solutions that satisfy the cardinality and which are, therefore, small and extremely fast to solve. Most algorithms start from the solution to the problem without the cardinality constraint. Since the time to solve a particular problem is typically a power-law function of the number of securities this means that these optimizers start by solving a disproportionately hard problem before paring down the number of securities to a reasonable amount.
3. Easily adaptable to more complicated problem forms – GA literature shows that GAs have been used to solve a wide variety of problems. A GA could easily accommodate our additional problem modifications.
4. Intuitive – they mimic the process of natural selection which is evidently a successful strategy for producing practical solutions to a variety of incalculable problems.
5. Robust – GAs will eventually converge to an optimal solution (Goldberg, 1989). Simple heuristics such as the paring and incrementing heuristics may generate solutions that are far from optimal and are simply an artifact of the particular problem's constraints.

6.3 PRACTICAL CONSTRUCTION OF A GENETIC ALGORITHM-BASED OPTIMIZER

After selecting the GA, two extra practical choices need to be made:

1. Design and implementation of the genetic algorithm.
2. Optimization of performance.

6.3.1 Design and implementation of the genetic algorithm

Genetic algorithms are search algorithms based on the mechanics of natural selection and natural genetics. There are a number of terms associated with GAs that refer to various features of the algorithm. Table 6.1 shows those GA terms and their equivalents in the investment universe. GAs use data structures called 'genes' to represent potential solutions. GAs combine survival of the 'fittest' among the genes with a randomized information exchange between genes to form a search algorithm that captures many of the intuitive features of a human-prompted search method. A simple genetic algorithm that yields good results takes the following form:

- develop an initial population of genes;
- determine fitness of the current population of genes;
- use the fitter members of the current population to breed a new population of genes;
- repeat steps 2 and 3 for a certain number of generations.

Table 6.1   *Correspondence between terms used in GA and the concepts they represent in portfolio construction*

GA term	Investment equivalent	Description
Population		A group of optimal portfolios for different portfolio universes.
Gene/Individual	Optimal portfolio for the portfolio universe	A gene is a combination of a chromosome, and the fitness value.
Chromosome	Portfolio universe	This is the list of securities used to construct the final portfolio
Allele	Individual security	The portfolio universe is constructed from a set of individual securities.
Fitness	Expected utility	This is a measure of how attractive a particular portfolio is to a fund manager.
Crossover		A way of combining two or more genes to form a third, hopefully fitter, gene
Mutation		A method for creating a new, hopefully fitter, gene from an existing gene

In every generation, a new set of genes is created using elements of the fittest genes of the previous generation and, on occasion, a random new element. GAs do not simply search through the potential solutions randomly; they efficiently exploit historical information to determine new search points with expected improved fitness.

In typical genetic algorithms, the next generation is bred using the following three operators:

- reproduction;
- crossover;
- mutation.

Reproduction is a process in which individual genes are copied according to their expected utility. Copying genes according to their utility means that genes with a higher value have a higher probability of contributing one or more off-spring in the next generation. The reproduction operator is an artificial version of natural selection, a Darwinian survival of the fittest among gene creatures. In natural populations fitness is determined by a creature's ability to survive predators, pestilence, and the other obstacles to adulthood and subsequent repro-duction. In our GA, the utility function (Equation (6.1)) is the final arbiter of the genes survival or otherwise.

Crossover is a process in which the fittest genes are mated at random. A selection of the information contained in the parents is used to create a child. This exchange of information should allow the algorithm to pick the best of both parents and generate a child that is likely to give a better solution to the current problem.

Finally, mutation is the occasional random alteration of a parent gene. By itself, mutation is a random walk through the gene space. Mutation helps the algorithm by preventing the gene pool from focusing on one particular type of solution. Instead, mutation occasionally generates new genes that are possibly better solutions of the current problem.

Therefore, implementing a genetic algorithm involves a couple of design decisions – selection of data structure to represent a particular solution (design of the chromosome), and determination of methods used as crossover and mutation operators.

A gene must represent the ability to trade in a subset of securities that satisfies the constraint on the number of holdings and the number of trades. We choose to represent a gene as three subsets of securities – securities to trade, securities to add, and securities to remove from the final portfolio. The set of additions was the set of securities that are not in the existing holdings, but we would like to add to the portfolio. The set of removals is the set of securities that are currently in the existing holdings, but whose position we would like to wind down. The trades are those securities that are currently in the existing holdings, but there are no preferences for the weight.

The methods used for the crossover and mutation operators must take the information from parent genes and generate new genes that are expected to have higher utilities. For crossover, we developed a method where multiple parents were selected. Securities were randomly selected from the parent gene and placed in the child gene. This process was repeated until a child gene that was feasible with respect to the cardinality constraints was created. The crossover method is similar to the Random Assorting Recombination operator described in Shapcott (1992). A particular security is more likely to be passed to the new gene if it appears in both copies of the parent gene. This ensures that the securities that are most important for reducing the tracking error will appear in the child. This attribute of the operator is sometimes referred to as 'respect' for the parent.

For mutation, we developed a method where we searched through the set of securities in the parent gene, and randomly replaced a small fraction of them. The likelihood that a particular security will be picked is in proportion to a weighting assigned by the system at the start of the process. This weighting is typically the weight of the security in the benchmark index.

6.3.2 Optimization of performance

There are various areas in which the performance of the final algorithm can be optimized. Two particular areas are more efficient evaluation of the utility function, and refinement of the GA parameters.

Efficient evaluation of the utility function

One of the most important areas is the efficient evaluation of the utility function. The genetic algorithm is only responsible for selecting the subset of securities that appears in the final solution. Once that subset has been selected, it is necessary to optimize the final portfolio using that subset as the investable universe. The resultant quadratic programming problem determines the utility of a particular gene. Hence, it is necessary to have an efficient quadratic programming routine to determine the utility value for that subset.

Recent developments in the linear programming field suggest that interior point methods may be the method of choice for quadratic programming (see e.g. Vanderbei, 1996). These methods guarantee convergence within a polynomial time.

Since we were working with factor models of the covariance matrix, we were able to make several changes to the problem formulation so that we could take advantage of sparsity. Using the method of Perold (1984), we added several extra variables to the problem to represent factor exposures. The addition of the linear constraints to represent the factor variance matrix significantly reduces the density of the final covariance matrix and improves the performance of the final algorithm. Therefore, it was advantageous to require a quadratic programming algorithm that could take advantage of the sparsity in the final problem formulation. Interior point quadratic programming methods are most efficient when the covariance matrix is diagonal. Performance decreases as the density of the covariance matrix increases. This sparsity can have a significant impact on the speed of the final algorithm. For example, inverting the covariance matrix can be a significant rate-limiting step in any quadratic optimization algorithm. Without adjusting for the sparsity of the covariance matrix, inversion can be an $O(n^3)$ process, so that the time inversion will require to complete is proportional to the number of inputs cubed.

Interior point methods have one drawback when applied to integer programming problems; so far good methods of 'warm-restarting' the algorithm have not been designed. In other words, it is not possible to start from a solution for a particular basket of securities and generate a solution to a problem that is significantly close in formulation. In our case, this is not a significant drawback, since the GA does not necessarily generate neighbouring solutions.

An additional benefit of sparse techniques is that fund managers often use sector constraints to construct the final portfolio. Sector constraints usually lead to a very sparse constraint matrix, since entries in the sector constraint matrix typically take the form of 1 for securities in a particular sector and 0 otherwise.

Refinement of the GA parameters

There are several parameters that may be altered to improve the performance of the algorithm. In this section, we attempt to find the best selection of parameters for optimization.

The GA uses three operators to build the next generation of individuals – reproduction, crossover, and mutation. In this section, we analyse what proportions of the next generation should be constructed using each operator. In order to do this we ran repeated trials of the GA using different proportions to determine which set of proportions was best. The trials consisted of 12 different optimization jobs in which the goal was to minimize tracking error using only a limited number of securities. Three benchmarks were used with four different limits on the number of securities in the final portfolio. The optimizer was allowed to choose any security in the benchmark. The three benchmarks were constructed from the following universes:

- UK: FTSE All-share;
- USA: S&P500;
- Japan: Nikkei 300.

Universes were constructed as of October 2001. These benchmarks were all capitalization weighted. The GA was allowed to construct a portfolio with 25, 50, 100, and 200 securities. Table 6.2 shows average times for the various jobs and demonstrates that the GA is capable of producing a reasonable solution to the problem quickly.

After all of the trials were run, we were left with various solutions for each of the 12 jobs. The lowest possible solution for each of the 12 combinations was determined and used as a baseline. For each job, we determined a score for the solution by calculating the difference between the tracking error and the lowest possible tracking error and then dividing this number by the standard deviation of tracking errors across all jobs.

We then examined how this score varied with three of the parameters in the GA – number of individuals chosen for reproduction, number of individuals chosen for mutation, and number of individuals chosen for crossover (Figure 6.4). The charts illustrate that better tracking errors are generated when the GA generates more mutants as a fraction of the next generation. This improvement levels off after the proportion of mutants is increased to approx. 70% of the next generation. After running the test, we increased the default

Table 6.2   *Average timing in seconds of the various jobs used to refine the GA parameters on an AMD 1.3 GHz machine with 256 MB Ram*

Number of stocks	FTSE	Nikkei	SP 500	Average
25	96	61	63	73.38
50	124	84	95	100.82
100	136	122	132	130.23
200	141	132	141	138.11

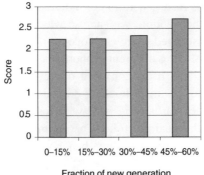

Fraction of new generation
produced via crossover

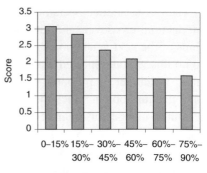

Fraction of new generation
produced via mutation

These three charts show the effect of changing the fraction of the next generation produced by a specific mechanism. The score is the average amount by which the solution exceeds the lowest possible tracking error (TE) for a particular job.

Score = (TE - Min. Possible TE)/ SD of TE

Hence, a lower score indicates a better quality of solution.

The graphs show that the most improvement is gained by increasing the number of mutations in the next generation

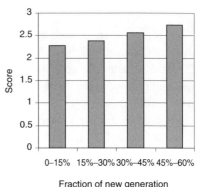

Fraction of new generation
reproduced

Figure 6.4 *Performance variation when different operators are emphasized for creating the new generation*

proportion of children created by mutation and decreased the proportion of children created by crossover in the next generation for the algorithm.

6.4   PERFORMANCE OF GENETIC ALGORITHM

Finally, we would like to test whether our GA is practically useful for building a final portfolio of securities. We would like to determine whether the solutions provided by the GA are practically useful. In order to do that, we will examine the results of a particular optimization to confirm that the portfolios constructed are sensible portfolios. We will also test whether the GA solutions provide portfolios that perform significantly better from a tracking error perspective.

We conducted practical tests of the GA solutions to answer the following three questions:

1. Do the portfolios generated by the GA have a significantly better tracking error than other portfolios satisfying the same limit on the number of holdings?
2. Are the portfolios generated by the GA practically sensible – i.e. do they display a normal distribution by size and sector?
3. Do the portfolios generated by the GA perform well in practice – i.e with an out-of-sample test?

The second and third test both the GA routine and the model of the covariance matrix in Equation (6.1) used to construct the final portfolios. The selection of a good model of the covariance matrix that is used to test the GA is a necessary but not sufficient condition for the GA to produce good results. Consequently, if the results with the GA are good, it confirms that the GA works well. The GA optimizer has been designed to work with all types of factor model – fundamental factor models, industry index models, and pure statistical models (see Connor and Korajczyk, 1995, for a review of the different types of factor modelling techniques available).

For this Chapter, the tests have been conducted using the EM applications statistical factor models. The factor models are constructed quarterly from 200 weeks of returns using EM ('Expectation Maximization') factor analysis techniques developed by Stroyny (1992). Factor models are estimated for various countries and regions. For each test, we selected the appropriate factor model for the job. For example, when building portfolios to track the FTSE All Share we selected the UK factor model. You can find further information about the factor model at www.emapplications.com.

To test whether the GA solutions are close to optimal we compared the GA solution to optimized baskets of securities satisfying the same limit on the number of holdings. We conducted a random search by constructing 1500 baskets of securities and optimizing the baskets. Figure 6.5 shows the distribution of tracking errors for these randomly generated baskets of securities. The randomly generated baskets had an average predicted tracking error of 6.2% with a standard deviation of 0.4%. On the other hand, the GA produced a tracking error of 3.2%. Not one of the random portfolios had a predicted tracking error that was close to the GA solution. The best randomly generated solution had a tracking error of 5.1%. If we assume that the random baskets had a normal distribution of tracking errors, then a portfolio with a tracking error of 3.2% or better would only be found in 1 in 10^{12} portfolios produced randomly. This is illustrated graphically in Figure 6.3.

In order to answer the second question and show that the portfolios generated by the GA are practically sensible we will review some of the portfolios created in a particular scenario. In our case, the scenario will be designing a portfolio to track the FTSE All Share, which contained 758 securities, in October 2001.

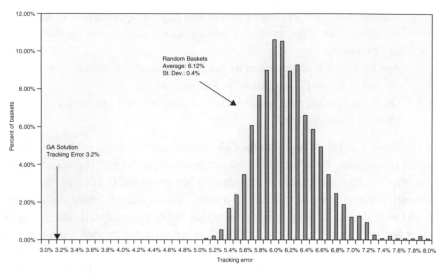

Figure 6.5   *The distribution of tracking errors for random subsets of 35 securities from a 500-security benchmark. After the subset has been randomly selected, an optimized portfolio of the 35 securities is chosen and the tracking error is calculated. Since the optimizer generates a tracking error of approx. 3.2%, this graph clearly shows that the GA returns a very good choice of portfolio. No randomly generated portfolio came close to the optimal solution*

We will use the GA to build portfolios containing 25, 50, 75, 100, and 125 securities. Figure 6.6 shows a list of statistics for each of those portfolios. The portfolios are constrained to have no more than 10% of the final weight in any particular security. Earlier, Figure 6.3 showed how the tracking error of the final portfolio changes with the number of securities. There is a very significant reduction in the estimated tracking error as we increase the number of securities from 25 to 50, but this reduction decreases as the number of securities increases.

Figure 6.7 shows a trade report giving the optimal portfolio of 25 securities to track the FTSE All Share. The portfolio is sorted by weight. This figure shows that the portfolio constructed by the GA is a reasonable portfolio and matches one's expectations of what a tracking portfolio should look like. The portfolio is constructed mostly from the larger-cap universe and contains significant positions in all of the largest securities.

Figure 6.8 shows the sector weights of the portfolio and the benchmark. The GA has produced portfolios that have sector weights that correspond very closely to the benchmark, even though no sector constraints were specified as part of the optimization process. The largest differences are seen on the 25 stock portfolio, but even then the sector weights do not differ from the benchmark by more than 2.6% (Energy Minerals sector).

As a final test we checked whether the portfolios produced by the genetic algorithm performed well out-of-sample. For this test, we constructed several

EM Applications Home Page

Tracking Error	Volatility Breakdown					Selected Portfolio Statistics	
		Total	Latent	Specific	R-Squared	Portfolio Alpha	0.00
2.76%	FTSE Tracker	16.65%	15.41%	6.32%	85.62%	Portfolio Beta	1.02
	FTSE All Share	16.06%	15.22%	5.13%	89.80%	Correlation	0.99
						Number of Trades	25
	Tracking Error	2.76%	1.17%	2.50%	17.94%	Number of Securities	25

Individual Portfolio Reports

Selected Portfolio	25 Stock Tracker

Trade Report	Trade Report for selected portfolio showing the trades used to create the portfolio
Optimized Portfolio Report	Report showing the composition of the final portfolio

Optimization Results

Portfolio Name	Tracking Error	Portfolio Volatility	Beta	Alpha	Number of Securities	Number of Trades	Turnover
1 25 Stock Tracker	2.76%	16.65%	1.02	0.00	25	25	100.00%
2 50 Stock Tracker	1.38%	16.21%	1.01	0.00	50	50	100.00%
3 75 Stock Tracker	0.90%	16.16%	1.00	0.00	75	75	100.00%
4 100 Stock Tracker	0.63%	16.12%	1.00	0.00	100	100	100.00%
5 125 Stock Tracker	0.46%	16.10%	1.00	0.00	125	125	100.00%

Summary Reports

Report Name	Available?	Description
Output Statistics	Yes	Table of Output Statistics for all portfolios
Valuation Report	Yes	Table of Valuation Attributes for all portfolios
Sector Report	Yes	Sector Report for all of the optimized portfolios
Efficient Frontier Report	Yes	Efficient Frontier Report for all of the optimized portfolios
Country Report	Yes	Country Report for all of the portfolios
Constraint Report	No	Constraint Report for all of the portfolios

Optimization

Repeat Optimization	Repeat the optimization with any changes made to the optimization job
Review Parameters	Review the optimization parameters used in the optimization process
Review Data	Review stock-level data used in the optimization process

Figure 6.6 *The EM Applications Optimizer uses Microsoft Excel to generate system reports. This is a typical report generated by the Optimizer. This is the main page of the report and shows links to other reports generated by the Optimizer. The report shows a scenario in which the optimizer has been run repeated times each time with a different number of securities allowed in the final portfolio*

portfolios with the GA. These portfolios were limited to 25, 35, 50, 75, and 100 securities and were designed to track an index. The index was constructed from 500 of the largest securities in the world. For each of these numbers of securities we constructed a portfolio without sector constraints and a portfolio that had sector constraints. We used the EM applications model from October 2000

EM Applications Trade Report
Optimization_FTSE_Tracker

Action	Stock Identifiers	Name	Shares Bought	Shares Bought	Shares Sold	Price	Portfolio Weight	Benchmark Weight	Active Weight	Buy Weight	Sell Weight
Buy	079805	Bp Ord Usd0.25	177933	177933	0	5.62	10.00%	9.41%	0.59%	10.00%	0.00%
Buy	092528	Glaxosmithkline Ord Gbp0.25	49659	49659	0	19.2	9.53%	8.84%	0.69%	9.53%	0.00%
Buy	071921	Vodafone Group Ord Usd0.10	557884	557884	0	1.5	8.37%	7.54%	0.82%	8.37%	0.00%
Buy	054052	Hsbc Hldgs Ord Usd0.50(Uk Reg)	95328	95328	0	7.17	6.84%	4.96%	1.88%	6.84%	0.00%
Buy	080341	Shell Trnspt&Trdg Ord Gbp0.25(Regd)	117127	117127	0	5.1	5.97%	3.72%	2.26%	5.97%	0.00%
Buy	098952	Astrazeneca Ord Usd0.25	16147	16147	0	31.65	5.11%	4.14%	0.97%	5.11%	0.00%
Buy	075478	Royal Bk Scot Grp Ord Gbp0.25	29602	29602	0	14.98	4.43%	3.16%	1.27%	4.43%	0.00%
Buy	079087	Scot & Southern En Ord Gbp0.50	67357	67357	0	6.48	4.36%	0.41%	3.95%	4.36%	0.00%
Buy	007820	Barclays Ord Gbp1	18356	18356	0	18.71	3.43%	2.30%	1.14%	3.43%	0.00%
Buy	023740	Diageo Ord Gbx28.935185	44999	44999	0	7.145	3.22%	1.80%	1.42%	3.22%	0.00%
Buy	087628	Bg Group Ord Gbp0.10	119278	119278	0	2.6225	3.13%	0.68%	2.45%	3.13%	0.00%
Buy	305875	Hbos Ord Gbp0.25	41612	41612	0	7.34	3.05%	1.93%	1.13%	3.05%	0.00%
Buy	010812	Boc Group Ord Gbp0.25	32560	32560	0	9.375	3.05%	0.34%	2.71%	3.05%	0.00%
Buy	087061	Lloyds Tsb Group Ord Gbp0.25	46641	46641	0	6.5	3.03%	2.65%	0.38%	3.03%	0.00%
Buy	061070	Cadbury Schweppes Ord Gbp0.125	67444	67444	0	4.415	2.98%	0.67%	2.31%	2.98%	0.00%
Buy	088470	Tesco Ord Gbp0.05	113906	113906	0	2.56	2.92%	1.31%	1.60%	2.92%	0.00%
Buy	024319	Six Continents Ord Gbp0.28	43442	43442	0	6.2	2.69%	0.40%	2.29%	2.69%	0.00%
Buy	014084	British Telecom Ord Gbp0.25	77298	77298	0	3.4	2.63%	2.15%	0.48%	2.63%	0.00%
Buy	071887	Rio Tinto Ord Gbp0.10	24259	24259	0	10.7	2.60%	0.84%	1.75%	2.60%	0.00%
Buy	088869	3I Group Ord Gbp0.50	35567	35567	0	7	2.49%	0.31%	2.18%	2.49%	0.00%
Buy	056540	Marks & Spencer Ord Gbp0.25	82985	82985	0	2.55	2.12%	0.54%	1.57%	2.12%	0.00%
Buy	070995	Prudential Ord Gbp0.05	29887	29887	0	7	2.09%	1.03%	1.07%	2.09%	0.00%
Buy	067760	Pearson Ord Gbp0.25	28138	28138	0	7.29	2.05%	0.43%	1.62%	2.05%	0.00%
Buy	023691	Reuters Group Ord Gbp0.25	33939	33939	0	5.99	2.03%	0.63%	1.40%	2.03%	0.00%
Buy	097404	Wpp Group Ord Gbp0.10	37778	37778	0	4.95	1.87%	0.42%	1.45%	1.87%	0.00%

Figure 6.7 *A sample optimizer trade report showing the portfolio of 25 securities to track the FTSE All Share produced by the GA. The weight in each security was capped at 10%. The shares bought and sold are based on a nominal portfolio value of £10m. As you would expect when setting out to construct such a portfolio, the final tracking portfolio is mostly constructed from high-cap securities that constitute a significant portion of the benchmark*

to construct these portfolios. We then constructed 200 random portfolios by selecting a random subset of securities and optimizing the portfolio against the benchmark.

We proceeded to test the performance of the portfolios by tracking the portfolios against the benchmark for the following year. In all cases, the out-of-sample performance of the GA portfolios was significantly better than any of the random baskets of securities. Table 6.3 shows the performance of the GA solutions compared to the performance of the random baskets for the year following (October 2000 to October 2001).

Even out of sample, the portfolios constructed by the GAs are still the best performers when measured by the realized tracking error – the standard deviation of the portfolio's returns relative to the benchmark. The GAs have the lowest predicted and realized tracking error given the number of securities in the final portfolio demonstrating conclusively that the GA portfolios are good choices.

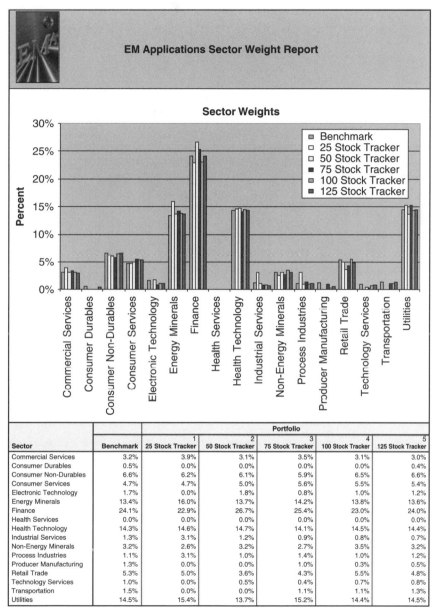

		Portfolio			
		1	2	3	4	5
Sector	Benchmark	25 Stock Tracker	50 Stock Tracker	75 Stock Tracker	100 Stock Tracker	125 Stock Tracker
Commercial Services	3.2%	3.9%	3.1%	3.5%	3.1%	3.0%
Consumer Durables	0.5%	0.0%	0.0%	0.0%	0.0%	0.4%
Consumer Non-Durables	6.6%	6.2%	6.1%	5.9%	6.5%	6.6%
Consumer Services	4.7%	4.7%	5.0%	5.6%	5.5%	5.4%
Electronic Technology	1.7%	0.0%	1.8%	0.8%	1.0%	1.2%
Energy Minerals	13.4%	16.0%	13.7%	14.2%	13.8%	13.6%
Finance	24.1%	22.9%	26.7%	25.4%	23.0%	24.0%
Health Services	0.0%	0.0%	0.0%	0.0%	0.0%	0.0%
Health Technology	14.3%	14.6%	14.7%	14.1%	14.5%	14.4%
Industrial Services	1.3%	3.1%	1.2%	0.9%	0.8%	0.7%
Non-Energy Minerals	3.2%	2.6%	3.2%	2.7%	3.5%	3.2%
Process Industries	1.1%	3.1%	1.0%	1.4%	1.0%	1.2%
Producer Manufacturing	1.3%	0.0%	0.0%	1.0%	0.3%	0.5%
Retail Trade	5.3%	5.0%	3.6%	4.3%	5.5%	4.8%
Technology Services	1.0%	0.0%	0.5%	0.4%	0.7%	0.8%
Transportation	1.5%	0.0%	0.0%	1.1%	1.1%	1.3%
Utilities	14.5%	15.4%	13.7%	15.2%	14.4%	14.5%

Figure 6.8   *Sector weights of various portfolios built by the GA. Each portfolio is constrained by the number of securities in the final portfolio. Portfolios are constructed with 25, 50, 75, 100, and 125 securities. This graph shows that even with very few securities used in the construction of the final portfolio, the final sector weights are still very close to the index*

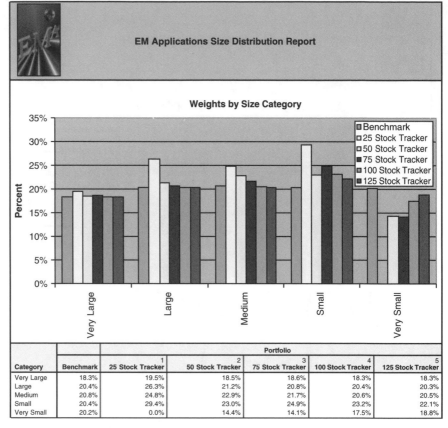

Figure 6.9 *The distribution of weights by size categories built by the GA. For this graph, securities were categorized into five groups – Very Large, Large, Medium, Small, and Very Small. Each of these groups was designed to contain approx. 20% of the benchmark. The graph shows that most of the portfolios match the size profile of the benchmark very closely. The only significant difference is for the 25 stock portfolio which has no securities in the Very Small category (i.e. securities that make up the bottom 20% of the index)*

Table 6.3 also shows the ratio of realized to predicted tracking error for both the GA portfolios and the random portfolios. All categories of portfolio had a higher volatility in the year following the construction of the model. This increase seems to be explained by the fact that the year following the model was a period of increasing volatility. For example, the SP 500 increased volatility in the following year. Over the model period, the SP 500 had a volatility of approx. 19%. This volatility increased to 23% in the year used for the out-of-sample trial (i.e. approx. a 20% increase in volatility over the model sample period and in line with the ratios in the table).

Table 6.3 *Comparison of performance of GA optimized portfolios with random baskets of securities. It shows that the GA's are still among the best possible portfolios when projected out of sample. The realized tracking error is calculated using the standard deviation of the relative weekly returns of the portfolio and the benchmark for the next year. Although all of the tracking errors are higher for the GA portfolios, it is worth noting that the returns data included 11 September 2001 and the WTC tragedy. Data from this period increased volatility for all portfolios*

Number of stocks	Genetic algorithm portfolios				Optimal portfolios of random subsets		
	Predicted tracking error	Realized tracking error	Over/ under performance	Ratio of realized to predicted tracking error	Lowest predicted tracking error	Lowest realized tracking error	Average ratio of predicted/realized tracking error
25	4.10%	4.59%	0.87%	1.12	5.72%	5.19%	1.13
35	3.09%	3.84%	0.54%	1.24	5.02%	4.76%	1.15
50	2.39%	3.06%	1.06%	1.28	4.08%	3.87%	1.17
75	1.74%	2.54%	−0.45%	1.46	3.35%	3.21%	1.22
100	1.33%	2.06%	−0.12%	1.54	2.91%	2.69%	1.23

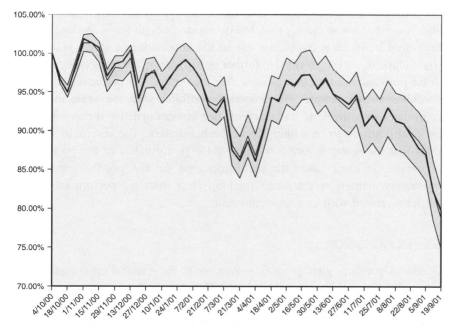

Figure 6.10 *The performance of 50-stock GA solutions to track the index. The lighter lines show the performance of the benchmark and the 95% confidence interval around the benchmark. The dark line shows the performance of the portfolio. The portfolio never exceeds the 95% confidence interval and ends up with a performance indistinguishable from the benchmark. The 50-stock GA solution had a predicted tracking error of 2.39%. The realized standard deviation of returns was 3.09%*

Table 6.4   *The performance of sector constrained portfolios out of sample. These portfolios are constrained to a limited number of securities in the final portfolio and to have a sector weight within 2% of the benchmark*

Number of stocks	GA portfolio with sector constraints		
	Predicted tracking error	Realized tracking error	Ratio of realized to predicted tracking error
25	4.29%	4.43%	1.03
35	3.29%	3.92%	1.19
50	2.52%	2.94%	1.16
75	1.81%	2.39%	1.32
100	1.34%	1.92%	1.44

Table 6.3 also shows that the ratio of realized to predicted tracking error increased as the number of stocks in the final portfolio increased. We noticed that the portfolios generated by the GA were closely matched on a country weight basis, but were not so closely matched on a sector weight basis. We believed that the period in question has seen a rise in the importance of sector volatility on world markets, and we decided to further investigate by adding sector constraints to the portfolio construction process. We then tested the performance of these portfolios out of sample. We generated portfolios with the same number of securities using the GA, but this time we constrained the sector weights of the final portfolio to be within 2% of the benchmark. The results in Table 6.4 show that the sector constraints improve the performance of the portfolio out of sample. In most cases, the performance of the GA portfolio with sector constraints actually has a better tracking error than the performance of the portfolio created without sector constraints.

6.5   CONCLUSIONS

Genetic Algorithms yield promising solutions to the practical optimization problems solved by fund managers routinely. However, there are a few areas where they could be improved. First, the GA needs to improve its feasibility detection. The current version of the optimizer uses an identical value of the utility function for all infeasible solutions. This makes feasibility detection difficult for all situations in which the set of feasible solutions is small. In this scenario, the GA does not distinguish between a solution that is close to feasibility and a solution that is very distant from feasibility. Second, the GA could be designed with improved rules for picking and discarding securities. Finally, a full comparison between methods such as these and a branch-and-bound style solution would be very instructive.

In spite of this, GAs offer a feasible way of constructing portfolios with a limited number of securities and/or trades efficiently. GAs are flexible enough to be able to solve various practical modifications of the simple cardinality constraint. For example, the optimizer has been adapted to allow a constraint on the number of trades as well as the number of securities. The optimizer has also been adapted to allow the user to force or deny inclusion to a particular security. GAs can be used on modern PCs to generate reasonable solutions in a fairly short time (two to three minutes).

REFERENCES

Bienstock, D. (1996) Computational study of a family of mixed-integer quadratic programming problems, *Math. Programming*, **74**, 121–40.

Chang, T-J., Meade, N., Beasley, J.E. and Sharaiha, Y.M. (2000) Heuristics for cardinality constrained portfolio optimization, *Computers and OR*, **27**, 1271–1302.

Connor, G. and Korajczyk, R.A. (1995) The Arbitrage Pricing Theory and Multifactor Models of Asset Returns. In *Finance, Handbooks in Operations Research and Management Science*, Vol. 9 (eds R. Jarrow, V. Maksimovic, and W. Ziemba) Amsterdam: North Holland.

Fletcher (1987) *Practical Methods of Optimization*, John Wiley & Sons.

Glover, F. and Laguna, M. (1997) *Tabu Search*, Kluwer Academic Publishers.

Goldberg, D.E. (1989) *Genetic Algorithms in Search, Optimization, and Machine Learning*, Addison-Wesley.

Grinold, R.C. and Kahn, R.N. (1994) *Active Portfolio Management*, McGraw Hill.

Holland, J.H. (1975) *Adaptation in Natural and Artificial Systems*, University of Michigan Press.

Kirkpatrick, S., Gelatt, C.D. and Vecchi, M.P. (1983) Optimization by Simulated Annealing, *Science*, **220**, 671–80.

Konno, H. and Yamazaki, H. (1991) Mean-Absolute Deviation Portfolio Optimization Model and its Application to Tokyo Stockmarket, *Management Science*, **37**, 519–631.

Mansini, R. and Speranza, M.G. (1999) Heuristic Algorithms for the portfolio selection problem with minimum transaction lots, *European Journal of Operational Research*, **114**, 219–33.

Markowitz, H.M. (1952) Portfolio Selection, *Journal of Finance*, **7**(1), 77–91.

Michaud, R.O. (1998) *Efficient Asset Management*, Harvard Business School Press.

Nemhauser, G.L. and Wolsey, L.A. (1988) *Integer and Combinatorial Optimization*, J. Wiley, New York.

Perold, A.F. (1984) Large-scale portfolio optimization, *Management Science*, **30**, 1143–60.

Shapcott (1992) Index Tracking: Genetic Algorithms for Investment Portfolio Selection, Report EPCC-SS92-24, Edinburgh Parallel Computing Centre.

Stroyny, A.L. (1992) Still More on EM Factor Analysis, Working Paper, University of Wisconsin-Milwaukee.

Vanderbei, R.J. (1996) *Linear Programming: Foundations and Extensions*, Kluwer Academic Publishers.

Chapter 7

Near-uniformly distributed, stochastically generated portfolios

RICHARD DAWSON AND RICHARD YOUNG

ABSTRACT

In modern science, experimental results without a control carry little weight. In the science of portfolio construction and financial modelling no such control currently exists. Thus it is very difficult to show conclusively the effect that a model, strategy, or individual (manager) has on the investment process.

A set of uniformly distributed, stochastically generated, portfolios that by construction incorporate no investment strategy, bias or skill form an effective control set for any portfolio measurement metric. This allows the true value of a strategy or model to be identified. They also provide a mechanism to differentiate between effects due to 'market conditions' and effects due to either the management of a portfolio, or the constraints the management is obliged to work within.

Presented here is a mechanism to generate a set of portfolios, with a near-uniform distribution over an n-dimensional search space, restricted by k linear constraints.

All algorithms discussed here have been implemented in C++ as part of Vestek-Quantec's (a Thomson Financial Company) Policy Guidelines Simulator (PGS). All results and simulations have been taken from PGS. Computing resource used was an AMD Athlon © 1000 Mhz with 256 Mb of memory, or equivalent.

7.1   INTRODUCTION – A TRACTABLE *N*-DIMENSIONAL EXPERIMENTAL CONTROL

In modern science experimental results without a control carry little weight. In the science of portfolio construction and financial modelling no such control currently exists. It is therefore very difficult to show conclusively the effect that a model, strategy, or indeed individual has on the real investment process. It is possible to do a comparison against other live portfolios but these will either have unknown construction methodologies or will have some other (possibly unknown) biases (Allen and Tan, 1998), Section 7.2 provides a review of existing research in persistence of performance, and also covers survivorship bias; Brown and Goetzmann (1995); Grinblatt and Titman (1992)).

The ideal solution would be to generate a set of portfolios, constrained in the same way as the portfolio(s) built with the theory or model under investigation, only without the information produced by the theory. It would then be possible to compare the distributions of the portfolio characteristics with and without the added information from the new theory, giving strong statistical evidence of the effects of the new information.

This set of Monte Carlo portfolios needs to be uniformly distributed over the solution space[1] so as not to introduce any biases. This is most easily done by first fully identifying the boundary of the solution space. Unfortunately the complexity of the shape of solution space grows geometrically with increasing number of assets (dimensions) and constraints.

To be able to generate a set of portfolios the solution space must be bounded in all dimensions and we impose the constraint that we must be fully invested, i.e. all portfolios have 100% total holding. So the number of constraints, k, has a lower bound of $n + 1$. This is the simplest case. Here there are $n + 1$ vertices, forming what might be described as a hyper-tetrahedron, more formally known as a simplex (Anderson, 19XX).

In reality all investment is done under many constraints. Not just those imposed by the owners of the money in the fund, and regulatory bodies, but also by the market (e.g. liquidity). In addition, an investment strategy is essentially a set of constraints that are carefully constructed to (hopefully) remove, in aggregate, poor performing regions of the solution space.

We must build a set of uniformly distributed points in an n dimensional space, bounded by k (orthogonal or non-orthogonal) linear constraints, without explicitly calculating the boundaries of the solution space. This is a well established academic problem in mathematical programming (Kai-Tai Fang, Guo-Liang Tain and Min-Yu Xie, 1991; Crosier, 1986; May and Smith, 1982; Rubin, 1984).

The central simplification used is not to map the solution space by identifying the vertices, and mapping how they are connected together with edges and how the edges are connected at the vertices. We do however build a list of the hyper-planes that the constraints define, these hyper-planes bound the solution space. Those planes that connect to each other are recorded, exactly where and how is not. These hyper-planes do fully define the solution space but this is not an explicit mapping of the solution space as no attempt is made to record the parameters of the equations that define the intersections of these planes. Hence the overall shape of the solution space remains unknown through out the procedure.

By not attempting to map the solution space explicitly we can only achieve an approximation to the ideal uniform distribution but it is now tractable in polynomial time.

Two algorithms are used in conjunction. First is an algorithm using dynamic constraints to build a portfolio that is in the solution space. The limitations and distortions created by this mechanism are identified. However it is efficient and fast and with appropriate optimizations will execute in $O(k_c n)$, where k_c is the number of child constraints (see Section 7.3, Dynamic Constraints).

A further algorithm is then presented that modifies the distributions produced by the dynamic constraints algorithm, reducing the majority of the distortions.

7.1.1   Order of calculation for determination of membership of solution

The order of this computation for a given point is very dependent on the constraints and varies between $O(k)$, where there are no general linear constraints only simple bounding constraints, tending to $O(nk)$ as the number of general linear (multiple asset) constraints dominates over the simple bounding constraints. However in either case the problem is tractable, and will not be addressed further here.

7.1.2   Other assumptions

No short holdings are allowed, and a portfolio must be fully invested so the widest holdings are 0–100%. Modifications to both algorithms that deal with shorting have been implemented by the authors, but are not detailed here for simplicity.

All the assets in the universe must be held in all portfolios. This restriction is only necessary for the local density algorithm not for the mapping of the solution space, or the actual generation of a portfolio in the solution space. It is a severe assumption. Practical implementations will need to formulate methodologies to relax this assumption.

7.2   APPLICATIONS

7.2.1   Constraint evaluation

Many investment companies impose in-house constraints on their managers, with the intention of controlling risk, or improving returns. The effects on the distribution of possible portfolios of different aspects of these constraints can be explored, along with the distribution of characteristics of those 'available' portfolios. This is particularly useful in identifying the range of tracking errors that is available to the fund managers.

For example, if a single set of portfolios is created and randomly rebalanced each month, the average turnover required simply to keep within the constraints can also be calculated, revealing the amount of freedom the fund manager actually has to stock pick.

7.2.2   Returns model evaluation

In evaluating an alpha model it is usual to look at the performance of only a handful of portfolios, often only one. Typically this portfolio will be built to express the full power of the model, i.e. containing the highest alpha stocks, perhaps after adjusting for risk. Unfortunately this does not reflect the reality of running a live portfolio, its market driven limits of liquidity, cash flows, changing alphas etc. It is possible to run paper portfolio to reflect this reality but it is both time consuming and difficult.

A broad and statistically powerful view of the model's performance can be achieved by comparing the characteristics of two sets of random portfolios. The first without the data from the alpha model, using only the standard in-house constraints, the second with the additional constraint that each portfolio must achieve above a certain aggregate alpha (as defined by the model under test) value. With thousands of portfolios generated for each set, standard statistical analysis could now be applied.

7.2.3   Manager performance

Currently the standard way of measuring the performance of a fund manager is by comparison with his/her peers. This is flawed for a number of reasons, but primarily because the peers are not managing under the same conditions nor with the same information. A more accurate measure would be against known no-skill portfolios that have been built and managed under the same limitations and constraints. One need only randomly rebalance a set of Monte Carlo portfolio to keep them within the constraints, to have such a set of no-skill portfolios. One would clearly expect a manager to beat the mean return of this set of portfolios.

7.2.4   Portfolio attribute benchmarking

An example will best explain the general nature of attribute benchmarking. A portfolio manager is given a fund to manage, with the client setting a range of limits, these limits are not to be broken, they include tracking error and turnover. After a year the fund manager has breached these limits five times and the fund is removed from their control. Is this justified? This question is currently answered subjectively. However if a set of random portfolios is generated and randomly rebalanced each month to stay within the constraints we can use the average breach count of these portfolios as a statistically meaningful benchmark. If these portfolios have on average only breached three times then the fund owner would seemed to be justified. If however the average breach count of these portfolios was seven, then the manager would have a strong defence, in that market conditions lead to unavoidable breaches.

There are many such measures used in portfolio management that currently have no benchmark, or only use a single portfolio (e.g. S&P500) as the benchmark. Using the market index is often both statistically useless, and comparably meaningless, as the S&P500 does not pay transaction costs, is not bound by in-house constraints, alpha models, limitations on holdings etc. that many funds are subject to.

7.3   DYNAMIC CONSTRAINTS

7.3.1   Overview

The problem is solved in percentage holding space. Cash is considered an asset, so the holdings in a portfolio must sum to 100%.

We start with an empty proto-portfolio, and a set of dynamic constraints. The dynamic constraints define the float for each asset and each constraint.
We randomly select an asset with a non-zero float, and then a random holding increase within the available float.
The process of asset selection and addition to the portfolio continues until all float on all assets in all constraints is used.

7.3.2   Definitions

Problem constraints:	The k constraints specified at the problem out set.
Dynamic constraints:	The k_c set of constraints that fully define the remaining solution space available to the proto-portfolio. They map the intersections between the problem constraints, and ultimately, give the Float available for each asset.
Float:	The amount an assets holding in the proto-portfolio may be increased by. It is the maximum distance between the solution space boundaries in this dimension, for this set of problem constraints, and given the current proto-portfolio.

Proto-portfolio: A portfolio with less than 100% holding,
                          i.e. incomplete.
Constraint minimum holding requirement:
                          The smallest weight that this constraint must hold
                          in order to be satisfied.

7.3.3   Mapping the solution space

In principle it is possible to entirely define the boundaries of the solution space
for any set of linear constraints. In practice, this rapidly becomes an unfeasible
task as the number of assets rises. Kai-Ta et al. (1991) presents a mechanism
to transform the solution space and calculates an exact solution. Rubin (1994)
also presents a mechanism for an exact solution, but both of these techniques
rapidly become intractable as the number of dimensions grows. The number of
asset combinations, for a problem with n assets is:

$$\sum_{k=1}^{n} \frac{n!}{k!(n-k)!} \qquad (7.1)$$

so for a 100 asset problem, there are of the order of 1×10^{30} different asset
combinations. Mapping a space of this complexity is beyond current computer
architecture.

Fortunately, for finance problems in the real world, the solution space is much
simpler than this. Most asset combinations are meaningless, of no interest to
fund managers. It is also possible to artificially reduce the number of assets
by combining them into asset patterns, reducing the number of combinations
still further.

Additionally, for the Monte Carlo mechanism described in this paper, there
is no need to completely calculate the solution space at every stage of portfolio
generation. Only those parts of the space that are relevant at the time need be
fully mapped.

7.3.4   Asset patterns – reducing the size of the problem

For a system of simple linear holding constraints, it is possible to calculate the
boundaries of the entire solution space, even for problems with a large number
(>1000) of assets. This is because different assets can be grouped into sets in
which they are indistinguishable from the other assets in that set. No esoteric
mechanism is required to determine what these sets are; they are readily defined
by Quantec's Asset Pattern.

This is an asset classification, consisting of three hierarchies: domicile country, asset class and currency. It is simple and intuitive classification, useful to fund managers as well as algorithmic engineers!

Assets with the same pattern (for instance UK Banking stocks quoted in UK £s) are indistinguishable from each other. This rationalization of the available asset combinations dramatically reduces the complexity of the solution space. To calculate the solution space for a FTSE100 simulation, 150 linear constraints completely describe the solution space when the assets are grouped by Quantec's asset classification scheme (100 single asset constraints, and 50 pattern (or asset set) constraints). This compares favourably with the theoretical limit.

Note that every problem has at least one constraint in common with every other problem – the portfolio constraint, or 100% holding constraint. This requires every portfolio to be fully populated, to have a total asset holding weight of 100%, and reduces the dimensionality of the solution space by one.

7.3.5   The constraint hierarchy

At this point, we have constructed a consistent system of linear inequalities. While this does completely describe the problem, on its own this information is not readily useful in the generation of portfolios. It is convenient to gather more information about the structure of the solution space; specifically how the linear constraints interact with each other. Generally speaking, the more information that we determine about the solution space in its initial state (all assets in the proto-portfolio having a holding weight of zero), the more efficient the later portfolio generation becomes.

A useful arrangement is to form a hierarchy, relating all the linear constraints from the simple asset holding constraints at the bottom, to the 100% portfolio holding constraint at the top. The key to building this hierarchy is to define the relationship between constraints in terms of the assets that make up those constraints.

Set theory is extremely useful for performing this sort of analysis and turns out to provide all the tools necessary to solve all problems associated with linear constraints. To avoid confusion however, the terminology used in the rest of this paper will be that of a hierarchy – a parent is a superset, a child is a subset.

7.3.6   Monte Carlo solutions

It is important to remember that this is not an optimization problem. Any point in the solution space is a good portfolio. Ideally, the algorithm will produce an even distribution of portfolios across the solution space, but in practice this is difficult to achieve without some form of post processing.

The portfolios are built by randomly selecting a single dimension (one asset) from the entire solution space, and determining the current limits on that dimension. The weight of that asset is increased in line with these limits, and this process is then repeated until all the constraints are satisfied. If these limits have been determined correctly, then each weight increase will move closer to satisfying one or more constraints, and will not violate any of the other constraints.

It transpires that these limits are potentially influenced by every constraint in the system. Those constraints that contain the asset in question apply their current maximum holding limits. Those constraints that do not contain the asset in question, restrict on the basis of their minimum holding requirements.

With judicious use of the hierarchy, many optimizations are possible that can substantially reduce the number of limiting constraints that need to be considered. However, calculating the current maximum and minimum holding limits of a constraint turns out not to be a trivial process. Determining a constraint's minimum holding requirement is a particularly interesting problem.

7.3.7   Pattern constraints

Determining a constraint's minimum holding requirement at a particular time in a Monte Carlo simulation is an important part of determining the shape of the solution space at that time. Dynamically recalculating the entire solution space every time an asset is added to the current Monte Carlo proto-portfolio is an arduous task however, made all the more complicated by the inevitable presence of pattern constraints that have some assets in common with other pattern constraints.

Changes in the weights of these shared assets can have subtle effects on the shape of the solution spaces as it changes dynamically. Calculating the contribution of these constraints to the overall solution space is mainly a matter of determining the pattern's minimum required holding weight. Several concepts need to be introduced here to fully understand how the linear holding constraints work:

Minimum child holding
Since the constraint hierarchy has been constructed in terms of the assets that each constraint affects, parent constraints will always constrain more assets than their children. This implies that, once shorting has been accounted for, all parent constraints have a greater or equal minimum and maximum holding requirement than their children.

However, the parent's minimum holding requirement is not independent of its children. Once an asset has been added to the proto-portfolio, new limits are calculated for all constraints and changes in child weights and limits can affect parent limits in sometimes complex ways.

A constraint's contribution to the problem is defined in terms of its minimum holding requirement. In fact there are three quantities that influence this minimum dynamic limit:

- The constraint's minimum holding limit. This is always the dominant quantity in the initial, unweighted solution space.
- The constraint's current holding weight.
- The constraint's minimum child contribution. The following example will explain what is meant by this:

Consider three constraints: a parent constraint with two child constraints, A and B. They have the following holding limits:

Parent constraint   20% –60%
Child A   5% –30%
Child B   10% –20%

First of all, consider the case where A and B do not share any assets (Figure 7.1).

How does increasing the weights of assets in the child constraints affect the minimum holding requirement of the parent?

If A has a weight of 12% and B 0%, then the parent's minimum holding requirement now becomes 22%, since B still requires at least another 10%.

A parent's minimum holding requirement due to its children is referred as the minimum child contribution and is the third quantity used to assess a constraint's contribution to the current problem. Whichever is the greater of these three

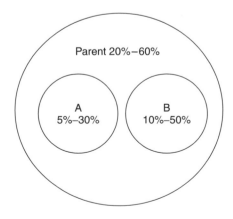

Figure 7.1   *Parent–child constraints, no intersections*

determines the constraint's contribution.

$$\text{Minimum dynamic limit} = \text{MAX}\left(\sum \text{Child contribution,}\right.$$

$$\left.\sum \text{Asset weights, initial holding limit}\right) \quad (7.2)$$

Constraint intersections – generation of implied constraints

Intersections between child constraints complicate the calculation of a parent's minimum holding limit and the above equation is no longer valid. Consider the case where A and B do have assets in common.

Single intersection

Any changes in the weight of the assets in the intersection A ∩ B affect the limits of both child A and B and hence the parent's child minimum.

If A has a weight of 18% and B 8%, and 3% of this is in the intersection what is the minimum contribution of the parent to the problem?

A's unique contribution is $18-3 = 15\%$;

B's unique contribution is $10-3 = 7\%$;

B's minimum holding (10) is greater than its weight (8), so use this in the calculation above. The intersection contribution is 3%.

So the parent's contribution is $15+7+3 = 25\%$, which in this case satisfies its minimum.

$$\text{Parent contribution} = \sum \text{Intersection contribution}$$

$$+ \sum \text{Unique child contribution} \quad (7.3)$$

Multiple intersections

Multiple intersections are exceedingly common and complicate matters only slightly.

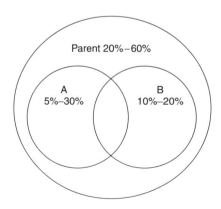

Figure 7.2   *Parent–child constraints, single intersections*

Consider a parent P, with three children, A, B and C.
In this case, there are up to four intersections possible:

$$A \cap B, A \cap C, B \cap C \text{ and } A \cap B \cap C.$$

Remember that the key to determining the current shape of the solution space is to find the parent constraint's minimum required holding value.

This implies that the intersection with the most number of assets must be dealt with first, reducing the minima of as many children as possible.

This does not change the previous sum, it merely imposes an order in which it must be done.

7.3.8 Generating a Monte Carlo portfolio

Having mapped the unweighted solution space, we are now able to generate portfolios. There are a number of ways in which this could be done, but the particular method described below takes advantage of the information that has been gathered about the empty solution space.

Essentially, assets are added one at a time into the proto-portfolio. Every time an asset weight is changed, the solution space is recalculated. Clearly, each iteration of this process shrinks the solution space until, when the portfolio constraint (100% holding) is finally met, the available space has shrunk to nothing. This 'dynamic constraint' mechanism proves to be efficient and amenable to optimizations.

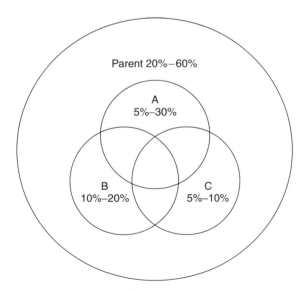

Figure 7.3 *Parent–child constraints, multiple intersections*

7.3.9   Portfolio generation with the dynamic constraints algorithm

Each constraint in the problem is considered in turn, starting with those at the bottom of the constraint hierarchy. Although the algorithm will still produce results no matter what order the constraints are satisfied in (and it is possible just to satisfy the portfolio constraint, all other constraints being met during this process), this tends to produce some bias when there are minimum holding constraints applied to single assets.

The method described below constructs a portfolio by satisfying minimum constraints, starting all assets with a weight of zero and increasing their weights. Other methods, such as giving all assets 100% weighting and then satisfying all the maximum constraints by reducing asset weightings are equally valid, although suffer from different problems.

1) Select the all the single asset constraints, and randomize their order.
2) Step through this randomized list of dynamic constraints and add each assets minimum holding to the proto-portfolio. (If the total holding in the proto-portfolio is >100% the problem constraints are infeasible.) Discard the list.
3) Select a dynamic constraint.
4) From the constraint in question, an asset is selected. The float, or amount by which the asset's weight can be increased, is determined, and a random weighting increase assigned, up to this float. Note that the float calculation ensures that no maximum limits are ever breached.
5) If the weight of the assets that make up that constraint is not greater than the constraint minimum, go to 4). Note that an asset may have its weight increased more than once.
6) Repeat from 3) until all constraints are satisfied.

When all have been satisfied, the final Monte Carlo portfolio consists of those assets with a non zero holding weight.

7.3.10   Number of holdings in a Monte Carlo portfolio

The latter half of this chapter concerns the theoretical distribution of portfolios across the solution space. The definition of a uniform distribution with portfolios of different sizes is unclear as they have different dimensionality, so the analysis is restricted to considering the distribution of portfolios with the same number of assets.

The only influences on the portfolio size in the dynamic constraints algorithm are the asset holding limits, with the average portfolio size clearly being related to the average asset weighting. When a particular portfolio size is desirable, some post processing of the fully weighted portfolio must be performed. One way of doing this is as follows:

If the portfolio is undersized, select an asset at random and find another asset that is affected by the same constraints. This asset should not be in the portfolio already. Assign a random portion of the first asset's weight to this new asset. Repeat this process until the portfolio contains the desired number of assets.

If the portfolio is oversized, select two assets in the portfolio that are affected by the same constraints. Reduce one of these assets' weight to zero and increase the other asset's weight according. The asset with no weight is discarded from the portfolio. Repeat this process until the portfolio contains the desired number of assets.

7.4 RESULTS FROM THE DYNAMIC CONSTRAINTS ALGORITHM

Calculating the expected distribution of holding sizes of an assets, given a uniform distribution of portfolios in the solution space is surprisingly difficult, even for simple cases. See Appendices 2 and 3.

Figure 7.4 shows the results for three assets as they are easily visualized. Further results are shown combined with just the dynamic constraints algorithm later without distorting the solution space.

7.4.1 Three asset results

As the solution space with three assets and the minimal constraints is a 2D triangle, we can show the full solution space and all the portfolios plotted within it.

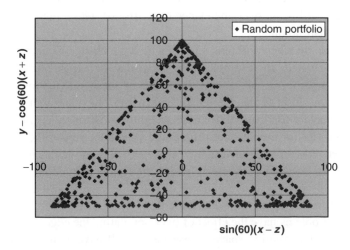

Figure 7.4 *Three assets with minimal constraints: 500 portfolio plot dynamic constraints*

The three dimensions (x, y, z) have been mapped to x^* and y^*

$$x^* = y - \cos(60°)(x - z)$$

$$x^* = \sin(60^o)(x - z)$$

The boundary preferring nature of the dynamic constraints algorithm can be easily seen with over population at the very small holding level and the very large.

An alternative way of viewing this is to look at the distribution of holdings in a single asset across all portfolios. See Appendices 2 and 3 for theoretical distribution and 'Results of the Dynamic Constraints with Local Density Control' for plot of the three asset dynamic constraints results.

7.5   PROBLEMS AND LIMITATIONS WITH DYNAMIC CONSTRAINTS ALGORITHM

As the proto-portfolio grows the amount left to add reduces, approaching zero asymptotically. This creates the tendency to over populate with very small holdings. Applying a cut off of say 10 basis points, as the smallest allowable holding in any one asset can reduce this effect. As the number of assets in the problem increases this limit must fall so as not to impose an artificial minimum holding limit on an asset that has a meaningful impact on the distribution of any portfolio metric.

Equally where the initial float for some or all the assets is very wide there is a tendency to over populate with large holdings. This is because the first asset to be added to the proto-portfolio will have a very large allowable range, in the extreme 0–100%, and its weight is a uniform distribution between these limits. So that there will be an over abundance of portfolios with a few large holdings and many small holdings.

While there are many different ways in which the change in an asset's weight could be calculated, for example using a normal or exponential distribution rather than a uniform one, and while some of these distributions will give results that are closer to the theoretical distribution, they are highly dependant on the parameters used to define these weighting distributions. In turn, these parameters differ for problems of different sizes. As the rest of the algorithm is unparameterized and it is unclear how these distribution parameters would be determined for complex problems in which the results are not already known it seems wise to apply a simple uniform distribution. The inaccuracies resulting from this approach are at least understood!

All these problems have the effect of over populating the edges and especially the corners of the solution space. These points will have a strong tendency to be the more extreme of the portfolios in the solution space.

It is worthy of note that in real world problems it is not normally allowable to have very large holdings in a single asset. For portfolios of 100+ assets it would be usual to have a maximum holding limit on each assets of 10% or less. These real world individual holding limits significantly reduce the distortions the raw dynamic constraints algorithm introduces.

7.6   IMPROVEMENTS TO THE DISTRIBUTION

There are many ways to improve the distribution once one has been established. Rubin (1985) describes the effects of the most obvious (Random Walk) over short runs of the type most likely to be used in portfolio generation. We use a variant of random walk, which reduces the rejection of points that 'walk' out of the solution space, and is tailored to the known deficiencies in the dynamic constraints algorithm.

7.6.1   Overview

It is a necessary condition of a uniform distribution that the density of portfolios over a smooth, continuous, convex subsection of the solution space is (broadly) the same as that over any other sub-section of the solution space. As the size of the sub-spaces tends towards the total space the portfolio densities in any two such sub-spaces will tend towards each other.

It is this property that is at the heart of the mechanism that is used to detect and correct variations in the population distribution over different regions of the solution space.

A particular (serious) problem arises with using local population density measurement at the boundary of the solution space. Any sub-space that extends outside the solution space will have an artificially low density, as there are no portfolios in the region of the sub-space that is outside the solution space. This will lead to over population at the edge of the solution space. It is difficult to compensate for this as the overall shape and location of the boundary of the solution space is unknown.

A technique is used to find the boundary of the solution space locally. The proportion of the hyper-surface of the sub-space that is outside the solution space is then used as an approximation to hyper-volume that is outside the solution-space. (See Boundary detection and Density correction, Section 7.6.2.)

7.6.2   Algorithm description

Definitions

Active list: The list of portfolios that have been created so far and
                                are deemed to be 'correctly' placed in the
                                solution space.

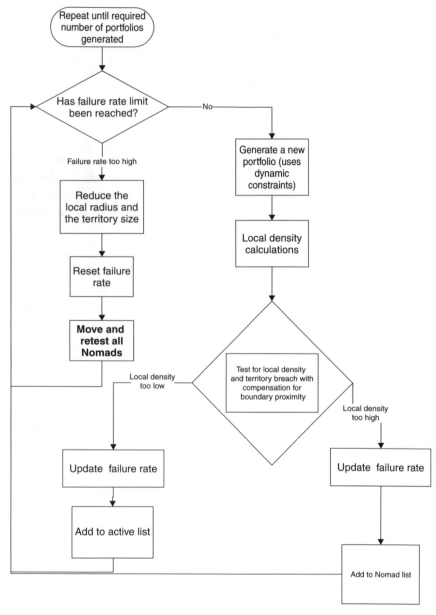

Figure 7.5   *Local density control algorithm*

Nomad: A portfolio that failed the local density, and/or territory
                              test, i.e. a portfolio not on the active list.
Failure rate: A rolling window of the past *p* attempts to place a
                              (new) portfolio onto the active list.

LocalRadius: The radius of the hyper-sphere that defines the sub-space for which we are calculating the population density. A hyper-sphere is used as the shape of the sub-space. Determining whether a point is inside the hyper-sphere is only a matter of comparing the radius of the hyper-sphere to the distance from the centre of the sphere to the point.

Territory size: The minimum distance between two portfolios.

Functional block outline

Failure rate limit reached:

    Test to see if the rate at which portfolios are added has fallen below some limit. This needs to be fairly low. The greater the inherent non-uniform distribution in the portfolio generation algorithm the lower this needs to be.[2] This is the test for saturation at the current local density limit.

Reduce LocalRadius and territory size:

    We have reached saturation with the current level of portfolio density, and minimum portfolio separation, so to add more portfolios we need to increase the allowable density.

Reset failure rate:

    Now we have increased the allowable density we reset the failure rate by deleting the existing history of attempted portfolio additions.

Move and retest all Nomads:

    Loop through each Nomad and as it does not fit in where it is attempt to move it to where it does. See Figure 7.5.

Generate a new portfolio:

    Run the previously described dynamic constraints algorithm to create a new random portfolio.

Local density calculations:

    Calculate the density of the portfolios in a hyper-sphere (of radius LocalRadius) around the current portfolio.

Test for local destiny, territory breach and boundary proximity correction.

    Is the portfolio density around the current portfolio lower than the current limit, even after compensating for the hyper-volume in the sub-space that is outside the solution space. (See Boundary detection and Density correction, Figure 7.6.)

Update failure rate.
Add to our rolling history of portfolio additions.

Boundary detection

A portfolio is defined as on the boundary of the solution space if any part of its local hyper-sphere is outside the solution space. Clearly, as the local density is allowed to increase and the radius of the hyper-sphere falls, portfolios that were once deemed on the edge will no longer be.

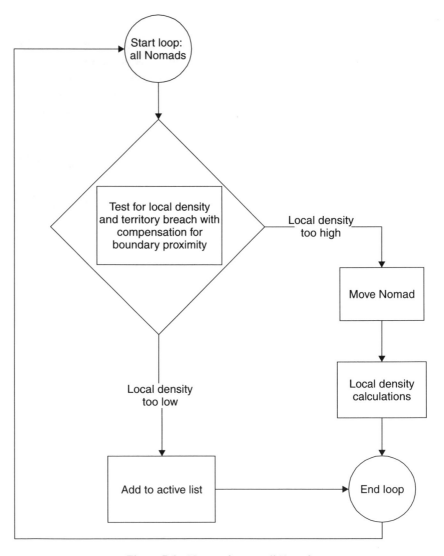

Figure 7.6 *Move and re-test all Nomads*

As we do not know where the edge of the solution space is it is not possible to look directly for its intersection with the hyper-sphere. Instead we take random points on the surface of the hyper-sphere and test to see if they are in the solution space. A single failure indicates this portfolio is on the edge. The more successes we have, the more confident we can be that no part of this portfolio's local hyper-sphere is outside the solution space.

Density correction

We are attempting to correct for the following effect:

If a hyper-sphere has a density of p portfolios per V_L (hyper-volume of $n - 1$ dimensions) but some fraction f_V falls outside the solution space then the density will be under stated and should be

$$\frac{p}{V_H(1 - f_V)} \tag{7.4}$$

As previously stated the boundary of the solution space is not explicitly known, and so it is not possible to directly calculate f_V.

We make the following simplifying assumption:

The fraction f_S of the surface of the local hyper-sphere that is outside the solution space is the same as the fraction f_V of the volume that falls outside.

This assumption is true as long as:

1) There are no sub-vertex[3] in the hyper-sphere and the boundary of the solution space passes through the centre of the sphere.
2) A single sub-vertex passes through the centre of the hyper-sphere.

As the portfolio get closer to the boundary of the solution space, and the sub-space becomes a smaller proportion of the total space, 1) becomes more likely and the approximation improves.

Where neither 1) nor 2) is true $f_S > f_V$ as the centre of the hyper-sphere is always on the inside of a convex shape.[4] The degree to which this helps control the over population of the boundary regions of the solution space is difficult to quantify.

We can now use a similar procedure to the boundary proximity detection to determine f_S: for a large number of random points

$$f_S = \frac{p_o}{p_i + p_o} \tag{7.5}$$

where p_o is number of random portfolio outside the solution space and p_i is the number of random portfolios inside the solution space.

Moving Nomads

Once a portfolio has been tested to see if it fits into the current active set of portfolios, and has failed, the question arises what to do with it. The most naive of answers is to throw it away and generate a new one. However the cost of moving a portfolio is $O(4n)$, whilst generating a new one is $O(nk_c)$ But how do we move the portfolio without breaking the constraints?

We could use a random walk. However the dynamic constraints algorithm is edge preferential, and hence this is the area of the solution space that will saturate first as a result most of the Nomad portfolios will be close to the edge of the solution space. A random walk on these portfolios will have a high likelihood of moving them out of the solution space. Although the Nomads will then either be removed from the solution space or moved away from an area of high density, on average smoothing any population density variations, we found that this was highly inefficient and becomes more so as the number of dimensions increases.

As the boundary of the solution space is convex, and the solution space itself is continuous, then all portfolios on a straight line drawn between two portfolios already known to be in the solutions space will also be in the solution space. This gives us an efficient mechanism to move a portfolio to a new position that is guaranteed to be in the solution space. To move a portfolio we randomly select another portfolio from the active list and make a small semi-random step towards it. The size of the step is controlled to be evenly distributed between 0 and $^{100}/_n$ per cent of the distance between the two portfolios. A Nomad may make as many steps as is required to find a space in the active set.

The tendency of Nomads to move towards the centre of the search space is the main counter to the edge preference in the dynamic algorithm. Further there is an (imperfect) self-correcting feature. If there is an over abundance of portfolios that are close to the edge of the solution space, then one of these is more likely to be selected to be moved towards. Also as the Nomad will, more likely than not, be moving from a position that is on the boundary of the solution space towards another, also on the boundary, the distance to move will tend to be large (or more precisely larger than a move from a boundary portfolio to a non-boundary). The result is that as the number of boundary portfolios increases so does the tendency of Nomad portfolios to take a big step away from the edge of the solution space.

7.7   RESULTS OF THE DYNAMIC CONSTRAINTS WITH LOCAL DENSITY CONTROL

All results presented here are with all parameters of the algorithm fixed. Improvements can be made by varying the parameters as the number of dimensions changes.

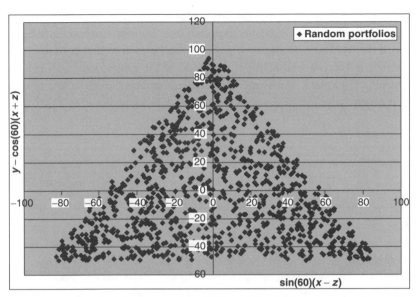

Figure 7.7 *Assets with minimal constraints: 1000 portfolio plot dynamic constraints and local density control*

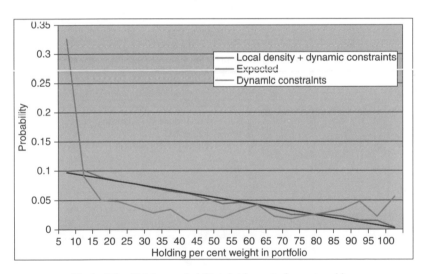

Figure 7.8 *Holding probability plot for a single asset problem*

Figure 7.7 shows a three-asset problem, mapped to two dimensions, with the local density control algorithm as described. The apparent voids and clusters are a feature of the random weight allocation, and whist always present their position and form changes from run to run.

These results can be presented as a 'probability vs percentage holding in a specified asset' plot. See Figure 7.8 showing this plot for the data set in

Figure 7.7, the data set presented in 'Results from the dynamic constraints algorithm' (see Figure 7.4) and the expected distribution. The boundary hugging nature of the dynamic constraints algorithm can be seen as higher than expected probability at the low and high holding ends of the graph.

Appendix 3 explains the shape and expected holding distribution in a three asset problem when each asset is limited to a holding between 0–50%. The

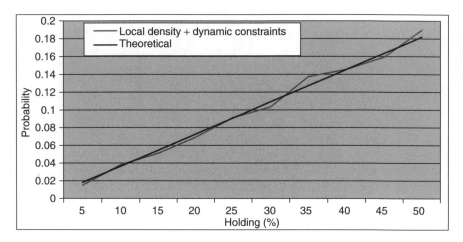

Figure 7.9   *Holding probability plot for a single asset in asset problem with 50% holding limit*

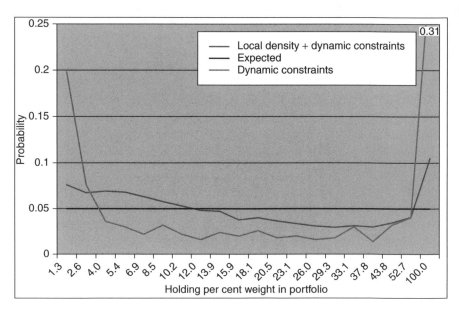

Figure 7.10   *Holding probability plot for an average asset in asset problem*

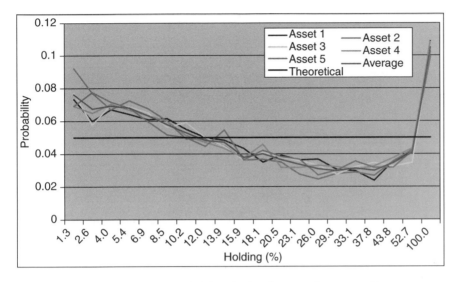

Figure 7.11 *Holding probability plot for all asset in five asset problem*

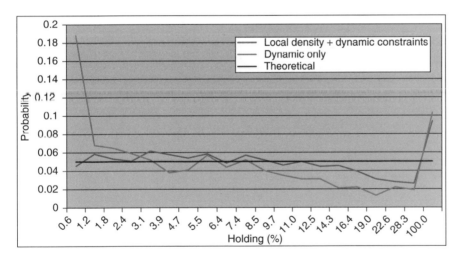

Figure 7.12 *Holding probability plot for a single asset in 10 asset problem*

results achieved are plotted against this theoretical expectation in Figure 7.9 (the Monte Carlo set consists of 1000 portfolios). This very simple case, demonstrates that the algorithm is at the very worst independent of the shape of the solution shape at low dimensionality. Unfortunately constructing the expected holdings distribution at higher (10 asset+) dimensionality is very hard, even with simple constraints, so this test of solution space shape independence has yet to be done at high dimensions.

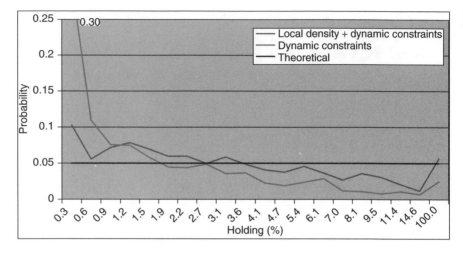

Figure 7.13   *Holding probability plot for a single asset in 20 asset problem*

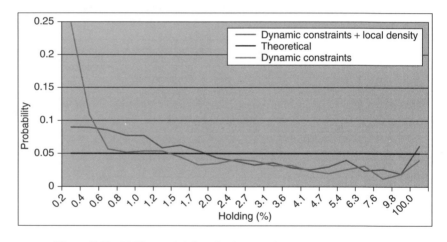

Figure 7.14   *Holding probability plot for a single asset in 30 asset problem*

When we move to higher dimensions it becomes necessary to scale the graph such that theoretical results form a constant probability.

The local density + dynamic constraints plot in Figure 7.10 is the average of all of the five assets. The plot in Figure 7.11 is all five assets from the same distribution and the average, it shows no significant bias between the assets. Although asset 2 does have a notably higher probability at low weights, repeated runs do not show persistence. These results were built from 2400 random portfolios, taking approximately 100 seconds to calculate.

At 10 assets (Figure 7.12) note the steeply exponential nature of the *x*-axis scale needed to keep the theoretical probability plot flat. Figure 7.12 shows an improvement over the five asset case. There are 1000 portfolios in this results set, taking about two minutes to calculate.

As can be seen from the 20 assets case (Figure 7.13), the correction the local density algorithm provides diminishes as the number of assets climbs. The probability of a very small holding (under 0.3%) is twice the theoretical (0.102). However the average error is only 0.016.

At 30 assets (Figure 7.14) the improvement from the local density algorithm is limited to the very small holdings. The plot is of 1000 assets taking approximately five minutes to calculate.

7.8 CONCLUSIONS

This paper has not attempted to make any new observations about the investment process. Rather it has provided a new tool to aid analysis of the investment process.

Monte Carlo analysis is a powerful tool used in almost every other scientific discipline, from climate modelling to cosmology. It is not a tool that has been readily applied to the investment process in the past, due to the perceived complexity of the problem. However over the last few years the power of desktop computers has risen sufficiently to make simple Monte Carlo modelling practical and once we began analysing the Monte Carlo modelling in detail, we found that it was not necessarily as intractable as first thought.

While the general problem of mapping a solution space for an n asset problem is exceedingly complex when n becomes large enough to be interesting ($\sim$30 assets for example), the problems found in portfolio construction are much simplified, and it is possible to build near-uniform distributions.

The time to build a set of 2000 simulated portfolios for problems of fewer than 30 assets is under 10 minutes. This is fast enough to be of practical use in 'what-if' analysis, constraint set design, portfolio metric benchmarking or Monte Carlo portfolio management.

As most real world problems will be done with no knowledge of the expected holdings distributions, or solution space shape, the lack of manual parameter tuning is a requirement in implementing real world systems. The algorithms presented here either have no parameters, or the parameters used throughout all the results are fixed, demonstrating that practical systems can be built.

7.9 FURTHER WORK

Calculating a reasonable estimate for whether a portfolio is close to the boundary of the solution space is both computationally intensive and frequently executed—the worst combination. An improvement here would allow both reductions in the execution time and the better estimates of the local density in the critical boundary areas.

The way Nomads move, both direction and distance, have much scope for research. A record could be kept of where portfolios have been recently successfully added. A Nomad could be moved close to this point, on the grounds that it had a low enough density to accommodate one portfolio, perhaps it can take another. The pattern of migration of the Nomads currently used does not seem to fit the problems as the dimensionality increases above 20 or so. Constricting a dynamic migration algorithm that is sensitive to the varying local densities is likely to bring better results over a wider range of dimensions and constraint sets.

It is very difficult to find ways to see how changes in the algorithm affect the distributions. A mechanism to 'eye-ball' the distributions would be very helpful in selecting profitable areas of future developments. If the linear constraints were set such that the solution space was a hyper-cube, then the portfolios could be projected down onto a 2D plot, one plot for each dimension. Like looking into a glass box from the top, the front and the side. If all n plots have even distributions then the distribution throughout the space must also be uniform. More importantly any distortions would be relatively easy to see.

The authors are not mathematicians by training, and much of the algorithm relies on extrapolation from three- and four-dimensional cases where the mathematics of geometric shapes is well established. Things that are simple at three dimensions seem to be absent from the mathematical literature in n dimensions, where n is 50 to 1000. For example whilst generalized polar co-ordinates are detailed (Muirhead, 1983), the hyper-sphere equivalent of the volume of a cap or spherical cone is not. Much of the work and ideas contained in this chapter would benefit greatly from a more rigorous and formal footing.

7.10   APPENDIX 1: REVIEW OF HOLDING DISTRIBUTION IN LOW DIMENSIONS WITH MINIMAL CONSTRAINTS

The minimal constraints, as defined in the assumptions, are all assets bounded between 0–100% and a single general linear constraint that forces all holdings to sum to 100%.

The combined effect of these constraints is to reduce the problem space to a $n - 1$ dimensional (hyper) volume.

Figure 7.15 shows a three asset example.

The shaded triangle is the solution space defined by three assets and the minimal constraints. It is important to note that whilst the solution space itself is two dimensional (it is just a 2D equilateral triangle), it lies in a way that cuts through three dimensions.

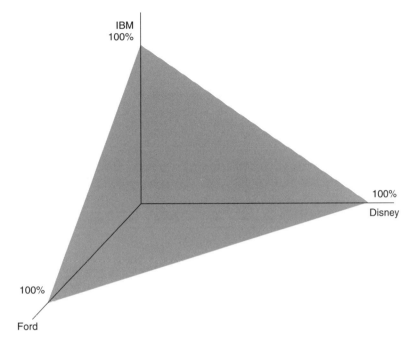

Figure 7.15 *Three asset example*

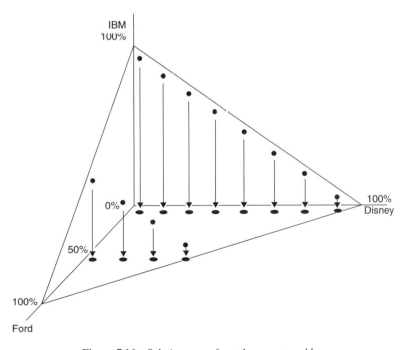

Figure 7.16 *Solution space for a three asset problem*

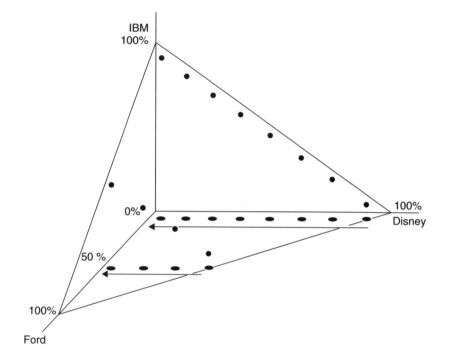

Figure 7.17   *Points collapsed onto Ford axis*

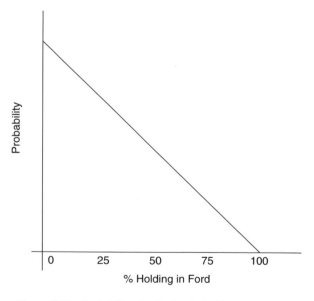

Figure 7.18   *Probability distribution for holding size in Ford*

The question we ask is: if I have three assets in a problem, with the minimal constraints, and I have a fair sample from my solution space how many port-folios will I have with holdings in asset 'A' of between 0 and 10, how many between 11 and 20 etc.? In short, what is the asset holding distribution?

As discussed above the solution space for a three asset problem with the default constraints is a equilateral triangle in three dimensions (Figure 7.15).

Figure 7.16 shows this solution space with a sub-set of equally distributed random points for clarity.

We now collapse those points onto the 'Ford' axis, through the other two dimensions. Figure 7.16, shows the first collapse and the arrows in Figure 7.17 the second.

The probability distribution for holding size in Ford is shown in Figure 7.18.

7.11 APPENDIX 2: PROBABILITY DISTRIBUTION OF HOLDING WEIGHT IN MONTE CARLO PORTFOLIOS IN N DIMENSIONS WITH MINIMAL CONSTRAINTS

This is a generalization of the three dimensional example in Appendix 1.

From Appendix 1 the total area of the search space with three assets is $\frac{1}{2}\sqrt{(3)}$.

If the minimum holding of an asset is r, then the area of the search space containing the portfolios with a weight of that of r or more is

$$\frac{1}{2}(1 - r)^2 \sqrt{(3)}$$

The probability of a portfolio having this asset with a weight of r or more is the ratio of these two areas:

$$P(x > r) = (1 - r)^2$$

We can extend this to calculate the probability of a portfolio holding being between r_1 and r_2 for a specified asset:

$$P(r_1 < x < r_2) = (1 - r_1)^2 - (1 - r_2)^2 \tag{7.6}$$

We can extend the above analysis into any number of dimensions, by noting that area of

$$x > r = k(1 - r)^{n-1}$$

Therefore by the argument above

$$P(x > r) = (1 - r)^{n-1} \tag{7.7}$$

And as before the probability of a holding being between two weights r_1 and r_2 is

$$P(r_1 < x < r_2) = (1 - r_1)^{n-1} - (1 - r_2)^{n-1} \tag{7.8}$$

7.12 APPENDIX 3: THE EFFECTS OF SIMPLE HOLDING CONSTRAINTS ON EXPECTED DISTRIBUTION OF ASSET HOLDING WEIGHTS

This is really a disguised question, the underlying issue being how do asset holding constraints change the shape of the solution space as it is the shape of the solution space that dictates the distribution of asset holdings?

The addition of constraints will either remove part of the solution space, or if that constraint is dominated, leave it unchanged. Application of number of constraints can dramatically alter the shape of the solution space, although as all the constraints are linear its boundary always remains convex.

An example of how dramatic a change in the expected distribution of holding weights it is possible to achieve even in the simple case of three assets is presented in Figure 7.19. Let us take the example in Appendix 1, and alter the default constraints (all three assets held between 0–100%) to all three assets held between 0–50%, a seemingly minor change.

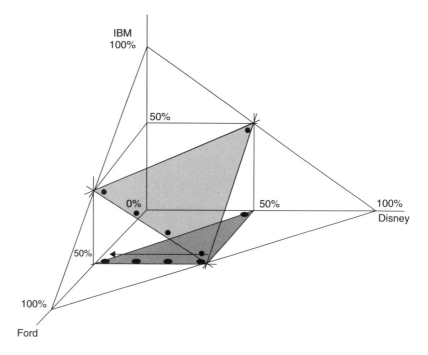

Figure 7.19 *Solution space, three assets, altered default constraints*

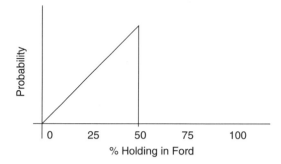

Figure 7.20 *Altered probability distribution for holding size in Ford*

But from Figure 7.19 we can see that the solution space is significantly smaller (light shaded). Its projection onto two dimensions is shaded darker. Note the number of portfolios we lose. The probability distribution this gives us is shown in Figure 7.20.

Previously (see Appendix 1) the closer to zero holding in an asset the more likely it became. Now, however, holdings closer to 50% are more likely, with the distribution falling off as the holding approaches 0%.

Adding constraints to the minimal case creates holding distributions that are surprisingly complex, particularly as the number of dimensions grows. For example, the four assets problem with no asset held more than 50% is very different to the three-dimension example above. It is symmetrical and there are no linear parts to the distribution function, but four quadric curves.

7.13 APPENDIX 4: PROPERTIES OF HYPER-SOLIDS

In general, the n-content (volume) of an n-dimensional hyper-sphere is:

$$\text{if } n \text{ is even}: (1/(n/2)!)\pi^{(n/2)}r^n \tag{7.9}$$

$$\text{if } n \text{ is odd}: ((2^{((n+1)/2)})/(n!!))\pi^{((n-1)/2)}r^n \tag{7.10}$$

Finding random points on the surface of a hyper-sphere can be done by finding a 'random' solution to:

$$n_1^2 + n_2^2 \ldots n_n^2 = R^2$$

where R is the radius of the sphere.

The visualization and understanding of hyper-solids helps in the understanding of the complexity of, say, a 40-dimension problem. The solution space of the minimal constraints is a hyper-simplex, see Anderson 'The Simplex – Minimal

Higher Dimensional Structures' for visualizations and a description of the complexity.

REFERENCES

Anderson, D. (1999) The Simplex – Minimal Higher Dimensional Structures http://w3.one.net/~monkey/mathematics/simplex/.

Allen, D.E. and Tan, M.L. (1998) A Test of the Persistence in the Performance of UK Managed Investment Funds, Edith Cowen University (Australia), Working Paper 98.12 (ISBN 0-7298-0426-7).

Brown, S.J. and Goetzmann, W.N. (1995), Performance Persistence, *Journal of Finance*, **50**, June, 679–98.

Crosier, R.B. (1986) The Geometry of Constrained mixture experiments, *Technometrics*, **28**, 95–102.

Grinblatt, M. and Titman, S. (1992) Persistence of Mutual Fund performance, *Journal of Finance*, **47**, (Dec) 1977–84.

Le Lionnais, F. (1983) *Les Nombres Remarquables*, Hermann, Paris, 58.

May, J.H. and Smith R.L. (1982) Random polytopes: their definition, generation and aggregate properties, *Mathematical Programming*, **24**, 39–54.

Muirhead, R. (1983) *Multivariate Analyses*, Wiley.

Rubin, P.A. (1984) Generating random points in a polytope, *Communications in Statistics Sections Simulation and Computation*, **13**, 375–96.

Rubin, P.A. (1985) Short-run Characteristics of Samples Drawn by Random Walks, *Communications in Statistics – Simulation*, **14**, 473–90.

NOTES

1. The space is defined as all the combinations of weights that all the assets in the investable universe can be held in. The solution space is all those combinations allowed by the constraints. So in this context 'space' is holding (% weight) space, and is flat. It is possible to conceive of other 'spaces' that are not flat that one may wish to have a uniform distribution over e.g. tracking error.

2. If the portfolio generation algorithm was perfect, than on average the entire solution space would saturate at the same time (for any given local density). However, as it is not we will have areas that saturate too early. Allowing a high number of failure gives the other areas time to 'catch up'. Whilst they are catching up the rejection of portfolios in areas of high local density prevents these areas from over saturating.

3. A sub-vertex can be thought of as a corner (meeting point of (hyper)surfaces of the solution space), of any dimensionality less than the full $(n - 1)$ required for a true vertex.

4. This can be shown for two and three dimensions. However it is unclear what happens when the number of dimensions passes five (the hyper-volumetric maxima) and seven (the hyper-surface maxima). (Le Lionnais, 1983).

Chapter 8

Modelling directional hedge funds – mean, variance and correlation with tracker funds

EMMANUEL ACAR

ABSTRACT

Many hedge fund managers use some kind of systematic approach to actively trade the markets. Modelling the returns generated by these dynamic strategies requires allowing for market inefficiencies. The first two moments, expected value and variance are derived analytically for a general class of trading rules with potential forecasting ability. The correlation coefficient between the active program and a tracker fund is subsequently derived allowing for mean-variance allocation. The use of theoretical formulae improves the accuracy of the parameter's estimates. Furthermore, this permits the construction of ex-ante optimal portfolios. When the underlying market shows a positive drift and the goal is to maximize the return-to-risk ratio on the investment, a portfolio including both a tracker fund and a long/short strategy will be superior to both investments considered separately. The forecasting model used to time the derivatives markets will have to take into account the tracker fund it is associated to if the goal is to provide the highest return-to-risk ratio. Finally, we provide an empirical application in the currency markets. We show how two popular overlay strategies can be added to a benchmark and how theoretical modelling can be used.

8.1 INTRODUCTION

Alternative investment has grown in popularity over the past few years. The main reason being the decline in stock markets and the lack of correlation between hedge fund returns and major indices. Still, theoretical work on hedge funds is at its infancy. The academic research can be roughly split into two areas. The first category studies the historical track records generated by these managers and attempts to replicate their performance using popular strategies. The fact is that many hedge fund managers base their trading decisions on models. They often receive the label of 'systematic' managers. Therefore it is not unreasonable to think that their returns can be replicated or at least explained by basic market factors. These studies are informative because they provide a better understanding of the trading process followed by hedge fund managers. In the Futures markets, trend-following indicators are especially used. However the range of explanatory factors is much wider in other markets and the reader is referred to Schneeweis and Spurgin (1998), Fung and Hsieh (2001), Mitchell and Pulvino (2001) and Martin (2001) for an in-depth analysis of hedge fund strategies. The second category of research concentrates on establishing the return distributions of dynamic strategies. Directional trading rules are typical examples of techniques affecting the distribution of return (Acar and Satchell, 1998). Extension of this work and its relevancy to hedge fund management has been investigated by Lundin and Satchell (2000). Generalization to active fund management and relative returns has been recently formulated in Hwang and Satchell (2001). Most of these studies use the assumption of no forecasting ability to achieve analytical developments. These results are useful because they provide the statistical means to build random walk tests, or value-at-risk estimators. Our goal is here to combine both parties, that is to reconcile empirical observations with analytical formulae. Modelling the returns generated by directional strategies, especially their expected value, requires allowing for market inefficiencies. More specifically, Section 8.2 establishes the first two moments of the returns generated by the directional predictor allowing for forecasting ability. Our theoretical work draws from Acar (1998) but generalizes the findings to a much broader class of active strategies including long/short, short only, long only and asymmetrical positioning. Section 8.3 studies the effect of combining a tracker fund with a hedge fund. Section 8.4 performs some Monte Carlo simulations to compare the efficiency of estimating mean-variance and correlation of hedge fund returns either directly or using our formulae. Section 8.5 discusses the issue of optimal allocation when the goal is to maximize the return-to-risk ratio of the portfolio. Finally, Section 8.6 provides an empirical application in the currency markets. We show how two popular overlay strategies can be added to a benchmark and how theoretical modelling can be used.

8.2   MEAN AND VARIANCE OF DIRECTIONAL STRATEGIES

Let us consider a money manager trading an underlying asset whose returns are denoted X. To generate his position, the trader uses a forecasting technique to predict the sign of the forthcoming returns. The forecast F decides if the asset is to be bought or sold. We study here the general trading process where units in quantity a are held when the forecast is positive and units in quantity b are hold when the forecast is negative. A rationale rule consists in buying the asset ($a \geq 0$) when the forecast is positive and selling the asset ($b \leq 0$) when the forecast is negative. However it could be that the strategy is constrained to be long only and that $a > b \geq 0$. To consider the most general case, we do not put any restrictions on the parameters a and b and the formulae developed in this section are also valid for any values of a and b including $a < b$ or $b = 0$. This is a significant generalization of Acar (1998) and Skouras (2001) who only consider symmetrical long/short strategies of the form $a = -b = 1$. The returns generated by the forecasting rule are denoted H. That is:

$$H = \begin{cases} aX & \text{if } F > 0 \\ bX & \text{if } F < 0 \end{cases} \tag{8.1}$$

The case $F = 0$ is considered of zero possibility.

The forecasting technique could be a technical indicator, an auto-regressive predictor or an exogenous variable. Two examples in the currency markets would be moving averages and interest rate differential (See Section 8.6 for further details). Here, we assume that the joint distribution of the underlying returns X and the forecast F is a bivariate normal distribution denoted by:

$$\begin{bmatrix} X \\ F \end{bmatrix} \sim N \left(\begin{bmatrix} \mu_x \\ \mu_f \end{bmatrix}, \begin{bmatrix} \sigma_x^2 & \rho_{xf}\sigma_x\sigma_f \\ \rho_{xf}\sigma_x\sigma_f & \sigma_f^2 \end{bmatrix} \right)$$

The random walk hypothesis would imply that there cannot be any correlation between the forecast and the forthcoming market returns. That is $\rho_{xf} = 0$. Appendix 1 demonstrates that under the assumption that the underlying market and the forecast follow a bivariate distribution, the directional strategy has for first two moments:

$$E(H) = \mu_x \left[a\Phi\left(\frac{\mu_f}{\sigma_f}\right) + b\Phi\left(-\frac{\mu_f}{\sigma_f}\right) \right] + \sigma_x \frac{(a-b)}{\sqrt{2\pi}} \rho_{xf} \exp\left(-0.5\frac{\mu_f^2}{\sigma_f^2}\right) \tag{8.2}$$

$$E(H^2) = \mu_x^2 \left[a^2\Phi\left(\frac{\mu_f}{\sigma_f}\right) + b^2\Phi\left(-\frac{\mu_f}{\sigma_f}\right) \right] + 2\mu_x\sigma_x \frac{(a^2-b^2)}{\sqrt{2\pi}} \rho_{xf} \exp\left(-0.5\frac{\mu_f^2}{\sigma_f^2}\right)$$

$$+ \sigma_x^2 \left[a^2 \left(\frac{\rho_{xf}^2}{\sqrt{2\pi}}\left(-\frac{\mu_f}{\sigma_f}\right) \exp\left(-0.5\frac{\mu_f^2}{\sigma_f^2}\right) + \Phi\left(\frac{\mu_f}{\sigma_f}\right) \right) \right.$$

$$\left. + b^2 \left(\frac{\rho_{xf}^2}{\sqrt{2\pi}}\left(\frac{\mu_f}{\sigma_f}\right) \exp\left(-0.5\frac{\mu_f^2}{\sigma_f^2}\right) + \Phi\left(-\frac{\mu_f}{\sigma_f}\right) \right) \right] \tag{8.3}$$

where Φ is the cumulative function of a normal distribution $N(0,1)$.

The variance is simply given by the relationship $\text{Var}(H) = E(H^2) - (E(H))^2$ and the standard deviation $\text{Std}(H) = \sqrt{\text{Var}(H)}$.

Equation (8.2) may explain some of the empirical results observed by Schneeweis and Spurgin (1998). They find that Commodity Trading Advisors, (CTAs) returns are positively correlated to factors such as market trends and currency movements, while hedge fund and mutual fund returns are best explained by the return to a buy and hold strategy in the markets the fund invests in. On the one hand, CTAs usually trade the futures markets, which over long period of time exhibit small drift. The profit generated by active programs has got to come therefore from the second block in Equation (8.2), the product of the market volatility with the correlation coefficient between forecast and future moves. On the other hand, in markets exhibiting strong drift, the first term in Equation (8.2) is more likely to be the dominant factor.

Higher moments of the hedge fund returns also accept exact analytical formulae. They are not reproduced here for length purpose but the interested reader is referred to Kotz et al. (2000: p. 315) or Chou and Owen (1984) who develop the explicit formulas for the cumulants of a variable of the bivariate normal distribution when the other variable is truncated below. These values are useful for obtaining, via the Cornish–Fisher expansion, approximation to percentage points of the hedge fund returns. An inspection of the cumulants (Kotz et al., 2000, p. 315) shows that the correlation coefficient between forecast and market significantly affects the mean of the hedge fund return, but its effect on higher moment decreases rapidly. This effect is particularly pronounced in Finance since the correlation coefficient is very unlikely to exceed 0.3. The amounts of skewness and kurtosis will be mostly a function of the trading units, the parameters a and b rather than the correlation coefficient between forecast and market. The less symmetrical the strategy, the bigger the magnitude of the skewness and kurtosis coefficients. In particular, 'polar' strategies ($a = 1, b = 0$ or $a = 0, b = -1$) are likely to generate returns deviating significantly from a normal distribution simply because of the abnormally large number of zero observations.

8.3 CORRELATION WITH TRACKER FUND

So far we have only considered systematic programs as an asset class in isolation of any other investment. In practice, directional hedge funds do not purely and simply replace traditional investments but complement them to form a fully diversified portfolio. Indeed, an interesting approach already adopted by a few large institutions, is to construct a portfolio including both a tracker fund and a hedge fund. The inclusion of hedge funds in a portfolio can potentially result in better risk-return tradeoffs due to the low correlation between hedge fund returns and the returns on the traditional asset classes like equities or bonds (Fung and Hsieh, 1997). However to realize an effective allocation between a tracker fund and a hedge fund, a crucial parameter is needed, the correlation coefficient between the two investments. As pointed out in Schneeweis and Spurgin (2000), it is important to realize that while hedge fund managers do not emphasize benchmark tracking this does not mean that their entire return is based solely on manager skill or is independent of the movement of underlying stock, bond or currency markets. The correlation coefficient with the tracker is clearly going to be negative for short only fund and positive for long only funds, whereas it may be closer to zero for market neutral hedge funds. It is notoriously difficult to estimate the correlation coefficient between hedge funds and benchmarks from historical returns. Previous research has identified a tendency for hedge fund and managed futures strategies to exhibit non-constant correlation with the US equity market. Schneeweis and Spurgin (1998) observed that many market-neutral strategies exhibit higher correlation with stock and bond benchmarks during the market declines, and lower correlation during rallies. Schneeweis and Spurgin (2001) outlines a simple econometric method of estimating changes in correlation from historical returns. Indeed, a precise quantification of the correlation coefficient is key for use in the asset allocation decision. A complementary approach is to establish the theoretical correlation coefficient. This can be achieved when the hedge fund trading process is modelled by Equation (8.1). We simply need to incorporate the tracker fund in our modelling process. Here, we explicitly assume that the joint distribution of the underlying returns X, the forecast F and the tracker fund T is a trivariate normal distribution denoted by:

$$\begin{bmatrix} X \\ F \\ T \end{bmatrix} \sim N \left(\begin{bmatrix} \mu_x \\ \mu_f \\ \mu_t \end{bmatrix}, \begin{bmatrix} \sigma_x^2 & \rho_{xf}\sigma_x\sigma_f & \rho_{xt}\sigma_x\sigma_t \\ \rho_{xf}\sigma_x\sigma_f & \sigma_f^2 & \rho_{ft}\sigma_f\sigma_t \\ \rho_{xt}\sigma_x\sigma_t & \rho_{ft}\sigma_f\sigma_t & \sigma_t^2 \end{bmatrix} \right)$$

The hedge fund returns H and the tracker fund T will not follow a bivariate normal distribution. However for mean variance allocation purposes, it is still important to assess the correlation coefficient between the tracker fund and the hedge fund Corr(T,H) which is the only parameter missing at this stage. The basic idea is that the covariance between the two variables can be deduced from the variance of the portfolio including both the tracker fund and the hedge fund. Let us note the portfolio $P = T + H$, $\delta_f = \mu_f/\sigma_f$ the return to risk ratio of the forecast and

$$g[\mu_x, \sigma_x^2, \delta_f, \rho_{xf}] = \mu_x^2 \Phi(\delta_f) + 2\mu_x\sigma_x \frac{\rho_{xf}}{\sqrt{2\pi}} \exp\left(-\frac{\delta_f^2}{2}\right)$$

$$+ \sigma_x^2 \left(\frac{-\rho_{xf}^2}{\sqrt{2\pi}} \delta_f \exp\left(-\frac{\delta_f^2}{2}\right) + \Phi(\delta_f) \right)$$

Appendix 2 shows that:

$$E(P) = \mu_t + E(H)$$

$$E(P^2) = g\left[\mu_t + a\mu_x, \sigma_t^2 + a^2\sigma_x^2\right.$$

$$\left. + 2a\rho_{xt}\sigma_t\sigma_x, \delta_f, \frac{\rho_{ft}\sigma_t + a\rho_{xf}\sigma_x}{\sqrt{\sigma_t^2 + a^2\sigma_x^2 + 2a\rho_{xt}}}\right]$$

$$+ g\left[\mu_t + b\mu_x, \sigma_t^2 + b^2\sigma_x^2 + 2b\rho_{xt}\sigma_t\sigma_x, -\delta_f,\right.$$

$$\left. -\left(\frac{\rho_{ft}\sigma_t + b\rho_{xf}\sigma_x}{\sqrt{\sigma_t^2 + b^2\sigma_x^2 + 2b\rho_{xt}}}\right)\right]$$

$$\text{Var}(P) = E(P^2) - (E(P))^2$$

$$\text{and Corr}(T,H) = \frac{\text{Var}(P) - \sigma_t^2 - \text{Var}(H)}{2\sigma_t\sqrt{\text{Var}(H)}} \tag{8.4}$$

It can be shown by developing (8.4) that the correlation coefficient between the tracker and the hedge fund will be equal to zero irrespective of the values of ρ_{xt}, ρ_{ft}, and ρ_{xf} when the following three conditions are met. Firstly, the underlying actively traded market X has zero mean $\mu_x = 0$. Secondly, the forecast has zero mean $\mu_f = \delta_f = 0$. Lastly, the trading process is long/short in equal quantities $b = -a$. This implies that we can think of combining a cash index fund with a derivatives program trading exclusively the index futures contracts. If the mean of the index futures contracts is zero as well as the mean of the forecast, then the correlation coefficient between the cash index and the short/long futures program will be zero. This intuitive result may not hold as soon as the market drift is different from zero or the strategy is not long/short in equal quantity ($b \neq -a$) and/or probability ($\mu_f \neq 0$).

8.4   PARAMETERS ESTIMATION

The benefit of a theoretical formula to estimate the hedge fund mean, variance and correlation with other asset classes is primarily in the improved understanding of the market conditions required for out-performance. Sensitivity analysis is rendered possible. Here we want to make a further point that by using theoretical formulae better estimates of mean, variance and correlation may be achieved. If we think of short-only hedge funds, active positioning may be infrequent and if we only have access to the hedge funds returns we may have very few observations. On the other hand, studying the forecasting strategy and its relation to the underlying market may be more valuable since this is similar to observing a distribution before truncation. Let us take the example of a normal random walk with no drift for all the variables, the underlying market, forecast and tracker fund. We further assume zero correlations between all the variables:

$$\begin{bmatrix} X \\ F \\ T \end{bmatrix} \sim N \left(\begin{bmatrix} 0 \\ 0 \\ 0 \end{bmatrix}, \begin{bmatrix} 1 & 0 & 0 \\ 0 & 1 & 0 \\ 0 & 0 & 1 \end{bmatrix} \right)$$

Of course the hedge fund will have zero expected value $E(H) = 0$ and variance $\text{Var}(H) = 0.5(a^2 + b^2)$. An informative experimentation is to use Monte-Carlo simulation to compare the estimates of the hedge fund moments either provided directly using the empirical observations for H or implied by the joint distribution of $[X, F, T]$. Measurement errors will affect both methodologies but the use of theoretical formulae may exacerbate or decrease those. Since very few hedge funds have more than ten years' track records of monthly returns, series of 36, 60 and 120 observations were simulated ten thousand times for two sets of strategies, long/short with equal quantity $a = -b = 1$ and short only strategies $a = 0, b = -1$.

For long/short strategies (Table 8.1), the use of analytical formulae only marginally improves the estimations of the mean and standard deviation. However the correlation coefficient between the tracker and the hedge fund converges towards its expected value of zero much more quickly as seen by a smaller range maximum minus minimum. For short only strategies (Table 8.2), the estimations implied from the joint distribution of X, F and T are more accurate than row observations for both the standard deviation of hedge fund returns and its correlation with the tracker fund. However the magnitude of improvement is reduced.

8.5 OPTIMAL ALLOCATION

Let us consider an investor holding a tracker fund and willing to add a hedge fund to its portfolio. His resulting portfolio will be $P = T + wH$. The weight w to be given to the hedge fund depends on the investor utility function. This section considers that the investor is willing to maximize his return divided standard deviation ratio $SR(P) = E(P)/\sqrt{\text{Var}(P)}$, the optimal weight w^* can be derived for given directional strategies using the steps similar to Elton et al. (1987). The results of the previous section can be used to establish $\mu_h = E(H), \sigma_h = \sqrt{\text{Var}(H)}$, and $\rho_{th} = \text{Corr}(T, H)$.

Table 8.1 *Long/short strategies*

	Observed from (H,T)			Implied from (X,F,T)		
	$E(H)$	$\text{Std}(H)$	$\text{Corr}(T,H)$	$E(H)$	$\text{Std}(H)$	$\text{Corr}(T,H)$
36 months						
Average	0.0027	0.9923	0.0007	0.0007	0.9972	0.0001
Standard deviation	0.1664	0.1197	0.1678	0.1339	0.1194	0.0312
Minimum	−0.7072	0.5525	−0.5699	−0.5761	0.5643	−0.1636
Maximum	0.6833	1.4890	0.5807	0.4775	1.4972	0.1747
60 months						
Average	−0.0013	0.9956	0.0001	−0.0010	0.9984	0.0000
Standard deviation	0.1275	0.0905	0.1307	0.1030	0.0904	0.0186
Minimum	−0.4794	0.5962	−0.4944	−0.4183	0.5973	−0.1205
Maximum	0.4792	1.3347	0.4421	0.3883	1.3450	0.1290
120 months						
Average	−0.0003	0.9987	−0.0004	−0.0006	1.0002	0.0000
Standard deviation	0.0911	0.0648	0.0910	0.0732	0.0647	0.0093
Minimum	−0.3492	0.7748	−0.3506	−0.2743	0.7757	−0.0511
Maximum	0.3395	1.2595	0.3402	0.3029	1.2602	0.0486

Table 8.2 *Short-only strategies*

	Observed from (H,T)			Implied from (X,F,T)		
	$E(H)$	$\text{Std}(H)$	$\text{Corr}(T,H)$	$E(H)$	$\text{Std}(H)$	$\text{Corr}(T,H)$
36 months						
Average	0.0007	0.6951	−0.0011	0.0009	0.7019	−0.0017
Standard Deviation	0.1169	0.1327	0.1692	0.1068	0.0960	0.1193
Minimum	−0.3855	0.2312	−0.5991	−0.3711	0.3751	−0.4396
Maximum	0.4075	1.1755	0.5997	0.4162	1.1104	0.4271
60 months						
Average	−0.0004	0.6999	0.0006	−0.0001	0.7043	0.0005
Standard Deviation	0.0911	0.1018	0.1287	0.0821	0.0737	0.0914
Minimum	−0.3597	0.3576	−0.4539	−0.3566	0.4586	−0.3316
Maximum	0.3403	1.0913	0.4897	0.3241	1.0041	0.3352
120 months						
Average	−0.0003	0.7048	−0.0005	−0.0004	0.7066	−0.0007
Standard Deviation	0.0648	0.0716	0.0918	0.0589	0.0521	0.0656
Minimum	−0.3161	0.3959	−0.3215	−0.2673	0.5124	−0.2550
Maximum	0.2680	0.9683	0.3710	0.2345	0.9344	0.2441

Under the assumptions that:

$$\left(\frac{\mu_h}{\sigma_h}\right) > \left(\frac{\mu_t}{\sigma_t}\right)\rho_{th} \text{ and } \left(\frac{\mu_t}{\sigma_t}\right) > \left(\frac{\mu_h}{\sigma_h}\right)\rho_{th},\ w^* = \frac{\left(\dfrac{\mu_h}{\sigma_h}\right) - \left(\dfrac{\mu_t}{\sigma_t}\right)\rho_{th}}{\left(\dfrac{\mu_t}{\sigma_t}\right) - \left(\dfrac{\mu_h}{\sigma_h}\right)\rho_{th}}\frac{\sigma_t}{\sigma_h}$$

(8.5)

The optimal weight may be larger than one, but since the allocation is made to a hedge fund, this would mean increasing the leverage used by the hedge fund manager. This is often possible given that the latter trades the derivatives markets.

An interesting question is to know if an actively managed fund is preferable to the combination of a tracker fund and a hedge fund or vice-versa. Indeed, it could be claimed that an actively managed fund can always be decomposed as the sum of a tracker fund and a hedge fund. The benefit generated by such decomposition is that it allows the asset allocator and/or investor to adjust the weightings between passive and active management. In the most general case, the number of degrees of freedom to build the trading rule is too large to bring a definite conclusion. However some comparison can be investigated analytically if we restrict ourselves to long/short strategies in equal quantity $a = -b = 1$. Let us consider an index returns X with positive mean μ_x, and standard deviation σ_x. We assume that there exists a futures market, X^* which differs from the underlying market only by the long-term drift. We do not suppose the existence of any risk premium. That is $X^* = X - \mu_x$. The question is which of the two portfolios produces the highest return to risk ratio, an actively managed fund on the index itself or a portfolio including the index and an actively managed index futures program. Let us establish the corresponding maximum returns–to–risk ratios for both investments.

8.5.1 Optimal long/short fund on the index itself X

Our long/short strategy is defined by:
$$H = \begin{cases} X & \text{if } F > 0 \\ -X & \text{if } F < 0 \end{cases}$$ where F is a forecast used to predict the index market X.

It is worthwhile noting that in this case $E(H^2) = E(X^2) = \mu_x^2 + \sigma_x^2$ and $\text{Var}(H) = \mu_x^2 + \sigma_x^2 - E(H)^2$. As a consequence, the forecast that maximizes returns will also minimize variance[1]. Acar (1998) shows that such a forecast needs to maximize ρ_{xf} and satisfies the equation $\dfrac{\mu_f}{\sigma_f} = \dfrac{\mu_x}{\sigma_x \rho_{xf}}$. If we denote H_{max} the returns derived by the optimal predictor, we obtain from Equation (8.1):

$$E(H_{max}) = \mu_x \left[1 - 2\Phi \left(-\frac{\mu_x}{\sigma_x \rho_{xf}} \right) \right] + \sigma_x \sqrt{\frac{2}{\pi}} \rho_{xf} \exp \left(-0.5 \frac{\mu_x^2}{\sigma_x^2 \rho_{xf}^2} \right)$$

$$SR(H_{max}) = \frac{E(H_{max})}{\sqrt{\mu_x^2 + \sigma_x^2 - E(H_{max})^2}}$$

It can be noted that $SR(H)_{\max}$ is an only function of the return to risk ratio $\delta_x = \mu_x/\sigma_x$ and ρ_{xf}.

$$SR(H_{\max}) = \frac{\delta_x\left[1 - 2\Phi\left(-\dfrac{\delta_x}{\rho_{xf}}\right)\right] + \sqrt{\dfrac{2}{\pi}}\rho_{xf}\exp\left(-0.5\dfrac{\delta_x^2}{\rho_{xf}^2}\right)}{\sqrt{\delta_x^2 + 1 - \left(\delta_x\left[1 - 2\Phi\left(-\dfrac{\delta_x}{\rho_{xf}}\right)\right] + \sqrt{\dfrac{2}{\pi}}\rho_{xf}\exp\left(-0.5\dfrac{\delta_x^2}{\rho_{xf}^2}\right)\right)^2}}$$

Figure 8.1 plots the maximum return-to-risk ratio generated by the directional forecast as a function of the return-to-risk ratio of the underlying market and the correlation between the forecast and the cash index market. When there is little correlation, the market timing ability is low and the optimal strategy is close from Buy and Hold. However the presence of positive correlation between forecast and the underlying market permits the directional hedge fund to exhibit a superior return-to-risk ratio. It is worthwhile noting that the excess returns are larger, the lower the drift in the cash market. In other words, fund managers have an incentive to trade a zero drift market when they are evaluated in terms of relative performance against a Buy and Hold benchmark.

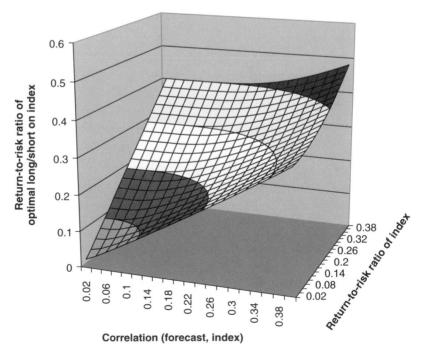

Figure 8.1 *Maximum return-to-risk ratio of optimal long/short strategy*

8.5.2 Optimal allocation between an index and the maximum return long/short futures fund

Before investigating the general portfolio of an index fund with a managed futures program, we consider first the case of a separate futures program. This means that the manager seeks to maximize first the return on the futures contract and does not take into consideration the fact that his trading may not be optimal when combined to an index fund. This is very often the case in practice. Hedge fund managers design vehicles, which have for goals to maximize risk-adjusted returns on a stand-alone basis. No hedge fund manager will modify their strategies as a function of the index fund they may be added to.

$$P = X + wH^* \text{ and } H^* = \left\{ \begin{array}{ll} X^* & \text{if } F > 0 \\ -X^* & \text{if } F < 0 \end{array} \right\}$$

where F is the forecast used to predict the Futures market X^*.

We have just seen that maximizing the returns on the long/short futures fund requires maximizing the correlation between the forecast and the futures markets (or the index itself) ρ_{xf} and satisfies the equation $\delta_f = \mu_f/\sigma_f = 0$. If we denote H^*_{max} the returns derived by the optimal predictor on the driftless futures markets, we obtain from Equation (8.2):

$$E(H^*_{\text{max}}) = \sigma_x \sqrt{\frac{2}{\pi}} \rho_{xf} \text{ and } \text{Var}(H^*_{\text{max}}) = \sigma_x^2 \left(1 - \frac{2}{\pi} \rho_{xf}^2 \right)$$

We also know from Section 8.3 that for long/short strategies in a driftless market $\text{Cov}(H^*_{\text{max}}, X^*) = \text{Cov}(H^*_{\text{max}}, X) = 0$.

The second step is to allocate the optimal weight w between tracker and hedge fund given by (8.5).

$$\tilde{w} = \frac{\sigma_x}{\mu_x} \frac{\sqrt{\frac{2}{\pi}} \rho_{xf}}{\left(1 - \frac{2}{\pi} \rho_{xf}^2 \right)}$$

Simple algebra provided in Appendix 3 shows that:

$$SR(P) = \frac{\delta_x^2 + \frac{2}{\pi} \rho_{xf}^2}{\sqrt{1 - \frac{2}{\pi} \rho_{xf}^2} \sqrt{\delta_x^2 + \frac{2}{\pi} \rho_{xf}^2 (1 - \delta_x^2)}}$$

It can be noted once more that $SR(P)$ is an only function of the return to risk ratio δ_x and ρ_{xf}. Figure 8.2 plots the return-to-risk ratio generated by

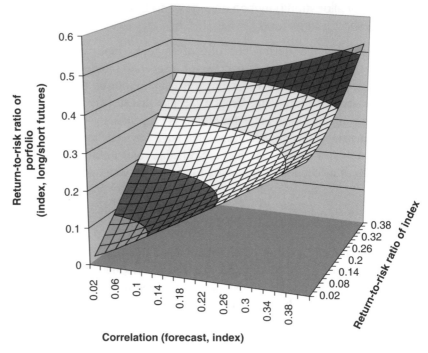

Figure 8.2   *Maximum return-to-risk ratio of optimal portfolio including the index and the long/short strategy maximizing returns on the futures markets*

the optimal combination of the tracker and the directional forecast maximizing return on the derivatives, as a function of the return-to-risk ratio of the underlying market and the correlation between the forecast and the forthcoming market returns.

Figure 8.3 specifies the weight actually given to the futures fund. Small values of the index fund tend to generate extremely large values on the derivatives position. They are not therefore being represented. As anticipated, the bigger the forecasting ability as measured by the correlation coefficient the bigger the allocation to the futures fund. This effect increases as the mean of the index fund decreases.

A close examination of the mathematical formulae would suggest that for $\rho_{xf} > 0, \delta_x > 0, SR(P) > SR(H_{max})$. The differences are the biggest when the drift and correlation coefficient are the highest. The maximum improvement is in the order of 0.05. This has important consequences since this suggests that going long/short in equal quantities (but not necessarily in equal probability) in a market with drift will be sub-optimal to combining a passive position and an active long/short program in the driftless market.

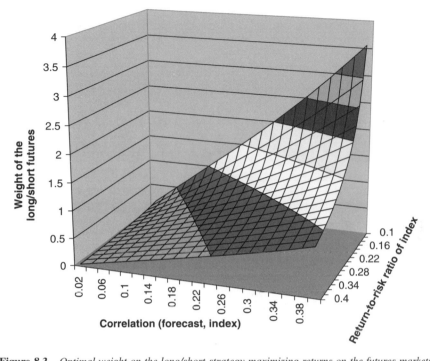

Figure 8.3 *Optimal weight on the long/short strategy maximizing returns on the futures markets within a portfolio including the index*

8.5.3 Optimal allocation between an index and a long/short futures fund

The reader should bear in mind that the previous portfolio had been constructed to first maximize the returns on the futures market. The derivatives program was then given the weight maximizing the return-to-risk ratio of a portfolio also including the cash market. This two separate steps process does not guarantee the reach of a global maximum. A joint study of the forecasting strategy and weight is necessary. Let us establish ratio $SR(P) = E(P)/\sqrt{\text{Var}(P)}$ in its most general form.

$$P = X + wH^* \text{ and } H^* = \begin{cases} X^* & \text{if } F > 0 \\ -X^* & \text{if } F < 0 \end{cases}$$

$$E(P) = \mu_x + wE(H^*), \quad \text{Var}(P) = \sigma_x^2 + w^2\text{Var}(H^*) + 2w\text{Cov}(H^*, X)$$

If we note $\delta_f = \mu_f/\sigma_f$, we know using (8.2), (8.3) and (8.4) that

$$E(H^*) = \sigma_x\sqrt{\frac{2}{\pi}}\rho_{xf}\exp(-0.5\delta_f^2), \quad E(H^{*2}) = \sigma_x^2$$

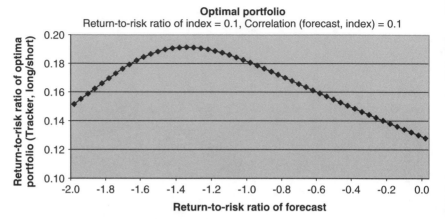

Figure 8.4   *Maximum return-to-risk ratio of optimal portfolio including the index and a long/short strategy as a function of the return-to-risk of the forecast when the return-to-risk ratio of the index = 0.1 and the correlation (forecast, index) = 0.1*

$$\text{Cov}(H^*, X) = \sigma_x^2 \left(-2\delta_f \sqrt{\frac{2}{\pi}} \rho_{xf}^2 \exp(-0.5\delta_f^2) + 4(\Phi(\delta_f) - 0.5) \right)$$

The function $\text{Cov}(H^*, X)$ is an increasing of δ_f irrespective of the value of the correlation ρ_{xf}. This is negative for $\delta_f < 0$, equal to zero when $\delta_f = 0$ and positive when $\delta_f > 0$. Let us only consider the case where both the index and the futures fund have positive expected value. That is $\delta_x > 0$ and $\rho_{xf} > 0$. The case $\delta_f > 0$ cannot lead to a maximum return to risk ratio for the all portfolio. Having $\delta_f > 0$ generates lower expected value on the futures fund than having $\delta_f = 0$ and higher correlation with the index. On the other hand, $\delta_f < 0$ may lead to a global maximum. Having $\delta_f < 0$ again generates lower expected value on the futures fund than having $\delta_f = 0$.

However, this time the correlation with the index is negative and it could be that the risk reduction compensates the decrease in returns. Injecting these results in Equation (8.5) suggests that the optimal weight will be an only function of δ_x, δ_f and ρ_{xf}. Figure 8.4 charts one example of $SR(P) = E(P)/\sqrt{\text{Var}(P)}$ as a function of δ_f for a given value of $\delta_x = 0.1$ and $\rho_{xf} = 0.1$. The maximum return-to-risk ratio of 0.19 is obtained for δ_f equal to approximately -1.36. This is a considerable improvement to the previous allocation that forced $\delta_f = 0$ and could only achieve a ratio of 0.13. Therefore the benefits of combining tracker and directional hedge funds will be greater if the directional strategy applied to the derivatives markets takes into account the tracker it is combined to[2]. This raises an important issue since in practise it is unlikely that the hedge fund manager will be willing to refine his/her strategy as a function of the asset it is associated to.

8.6   AN EMPIRICAL APPLICATION TO THE CURRENCY MARKETS

This Section investigates the explanatory power of our theoretical modelling. Attention is restricted to the mean, standard deviation of the directional hedge fund as well as its correlation with the tracker fund. For illustrative purposes, we consider a hedge fund trading currency. The underlying markets X is therefore the spot currency appreciation plus the carry in percentage terms over a month. The first forecasting strategy AR1 is based on an autoregressive model of length one. This trend-following strategy simply says buy the currency after a monthly appreciation and sell it after a depreciation. The second strategy FRB is the forward rate bias, formally defined as buy the currency pair if the forthcoming monthly carry is positive and sell it if this is negative. We express the forecasting strategy in terms of carry rather than hedged returns (the opposite) such that the correlation between forecast and forthcoming returns is sought to be positive. Tables 8.3 and 8.4 provide summary statistics respectively on the underlying currency markets X and the forecasting strategies F.

Both strategies have been studied by academics and applied by currency fund managers over the past twenty years. Strange (2001) gives an example of how these trading rules can be applied to hedge the currency exposure of international portfolios. In our first example, the benchmark will be a 50% hedged bond benchmark. We can then add a long/short currency overlay on 50% of the position $a = -b = 0.5$, denoted 0.5 l/s in Table 8.5. The second benchmark will be an unhedged bond benchmark, to which we add a short only currency overlay $a = 0, b = -1$. Our last benchmark will be a fully hedged bond benchmark, to which we add a long only currency overlay $a = 1, b = 0$.

Table 8.3   *Underlying currency markets X, monthly statistics from end May 1987 to end July 2002*

	$/Euro	$/Yen
Mean (X)	0.073%	0.151%
Stdev(X)	3.179%	3.657%

Table 8.4   *Forecasting strategies F*

	$/Euro		$/Yen	
	AR(1)	FRB	AR(1)	FRB
Mean (F)	0.073%	0.025%	0.151%	0.264%
Stdev(F)	3.179%	0.242%	3.657%	0.208%
Corr(F,X)	0.139	0.128	0.019	0.191

Table 8.5   *Directional overlay program H and combination with benchmark T*

	Dollar bond investments from a Euro base						Dollar bond investments in Yen					
	AR(1)			FRB			AR(1)			FRB		
	0.5 l/s	short	long	0.5 l/s	short	long	0.5 l/s	short	long	0.5 l/s	short	long
Mean (H)	0.289%	0.252%	0.325%	0.211%	0.175%	0.248%	0.243%	0.168%	0.319%	0.234%	0.159%	0.310%
From model	0.177%	0.141%	0.214%	0.165%	0.128%	0.201%	0.030%	−0.045%	0.106%	0.184%	0.109%	0.260%
Stdev(H)	1.563%	2.410%	2.032%	1.576%	2.017%	2.439%	1.814%	2.504%	2.645%	1.815%	1.094%	3.475%
From model	1.580%	2.218%	2.264%	1.581%	2.146%	2.334%	1.830%	2.543%	2.630%	1.821%	1.196%	3.448%
Mean(T)	0.675%	0.711%	0.638%	0.675%	0.711%	0.638%	0.474%	0.550%	0.398%	0.474%	0.550%	0.398%
Stdev(T)	1.871%	3.214%	1.315%	1.871%	3.214%	1.315%	2.139%	3.758%	1.308%	2.139%	3.758%	1.308%
Corr(T,X)	0.723	0.915	−0.180	0.723	0.915	−0.180	0.794	0.938	−0.100	0.794	0.938	−0.100
Corr(T,F)	0.052	0.099	−0.095	−0.024	0.049	−0.189	0.013	0.016	−0.006	0.066	0.131	−0.158
Corr(T,H)	−0.072	−0.685	−0.062	−0.191	−0.562	−0.088	0.050	−0.645	−0.066	0.715	−0.231	−0.040
From model	0.014	−0.643	−0.130	0.060	−0.622	−0.134	0.027	−0.652	−0.072	0.629	−0.308	−0.090

Empirically, we analyse a dollar bonds index (SSB all maturities) from two different bases, Euro (Deutschmark prior to 1999) and Yen, over the period end of May 1987 to July 2002. Table 8.5 indicates the monthly returns achieved by the active overlay programs on a stand alone basis, H as well as its correlation with the passive benchmark. Overall, the estimates implied from the joint distribution of (X, F, T) are close to direct observations (Table 8.5), especially the standard deviation of the overlay program as well as the correlation with the benchmark. Expected value derived from the model are lower than observed in the markets suggesting that assuming multivariate normal distributions can only be a first approximation and that further research is needed to model more closely the expected value of directional strategies.

8.7   CONCLUSIONS

Systematic programs are popular among commodity trading advisors and hedge fund managers. A better understanding of directional strategies can be achieved using stochastic modelling. The first two moments, expected value and variance, are derived analytically for a general class of trading rules. The correlation coefficient between the active program and a tracker fund is subsequently derived allowing for mean-variance allocation. When the underlying markets show a positive drift and the goal is to maximize the return to risk ratio on the investment, a portfolio including both a tracker fund and a long/short strategy will be superior to both investments considered separately. The forecasting model used to time the derivatives markets will have to take into account the tracker fund it is associated to if the goal is to provide the highest return-to-risk ratio. An avenue for further research would include the consideration of non-symmetrical directional strategies. Indeed in a market with positive drift, it could well be that an asymmetrical strategy outperforms the combination of tracker fund with an actively managed futures contract. This will involve redefining the risk analytics and going beyond the traditional mean-variance analysis which cannot capture the risk of dynamic strategies such as shorting options or take profits rules.

An empirical application to the currency markets suggests that the theoretical model explains both the standard deviation of returns generated by the active program as well as its correlation with a tracker fund. Expected values are underestimated in sample. These results indicate that assuming multivariate normal distributions can only be a first approximation and that further research is needed.

8.8 APPENDIX 1: MEAN AND VARIANCE OF DIRECTIONAL STRATEGIES

$$H = \begin{Bmatrix} a\,X & \text{if } F > 0 \\ b\,X & \text{if } F < 0 \end{Bmatrix}$$

Let us note the trading signal $B = \begin{Bmatrix} a & \text{if } F > 0 \\ b & \text{if } F < 0 \end{Bmatrix}$

$$H - BX$$

$$\begin{bmatrix} X \\ F \end{bmatrix} \sim N\left(\begin{bmatrix} \mu_x \\ \mu_f \end{bmatrix}, \begin{bmatrix} \sigma_x^2 & \rho_{xf}\sigma_x\sigma_f \\ \rho_{xf}\sigma_x\sigma_f & \sigma_f^2 \end{bmatrix}\right)$$

Let us note $X^* = (X - \mu_x)/\sigma_x$ and $F^* = (F - \mu_f)/\sigma_f$ the standard normalized variables.

$$H = BX = B(\mu_x + \sigma_x X^*) = \mu_x B + \sigma_x B X^*$$

$$E(H) = \mu_x E(B) + \sigma_x E(BX^*)$$

$$E(H) = \mu_x \left[a\Phi\left(\frac{\mu_f}{\sigma_f}\right) + b\Phi\left(-\frac{\mu_f}{\sigma_f}\right) \right] + \sigma_x \left(\int_{X^*} \int_{F^* > -\frac{\mu_f}{\sigma_f}} aX^* \right.$$

$$\left. + \int_{X^*} \int_{F^* < -\frac{\mu_f}{\sigma_f}} bX^* \, \text{prob}(X^*, F^*) \right)$$

Using the results of Kotz et al. (2000, p. 311-2 as well as p. 315) on truncated bivariate distributions

$$E(H) = \mu_x \left[a\Phi\left(\frac{\mu_f}{\sigma_f}\right) + b\Phi\left(-\frac{\mu_f}{\sigma_f}\right) \right] + \sigma_x \left(\frac{a}{\sqrt{2\pi}} \rho_{xf} \exp\left(-0.5\frac{\mu_f^2}{\sigma_f^2}\right) \right.$$

$$\left. - \frac{b}{\sqrt{2\pi}} \rho_{xf} \exp\left(-0.5\frac{\mu_f^2}{\sigma_f^2}\right) \right)$$

$$E(H) = \mu_x \left[a\Phi\left(\frac{\mu_f}{\sigma_f}\right) + b\Phi\left(-\frac{\mu_f}{\sigma_f}\right) \right] + \sigma_x \frac{(a-b)}{\sqrt{2\pi}} \rho_{xf} \exp\left(-0.5\frac{\mu_f^2}{\sigma_f^2}\right)$$

$$H^2 = \mu_x^2 B^2 + 2\mu_x\sigma_x B^2 X^* + \sigma_x^2 B^2 X^{*2}$$

$$E(H^2) = \mu_x^2 E(B^2) + 2\mu_x\sigma_x E(B^2 X^*) + \sigma_x^2 E(B^2 X^{*2})$$

$$E(B^2) = a^2\Phi\left(\frac{\mu_f}{\sigma_f}\right) + b^2\Phi\left(-\frac{\mu_f}{\sigma_f}\right)$$

Using Kotz et al. (2000, p. 311)

$$E(B^2 X^*) = \frac{(a^2 - b^2)}{\sqrt{2\pi}} \rho_{xf} \exp\left(-0.5\frac{\mu_f^2}{\sigma_f^2}\right)$$

Using Kotz et al. (2000, p. 312)

$$E(B^2 X^{*2}) = a^2 \left(\frac{\rho_{xf}^2}{\sqrt{2\pi}} \left(-\frac{\mu_f}{\sigma_f}\right) \exp\left(-0.5\frac{\mu_f^2}{\sigma_f^2}\right) + \Phi\left(\frac{\mu_f}{\sigma_f}\right) \right)$$

$$+ b^2 \left(\frac{\rho_{xf}^2}{\sqrt{2\pi}} \left(\frac{\mu_f}{\sigma_f}\right) \exp\left(-0.5\frac{\mu_f^2}{\sigma_f^2}\right) + \Phi\left(-\frac{\mu_f}{\sigma_f}\right) \right)$$

Therefore:

$$E(H^2) = \mu_x^2 \left[a^2\Phi\left(\frac{\mu_f}{\sigma_f}\right) + b^2\Phi\left(-\frac{\mu_f}{\sigma_f}\right) \right] + 2\mu_x\sigma_x \frac{(a^2 - b^2)}{\sqrt{2\pi}} \rho_{xf} \exp\left(-0.5\frac{\mu_f^2}{\sigma_f^2}\right)$$

$$+ \sigma_x^2 \left[a^2 \left(\frac{\rho_{xf}^2}{\sqrt{2\pi}} \left(-\frac{\mu_f}{\sigma_f}\right) \exp\left(-0.5\frac{\mu_f^2}{\sigma_f^2}\right) + \Phi\left(\frac{\mu_f}{\sigma_f}\right) \right) \right.$$

$$\left. + b^2 \left(\frac{\rho_{xf}^2}{\sqrt{2\pi}} \left(\frac{\mu_f}{\sigma_f}\right) \exp\left(-0.5\frac{\mu_f^2}{\sigma_f^2}\right) + \Phi\left(-\frac{\mu_f}{\sigma_f}\right) \right) \right]$$

8.9   APPENDIX 2: CORRELATION WITH TRACKER FUND

Here, we explicitly assume that the joint distribution of the underlying returns X, the forecast F and the tracker fund T is a trivariate normal distribution denoted by:

$$\begin{bmatrix} X \\ F \\ T \end{bmatrix} \sim N \left(\begin{bmatrix} \mu_x \\ \mu_f \\ \mu_t \end{bmatrix}, \begin{bmatrix} \sigma_x^2 & \rho_{xf}\sigma_x\sigma_f & \rho_{xt}\sigma_x\sigma_t \\ \rho_{xf}\sigma_x\sigma_f & \sigma_f^2 & \rho_{ft}\sigma_f\sigma_t \\ \rho_{xt}\sigma_x\sigma_t & \rho_{ft}\sigma_f\sigma_t & \sigma_t^2 \end{bmatrix} \right)$$

Let us note the portfolio $P = T + H$.

$$E(P) = \mu_t + E(H)$$

$E(P^2)$ can be developed using the argufies which were invoked to establish $E(H^2)$. Indeed, we only need to remark that:

$$P = \begin{cases} T + aX = Y & \text{if } F > 0 \\ T + bX = Z & \text{if } F < 0 \end{cases}$$

Therefore both $[Y,F]$ and $[Z,F]$ also follow bivariate normal distributions.

$$Y \sim N(\mu_t + a\mu_x, \sigma_t^2 + a^2\sigma_x^2 + 2a\rho_{tx}\sigma_t\sigma_x)$$

$$\text{Cov}(Y,F) = \text{Cov}(T,F) + a\text{Cov}(X,F)$$

$$\text{Corr}(Y,F) = \frac{\rho_{tf}\sigma_t + a\rho_{xf}\sigma_x}{\sqrt{\sigma_t^2 + a^2\sigma_x^2 + 2a\rho_{tx}\sigma_t\sigma_x}}$$

Similarly, $Z \sim N(\mu_t + b\mu_x, \sigma_t^2 + b^2\sigma_x^2 + 2b\rho_{tx}\sigma_t\sigma_x)$ and

$$\text{Corr}(Z,F) = \frac{\rho_{tf}\sigma_t + b\rho_{xf}\sigma_x}{\sqrt{\sigma_t^2 + b^2\sigma_x^2 + 2b\rho_{tx}\sigma_t\sigma_x}}$$

We know from Appendix 1, that by choosing a value of $a = 1, b = 0$ in Equation (8.3):

$$E(H^2)|_{a=1,\ b=0} = \int_X \int_{F>0} X^2 = \mu_x^2\Phi(\delta_f) + 2\mu_x\sigma_x\frac{\rho_{xf}}{\sqrt{2\pi}}\exp\left(-\frac{\delta_f^2}{2}\right)$$

$$+ \sigma_x^2\left(\frac{-\rho_{xf}^2}{\sqrt{2\pi}}\delta_f\exp\left(-\frac{\delta_f^2}{2}\right) + \Phi(\delta_f)\right)$$

If we note $g[\mu_x, \sigma_x^2, \delta_f, \rho_{xf}]$ this function, we obtain:

$$E(P^2) = g\left[\mu_t + a\mu_x, \sigma_t^2 + a^2\sigma_x^2\right.$$

$$+ 2a\rho_{tx}\sigma_t\sigma_x, \delta_f, \frac{\rho_{tf}\sigma_t + a\rho_{xf}\sigma_x}{\sqrt{\sigma_t^2 + a^2\sigma_x^2 + 2a\rho_{tx}}}\right]$$

$$+ g\left[\mu_t + b\mu_x, \sigma_t^2 + b^2\sigma_x^2 + 2b\rho_{tx}\sigma_t\sigma_x, -\delta_f,\right.$$

$$\left.-\left(\frac{\rho_{tf}\sigma_t + b\rho_{xf}\sigma_x}{\sqrt{\sigma_t^2 + b^2\sigma_x^2 + 2b\rho_{tx}}}\right)\right]$$

$$\text{Var}(P) = E(P^2) - (E(P))^2$$

$$\text{and Corr}(T,H) = \frac{\text{Var}(P) - \sigma_t^2 - \text{Var}(H)}{2\sigma_t\sqrt{\text{Var}(H)}}$$

8.10 APPENDIX 3: OPTIMAL ALLOCATION

8.10.1 Optimal allocation between an index and the maximum return long/short futures fund

If we denote H_{max}^* the returns derived by the optimal predictor on the dritfless futures markets, we obtain from Equation (8.1):

$$E(H_{max}^*) = \sigma_x\sqrt{\frac{2}{\pi}}\rho_{xf} \text{ and } \text{Var}(H_{max}^*) = \sigma_x^2\left(1 - \frac{2}{\pi}\rho_{xf}^2\right)$$

We also know from Section 8.3 that for long/short strategies in a driftless market $\text{Cov}(H_{max}^*, X^*) = \text{Cov}(H_{max}^*, X) = 0$.

The second step is to allocate the optimal weight w between tracker and hedge fund given by (8.5).

$$\tilde{w} = \frac{\sigma_x}{\mu_x}\frac{\sqrt{\frac{2}{\pi}}\rho_{xf}}{\left(1 - \frac{2}{\pi}\rho_{xf}^2\right)} = \frac{1}{\delta_x}\frac{\sqrt{\frac{2}{\pi}}\rho_{xf}}{\left(1 - \frac{2}{\pi}\rho_{xf}^2\right)}$$

As a consequence:

$$E(P) = \mu_x + \frac{1}{\delta_x}\frac{\frac{2}{\pi}\rho_{xf}^2\sigma_x}{1 - \frac{2}{\pi}\rho_{xf}^2} = \sigma_x\left(\delta_x + \frac{1}{\delta_x}\frac{\frac{2}{\pi}\rho_{xf}^2}{1 - \frac{2}{\pi}\rho_{xf}^2}\right)$$

$$E(P) = \mu_x + \sigma_x\frac{\frac{2}{\pi}\rho_{xf}^2}{1 - \frac{2}{\pi}\rho_{xf}^2} = \sigma_x\left(\frac{\delta_x^2 + \frac{2}{\pi}\rho_{xf}^2}{\delta_x\left(1 - \frac{2}{\pi}\rho_{xf}^2\right)}\right)$$

$$\text{Var}(P) = \sigma_x^2 + \tilde{w}^2\left(1 - \frac{2}{\pi}\rho_{xf}^2\right)\sigma_x^2 = \sigma_x^2\left(1 + \frac{\frac{2}{\pi}\rho_{xf}^2}{\delta_x^2\left(1 - \frac{2}{\pi}\rho_{xf}^2\right)}\right)$$

$$\text{Var}(P) = \sigma_x^2\frac{\delta_x^2 + \frac{2}{\pi}\rho_{xf}^2(1 - \delta_x^2)}{\delta_x^2\left(1 - \frac{2}{\pi}\rho_{xf}^2\right)}$$

$$SR(P) = \frac{\delta_x^2 + \frac{2}{\pi}\rho_{xf}^2}{\sqrt{1 - \frac{2}{\pi}\rho_{xf}^2}\sqrt{\delta_x^2 + \frac{2}{\pi}\rho_{xf}^2(1 - \delta_x^2)}}$$

REFERENCES

Acar, E. (1998) Expected returns of directional forecasters, in Acar and Satchell eds, *Advanced Trading Rules*, Butterworth-Heinemann, Oxford, 51–80.

Acar, E. and Satchell, S.E. (1998) The portfolio distribution of directional strategies, in E. Acar and S.E. Satchell eds, *Advanced Trading Rules*, Butterworth-Heinemann, Oxford, 103–11.

Chou, Y.M. and Owen, D.B. (1984) An approximation to percentiles of a variable of the bivariate normal distribution when the other variable is truncated, with applications, *Communications in Statistics-Theory and Methods*, **13**, 2535–47.

Elton, E.J., Gruber, M.J. and Rentzler, J.C. (1987) Professionally Managed, Publicly Traded Commodity Funds, *Journal of Business*, **60**(2), 175–99.

Fung, W. and Hsieh, D.A. (1997) Empirical characteristics of dynamic trading strategies: The case of hedge funds, *The Review of Financial Studies* **10**, 275–302.

Fung, W. and Hsieh, D.A. (2001) Asset-Based Hedge-Fund Styles and Portfolio Diversification, *Financial Analyst Journal*, forthcoming.

Hwang, S. and Satchell, S.E (2001) VaR versus Tracking Error, the strengths and weaknesses of two performance measures, in E. Acar eds, *Added Value in Financial Institutions, Risk or Return?*, 13–28.

Kotz, S., Balakrishnan, N. and Johnson, N.L. (2000) *Continuous Multivariate Distributions: Volume 1: Models and Applications*, Second Edition, Wiley & Sons.

Lundin, M. and Satchell, S.E. (2000) The Long and the Short of it, *Risk Magazine*, August, 94–8.

Martin, G. (2001), Making Sense of Hedge Fund Returns: A New Approach in Acar eds, *Added Value in Financial Institutions: Risk or Return*, Pearson, 165–82.

Mitchell, M. and Pulvino, T. (2001) Characteristics of Risk and Return in Risk Arbitrage, *Journal of Finance*, **55**(6), 2135–75.

Schneeweis, T. and Spurgin, R. (1998) Multi-Factor Analysis of Hedge Fund, Managed Futures and Mutual Fund Return and Risk Characteristics, *Journal of Alternative Investments*, **1**, 1–24.

Schneeweis, T. and Spurgin, R. (2000) Hedge Funds: Portfolio Risk Diversifiers, Return Enhancers or Both ?, Working paper, CISDM.

Schneeweis, T. and Spurgin, R. (2001) A method of estimating changes in correlation between assets and its application to hedge fund investment, *Journal of Asset Management*, **1** (3), 217–29.

Skouras, S. (2001) Risk Neutral Forecasting, Working paper, Santa Fe University.

Strange, B. (2001) Currency Matters, *European Pension News*, 28 May, Currency Overlay Supplement, 19–21.

NOTES

1. Strictly speaking the forecast the forecast maximizing the absolute value of the expected return will minimize variance. However if the predictor generates a loss, it is always possible to establish the reverse strategy generating the maximum gain.
2. The improvement will only affect investors exhibiting a quadratic utility function. Different values of δ_f will generate different skewness and kurtosis coefficients.

ACKNOWLEDGEMENTS

I would like to thank Stacy Williams for useful comments and suggestions. All errors remain mine.

Chapter 9

Integrating market and credit risk in fixed income portfolios

ALLA GIL AND YURI POLYAKOV

ABSTRACT

This paper proposes an original approach to the simultaneous assessment of market and credit risk. This approach combines the advantages of major existing models and uses all sources of information relevant to credit risk. We model credit spread as jump-diffusion process (as in reduced form approach) and use rating transition matrices for parameter calibration. We estimate recovery rates externally using the value of the firm model (as in structural approach).

We expand this methodology to a portfolio level and apply a novel algorithm for portfolio optimization.

This chapter provides a portfolio manager with a practical and comprehensive tool to quantify and compare the different portfolio strategies. It addresses the main issues that a manager of a credit risky portfolio of fixed income instruments faces.

9.1 INTRODUCTION

Traditional portfolio optimization has boiled down to construction of the efficient frontier – the family of portfolios with the lowest risk for a given level of return – without explicitly taking into consideration credit (and default) risk. The two obvious reasons for this omission have been the difficulty of evaluating this non-traditional risk and the lack of means for dealing with it. The portfolio manager could only take on the risk associated with fixed income instruments and try to diversify it as much as possible within the preferred credits and industries.

The development of credit derivatives markets in the past decade has brought new flexibility to measuring and managing credit risk. Now portfolio managers can afford to buy and hold any names that have good prospects while unloading exactly that portion of credit risk that they are uncomfortable with.

In order to use these newly created opportunities efficiently, one has to evaluate market and credit risk consistently with each other. This means employing the models that can verify whether the different types of risk offset or enhance each other on the portfolio level. Let us consider an example of a portfolio consisting of an emerging market (EM) bond and a currency swap paying this EM currency and receiving US$. This is a typical example of market and credit risks offsetting each other. Since a country event drives both credit and foreign exchange exposures, they are highly correlated. As credit spread increases and the bond loses value, the currency swap gets deeply in the money thus compensating for loss. Of course, such risk offsetting is possible only if the swap counter-party does not default at the same time as underlying EM bond (which can happen if the swap was with the bank from the same EM country).

This paper starts by discussing the differences between market and credit risk management and measurement and the challenges facing the portfolio manager who is trying to assess the exposures on an integrated basis (Sections 9.2 and 9.3). Section 9.4 outlines our original approach to consistent estimation of market and credit risk. It focuses on the risks associated with a single name and prepares for the portfolio approach outlined in Section 9.5. There we offer a new evaluation tool for comparing different portfolio strategies and an original optimization approach to determining the most efficient credit risk profile.

9.2   HOW TO MEASURE MARKET AND CREDIT RISK

Traditionally, market risk was measured using Value-at-Risk methodology (VaR) for 95% confidence interval. This methodology is based on historical changes in the portfolio value. Since historical performance does not give an adequate future forecast, many VaR methodologies today are based on Monte Carlo simulations to cover feasible dynamics of relevant environments. At the same time historical information should not be ignored but can be taken into account in the form of covariance matrix.

Credit risk was traditionally measured not on the portfolio level but on name-by-name or industry-by-industry basis. Though this approach provided fundamental depth, it did not take into account correlations between the instruments in the portfolio. At the same time, the conventional VaR methodology was not appropriate for measuring credit risk. The distribution of portfolio value due to credit risk uncertainty is very asymmetric and has fat tails. It is possible to parameterize it using extreme value theory but the results of such calibration are not intuitive.

In recent years there have been several approaches to credit risk evaluation on a portfolio level:

- CreditMetrics[1] and KMV[2] use equity information and the 'value of the firm' concept;
- CreditRisk+[3] developed by CSFB uses an actuarial approach; and
- CreditPortfolioView[4] developed by McKinsey & Co, based on econometric models.

All these methodologies take into consideration correlations within the portfolio, they construct loss distribution functions and they are based on the historical information.[5] However they lack flexible transparent connection with the current market pricing.

We propose an approach that combines valuable, stable, and reliable historical information with the market observable implied dynamics of credit spreads and yield curves. This methodology is consistent with pricing and hedging, providing a portfolio manager with a practical tool to compare and quantify different market strategies.

We use loss distribution function of the portfolio to generalize VaR approach so as to make it applicable to credit (and default) losses as well as other market uncertainties.

The function in Figure 9.1 clearly demonstrates that expected loss (represented by average portfolio credit spread and credit rating) does not fully explain all portfolio risks. Unexpected loss defined by correlations among portfolio instruments is another important risk indicator. This function allows us to determine the amount of losses incurred in the portfolio with any given confidence interval. The losses include changes in the market environment (yield curves, exchange rates, credit spreads) as well as losses due to defaults (when the value of investment drops significantly).

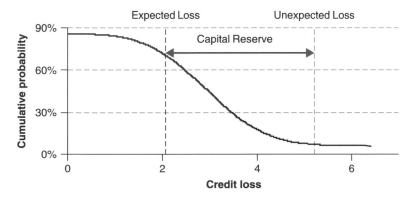

Figure 9.1 *Cumulative loss function*

9.3   THE WAYS OF CONSTRUCTING LOSS DISTRIBUTIONS

In the credit risk-free interest rate world, there are many different models (with different numbers of factors and parameters) but all of them are focused on modelling the yield curve. There is a much bigger variety of approaches to modelling credit risk. Different sets of market information are used: equity prices and the value of the firm notion, corporate bond prices, historical probabilities of defaults and rating transition matrices – and this is not a complete list.

It is possible to distinguish two major directions in modelling credit risk:

- structural approach based on the traded equity prices and the fundamental analysis of the balance sheet of a firm;
- reduced-form approach derived from the market credit spreads.

Each of these approaches uses only a subset of market data relevant to credit risk. Since information related to credit is very scarce, in order to construct a comprehensive model it would be advantageous to use all available sources.

We propose to use a combination of the best features of existing models. Such an approach combines all available sources of information and allows us to include market risk into consideration.

Let us discuss conceptually what features are critically important for modelling credit risk on a portfolio level.

There are important differences between strategic modelling of portfolios and pricing credit derivatives instruments. All the pricing models have to be arbitrage free and allow the replication of the derivatives payoff with the underlying securities pricing. If a portfolio manager strictly believes in absence of arbitrage in the market, all the investments would have the same fair value. On the other hand strategic modelling of portfolio trends contains the asset allocation views where the curve projections may deviate from the implied forwards.

Changing economic and market environment quite often causes the realized future trends to be far away from the projected ones. To make longer term assessment of portfolio risk, a portfolio manager should be able to stress-test the input assumptions (interest rates and credit spread trends as well as their covariance characteristics) and make sure that the models used for constructing the distributions of portfolio values are consistent with the pricing methodologies.

One of the important issues in modelling credit risk is understanding how a bond can arrive to a default event. From the observations we can say that high investment grade companies are most likely to default by a catastrophic event, which is totally unpredictable. By contrast, a lower grade company could be driven into bankruptcy even by a regular market move, so one can clearly see the default event coming. This means that the rating of the company should define a number of parameters for evaluating the losses in the portfolio value. In particular, since lower-graded companies depend more on the general health of the economy, they will have a higher joint correlation of default than more stable established companies even from the same industry group.

The credit rating of a company gets re-evaluated on a regular basis by different agencies (like Moody's or Standard & Poors), who publish historical probabilities of default and credit rating transition matrices. However, results of credit risk models based on these rating transition matrices are not entirely accurate.

Because the credit ratings do not change often, the existing ratings generally lag behind the continuously changing credit quality. The market anticipates changes in credit ratings and announcements of such a change usually do not cause abrupt changes in affected bonds prices, because they have already been lowered (or lifted) to the corresponding level. Credit risk as reflected in the traded bond prices changes continuously. The smooth changes in credit quality really represent market risk. Portfolio managers associate credit risk with the events that cause abrupt and significant losses in the portfolio (like defaults).

Hence a diffusion process might be a better choice for modelling the changes in credit quality than the counting process implied by rating transition matrices. In addition, credit ratings do not change much with economic conditions because the rating agencies always have 'normal' conditions in mind, while continuous correlated spread processes containing the liquidity component can take this issue into account.

By separating the dynamics of the credit spreads $s(t)$ into two components, diffusive changes in credit quality $\phi(t)$ and jumps to default $\varphi(t)$, we will have the flexibility of changing the proportion between them depending on the current level of spread

$$s(t) = \phi(t) \mid \varphi(t)$$

This proportional split into components $\phi(t)$ and $\varphi(t)$ can be calibrated using the rating transition matrix approach suggested by Jarrow et al. (1994).

The jump component $\varphi_i(t)$ represents the rate of arrival of the unexpected Poisson event – default trigger (Madan and Unal, 1998 and Duffie and Singleton, 1997).

To incorporate liquidity premium into this modelling approach we can assume that each credit instrument comes with a convenience yield modelled as a process $\lambda(t)$.

To summarize, we represent market risk by the underlying yield curves, liquidity premium $\lambda(t)$, and a diffusion component $\phi(t)$. Credit (default) risk is associated with the jump component $\varphi(t)$. By simulating interest rate and credit curves simultaneously and by identifying the components of credit risk on each path, we obtain consistent measures for market and credit risk.

9.4   COMPONENTS OF CREDIT RISK

Credit spreads of tradable securities are directly observable indicators of the credit risk. They reflect the combined market information on the liquidity risk associated with the given instrument maturity, the expected recovery rate in the event of default, the probability of being downgraded as well as the probability of default. The ability to evaluate those components is absolutely critical for the correct pricing and risk management. Most of existing approaches recognize the existence of these components. But they either try to calibrate all of them to the market traded instruments or focus on some of these components while virtually ignoring the others. The simultaneous calibration is not always practical; first, because the credit derivatives markets are not developed enough to produce the satisfactory information for such calibration; second, the parameters estimation obtained as a result of this calibration quite often is not robust and not intuitive.

We propose a model that identifies different types of parameters and calibrates all of these types sequentially using market data most appropriate for the respective type.

Obtaining intuitive results is one of the most important features in assessing credit risk exactly because we have very limited information about a particular credit traded on the market. Relying on other sources of information becomes very critical. This works quite well for estimating the components of the credit spread because they all reflect different aspects of risk.

9.4.1   Liquidity component

In this context, the liquidity component represents the portion of credit spread that is not associated with the risk of default. Quite often the widening of the credit spread means lack of liquidity in the market, while the probability of default does not increase. This component depends on the maturity of the trade, shape of the risk-free yield curve and its volatility, the collateral and termination conditions of the trade. The liquidity component can be estimated by considering the spreads of illiquid but credit risk-free instruments. Since Libor, government agency, AAA-industrial curves are all constructed from the instruments that are traded at some spread to Treasury curve, we can consider this spread, λ, to be the liquidity part of the total credit spread. In doing so we recognize that the spread λ does not represent the credit risk but other pressures on the market that are not directly associated with credit.

Let us consider a one-period zero-coupon bond. If this is a risk-free bond, its price, B_0, can be determined as

$$B_0 = E\{e^{-\int_0^t y(v)\,dv}\}$$

where the process $y(v)$ is the risk-free (Treasury) yield and t is time to maturity. B_0 represents a discount factor for risk-free liquid cash flows.

If D_0 is similar discount factor implied from Libor curve then

$$D_0 = E\{e^{-\int_o^t (y+\lambda)(v)\,dv}\} = E\{e^{-\int_o^t y(v)\,dv}e^{-\int_o^t \lambda(v)\,dv}\} \tag{9.1}$$

D_0 is utilized to discount risk-free but illiquid cash flows, where the extra discounting, $E\{e^{-\int_o^t \lambda(v)\,dv}\}$, represents liquidity risk.

Let us consider a corporate bond trading at spread S to Treasury curve. We can decompose S as $S = \lambda + s$, where λ is the spread to Libor and s is the remaining part of the total spread S, representing the specific credit risk of the issue. The risky discount factor D_1 can be expressed then using Equation (9.1) as

$$D_1 = E\{e^{-\int_o^t (y+S)(v)\,dv}\} = E\{e^{-\int_o^t (y+\lambda+s)(v)\,dv}\} = E\{e^{-\int_o^t y(v)\,dv}e^{-\int_o^t \lambda(v)\,dv}\}$$

$$= E\{e^{-\int_o^t y(v)\,dv}e^{-\int_o^t \lambda(v)\,dv}e^{-\int_o^t s(v)\,dv}\}$$

Assuming independence of credit spread to the risk-free but illiquid curve (i.e. Libor) with the Libor rate we obtain the following:

$$D_1 = E\{e^{-\int_o^t y(v)\,dv}e^{-\int_o^t \lambda(v)\,dv}\}E\{e^{-\int_o^t s(v)\,dv}\} = E\{e^{-\int_o^t s(v)\,dv}\}D_0 \tag{9.2}$$

We can see from the Equation (9.2) that the risky discount factor D_1 can be obtained as an extra discounting of a credit risk-free but illiquid discount factor, D_0. Thus D_0 incorporates the general liquidity component carried but almost all credit risky instruments. It represents supply–demand pressures, popularity of some specific maturities, but it is not name specific and does not reflect credit worries.

A natural question that appears in this situation is how to deal with a liquidity component specific to an industry group and/or credit rating?

We do know that the lower the credit rating, the less liquid corporate bond is. Also it is a known fact that some industries get out of fashion (usually when in trouble) and are traded at a huge liquidity spreads. But all of these considerations are credit specific so they should not be considered as liquidity but as a portion of specific credit spread.

9.4.2 Probability of default

The extra discounting in the Equation (9.2) represents the risk of not receiving the promised cash flows at maturity. It has to be equal to the expected outcome at maturity of zero-coupon bond. For a one-period bond, there are two possible outcomes:

- with the probability of default the owner of the bond will receive only a fraction R (recovery rate) of a promised cash flow (US\$1, par value);
- if default does not occur, the full promised cash flow will be paid.

Let p be the probability of default and respectively $(1 - p)$ the probability of surviving to maturity. Then the expected outcome of cash flows for one-period zero-coupon bond is $pR + (1 - p)$. The present value of this expected outcome equals to $D_0\{pR + (1 - p)\}$. Assuming no-arbitrage condition, we can equate this present value with the risky discount factor from the Equation (9.2).

$$D_1 = D_0[pR + (1 - p)]$$

or in a simplified form with a constant s in Equation (9.2),

$$e^{-st} D_0 = D_0[pR + (1 - p)]$$

from where

$$e^{-st} = pR + (1 - p) \tag{9.3}$$

Consider the first order approximation, $e^{-st} = 1 - st$, the Equation (9.3) becomes

$$1 - st = pR + 1 - p$$

or over one-year period with $t = 1$

$$s = p(1 - R) \tag{9.4}$$

The right-hand side of equation represents the expected loss in the event of default – with the probability p the owner of the bond receives only recovery R instead of promised par, thus loosing $1 - R$. The expected loss is also equal to the expected payoff in default protection. So the Equation (9.4) illustrates a well-known fact – the credit spread received above the risk-free rate has to be paid out in order to obtain default protection. In absence of arbitrage and transaction costs, the combination of risky zero-coupon bond and the default protection for this investment is equivalent to the risk-free bond.

The Equation (9.4) has two unknowns: the probability of default, p, and the recovery rate, R. The only known variable is spread s that can be observed on the market (or more precisely, obtained from the observable credit spread S and liquidity λ). Since we do not have enough market instruments to calibrate the unknowns, we have to choose which one to estimate using some external information. The proposed solution is to use the fundamental (structural) analysis of a firm for the recovery rate evaluation.

9.4.3 Recovery rate

According to the rating agencies, recovery rate is the price of a bond 30 days after default. The 30-day interval was chosen to let the price of a distressed bond calm down after the bankruptcy announcement. This price reflects the expected payoff of the obligation in the bankruptcy court proceedings. Rating agencies also publish statistical tables on the historical recovery rates. The historical average rate has been around 40% of par. But it varies significantly by the seniority of the obligation as it is demonstrated in the Table 9.1.

Other factors determining the expected recovery rate are industry affiliation and company assets. For example, US non-financial assets, on average, recover 41.7% while US banks only 22%.[7]

Expected recovery also depends on general economic conditions.[8] If many defaults occur together, the recovery rate might be much lower than the average historical level and investors would care about it much more. Recovery rates do not depend much on the maturity of the underlying treasury or on the original credit rating (it is almost always below investment grade just prior to default).

So we have taken a historical average recovery rate from the statistical tables. Now it can be plugged into the Equation (9.4). The spread s we can observe on the market. Thus Equation (9.4) can be used to extract the implied probability of default p:

$$p = s/(1 - R) \qquad (9.5)$$

Since we do not know the recovery rate with certainty, only the historical average, we might want to stress-test our assumption. The structural approach helps to obtain recovery rates on all defaults paths. In order to identify the possible constraint for this parameter, let us assume that the recovery rate is very close to 100%. Then the probability implied from the Equation (9.5), can become greater than 1.0 which is not possible. This paradox can be explained with the following reasoning. When the recovery rate is close to 100%, the owner of the bond under consideration receives the same cash flows whether the bond defaults or not. This means that the bond is practically risk-less. Its cash flows are equivalent to the cash flow of the bond with price D_0. Then in the absence of arbitrage its price, D_1, should be equal to D_0, that is spread

Table 9.1 *Average recovery rates 1970–2000*[6]

Seniority Security	Senior Secured Bonds	Senior Unsecured Bonds	Senior Subordinate Bonds	Subordinate Bonds	Junior Subordinate Bonds
	52.6%	46.9%	34.7%	31.6%	22.5%

$s = 0$ (Equation (9.1)). But we do not control the spread, it is implied from the bond's prices it is given by the market. This means that stress-testing of recovery assumption should be done with this restriction: the probability in the Equation (9.5) must be between 0 and 1.

The same intuition lies behind the following paradox: Equation (9.5) implies that when recovery rate increases the probability of default grows too. Everybody understands this is not the case: higher recovery means less risk and respectively lower probability of default. Again, the higher recovery rate and lower risk of losses will be reflected in the lower credit spread with which the instrument is traded. More narrow credit spread will cause reduction in the default probability. But if spread is out of our control and we manipulate only the recovery assumption, the higher recovery will mean the higher implied probability of default for the same level of spread.

9.4.4   Value of the firm approach[9]

In evaluating the future uncertainties in portfolio value, it is important to simulate the dynamics of recovery rates for obligations of different seniorities. Some modification of a classic value of the firm model provides the best platform for this task.

In its original form this model makes the following assumptions:

- Interest rates are deterministic (this assumption can be relaxed).
- The value of the firm follows a log-normal diffusion process.
- Default occurs if the value of the firm's assets falls below liability level (Figure 9.2).

This model provides a very intuitive approach, which is easy to implement. But since the value of the firm is an unobservable and non-traded entity, all the

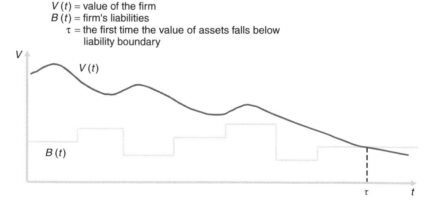

Figure 9.2   *The dynamic of a firm's assets and liabilities (1)*

parameters for its dynamics have to be backed out from the traded equity of the firm the equity/liability ratio of the balance sheet.

$$\sigma_E = \frac{V_A}{V_E} \sigma_A K$$

where σ_E and σ_A are respectively firm's equity and asset volatilities, V_A and V_E are the market values of firm's assets and equity ($V_A = V_E + V_L$, where V_L is the market value of the debt), and K is a coefficient defined by firm's capital structure.

Thus this model relies entirely on the equity information and ignores the corporate bond market and the traded credit spreads. This model also assumes that the firm's liabilities are strongly prioritized in bankruptcy proceedings, that is the holders of more senior obligations do not get hurt until all subordinate layers of debt are completely wiped out.

This is usually not the case – once the default is announced it affects all debt holders, but the senior obligations will provide a much higher recovery than the subordinate ones.

Also even on the paths where the value of the firm closes the liability level, default is not necessarily recorded right away. The modification is implemented in KMV[10] – if there is no obligatory cash flow at the time of the crossing, the default event is not going to be noticed by the market. Default is recorded only when a payment is missed. Thus the value of the firm has a chance to either recover or deteriorate further before the cash flow is due. If the asset value remains below the liability level, the default event will be recorded and the total recovery on company's debt will be the value of the firm at this point (Figure 9.3).

When default happens, the debt owners take over the firm at no cost and the available value of the assets is distributed proportionally to the seniority of the obligation:

$$R_k(p) = \{V_A(p) | V_A \leq V_L \,\&\, t > \tau\} \frac{\overline{R}_k}{\sum_j \overline{R}_j}$$

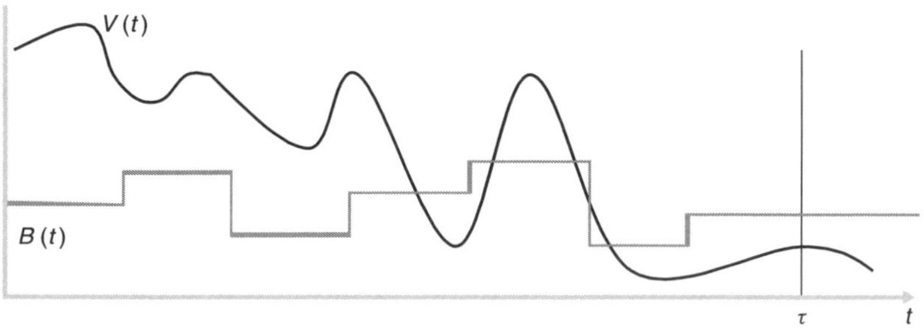

Figure 9.3 *The dynamic of a firm's assets and liabilities (2)*

where $R_k(p)$ is a recovery rate of an obligation with the seniority k on a random path p where the value of the firm V_A falls below the level of liabilities V_L and the cash flow scheduled at time τ is overdue. $\overline{R}_j$ here is average historical recovery level for a given industry group and seniority level[11].

That is why the structural approach is best suited for backing out the recovery rates. It models the behaviour of the firm's assets V_A. So for every simulation path where the default occurs (that is $V_A(t) < V_L(t)$ and at the same time the cash flow scheduled at time τ has been missed), this approach can determine exactly how much assets can be used to pay off the debt holders. Then using average historical recovery ratios between the different seniority pieces it is possible to determine how much exactly each obligation will recover for this specific default path.

9.4.5   Rating transition matrix approach

Once the recovery rate has been estimated, the next important step is to identify what portion of the credit spread is due to risk premium charged for the smooth changes in the credit quality, spread volatility and the possibility of downgrade. The remaining portion is due to the probability of jump to default. Such separation is appropriate for the well-established markets as in the emerging markets there can be more than one jump.

We propose to use rating transition matrices to calibrate the split of credit spread movements into diffusive and jumpy parts. The original approach has been proposed by Jarrow, Lando, and Turnbull[12] in order to consider the information published by the rating agencies and reflecting changes in credit quality.

This model assumes that the bankruptcy process is a finite state Markov process where the states are the firm's credit ratings. Since the observable rating transition probabilities are the historical (actual) ones, JLT adjusts them to risk-neutral rating transition probabilities.

Let $Q(t, t+1) = \{q_{ij}\}$ be a historical rating migration matrix, where q_{ij} is the actual probability of going from the state i to the state j in one tine step; $\tilde{Q}(t, t+1) = \{\tilde{q}_{ij}\}$ is the equivalent martingale probability matrix; π_i are the risk premium adjustments such that

$$\tilde{q}_j(t, t+1) = \pi_i(t)q_j \tag{9.6}$$

for all $i, j, i \neq j$.

The probability that default occurs after time T is $\tilde{Q}_t^i(\tau > T) = \sum_{j \neq K} \tilde{q}_j(t, T) = 1 - \tilde{q}_K(t, T)$, where K is default state. In this model $\tilde{q}_K(t, T)$ is deduced from the term structure of credit spreads assuming constant recovery; the adjustment coefficients are calculated from default state $\pi_i(t) = \tilde{q}_K(t, T)/q_K(t, T)$, and $\tilde{q}_j$ for $j \neq K$ are derived from Equation (9.6).

This approach has a lot of attractive features. It is easy to implement because of availability of historical credit ratings transition matrices. But it does not fully reflect the dynamics of the changes in credit quality. Also it is not practical to use this approach for the portfolio – it is not feasible to follow all of the states and their combinations in the correlated credit spread environment.

As a result we have come up with the following methodology for the total risk assessment:

- Liquidity for all of the instruments is incorporated in Libor spread to Treasury. Corporate spreads to Libor contain industry, credit rating and name specific pressures only.
- Corporate spread to Libor combines the information on recovery rates, rating transition probability and possible defaults, as well as risk premium for spread volatility.
- In order to cope with the lack of substantial term structure for each instrument in the portfolio, we combine into a single credit curve all the issuers belonging to the same industry group, credit rating and seniority level.
- Recovery rates are estimated from the fundamental (structural) approach.
- We use jump-diffusion process for credit spreads – calibration of the respective parts is done through rating transition matrix methodology.

9.5 PORTFOLIO APPROACH

9.5.1 Modelling joint defaults

Now that we have identified the steps in modelling the individual risk exposures, we need to combine them on the portfolio level. In order to obtain the risk picture for the entire portfolio, we need to introduce correlation between the instruments.

Ideally we would like to obtain a full correlation matrix between the credit spreads of all the instruments in the portfolio. But it is not feasible in practice as there are not enough instruments on the market to calibrate all the correlations. Moreover there is not enough historical information either.

The proposed solution to overcome this obstacle is to aggregate the issuers by their industry groups and credit ratings. It is possible to obtain substantial information renewed weekly[13] for these integrated entities. The correlations within industry (on average 70% on log-normal basis) are higher than between the industries (on average 10–20%). In addition the correlations can be made dynamic as the highly rated issuers usually have lower default correlation (they can withstand systematic stresses from the market), while deteriorated below investment grade companies can be driven out of business by a regular market volatility (rising interest rates, etc.).

Historical correlations of credit spreads contain not just default correlation but the systematic spread moves as well. Two large companies in the same business can be quite highly correlated but if one of them defaults by internal catastrophic event (that has nothing to do with their business cycle), it does not mean the second one is in worse shape as well. Surely, there will be a temporary increase in spread just by continuity of the correlation effect. But once the panic on the market settles down, the other company is going to thrive without a major competitor.

The observable correlations extracted from the historical time series are the ones containing both systematic (general market movements) and idiosyncratic (industry and name specific) components. The first component will affect mostly market risks for the portfolio, the latter – fat-tailed credit and default risk. Our approach to separating credit spreads into jumpy and diffusive components takes care of this correlation issue as well. When the spreads are simulated we use the correlation coefficients with both components. Then each spread sample on the path is split into diffusive and jumpy parts and the jump component only serves as rate of arrival of default event for another simulation series.

9.5.2   Monte carlo simulation of portfolio values

We assume joint log-normal distribution of credit spreads based on historical volatilities and correlations. The observable credit curves are constructed using industry, credit rating and seniority association.

The credit spread samples on a random path are obtained as:

$$s_i(t) = \hat{s}_i(t)e^{-\frac{\sigma^2}{2}t + \sigma\sqrt{t}z_i} \qquad (9.7)$$

where $s_i(t)$ is a credit spread for the i-th obligor in the portfolio; σ_i is credit spread volatility; z_i is a standard normal random variable.

Then the credit spread is represented in the following form:

$$s_i(t) = \phi_i(t) + \varphi_i(t) \qquad (9.8)$$

Here $\phi_i(t)$ is the diffusive component of the spread, and $\varphi_i(t)$ is the rate of arrival of default events.

$\phi_i(t)$ is used for mark-to-market of the corresponding instrument while $\varphi_i(t)$ gives us the probability of default.

To determine how the spread in Equation (9.8) is split between these two components we use the historical rating transition matrices.

In order to simulate the default events in the portfolio, we interpret the probability of default on the path obtained from $\varphi_i(t)$ as area under standard log-normal distribution of spread and finding z-score b_i corresponding to default.

$$1 - p_i = \frac{1}{\sqrt{2\pi}} \int_{-\infty}^{b_i} e^{-\frac{v_i^2}{2}} \, dv_i$$

Thus $b_i = N^{-1}(p_i)$ corresponds to the default boundary of the i-th instrument in the portfolio. In terms of Monte Carlo simulation this means that we can define default path as a path where simulated credit spread crosses the unknown default boundary. Then the ratio of the number of default paths to the total number of paths can be expressed as cumulative normal distribution function of this unknown boundary and it should be equal to the probability of default.

Once all default boundaries have been identified, on each path obtained by simulating the correlated portfolio assets, we can see whether any defaults took place and what losses are associated with them on each time interval.

Illustrative example of portfolio distribution
Let us consider the following portfolio example. It has 20 instruments with average credit rating of Aa3 and an average spread over Libor of 34 basis points (b.p.). This portfolio is fairly concentrated: 65% of the total portfolio value is allocated to Financial, Utility and Telecom sectors. All instruments have fixed rates. We assume that when an instrument matures it is rolled over into a similar tenor/credit quality security with a coupon composed of the par rate prevailing at that time and respective credit spread.

After simulating yield curve environment and credit spreads on a five-year time interval, observing the value of the portfolio on each path (including default paths) and discounting it back to today, we obtain the expected value of the portfolio of US$2.32bn. Because of the uncertainty in market environment, 1% of simulated outcomes falls below US$2.004bn. The difference (US$316m) represents the total risk – losses that can happen because of reinvestment risk, rating migration and possible defaults. Out of this US$316m, US$46m are the losses that occur due to defaults only. This has been calculated by analysing the default subset of all possible outcomes (paths that resulted in defaults).

On these paths the average loss value of the portfolio is US$1.2m and the worst case outcome (with 99% confidence interval) is US$47.2m. Since the capital reserve should cover the losses above and beyond the expected loss (which is covered by the portfolio revenues), we obtain the difference of US$46m (Table 9.2).

Table 9.2   *Portfolio risk analysis*

Various measures US$m	Current
Expected portfolio value	2.320
Credit risk capital reserve	46
Total risk capital reserve	316
99% worst case portfolio value	2.004
Average credit loss	1.2
99% worst case credit loss	47.2
Average portfolio spread	34
Average portfolio rating	Aa3

In this example the credit risk component (US$46m) represents a small portion of the total risk (US$316m) because this portfolio has a relatively high average credit rating (Aa3). At the same time it is exposed to significant mark-to-market risk because it is composed of fixed rate instruments.

In the next section we will demonstrate how this portfolio can be improved by achieving simultaneously a higher average credit spread and a lower risk measured by amount of capital that needs to be reserved for possible credit losses.

9.5.3   Optimizing portfolio credit risk profile

The loss distribution function of the portfolio is determined by the composition of weights of the portfolio instruments $\{w_n\}$. The whole universe of feasible names for the optimization is described by the credit curves V_j with the same probability of default per curve. The instruments belonging to the same curve have a higher correlation than between the curves but it does not mean they will necessarily default together.

The objective function for optimization depends on the result of the current portfolio analysis. For risky portfolios with relatively high yield, the major objective would be to reduce the risk without sacrificing the return. On the contrary, for higher investment grade portfolios, the manager would be more interested in boosting up the returns without jeopardizing current risk characteristics and without major deviation from the benchmark.

The benchmark considerations traditionally have been very strong for portfolio managers – as long as they outperform it they are in a good shape. That is why portfolio optimization has focused on asset allocation, not on risk characteristics – they were given by a benchmark and the portfolio manager did not have incentives to improve them.

But since 2000, we have observed a lack of performance both in equity and fixed income portion of the portfolio. It resulted in serious reduction in capital reserve. Now the portfolio manager wants to follow (and outperform) the benchmark only on the way up. But it is also very important for him to know not just the relative risk expressed as the deviation from the benchmark but the absolute level of risk as well.

Our approach to optimization treats the benchmark considerations as constraint but primarily focuses on the smoothing the volatility of charge-offs in the portfolio by providing a longer-term strategic optimal direction.

We consider n-dimensional space of portfolio weights $\{w_1, w_2, \ldots, w_n\}$ (where n is the number of current and feasible instruments in the portfolio).

One of the most popular objectives for strategic optimization is to minimize risk $W(w_1, w_2, \ldots, w_n)$ as defined by portfolio loss that might be exceeded only 1% of the time (99% worst case outcome). At the same time the portfolio return $E(w_1, w_2, \ldots, w_n)$ should remain at least at the current level. Optimization is also subject to investment, market and accounting constraints. Restrictions on the deviation from the benchmark can be viewed as type of investment constraints.

The objective function is computed algorithmically, that is for every set of weights $\{w_n\}$ we calculate the whole loss distribution function, its expected level and 99%-confidence interval. The optimization algorithm (see Appendix) chooses the next set of weights, etc.

When the optimization methodology described above is applied to the illustrative example, the following changes to the credit spectrum composition of the portfolio are suggested (see Figure 9.4)

As a result of proposed changes the credit risk of the portfolio was reduced from US$46m to US$22m while average credit spread increase from 31 to 45 b.p. per annum. The original and optimized distributions of the portfolio value are illustrated in Figure 9.5.

The results of the portfolio modification represent the minimum necessary increase in granularity of portfolio composition.

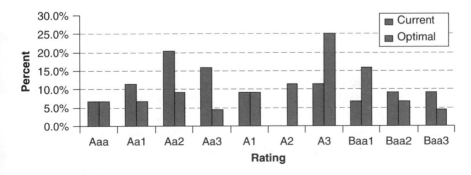

Figure 9.4 *Rating concentration (current v optimal portfolio)*

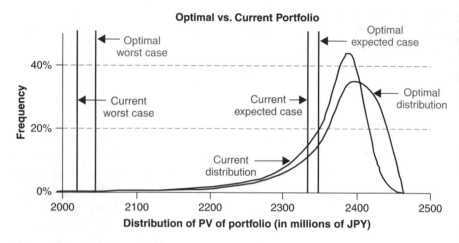

Figure 9.5 *Original and optimized distributions of portfolio value*

9.6 CONCLUSIONS

The proposed approach has a number of advantages over the existing models for analysing and optimizing credit risky portfolios.

It evaluates market and credit risk simultaneously with a clear dynamic modelling of their effect on each other. This is achieved by estimating the components of risk sequentially using relevant market data for parameter calibration. At each step we apply some modification of one of the existing models to evaluate the component of risk for which this model is suited the best. Along the way we consider all the information on credit risk contained in observable market sources. This allows us to combine the best features of existing approaches and overcome their shortcomings.

As a result of risk assessment on a portfolio level we generate loss distribution function by combining historical information and future dynamics of credit and yield curves. This procedure can easily accommodate different views on market projections, asset allocation strategies and stress-testing.

While constructing loss distribution function we directly simulate default events thus producing fat-tailed distributions naturally, without imposing an inflexible parametric structure.

Then it is possible to estimate tracking error with respect to portfolio benchmark and the absolute losses with a given confidence interval. This helps the portfolio manager to identify risk tolerance on the portfolio level and design flexible strategies to eliminate undesirable portions of loss distribution.

Because we assess risk consistently with pricing and hedging methodology, we are able to provide clear risk/return trade-offs in modification of portfolio composition. Thus the portfolio manager can formulate objectives and constraints for a strategic portfolio optimization.

To solve this problem, we suggest a unique optimization approach that utilizes gradient-based methods for non-smooth and non-convex function. The proposed method can be immediately applied to a given problem, while the standard optimization algorithms require that the problem be modified first to satisfy restrictions. This methodology has been successfully applied to a number of actual investment and loan portfolios.

9.7 APPENDIX

The original methodology used for optimizing credit risk profile has been derived from a technique for construction of algorithms for unconstrained minimization of function of many variables under conditions of imperfect initial information. It may be the case that the objective function $f(x)$ is given by its values alone. No other information is necessary for the algorithm to work. The objective function may also be non-smooth and non-convex, with non-unique optimum.

Existing methods for such kinds of problems, as a rule, are oriented to estimating the first and second order differential characteristics (or their generalized concepts), which are used in the effective algorithms of smooth optimization. Usually probabilistic algorithms (varieties of random search) and deterministic ones (using finite-difference approximations of derivatives) are based on different principles. Schemes of looking through the feasible directions of search both probabilistic and deterministic (as in polytope algorithm) are based on still different (heuristic) principles. But the absence of a unified basis for the construction of the indicated classes of algorithms makes it difficult to develop them using various kinds of initial and current information.

The method suggested here allows us to obtain all these algorithms from the common gradient basis. Instead of finding derivatives of the objective function our method differentiates the specially constructed potential function. This potential function satisfies some classic partial differential equations. Our approach is based on replacing the original problem with its randomized equivalent.

We reformulate the initial problem and obtain the whole series of essential algorithmic structures which are usually connected with different classes of models. In our approach they can be derived as special cases of a family of methods with the invariant algorithmic kernel.

We start with randomization of variable as one of the ways of looking through feasible directions. But now the objective function becomes a random variable and its minimization is meaningless. Thus a different formalization of the problem is necessary.

9.7.1　Random reformulation of the initial problem and the first order variation of the objective functional

For this purpose the initial problem

$$\min_{x \in R^n} f(x) = f(x_1, x_2, \ldots, x_n) \tag{9.9}$$

is converted into a randomized one:

$$\min_{x \in \{X\}} F(X) = E[f(X)] \tag{9.10}$$

where $\{X\}$ is the set of random vectors, and E is the operation of expectation. Here deterministic vectors are included in the set of random ones and correspond to concentrated distributions. The problems (9.9) and (9.10) are equivalent in a certain sense.

In order to identify the gradient basis for algorithm solution of problem (9.10), we consider the variation of objective functional $F(X)$. Consider the following equation for the functional derivative $\delta_Y F(X^0)$ at the point X^0 with respect to direction of random vector Y:

$$\delta_Y F(X^0) = \frac{d}{d\varepsilon}[F(X^0 + \varepsilon Y)]_{\varepsilon=0} = \frac{d}{d\varepsilon}\left[\int_{R^n} f(x) p_{X^\varepsilon}(x)\,dx\right]_{\varepsilon=0} \tag{9.11}$$

where the distribution density $p_{X^\varepsilon}(x)$ of the random vector $x^\varepsilon = x^0 + \varepsilon Y$ can be expressed through joint distribution density $p_{X^0, Y}(x, y)$ of vectors X^0 and Y:

$$p_{X^\varepsilon}(x) = \int_{R^n} p_{X^0, Y}(x - \varepsilon y, y)\,dy \tag{9.12}$$

Let us assume that the integral in (9.12) is differentiable with respect to parameter ε (which can always be achieved by choosing appropriate classes of distribution densities $p(x, y)$).

Then taking (9.12) into account we can get:

$$\delta_Y F(X^0) = \frac{d}{d\varepsilon}\left[\int_{R^n} f(x)\left(\int_{R^n} p_{X^0, Y}(x - \varepsilon y, y)\,dy\right)dx\right]_{\varepsilon=0}$$

$$= \int_{R^n} \frac{d}{d\varepsilon}[A_\varepsilon f(y)]_{\varepsilon=0}\,dy \tag{9.13}$$

where

$$A_\varepsilon f(y) = \int_{R^n} p_{X^0, Y}(x - \varepsilon y, y) f(x)\,dx \tag{9.14}$$

For further transformation it is convenient to use the following property of divergence operator:

$$\left[\frac{d}{d\varepsilon} p_{X^0,Y}(x - \varepsilon y, y)\right]_{\varepsilon=0} = \langle -\nabla_x p_{X^0,Y}(x, y), y\rangle$$
$$= -\text{div}_x[p_{X^0,Y}(x, y)y] \tag{9.15}$$

where $\langle \cdot, \cdot \rangle$ - denotes the scalar product, ∇ is the gradient operator. Introduce the conditional distribution density

$$p_{Y|X^0 x}(y) = p_{X^0,Y}(x, y)/p_{X^0}(x), \; p_{X^0}(x) = \int_{R^n} p_{X^0,Y}(x, u) \, du \tag{9.16}$$

Then directional derivative $\delta_Y F(X^0)$ can be written in the following way:

$$\delta_Y F(X^0) = -\int_{R^n} f(x) \text{div}_x[p_{X^0}(x)\overline{y}(x)] \, dx \tag{9.17}$$

where

$$\overline{y}(x) = E(Y|X^0 = x) = \int_{R^n} y p_{Y|X^0=x}(y) \, dy \tag{9.18}$$

At the same time, differentiating the identity

$$\int_{R^n} p_{X^\varepsilon}(x) \, dx = 1$$

with respect to ε when $\varepsilon = 0$ we will get:

$$\int_{R^n} \text{div}_x[p_{X^0}(x)\overline{y}(x)] \, dx = 0 \tag{9.19}$$

This leads to the final expression for directional derivative:

$$\delta_Y F(X^0) = -\int_{R^n} [f(x) - C] \text{div}_x[p_{X^0}(x)\overline{y}(x)] \, dx \tag{9.20}$$

where C is an arbitrarily chosen constant.

So, the derivative of the functional $F(X)$ (9.10) at the point X^0 (characterized by density $p_{X^0}(x)$) with respect to direction of random vector Y, which is characterized by vector field $\overline{y}(x)$ (9.18), is determined up to the constant C.

9.7.2 The concept of gradient in the non-smooth extreme problem

In order to define the gradient basis for problems where only the values of objective function $f(x)$, $x \in R^n$, are available, we have to choose vectors Y, which maximize the directional derivative $\delta_Y F(X^0)$. After imposing additional restrictions on vector Y using Cauchy inequality, we obtain the following condition for maximization:

$$\text{div}\lfloor p_{X^0}(x)\overline{y}(x)\rfloor = -\lambda[f(x) - C]p_U(x) \tag{9.21}$$

where parameter C is determined according to (9.19) as

$$C = \int_{R^n} f(x)p_U(x)\,dx \tag{9.22}$$

For the constructive description of the set of solutions for the Equation (9.21), we will decompose finite, or vanishing at infinity, vector field $p_{X^0}(x)\overline{y}(x)$ into the potential $\nabla\phi_0$ and zero-divergent W_0 components.

$$p_{X^0}(x)\overline{y}(x) = \nabla\phi_0(x) + W_0, \quad \text{div}\,W_0 = 0 \tag{9.23}$$

Under an additional condition $\phi_0|_\infty = 0$, this representation is unique.

Then, according to (9.21), the potential function $\phi_0(x)$ will satisfy the equation

$$\Delta\phi_0(x) = -\lambda[f(x) - C]p_U(x) \tag{9.24}$$

This represents a Poisson equation with respect to scalar function $\phi_0(x)$. The uniqueness condition for the solution of this equation (that the vector field vanishes at infinity) can be easily satisfied because of the properties of distribution density $p_{X^0}(x)$. It has the following form:

$$\phi_0(x) = -\lambda \int_{R^n} L(x, \xi)[f(\xi) - C]p_U(\xi)\,d\xi \tag{9.25}$$

where $L(x, \xi)$ is the fundamental solution of a Laplace equation:

$$L(x, \xi) = \begin{cases} -\dfrac{1}{(n-2)\omega_n|x-\xi|^{n-2}}, & n > 2 \\[2mm] \dfrac{1}{2\pi}\ln|x-\xi|, & n = 2 \end{cases} \tag{9.26}$$

Here ω_n is the surface area of unity sphere in R^n space.

As a result the gradient of the potential component $\phi_0(x)$ in (9.23) can be expressed as:

$$\nabla\phi_0(x) = -\lambda \int_{R^n} \nabla_x L(x, \xi)[f(\xi) - C]p_U(\xi)\,d\xi$$
$$= -\lambda E[\nabla_x L(x, U)[f(U) - C]] \tag{9.27}$$

$\nabla\phi_0$ here represents the generalized gradient for the direction of update under general assumptions about the objective function $f(x)$.

9.7.3 Constructing optimization algorithm

The iterative procedure in random vector space has the following form:

$$X^{N+1} = X^N + \alpha_{N+1}Y^{N+1} \quad (N = 0, 1, 2, \ldots) \tag{9.28}$$

This update can be rewritten in distribution characteristics:

$$E(X^{N+1}) = E(X^N) + \alpha_{N+1}E(Y^{N+1}) \tag{9.29}$$

or representing $E(Y^{N+1})$ as $E(Y^{N+1}) = E_{X^{N+1}}E\lfloor Y^{N+1}|X^N\rfloor$, we get

$$E(X^{N+1}) = E(X^N) + \alpha_{N+1}E_{X^N}E(Y^{N+1}|X^N) \tag{9.30}$$

Expectation of the random vector Y can be estimated from

$$E(Y|X) = \bar{y}(X) = \nabla\phi(X)/p(X) \tag{9.31}$$

Denoting the estimation of EX^{N+1} as $\hat{m}^{N+1}$ we can represent (9.30) in the following form:

$$\hat{m}^{N+1} = m^N + \alpha_{N+1}\bar{E}_X[\bar{y}(x)] \tag{9.32}$$

where $m^N = EX^N$, $\bar{E}$ is some statistical estimation of expectation.

Since expectations should concentrate in the potentially optimal area of search, we use only successful updates from the previous point m^N to calculate the statistical estimation of the next point $\hat{m}^{N+1}$. Such strategy assigns a higher probability to realizations with high potential. Degree of future prospect is determined by deviation of the objective function value in this realization from the moving average C. Then an estimation of expectation of X can be calculated as $\sum_j \gamma_j x^j$ where γ_j are the weights proportional to $|\hat{f}(x^j)|$, $\hat{f}(x^j) = f(x^j) - C$, $\gamma_j > 0$, $\sum_j \gamma_j = 1$.

Let us consider some specifics of search strategy in case of successful ($\hat{f} > 0$) and unsuccessful ($\hat{f} < 0$) realizations for estimation of the direction of update. Recalling the representation (9.23) and assigning for simplicity $W = 0$, we choose $E[\nabla\phi(X^N)/p_N]$ as direction of update Y. Then the iterative search procedure can be rewritten as

$$\hat{m}^{N+1} = m^N + \alpha_{N+1}\bar{E}_X E_U \left\{ \frac{\hat{f}(U)}{\omega_n|U - X^N|^n p(X^N)}(X^N - U) \right\} \tag{9.33}$$

If we limit the expectation estimation to just one realization u of random vector U and substitute the mean m^N as one of realizations of a random vector X, (9.33) becomes

$$\hat{m}^{N+1} = m^N + \alpha_{N+1} \frac{\hat{f}(u)}{\omega_n |u - m^N|^n p(m^N)} (m^N - u) \tag{9.34}$$

The suggested scheme is some adaptive expansion of well-known polytope method.[14] This method starts with initial set of $n+1$ points in R^n space that are sorted in order of increasing values of objective function. The 'worst' point x^{n+1} (with the highest function value) is symmetrically reflected with respect to centre of gravity of others

$$x^{n+1,1} = h + \alpha(h - x^{n+1}), h = \frac{1}{n} \sum_{i=1}^{n} x^i, \alpha > 0$$

If this reflection step has found the best (so far) point, that is $f(x^{n+1,1}) < f(x^1)$, then an expansion of polytope is performed:

$$x^{n+1,2} = h + \beta(x^{n+1,1} - h), \beta > 1$$

If it can not improve the current polytope at all ($f(x^{n+1,1}) > f(x^n)$) a contraction procedure is carried out:

$$x^{n+1,2} = h + \gamma(x^{n+1,1} - h), 0 < \gamma < 1$$

If the reflected point is neither the 'best' nor the 'worst' ($f(x^1) < f(x^{n+1,1}) < f(x^n)$), then the vertex x^{n+1} is replaced with $x^{n+1,1}$ and all vertices are resorted and enumerated again to retain the ascending order.

In our iteration procedure if realization u is potentially optimal ($\hat{f}(u) < 0$) then the search moves from m^N in the direction $m^N - u$, which corresponds to expansion in the polytope method. Otherwise the search moves in the opposite direction as in reflection stage. If the point $\hat{m}^{N+1}$ as a result of update (9.34) satisfies the condition $f(\hat{m}^{N+1}) < 0$, then we assign $m^{N+1} = \hat{m}^{N+1}$, $C_N = f(m^N)$ and move forward. If the trial point in (9.34) gave an unsuccessful estimation $\hat{m}^{N+1}$ (that is $f(\hat{m}^{N+1}) \geq 0$), then we can try the same direction with shorter step size α_{N+1}. This would correspond to contraction stage in polytope method. If a number of such attempts didn't give successful value of $\hat{m}^{N+1}$, then we obtain a new realization u of random vector U.

The current mean m^N in (9.34) can be interpreted as a centre of gravity at the iteration N. To assign the new value to m^{N+1} we can also use several estimations of $\hat{m}^{N+1}$, satisfying the condition $f(\hat{m}^{N+1}) < 0$ and corresponding to different realizations of the random vector U. This would correspond to the modification of polytope method where several vertices are reflected on the each iteration. The parameter C can be evaluated from the Equation (9.22). Thus the described iterative procedure can provide a natural regular empowerment of traditional heuristic polytope method.

We propose the following algorithm to implement this version of generalized gradient algorithm based on randomization of initial problem and use of potential theory:

1. Choose an initial point X^0 (weights in the current portfolio).
2. Obtain K realization of a random vector U^N, $\{U^{N,i}\}$, $i = 1, 2, \ldots, K$ (they may be interpreted as vertices of a polytope with $K = n + 1$).
3. Calculate the values of objective function in that vertices $f(U^{N,i})$.
4. Sort these vertices in the order of increase of function values.
5. Calculate the mean level $C_N = \frac{1}{K} \Sigma_i^K f(U^{N,i})$.
6. Calculate the initial expected value m^N (centre of gravity).
7. Perform (9.34) for each of the realizations of a random vector U^N, $\{U^{N,i}\}$, $i = 1, 2, \ldots, K$, reconciling the step size in case of an unsatisfactory result:

$$\hat{m}^{N+1,i} = m^N + \alpha_{N+1} \frac{\hat{f}(U^{N,i})}{\omega_n |U^{N,i} - m^N|^n} (m^N - U^{N,i})$$

8. Verify a stopping rule for a given tolerance level

$$D^N = \frac{1}{K} \sum_{i=1}^{K} [f(U^{N,i}) - C_N]^2 < \varepsilon$$

If it is not satisfied revert to step 4 after respectively updating the vertices.

To strengthen local properties of the algorithm the centre of gravity can be calculated using weights proportional to their successful deviation from the mean level:

$$m^N = \frac{1}{M} \sum_{j=1}^{M} \gamma_j U^{N,j}, \ \hat{f}(U^{N,j}) < 0, \gamma_j = \frac{|\hat{f}(U^{N,j})|}{\sum_{i=1}^{n} |\hat{f}(U^{N,i})|}$$

For emphasizing global properties of the algorithm we can overstate level C, assigning $C = f(U^{N,K-1})$. This would make more realizations to satisfy the condition of local improvement and allow algorithmic search to get out of local extreme neighbourhoods.

REFERENCES

Acharya, V., Das, R. and Sundaram, R. (2000) Pricing credit derivatives with rating transitions, Working paper, November.

Altman, E., Resti, A. and Sironi, A. (2001) Analyzing and Explaining Default Recovery Rates, Working Paper (Report submitted to ISDA).

Amner, J. and Packer, F. How consistent are credit ratings? A geographic and sectoral analysis of default risk, Working Paper.

Black, F. and Scholes, M. (1973) The pricing of options and corporate liabilities, *Journal of Political Economy*, **81**, 637–54.

Black, F., Derman, E. and Toy, W. (1990) A one factor model of interest rates and its application to treasury bond options, *Financial Analysts' Journal*, 33–9.

Bohn, J.R. (1999) A survey of contingent-claims approaches to risky debt valuation, Working paper, June.

Brace, A., Gatarek, D. and Musiela, M. (1997) The market model of interest rate dynamics, *Mathematical Finance*, **7**(2), 127–55.

Cox, J., Ingersoll, J.E. and Ross, S.A. (1985) An inter-temporal general equilibrium model of asset prices, *Econometrica*, **53**, 363–84.

CreditMetrics™ Technical Document, www.riskmetrics.com/cmtdovv.html

Credit Suisse Financial Products (1997) *CreditRisk + −A Credit Risk Management Framework*.

Das, S.R. (1995) Credit risk derivatives, *Journal of Derivatives*, **2**(3), 7–23.

Das, S. ed. (1998) *Credit Derivatives: Trading and Management of Credit and Default-Risk*, Wiley Frontiers in Finance, John Wiley & Sons, New York, Chichester, Singapore.

Das, S.R. and Tufano, P. (1994) Pricing credit-sensitive debt when interest rates, credit ratings and credit spreads are stochastic, Working paper, Harvard Business School, December.

Das, S.R. and Sundaram, R.K. (1998) A direct approach to arbitrage-free pricing of credit derivatives, Working Paper 6635, National Bureau of Economic Research, July.

Duffie, D. and Singleton, K.J. (1997) An econometric model of the term structure of interest-rate swap yields, *The Journal of Finance*, **52**(4), 1287–1322, B.3. 131.

Duffie, D. and Singleton, K.J. (1999) Modeling term structures of defaultable bonds, *Review of Financial Studies*, **12**(4), 687–720.

FITCH (2001) *Bank Loan and Bond Recovery Study: 1997–2001*, O'Shea, S., Bonelli, S. and Grossman, R. March 19.

Flesaker, B., Houghston, L., Schreiber, L. and Sprung, L. (1994) Taking all the credit, *Risk Magazine*, **7**, 105–8.

Gil, A. (1987) *Computational Aspects of Randomized Optimization Algorithms, Processing of Signals in Management Systems and Information Networks*, Voronezh, Voronezh University Press.

Gil, A., Kaplinsky, A. and Propoi, A. (1988) *The use of Potential Theory in Control Theory Approach to Construction of Optimization Algorithms Using Reflection and Extension Operations*, Optimization Methods and Models, Moscow, All-Union Institute of Systems Research Press.

Gill, P.E., Murray, W. and Wright, M. H. (1981) *Practical Optimization*. Academic Press, London.

Heath, D., Jarrow, R. and Morton, A. (1992) Bond pricing and the term structure of interest rates: A new methodology for contingent claims valuation, *Econometrica*, **60**, 77–105.

Ho, Thomas S.Y. and Sang-Bin Lee (1986) Term structure movements and pricing interest rate contingent claims, *Journal of Finance*, **41**, 1011–29.

Hull, J. and White, A. (1993) One factor interest rate models and the valuation of interest rate derivative securities, *Journal of Financial and Quantitative Analysis*, **28**, 235–254.

Hull, J. and White, A. (2000) Valuing Credit Default Swaps II: Modeling default correlations, Working paper, April.

Jamshidian, F. (1995) A simple class of square-root interest-rate models, *Applied Mathematical Finance*, **2**, 61–72.

Jamshidian, F. (1997) LIBOR and swap market models and measures, *Finance and Stochastics* **1**(4), 293–330, B. Bibliography 132.

Jarrow, R. and Madan, D. (1995) Option pricing using the term structure of interest rates to hedge systematic discontinuities in asset returns, *Mathematical Finance*, **5**(4), 311–36,10.

Jarrow, R.A. and Turnbull, S.M. (1995) Pricing derivatives on financial securities subject to credit risk, *Journal of Finance*, **50**, 53–85.

Jarrow, R.A., Lando, D. and Turnbull, S.M. (1997) A Markov model for the term structure of credit risk spreads, *Review of Financial Studies*, **10**(2), 481–523.

Kealhoffer, S. (1995) Managing Default Risk in Derivative Portfolios. In *Derivative Credit Risk: Advances in Measurement and Management*, Renaissance Risk Publications, London.

Leland, H.E. (1994) Risky debt, bond covenants and optimal capital structure, *Journal of Finance*, **49**, 1213–52.

Longstaff, F. and Schwartz, E. (1992) Interest rate volatility and the term structure: A two factor general equilibrium model, *Journal of Finance*, **47**, 1259–82.

Longstaff, F. and Schwartz, E. (1995) The pricing of credit risk derivatives, *Journal of Fixed Income*, **5**(1), 6–14, June.

Madan, D. and Unal, H. (1998) Pricing the risks of default, *Review of Derivatives Research*, **2**(2/3), 121–60.

Merton, R.C. (1974) On the pricing of corporate debt: The risk structure of interest rates, *Journal of Finance*, **29**, 449–70.

Moody's (2001) *Default and Recovery Rates of Corporate Bond Issuers: 2000*, Hamilton, D., Gupta, G. and Berhault, A. February.

Schonbucher, P.J. (1998) Term structure modeling of defaultable bonds, *Review of Derivatives Studies*, Special Issue: Credit Risk, **2**(2/3), 161–192.

Schonbucher, P.J. (2000) A LIBOR market model with default risk, Working paper, December 1999. Revised April.

Ugur Kolyuoglu, H. and Hickman, A. (1998) Reconcilable differences, *Risk Magazine*, October.

Vasicek, O. (1977) An equilibrium characterizations of the term structure, *Journal of Financial Economics*, **5**, 177–88.

Wilson T. (1997) Portfolio credit risk, *Risk September*, 111–7 and *Risk October*, 56–61.

Zhou, C. (1997a) A jump-diffusion approach to modeling credit risk and valuing defaultable securities, Finance and Economics Discussion Paper Series 1997/15, Board of Governors of the Federal Reserve System, March.

Zhou, C. (1997a) Default Correlation: an analytical result, Finance and Economics Discussion Paper Series 1997/15, Board of Governors of the Federal Reserve System, May.

NOTES

1. CreditMetrics™ Technical Document
2. Stephen Kealhoffer (1995)
3. Credit Suisse Financial Products (1997)
4. Wilson (1997)
5. See detailed comparison of these methodologies in Koyluoglu, Hickman (1998)
6. Moody's 2001
7. Amner and Packer Working Paper
8. Altman, Resti, and Sironi (2001)
9. R. Merton (1974)
10. Kealhoffer (1995)
11. Moody's, 2001
12. Jarrow, Lando and Turnbull (1997)
13. CreditMetrics™, www.riskmetrics.com
14. Gill, Murray and Wright (1981)

Chapter 10

Incorporating skewness and kurtosis in portfolio optimization: a multidimensional efficient set

GUSTAVO M DE ATHAYDE AND RENATO G FLÔRES, JR

ABSTRACT

We develop mathematical tools that make the algebra of multivariate higher moments very tractable. Based on them, a multidimensional portfolio frontier is created, incorporating skewness and using kurtosis instead of variance. Although both these moments describe dispersion, the former is a much more efficient instrument to capture extreme variations than the latter. A complete characterization of this portfolio set is made. Interesting properties make the construction of the portfolio frontier a task easier than supposed.

10.1 INTRODUCTION

Most models in finance are based on mean-variance analysis. Risk premium is therefore derived from the second moment of a random variable. The basic assumption of this kind of modelling is that agents are not so concerned about moments higher than the variance. In practice, however, it is known that these moments have an influence in investors' decisions. This might explain the bad empirical performance of the CAPM, as it is based on the assumption that the investors' goal is to minimize the variance, or maximize the expected return of their portfolio. Literature on this subject can be found in Markowitz (1952), Sharpe (1964), Lintner (1965), Mossin (1966) and Merton (1972).

In general, agents not only care about higher moments, but also their preferences seem to follow some standard behaviour. They are willing to trade a highly probable loss of a few cents, for a neglectable chance of winning a fortune. Intuition therefore suggests that agents prefer the highest odd moments. As far as even moments, the wider the tails of the returns distribution, the higher they will be. They capture, above all, the dispersion of the payoffs and, in general, people dislike them.

In fact, all the utility functions that are strictly increasing and concave have expected utilities that increase with odd moments and decrease with even moments. When restricting ourselves to expected utility, mean-variance analysis may be justified by either a quadratic utility function or by a Taylor approximation of a more general and acceptable utility function. The first approach has some theoretical problems, like a region in which more money would decrease investors' utility, while the second, in view of the arguments above, can often be considered a rough approximation. Further, classical discussions on these subjects may be found in Pratt (1964), Pratt and Zeckhauser (1987) Samuelson (1970) and Tsiang (1972).

Another argument in favour of mean-variance analysis is the assumption that asset returns are normally distributed.[1] Since all the odd moments are null, the optimization of the investor would be restricted to minimizing even moments. However, in the normal family, minimizing variance implies minimizing all the even moments, because any even moment of a normal distribution is given by.

$$(\sigma^2)^n \prod_{i=1}^{n} (2i - 1)$$

where $2n$, $n \geq 1$, is the order of the moment.

It turned out that normality of asset returns has been widely rejected in empirical tests (see for instance Eftekhari and Satchell, 1996, Mandelbrot, 1997). Skewness and fat tails are present on the conditional or unconditional distributions of returns. Additional facts, like the worldwide presence of the 'smile' effect on options quotations, can also be pointed out as a clear rejection of normality on asset returns.

Another argument in favour of the use of higher moments is the current concern with the downside risk of portfolios, and measures of risk like the VaR (value at risk). They all emphasize the worst states of the world, i.e. the left tails of the distributions. The higher the odd moments, and the lower the even ones, the lower this kind of risk will be.

Most of the models that dealt with higher moments were focused solely on the CAPM, or on simple microeconomic approaches, assuming a representative agent who chooses one single portfolio, which becomes the market portfolio. The great inconvenience of these approaches[2] is that they are unable to analyse the technical properties of the portfolio set per se. In other words, we know the technical characteristics of the Markowitz portfolio frontier that depend solely on the distribution of assets returns – namely, its means and covariances – as two-fund separation. In the approach described above, it is impossible to develop this analysis. The solution is always dependent on the utility function used. Not surprisingly, the optimal portfolio set is bypassed. In contrast to the Markowitz solution, that allows you to have several different investors with different risk tolerances, these models need to assume that all the investors demand exactly the same optimal portfolio. In the classical portfolio frontier, investors could choose several points in the portfolio frontier, or in the capital market line. Therefore it should be clear that when we choose to avoid the characterization of the portfolio set, and move to the representative agent approach, heterogeneity of investor behaviour towards risk is a fair assumption that will need to be discarded.

Apparently, the main difficulty of working with higher moments was the lack of mathematical tools that could reproduce the non-linear algebra they require. Some attempts were made to rewrite the problem in a typical linear algebra setting, as Kraus and Litzenberger (1976) and Simaan (1993). Both papers simply considered a vector containing the coskewness between each single asset and the optimal portfolio, so the inner product of the optimal portfolio and this vector would give us the skewness of the optimal portfolio. However, the optimal portfolio is the vector to be found, making their approach quite dubious. On one hand the portfolio is endogenous, and on the other it is taken as given a priori.

In this paper, we construct a portfolio frontier similar to the mean-variance-skewness in Athayde (2001), the only difference is that instead of using variance, we will use kurtosis. The goal to minimize kurtosis, instead of variance, is very interesting. Both capture dispersion, volatility and, to some extent, risk. However the fourth moment puts much more weight on extreme values (like crises) than variance does. Therefore, controlling kurtosis would imply controlling huge dispersions, and not putting much weight on small changes. If we think in terms of VaR, or even extreme values, kurtosis seems to be a much better indicator of that kind of risk.

Differently from the mean-variance case, that only requires linear algebra, higher moments require the use of the so-called tensors, which can be seen as a generalization of matrices. For instance, the skewness version of the covariance matrix has a three-dimensional cubic shape. In case we have n different assets, it will have dimension $n \times n \times n$. The kurtosis will be represented by a four-dimensional figure with dimensions $n \times n \times n \times n$, and so on. Needless to say, the mathematics becomes far more cumbersome than in the classical case. These 'multidimensional matrices' are called tensors. While matrices are defined in terms of only two co-ordinates, they can have several different co-ordinates. Although they are quite popular in physics – Einstein developed the tensorial notation when working on the Theory of Relativity – they are not so familiar to economists. Nonetheless, their use in the problems we will be dealing with is also cumbersome. We developed a friendlier notation, to bring the style closer to simple linear algebra. The following section explains these new mathematical tools, fully developed in Athayde (2001).

10.2   THE ALGEBRA OF MULTIVARIATE MOMENTS

The variance of a portfolio made of n assets, each one with a weight α is given by:

$$\sigma_{p^2} = \sum_{i=1}^{n} \sum_{j=1}^{n} \alpha_i \alpha_j \sigma_{ij} = [\alpha_1 \quad \alpha_2 \quad \cdots \quad \alpha_n] \begin{bmatrix} \sigma_{11} & \sigma_{12} & \cdots & \sigma_{1n} \\ \sigma_{21} & \sigma_{22} & \cdots & \sigma_{2n} \\ \vdots & \vdots & \ddots & \vdots \\ \sigma_{n1} & \sigma_{n2} & \cdots & \sigma_{nn} \end{bmatrix} \begin{bmatrix} \alpha_1 \\ \alpha_2 \\ \vdots \\ \alpha_n \end{bmatrix}$$

While the skewness is given by:

$$\sigma_{p^3} = \sum_{i=1}^{n} \sum_{j=1}^{n} \sum_{k=1}^{n} \alpha_i \alpha_j \alpha_k \alpha_{ijk}$$

Notice that the formula above suggests a product of vectors and matrices, in which the matrix of the third moment would have a cubic shape, like the n matrices below one above the other.

$$\begin{bmatrix} \sigma_{111} & \sigma_{121} & \cdots & \sigma_{1n1} \\ \sigma_{211} & \sigma_{221} & \cdots & \sigma_{2n1} \\ \vdots & \vdots & \ddots & \vdots \\ \sigma_{n11} & \sigma_{n21} & \cdots & \sigma_{nn1} \end{bmatrix} \begin{bmatrix} \sigma_{112} & \sigma_{122} & \cdots & \sigma_{1n2} \\ \sigma_{212} & \sigma_{222} & \cdots & \sigma_{2n2} \\ \vdots & \vdots & \ddots & \vdots \\ \sigma_{n12} & \sigma_{n22} & \cdots & \sigma_{nn2} \end{bmatrix} \cdots \begin{bmatrix} \sigma_{11n} & \sigma_{12n} & \cdots & \sigma_{1nn} \\ \sigma_{21n} & \sigma_{22n} & \cdots & \sigma_{2nn} \\ \vdots & \vdots & \ddots & \vdots \\ \sigma_{n1n} & \sigma_{n2n} & \cdots & \sigma_{nnn} \end{bmatrix}$$

Each one of these matrices would be pre- and post-multiplied by the vector of weights α, resulting in n scalars, therefore forming a vector with dimension n. This vector would be multiplied again by the same vector α, resulting in a scalar, that will be the third moment of the portfolio α.

This approach can be extended towards higher moments, where kurtosis would be given by a matrix with equal borders, with a four dimensional shape. In other words a matrix with dimensions $n \times n \times n \times n$. This matrix would be multiplied four times by the vector α until it has been reduced to a scalar:

$$\sigma_{p^4} = \sum_{i=1}^{n} \sum_{j=1}^{n} \sum_{k=1}^{n} \sum_{l=1}^{n} \alpha_i \alpha_j \alpha_k \alpha_l \alpha_{ijkl}$$

These multidimensional matrices are in fact the tensors, and their typical notation is quite different from the one to be developed. In order to make them easier to handle, we shall adopt the following technique. For the skewness, instead of a cubic matrix $n \times n \times n$, a $n \times n^2$ matrix, formed by putting each of the $n \times n$ matrices side by side, can be used:

$$[M_3] = \begin{bmatrix} \sigma_{111} & \sigma_{121} & \cdots & \sigma_{1n1} & \sigma_{112} & \sigma_{122} & \cdots & \sigma_{1n2} & & \sigma_{11n} & \sigma_{12n} & \cdots & \sigma_{1nn} \\ \sigma_{211} & \sigma_{221} & \cdots & \sigma_{2n1} & \sigma_{212} & \sigma_{222} & \cdots & \sigma_{2n2} & & \sigma_{21n} & \sigma_{22n} & \cdots & \sigma_{2nn} \\ \vdots & \vdots & \ddots & \vdots & \vdots & \vdots & \ddots & \vdots & \cdots & \vdots & \vdots & \ddots & \vdots \\ \sigma_{n11} & \sigma_{n21} & \cdots & \sigma_{nn1} & \sigma_{n12} & \sigma_{n22} & \cdots & \sigma_{nn2} & & \sigma_{n1n} & \sigma_{n2n} & \cdots & \sigma_{nnn} \end{bmatrix}$$

Notice that, using the following decomposition of the matrix $[M_3]$:

$$\underset{nxn^2}{[M_3]} = \begin{bmatrix} \underset{nxn}{[M_{31}]} & \underset{nxn}{[M_{32}]} & \cdots & \underset{nxn}{[M_{3n}]} \end{bmatrix}$$

where

$$\underset{nxn}{[M_{3k}]} = \begin{bmatrix} \sigma_{11k} & \sigma_{12k} & \cdots & \sigma_{1nk} \\ \sigma_{21k} & \sigma_{22k} & \cdots & \sigma_{2nk} \\ \vdots & \vdots & \ddots & \vdots \\ \sigma_{n1k} & \sigma_{n2k} & \cdots & \sigma_{nnk} \end{bmatrix}$$

the skewness of a portfolio α will be given by:

$$\sigma_{p^3} = \underset{1xn}{[\alpha]'} \begin{bmatrix} \underset{nxn}{[M_{31}]} & \underset{nxn}{[M_{32}]} & \cdots & \underset{nxn}{[M_{3n}]} \end{bmatrix} \begin{bmatrix} \underset{1xn}{\alpha_1[\alpha]} \\ \underset{1xn}{\alpha_2[\alpha]} \\ \vdots \\ \underset{1xn}{\alpha_n[\alpha]} \end{bmatrix} = \underset{1xn}{[\alpha]'} \underset{nxn^2}{[M_3]} \underset{n^2x1}{[\alpha \otimes \alpha]}$$

where $\otimes$ refers to the kroenecker product.

By analogy, the kurtosis could be written in the following manner:

$$\sigma_p^4 = \underset{1xn}{[\alpha]'} \underset{nxn^3}{[M_4]} \underset{n^3x1}{[\alpha \otimes \alpha \otimes \alpha]}$$

Moreover, as shown in Athayde (2001):

$$\frac{\partial \sigma_{p^3}}{\partial \alpha} = 3 \underset{nxn^2}{[M_3]} \underset{n^2x1}{[\alpha \otimes \alpha]} \qquad \frac{\partial \sigma_{p^4}}{\partial \alpha} = 4 \underset{nxn^3}{[M_4]} \underset{n^3x1}{[\alpha \otimes \alpha \otimes \alpha]}$$

$$\frac{\partial^2 \sigma_{p^3}}{\partial \alpha \partial \alpha'} = 3 \underset{nxn^2}{[M_3]} \underset{n^2x1}{[\alpha \otimes I]} \qquad \frac{\partial^2 \sigma_{p^4}}{\partial \alpha \partial \alpha'} = 4 \underset{nxn^3}{[M_4]} \underset{n^3x1}{[\alpha \otimes \alpha \otimes I]}$$

Another way to look at these properties is to think in the same manner in which the covariance matrix is constructed. The latter can be interpreted as the sum of several n-dimensional vectors, each one multiplied by their transpose (which would ensure the positive definiteness property), creating a matrix with dimension $n \times n$. The skewness matrix (tensor) is also a sum of the products of several vectors with dimension n (representing n asset returns at a specific date), multiplied by themselves in an orthogonal way and multiplied again in another orthogonal way, generating a figure with dimensions $n \times n \times n$.

No wonder the skewness matrix (tensor) is symmetric in a three-dimensional way. This symmetry guarantees many interesting properties. The same goes for kurtosis and all the higher moments. All these matrices (tensors) will be symmetric if we keep one or more of its co-ordinates fixed.

10.3   THE PORTFOLIO FRONTIER: EXPECTED RETURN, SKEWNESS AND KURTOSIS

The aim of this section is to provide the characteristics, the shape and the ways to assure the investor he is on the efficient set of portfolios. By this, we will be referring to the points on the surface where one cannot get better in any moment, without getting worse on another. Ingersoll (1975) made an effort in this direction, giving a clue of the shape of a portfolio frontier with the first three moments. Moreover, characterization of the efficient set seems a much more plausible approach if we are interested in practical problems, such as asset allocation or fund managing. Use of criteria such as utility functions may not seem reasonable for fund managers, especially those who need to provide reports to clients on their criteria to select portfolios.

Our aim is to provide a characterization of the set of portfolios that:

Property 1 – For a given expected return and skewness, they have the lowest kurtosis.

Property 2 – For a given expected return and kurtosis, they have the highest skewness.

Property 3 – For a given skewness and kurtosis, they have the highest expected return.

The first step we shall take is to ensure Property 1. Therefore we will be minimizing kurtosis for a given skewness and expected return:

$$\text{Min } \alpha^{\cdot}[M_4](\alpha \otimes \alpha \otimes \alpha) + \lambda[E(r_p) - ([\alpha]^{\cdot}[M_1] + (\alpha^{\cdot}[1] - 1)r_f)]$$

$$+ \gamma(\sigma_{p^3} - [\alpha]^{\cdot}[M_3][\alpha \otimes \alpha])$$

The first order conditions are given by:

$$4[M_4][\alpha \otimes \alpha \otimes \alpha] = \lambda[x] + 3\gamma[M_3][\alpha \otimes \alpha] \tag{10.1}$$

$$E(r_p) - r_f = \alpha \cdot ([M_1] - [1]r_f) = \alpha \cdot [x] \tag{10.2}$$

$$\sigma_{p^3} = [\alpha] \cdot [M_3][\alpha \otimes \alpha] \tag{10.3}$$

Pre-multiplying (10.1) by $[x] \cdot [[M_4](\alpha \otimes \alpha \otimes I)]^{-1}$ and using (10.2), we'll have:

$$4R = \lambda A_{(-2)} + 3\gamma A_{(0)} \tag{10.4}$$

Pre-multiplying (10.1) by $([M_3][\alpha \otimes \alpha]) \cdot [[M_4](\alpha \otimes \alpha \otimes I)]^{-1}$ and using (10.3), we'll have:

$$4\sigma_{p^3} = \lambda A_{(0)} + 3\gamma A_{(2)} \tag{10.5}$$

In the expressions above, we have used the following conventions:

$$R = E(r_p) - r_f$$
$$A_{(-2)} = [x] \cdot [[M_4](\alpha \otimes \alpha \otimes I)]^{-1}[x]$$
$$A_{(0)} = [x] \cdot [[M_4](\alpha \otimes \alpha \otimes I)]^{-1}[M_3](\alpha \otimes \alpha)$$
$$A_{(2)} = ([M_3][\alpha \otimes \alpha]) \cdot [[M_4](\alpha \otimes \alpha \otimes I)]^{-1}[M_3](\alpha \otimes \alpha)$$

The subscripts of the A's terms were chosen to correspond to the degree of homogeneity of the term with respect to the vector α.

Making use of (10.4) and (10.5), we have that the (implied) solution for the problem will be given by:

$$[M_4](\alpha \otimes \alpha \otimes \alpha) = \frac{A_{(2)}R - A_{(0)}\sigma_{p^3}}{A_{(-2)}A_{(2)} - (A_0)^2}[x]$$
$$+ \frac{A_{(-2)}\sigma_{p^3} - A_{(0)}R}{A_{(-2)}A_{(2)} - (A_0)^2}[M_3](\alpha \otimes \alpha) \tag{10.6}$$

Proposition 1: *$[[M_4](\alpha \otimes \alpha \otimes I)]$ is positive definite, and $A_{(-2)}$ and $A_{(2)}$ are positive.*

Proof: We can pre and post-multiply it by a vector β, resulting in:

$$\beta \cdot [[M_4](\alpha \otimes \alpha \otimes I)]\beta = \sigma_{\alpha\alpha\beta\beta} > 0$$

Thus we can also say that $A_{(-2)}$ and $A_{(2)}$ are positive, because the inverse of a positive matrix will also be positive definite.

Q.E.D.

The kurtosis of the solution portfolios will be given by:

$$\sigma_{p^4} = \frac{A_{(2)}R^2 - 2A_{(0)}R\sigma_{p^3} + A_{(-2)}(\sigma_{p^3})^2}{A_{(-2)}A_{(2)} - (A_0)^2} \tag{10.7}$$

Due to Proposition 1, $A_{(-2)}$ and $A_{(2)}$ are positive, as well as both the numerator and the denominator of (10.7):

$$\{[M_3](\alpha \otimes \alpha)R - [x]\sigma_{p^3}\}'[[M_4](\alpha \otimes \alpha \otimes I)]^{-1}\{[M_3](\alpha \otimes \alpha)R - [x]\sigma_{p^3}\}$$

$$= A_{(2)}R^2 - 2A_{(0)}R\sigma_{p^3} + A_{(-2)}(\sigma_{p^3})^2 > 0$$

$$\{[M_3](\alpha \otimes \alpha)A_{(0)} - [x]A_{(2)}\}'[[M_4](\alpha \otimes \alpha \otimes I)]^{-1}\{[M_3](\alpha \otimes \alpha)A_{(0)}$$

$$- [x]A_{(2)}\}$$

$$= A_{(-2)}[A_{(-2)}A_{(2)} - (A_0)^2] > 0$$

For the rest of this chapter we will make use of what we call the 'standardized moments'. They are the cubic root of skewness – denoted by y_3 – and the fourth root of kurtosis – denoted by y_4.

Proposition 2:   *For a given scalar k, all the minimum kurtosis portfolios that have the property that* $\sigma_{p^3} = k^3 R^3$, *or* $y_3 = kR$, *are given by* $\alpha = \overline{\alpha}R$, *where* $\overline{\alpha}$ *is the minimum kurtosis portfolio when for R = 1 and* $y_3 = kR$.

Proof: Making use of (10.7), when $\sigma_{p^3} = k^3 R^3$, or $y_3 = kR$:

$$[M_4](\alpha \otimes \alpha \otimes \alpha) = \frac{A_{(2)}R - A_{(0)}k^3 R^3}{A_{(-2)}A_{(2)} - A_{(0)}^2}[x]$$

$$+ \frac{A_{(-2)}k^3 R^3 - A_{(0)}R}{A_{(-2)}A_{(2)} - A_{(0)}^2}[M_3](\alpha \otimes \alpha) \tag{10.8}$$

For the case when $R = 1$, we will have:

$$[M_4](\overline{\alpha} \otimes \overline{\alpha} \otimes \overline{\alpha}) = \frac{\overline{A}_{(2)} - A_{(0)}k^3}{\overline{A}_{(-2)}\overline{A}_{(2)} - A_{(0)}^2}[x]$$

$$+ \frac{\overline{A}_{(-2)}k^3 - \overline{A}_{(0)}}{\overline{A}_{(-2)}\overline{A}_{(2)} - \overline{A}_{(0)}^2}[M_3](\overline{\alpha} \otimes \overline{\alpha}) \tag{10.9}$$

where $\bar{\alpha}$ is the solution to this problem. Replace now α by $\bar{\alpha}R$ in (10.8):

$$[M_4](\bar{\alpha} \otimes \bar{\alpha} \otimes \bar{\alpha})R^3 = \frac{\overline{A}_{(2)}R^3 - \overline{A}_{(0)}k^3R^3}{\overline{A}_{(-2)}\overline{A}_{(2)} - \overline{A}_{(0)}^2}[x]$$

$$+ \frac{\overline{A}_{(-2)}k^3R - \overline{A}_{(0)}R}{\overline{A}_{(-2)}\overline{A}_{(2)} - \overline{A}_{(0)}^2}[M_3](\bar{\alpha} \otimes \bar{\alpha})R^2$$

After cancelling the R's, we will be back to (10.9).

Q.E.D.

This means that in the direction $y_{p^3} = kR$, the kurtosis will be given by:

$$\sigma_{p^4} = \bar{\alpha}'R[M_4](\bar{\alpha}R \otimes \bar{\alpha}R \otimes \bar{\alpha}R) = \overline{\sigma}_{p^4}R^4 \Rightarrow y_{p^4} = \overline{y}_{p^4}\|R\|$$

and the standardized kurtosis will be a linear function of the modulus of R in a given direction k, in the $R \times y_3$ plane. Therefore, all the minimum kurtosis portfolios whose R and y_3 are such that $y_3 = kR$ will be described as:

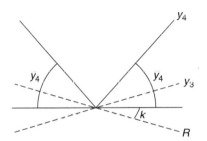

Figure 10.1 *Minimum kurtosis portfolios*

When we take into consideration all the possible angles k, the surface of the minimum kurtosis portfolio could take several shapes, shown in Figure 10.2:

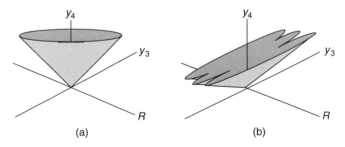

(a)   (b)

Figure 10.2 *Various shapes of minimum kurtosis portfolios*

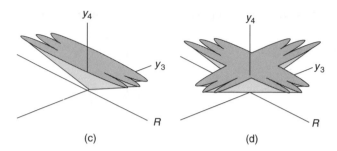

Figure 10.2   *(continued)*

The areas in light grey represent the bottom surface of the whole portfolio set, and they are formed by the set of minimum kurtosis portfolios described in Figure 10.1. In Figure 10.2(d) we would have some directions that would give us local maxima R and Y_3, for a given level of Y_4. In Figure 10.2(c) there would be several maxima R and only one direction that would give us a maximum Y_3. In Figure 10.2(b) we would have several local maxima Y_3 and only one maximum R. Finally, Figure 10.2(a) represents the ideal situation where there is only one maximum R and one maximum Y_3 for a given Y_4. It will be shown that the cases described in Figures 10.2(c) and 10.2(d) will never happen.

Because of Proposition 2, in case we want to find the set of minimum kurtosis portfolios that have the highest R or Y_3 it suffices to find a portfolio that lies on that specific direction. The desired set will be made of multiples of these portfolios.

But how do we find these specific directions? Consider the case where we want to minimize kurtosis subject only to R:

$$\text{Min } \alpha'[M_4](\alpha \otimes \alpha \otimes \alpha) + \lambda(R - \alpha'[x])$$

The first order conditions are:

$$4[M_4](\alpha \otimes \alpha \otimes \alpha) = 4[M_4](\alpha \otimes \alpha \otimes I)\alpha = \lambda[x] \tag{10.10}$$

$$R = \alpha'[x]$$

Pre-multiplying (10.10) by $[x]'[[M_4](\alpha_R \otimes \alpha_R \otimes I)]^{-1}$:

$$\lambda = \frac{4R}{A_{(-2)}}$$

Substituting λ in (10.10) we have that the solution is given by:

$$[M_4](\alpha_R \otimes \alpha_R \otimes \alpha_R) = \frac{R}{A_{(-2)}}[x] \tag{10.11}$$

Consider now the case of $\bar{\alpha}$, which is the portfolio that solves the problem for the case where $R = 1$:

$$[M_4](\bar{\alpha} \otimes \bar{\alpha} \otimes \bar{\alpha}) = \frac{1}{A_{(-2)}}[x] \tag{10.12}$$

If we try the solution $\alpha = \bar{\alpha}R$ for (10.11), we will see that it fits. This shows us that we only need to find one portfolio $\bar{\alpha}$ to generate the whole set of minimum kurtosis portfolios for a given R.

Since it is possible to show that kurtosis is strictly convex in its entire domain (Proposition 1), and we have only a linear constraint, we can ensure the solution is unique. Any numerical procedure can be applied.

Pre-multiplying the equation above by $([M_3][\alpha \otimes \alpha])\cdot[[M_4](\alpha \otimes \alpha \otimes I)]^{-1}$, we have:

$$\sigma_{p^3} = \frac{A_{(0)}R}{A_{(-2)}}$$

In view of (10.6), we see that this skewness will make the LaGrange multiplier of the skewness constraint null. Another aspect of interest is that the skewness of the portfolios that lie on this direction will be homogeneous of degree 3 with respect to R. These portfolios will also have a fixed k on the $R \times y_3$ space, and therefore a kurtosis behaviour just like in Figure 10.1:

$$k = \left(\frac{\overline{\Lambda}_{(0)}}{\overline{A}_{(-2)}}\right)^{1/3}$$

$$\sigma_{p^4} = \bar{\sigma}_{p^4}R^4, \qquad \text{or } y_{p^4} = \bar{y}_{p^4}\|R\|$$

This direction, by duality, will also be giving us the highest (in absolute value) R for a given kurtosis. It also divides the minimum kurtosis set in two parts. Since we want the highest possible skewness, we will always work with the upper half of the surface. By doing so, we will be ensuring Property 2. Thus, we already have achieved two of our three desired properties.

The second case is the highest skewness one. Just like in the previous case, this direction will be the one that gives us the lowest kurtosis subject only to a given skewness. Let us call these portfolios α:

$$\text{Min } \alpha'[M_4](\alpha \otimes \alpha \otimes \alpha) + \lambda(\sigma_{s^3} - \alpha'[M_3][\alpha \otimes \alpha])$$

The first order conditions are:

$$4[M_4](\alpha \otimes \alpha \otimes \alpha) = 4[M_4](\alpha \otimes \alpha \otimes I)\alpha = \lambda3[M_3][\alpha \otimes \alpha] \tag{10.13}$$

$$\sigma_{p^3} = \alpha'[M_3][\alpha \otimes \alpha]$$

Pre-multiplying (10.13) by $([M_3][\alpha \otimes \alpha]) \cdot [[M_4](\alpha \otimes \alpha \otimes I)]^{-1}$, we will have:

$$\lambda = \frac{4\sigma_{p^3}}{3A_{(2)}}$$

Substituting λ in (10.13) we have the solution:

$$[M_4](\alpha \otimes \alpha \otimes \alpha) = \frac{\sigma_{p^3}}{A_{(2)}}[M_3][\alpha \otimes \alpha] \tag{10.14}$$

Consider the case of $\bar{\alpha}$, which is the portfolio that solves the problem for the case where $\sigma_{p^3} = 1$:

$$[M_4](\bar{\alpha} \otimes \bar{\alpha} \otimes \bar{\alpha}) = \frac{1}{\bar{A}_{(2)}}[M_3][\bar{\alpha} \otimes \bar{\alpha}] \tag{10.15}$$

If we try the solution $\alpha = y_{p^3}\bar{\alpha}$ for (10.14), we see that it fits. This shows us that we only need to find one portfolio $\bar{\alpha}$ to generate the whole set of minimum kurtosis portfolios for a given skewness. It can also be easily verified that:

$$R = \frac{\sigma_{p^3}}{A_{(2)}}A_{(0)} \quad k_p = \left(\frac{\bar{A}_{(0)}}{\bar{A}_{(2)}}\right)^{1/3} \quad \sigma_{p^4} = \bar{\sigma}_{p^4}(y_{p^3})^4 \Rightarrow y_{p^4} = \bar{y}_{p^4}\|y_{p^3}\|$$

The first relation makes the first constraint in (10.6) redundant. Meaning that it applies to the general case, being a particular case where the constraint on R does not count.

Unfortunately, there can be several solutions to (10.15), because now we have a non-linear constraint. Some of them will be a local maximum of skewness (in modulus) and some will be local minimum (in modulus). This situation is well described in Figure 10.2(b), which is the most common profile of our minimum kurtosis surface. For a fixed level of kurtosis, we shall have only one direction with the highest R, and a few others with local maxima skewness.

In case we want to verify if the portfolio is a local maximum/minimum, we must look at the determinants of the bordered Hessian below, and verify if they are all positive.

$$\begin{bmatrix} 12[M_4](\alpha \otimes \alpha \otimes I) - \dfrac{8}{A_{(-2)}}[M_3](\alpha \otimes I) & -3[M_3](\alpha \otimes \alpha \otimes I) \\ -3[M_3](\alpha \otimes \alpha \otimes I)' & 0 \end{bmatrix}$$

Let us now consider the figure below (which is a common shape), which represents an isoquant of kurtosis, with three directions on the $R \times y_3$ plane – one with the highest R and two with the highest (local) skewness. The direction

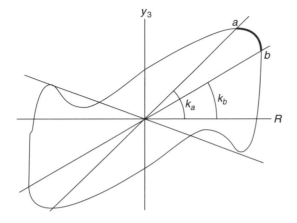

Figure 10.3 *Isoquant of kurtosis (1)*

with the highest R (k_b) will divide the isoquant in two halves, and we shall select only the upper half, because for a given R, the upper half of the isoquant will always have higher skewnesses than the lower half – ensuring Property 2.

If we take the direction of highest skewness (k_a), we can make a similar analysis. It divides the isoquant in two parts. We shall choose the portfolios on the right side of this direction, because the right side will give us always higher R's than the left part for a given level of skewness – ensuring Property 3. The area that ensures us all those three properties mentioned at the beginning of this section is the area in bold and between points a and b.

In this case, all we should do is:

1 Minimize kurtosis with respect to R only.
2 Minimize kurtosis with respect to skewness only.
3 Get k_a and k_b.
4 Minimize kurtosis with respect to R and skewness, only in the directions between k_a and k_b.

However, let us say that our picture looks in fact like that in Figure 10.4. The optimal area will be the one in bold (between points a and b, c and d). This is the area that, for a minimum kurtosis isoquant, will also have the highest skewness for a given R, and the highest R for a given skewness. To reach this area, we should:

1 Minimize kurtosis with respect to R only – we will get k_d
2 Minimize kurtosis with respect to skewness only – we will get k_a and k_c.

In case the highest local skewness is not the one furthest to the right (like in Figure 10.4), then we will need to go a bit further. First of all, the area in between the direction with the highest R and the highest local skewness

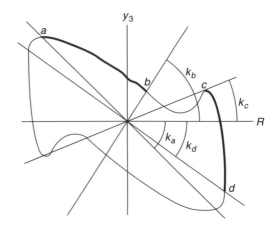

Figure 10.4   *Isoquant of kurtosis (2)*

furthest to the right is optimal. Therefore minimizing kurtosis with respect to angles between k_c and k_d, guarantees optimal portfolios – in the sense they have the three properties desired.

So far the procedure is the same as in the former case. We could stop here in case the investor is not so sensitive to skewness. In case he is, there is still another region (between points a and b) that is also considered to be optimal. In this region, he could get higher skewnesses at the cost of R. To get to this region he should start in the direction of the portfolio with the highest skewness (k_a) and keep minimizing kurtosis on directions with higher angles k, moving on the isoquant until he reaches point b. Once point b is reached, one gets k_b. Then the optimal sets are completely defined. You just need to keep minimizing kurtosis with respect to R and skewness, provided these two lie in the directions between k_a and k_b, and in the directions between K_c and K_d. To get the whole optimal surface, just scale the isoquants.

10.4   CONCLUSION

In this chapter we provided mathematical tools to deal with higher moments. Specifically, we showed how to construct a portfolio frontier that takes into consideration expected return, skewness and kurtosis. The properties of this portfolio frontier are analysed; showing some features that make far easier to achieve the optimal set of portfolios.

REFERENCES

Athayde, G. (2001) A Few More Moments to Finance Theory: Introducing Higher Moments in Investment Theory and econometrics, PhD Dissertation, EPGE/Fundação Getulio Vargas. Rio de Janeiro.

Chamberlain, G. (1983) A Characterisation of the Distributions that Imply Mean-Variance Utility Functions, *Journal of Economic Theory*, **29**, 185–201.

Eftekhari, B. and Satchell, S. (1996) Non-Normality of Returns in Emerging Markets, *Research in International Business and Finance*, Supplement 1, 267–77.

Ingersoll, J. (1975) Multidimensional Security Pricing, *Journal of Financial and Quantitative Analysis*, December, 785–98.

Kraus, A. and Litzenberger, R.H. (1976) Skewness preference and the valuation of risk assets, *Journal of Finance*, **31**, 1085–100.

Lintner, J. (1965) The Valuation of Risk Assets and The Selection of Risky Investments in Stock Portfolios And Capital Budgets, *Review of Economics and Statistics*, **47**, 13–37.

Mandelbrot, B. (1997) *Fractals and Scaling in Finance*, Springer.

Markowitz, H. (1952) Portfolio Selection, *Journal of Finance*, **7**, 77–91.

Merton, R. (1972) An Analytical Derivation of the Efficient Portfolio Frontier, *Journal of Financial and Quantitative Analysis*, **7**, 1851–72.

Mossin, J. (1966) Equilibrium in a Capital Asset Market, *Econometrica*, **35**, 768–83.

Pratt, J. (1964) Risk Aversion in the Small and in The Large, *Econometrica*, **32**, 122–36.

Pratt, J. and Zeckhauser, R. (1987) Proper Risk Aversion, *Econometrica*, **55**, 143–54.

Samuelson, P.A. (1970) The Fundamental Approximation Theorem of Portfolio Analysis in Terms of Means, Variances and Higher Moments, *Review of Economic Studies*, **32**(4), 112.

Sharpe, W. (1964) Capital Asset Prices: A Theory of Market Equilibrium under Conditions of Risk, *Journal of Finance*, **19**, 425–42.

Simaan, Y. (1993) Portfolio Selection and Asset pricing Three Parameter Framework, *Management Science*, **5**, 568–77.

Tsiang, S. (1972) The Rationale of The Mean-Standard Deviation Analysis, Skewness Preference, and the Demand for Money, *American Economic Review*, **62**, 354–71.

NOTES

1. A broader discussion of this subject can be found in Chamberlain (1983).
2. With the exception of Ingersoll (1975) and Bawa and Lindenberg (1977).

Chapter 11

Balancing growth and shortfall probability in continuous time active portfolio management

SID BROWNE

ABSTRACT

Active portfolio management is concerned with objectives related to the outperformance of the return of a target benchmark portfolio. Here we consider an objective that relates the *probability* of achieving a given performance objective to the *time* it takes to achieve the objective, in this way balancing risk and return. As a special case, our analysis includes the case where the investor wants to minimize the expected time until a given performance goal is reached subject to a constraint on the shortfall probability. We find that this purely probabilistic based objective is equivalent to maximizing a Hyperbolic Absolute Risk Aversion utility function with particular parameter values, thus extending the class of equivalences between utility (i.e. subjective) and probabilistic (i.e. objective) based portfolio optimization.

11.1 INTRODUCTION

The goal of active portfolio managers is to beat an index, while passive managers track an index. An index, as used here, refers to some specific portfolio strategy. As such, the goal of the active manager can be restated as to beat another given portfolio strategy.

In this chapter, the objectives of interest relate to non-standard goal type objectives. More specifically, for a given investment 'goal' and 'shortfall' level, we consider the objectives of maximizing the probability of achieving the goal before the shortfall, as well as minimizing the expected time until goal reached. Such objectives have their roots in the classical work of Dubins and Savage (1965). This paper deals with dynamic multi-period models in continuous time. One-period models of active portfolio management are covered in Grinold and Kahn (1995).

For fixed finite–time horizon problems, the active portfolio problem with the maximal probability objective has been studied in Browne (1999b, 1999c), where it was shown that option strategies are optimal but are then very 'risky' in the sense that they replicate a binary option.

Alternatively, over an infinite horizon, the maximal probability objective as well as the minimum time objective both have a constant proportions strategy as the optimal policy (Browne, 1999a). Recall that constant proportions dictates that the asset mix always be held constant in terms of the proportion of wealth invested. To implement such a strategy, one needs to sell an asset after an appreciation and buy after a depreciation. These probabilistic based objectives are also shown to have an equivalence, for the case of a stationary coefficient model, to utility based objectives for particular Constant Relative Risk Aversion (CRRA) utility functions. In spite of these optimality characteristics, constant proportions is considered 'too simple' an idea to be used by many professional investors.

In this chapter, we consider a goal related objective for the risk/return tradeoff, where we consider risk to be the shortfall probability, and return to be related to the time it takes to reach an investment goal. Thus we combine growth and risk in a single dynamic optimization framework. For our objective, it turns out that the policy is no longer constant proportions, and provides a framework that allows explicit consideration of risk-constraints (see Browne (2000b) for a more mathematical treatment of many of these issues). Moreover, it is related to optimizing a particular extended Hyperbolic Absolute Risk Aversion (HARA) utility function.

11.2   SOME BASICS

Our results are stated here in terms of a basic and simple continuous time model, but a more general framework is provided in Browne (1999a).

Here the investor can split and adjust his wealth dynamically, and without cost, between a risky stock and a riskless asset (the money market). The price of the risky stock follows a geometric Brownian motion,

$$dS_t = \mu S_t \, dt + \sigma S_t dW_t \tag{11.1}$$

while the price of the riskless asset is given by

$$dB_t = r B_t \, dt \tag{11.2}$$

A portfolio allocation (trading) strategy is given by a suitably admissible integrable process $\{\pi_t, t \geq 0\}$, where the interpretation of π_t is the fraction of wealth invested in risky stock at time t.

The wealth process associated with strategy $\{\pi_t, t \geq 0\}$ is denoted for the sequel by $\{X_t^\pi t \geq 0\}$. Observe that this wealth process satisfies (see Merton, 1990)

$$dX_t^\pi = \pi_t X_t^\pi \frac{dS_t}{S_t} + (1 - \pi_t) X_t^\pi \frac{dB_t}{B_t}$$
$$= [r + \pi_t(\mu - r)] X_t^\pi dt + \pi_t \sigma X_t^\pi dW_t$$

Observe too that for $\pi_t = 0$ for all t, we recover the riskless asset $X_t^0 = B_t$, while or $\pi_t = 1$ for all t (referred to as the 'buy and hold' strategy), $X_t^1 = S_t$.

11.2.1   Constant proportions and optimal growth

For the model under consideration here, a constant proportions strategy is optimal for a variety of objectives, both utility based (see Merton, 1990) as well as goal based (see Heath et al., 1987 and Browne, 1995, 1997). A constant proportions strategy has $\pi_t = \pi$ for all t, for some constant π. See Perold and Sharpe (1988) for an interesting discussion of such strategies from a practitioner viewpoint. Observe that for constant π, wealth X_t^π, is the geometric Brownian motion

$$X_t^\pi = X_0 \cdot \exp\left\{\left(r + \pi(\mu - r) - \frac{\pi^2 \sigma^2}{2}\right) t + \pi \sigma W_t\right\} \tag{11.3}$$

Constant proportions is the optimal portfolio strategy for maximizing expected terminal utility of wealth, with $U(x) = x^\alpha$ for $\alpha < 1$, or $U(x) = \ln(x)$ (Merton 1990). The resulting optimal fractions are $(1 - a)^{-1} \pi^*$ and π^* accordingly, where the constant π^* is defined as

$$\pi^* = \frac{\mu - r}{\sigma^2} \tag{11.4}$$

It is also well known that for any t, the 'growth rate' $\frac{1}{t} E \ln(X_t / X_0)$, is maximized by π^*. More pertinent to our interests here, π^* also minimizes the expected time to reach any given (upper) investment goal (see Heath et al., 1987 and Browne, 1997). For these reasons, it is sometimes called the 'optimal growth' strategy. (Further optimality properties of π^* are reviewed in Merton (1990, chapter 6) and Browne, 1998).

The wealth under the optimal growth strategy π^* is given by

$$X_t^* = X_0 \exp\left\{\left(r + \frac{(\sigma \pi^*)^2}{2}\right) t + \sigma \pi^* W_t\right\} \tag{11.5}$$

This wealth process is intimately related to the Girsanov martingale for Brownian motion. In particular, for any other strategy $\{\pi_t, t \geq 0\}$, the wealth process X_t^π satisfies

$$E\left(\left.\frac{X_{t+s}^\pi}{X_{t+s}^*}\right|\mathcal{F}_t\right) \leq \frac{X_t^\pi}{X_t^*} \longrightarrow 0, \quad \text{as } t \to \infty \tag{11.6}$$

$\mathcal{F}_t$ is the relevant history at time t, while for any constant π

$$\frac{X_t^\pi}{X_t^*} = \exp\left\{-\frac{\sigma^2}{2}(\pi^* - \pi)^2 t - \sigma(\pi^* - \pi)W_t\right\} \tag{11.7}$$

Equation (11.6) exhibits the supermartingale structure as well as the asymptotic dominance of the optimal growth of wealth.

This fact is intimately related to the pricing of derivative securities, in that if there is a contingent claim that will pay $g(X_T^1)$ at time T (recall that X_t^1 is the price of the risky stock at time t), then the time t 'fair' (Black & Scholes, 1973) price of the contingent claim can be expressed as $X_t^0 E\left(\left.\frac{g(X_T^1)}{X_T^*}\right|\mathcal{F}_t\right)$, where X_t^0 is the price of the riskless asset at time t.

11.3   ACTIVE PORTFOLIO MANAGEMENT

The components of the active portfolio management problem are the controlled wealth process,

$$dX_t^\pi = X_t^\pi[(r + \pi_t(\mu - r))\,dt + \pi_t\sigma\,dW_t^{(1)}] \tag{11.8}$$

as well as a benchmark target process,

$$dY_t = Y_t[\mu_Y\,dt + \sigma_Y dW_t^{(2)}] \tag{11.9}$$

where $W^{(1)}$ and $W^{(2)}$ are two correlated Brownian motions with $E(W_t^{(1)} W_t^{(2)}) = \rho t$. For example Y could be an exogenous process, such as inflation, or some other economic index, or the wealth process associated with a trading strategy that encompasses other assets not included in the investment opportunity set of the ordinary investor.

The sufficient statistic for our problem is the ratio of the controlled wealth to the target benchmark, X_t^π / Y_t, which is stochastically equivalent to the process Z_t^π defined by

$$dZ_t^\pi = Z_t^\pi(m(\pi_t)\,dt + v(\pi_t)d\tilde{W}_t) \tag{11.10}$$

where the drift function is given by

$$m(\pi) = \pi(\mu - r - \sigma^2\beta) - (\mu_Y - r - \sigma_Y^2)$$

and the diffusion function is given by

$$v^2(\pi) = \pi^2\sigma^2 + \sigma_Y^2 - 2\pi\sigma^2\beta$$

where $\beta = \rho\sigma_Y/\sigma$.

For two constants l and u, with $l < u$, we say that investment goal u reached at t if $Z_t^\pi = u$, and that the shortfall level l reached at t if $Z_t^\pi = l$.

- If $\rho^2 < 1$, then the market is 'incomplete' and no perfect hedge exists in the sense of eliminating the variance of the ratio process.
- If $\rho^2 = 1$, and Y is traded, then the 'no arbitrage' condition implies that

$$\frac{\mu - r}{\sigma} = \frac{\mu_Y - r}{\sigma_Y}$$

which in turn implies that

$$\mu_Y = r + \pi(\mu - r), \text{ and } \sigma_Y = \pi\sigma, \text{ for some } \pi \qquad (11.11)$$

As noted earlier, it is known that constant allocations strategies are optimal for many 'goal' based objectives. In particular, Browne (1999a) showed that such strategies are optimal for minimizing the shortfall probability (i.e. maximizing the probability of reaching goal before shortfall), minimizing the expected time to reach the goal in the superfair case (also for maximizing the expected time to reach the shortfall in the subfair case) as well as maximizing (minimizing) the expected discounted reward (cost) of reaching goal (shortfall). We discuss some of these results directly.

11.3.1   The incomplete market case: diffusion minimization and probability maximization

Observe now that choosing π_t to pointwise minimize the diffusion function gives the constant proportions strategy

$$\pi_t^{min-diff} = \beta$$

with resulting diffusion parameter $v^2(\beta) = \sigma_Y^2(1 - \rho^2)$. We will call this the diffusion minimizing strategy.

From Browne (1997), we know that the probability maximizing strategy (of reaching the goal before the shortfall) is given by the pointwise maximizer of the ratio of the drift to the diffusion, i.e.

$$\pi_t^{max-prob} = \arg\min_{\pi_t} \frac{m(\pi_t)}{v^2(\pi_t)}$$

Performing the maximization for this case yields the following constant proportions strategy

$$\pi^{max-prob} = M - \sqrt{M^2 + S^2 - 2\rho SM} = M - \sqrt{M^2 + S^2 - 2\beta M}$$

where

$$M = \frac{\mu_Y - r - \sigma_Y^2}{\mu - r - \sigma^2\beta} \quad \text{and} \quad S = \frac{\sigma_Y}{\sigma}$$

It is of interest now to compare the strategy of the probability maximizer with that of a diffusion minimizer: in particular, observe that a probability maximizer invests less than a diffusion-minimizer. This can be seen by noting that $\pi^{max-prob} \leq \pi^{min-diff}$ can be rearranged to give $M - \beta \leq \sqrt{M^2 + S^2 - 2\beta M}$, and squaring both sides shows that this inequality holds if $\beta^2 \leq S^2$, which of course holds by definition, since $\beta^2 = \rho^2 S^2$.

11.3.2 Minimizing/maximizing expected time

Consider now an investor whose sole interest lies in achieving a given investment goal (e.g. increase wealth by 10%) in a short a period of (expected) time as possible, or to maximize the expected time to a given shortfall level. The solution to the these goal problems depends on the sign of the 'favourability' parameter θ, where

$$\theta := \frac{1}{2}\left[\sigma_Y^2 + \left(\frac{\mu - r}{\sigma}\right)^2\right] - (\mu_Y - r)$$

Observe that θ is independent of ρ. The interpretation of θ is the difference between the maximal possible growth rate for an ordinary investor (see e.g. Merton, 1990, chapter 6), given by $\frac{1}{2}((\mu - r)/\sigma)^2$ – and the growth rate of the benchmark itself, given by $\mu_Y - r - \sigma_Y^2/2$.

The ordinary optimal growth strategy, $\pi^* \equiv (\mu - r)/\sigma^2$, is again optimal for the active portfolio problem with a benchmark, and in particular, if $\theta > 0$, then π^* minimizes expected time to goal, while if $\theta < 0$, then π^* maximizes expected time to shortfall.

Worst case (for the benchmark) bounds for many of these goal type problems can be obtained from the game theoretic analysis of Browne (2000a), who considered a stochastic differential game between two investors, each of whom is restricted from investing in the other one's investment opportunity. The games have nontrivial values if and only if $\rho^2 < 1$.

11.3.3 Active Portfolio Management: the complete market case with $\rho^2 = 1$

When $\rho^2 = 1$, the market is complete and as mentioned earlier, to preclude arbitrage, we must have

$$\mu_Y = r + \pi(\mu - r) \quad \text{and} \quad \sigma_Y = \pi\sigma$$

where π is the 'benchmark' strategy.

If the objective is to maximize the probability of beating benchmark return by a fixed deadline T, then the optimal strategy is to replicate a binary (digital) option (Browne, 1999b, 1999c), which is risky in the sense it can lead to substantial shortfalls. The infinite horizon probability maximizing problem becomes trivial since the investor can reach the goal with probability 1 (so long as $\pi \neq \pi^*$). Similarly, the expected time to the shortfall can be made infinite, and π^* will minimize the expected time to goal.

However, there are some significant disadvantages to using the ordinary optimal growth policy π^* in the active case with a benchmark. In particular, the optimal growth strategy is independent of the benchmark policy π. More importantly, for the optimal growth strategy, the probability of reaching the goal before the shortfall is independent of benchmark policy, as well as any other parameter of interest.

In particular, recall that the ratio of the optimal growth wealth to the benchmark is the geometric Brownian motion

$$dZ_t(\pi^*, \pi) = Z_t(\pi^*, \pi)[\gamma \, dt + (\pi^* - \pi)\sigma dW_t]$$

where $\gamma = \sigma^2(\pi^* - \pi)^2/2$, for which the probability of reaching the goal u before the shortfall l, starting from z is

$$\theta(z) = \frac{u}{z}\left(\frac{z-l}{u-l}\right)$$

Observe that this is independent of all parameters in the model. The expected time to exit the strip (l, u) is given by

$$\gamma^{-1}\left[\theta(z)\ln\left(\frac{u}{l}\right) - \ln\left(\frac{z}{l}\right)\right]$$

Note that this does depend on the benchmark policy π as well as all other parameters through the constant γ.

As such, we now move on to consider a new objective which is a linear tradeoff between shortfall probability and expected time to the goal.

11.4 TRADING OFF RISK AND RETURN IN ACTIVE PORTFOLIO MANAGEMENT: FRACTIONAL OBJECTIVES

For given constants α and β, consider now an objective that tradeoffs the expected time to a goal with the probability of a shortfall. Analytically, if τ^f is the first escape time from the strip (l, u), then successful escape (in terms of reaching the goal) is exit through the upper barrier u, and hitting the lower barrier first, l, results in a shortfall. We are interested in maximizing a linear tradeoff between these two:

$$\sup_f \{ \alpha P_z(Z^f_{\tau^f} = u) - \beta E_z(\tau^f) \}$$

where $\{ f_t, t \geq 0 \}$ is a control policy. As shown in Browne (2000b), the optimal portfolio strategy for this objective is no longer constant. In particular, the optimal portfolio strategy is given by

$$f^*(Z_t) = \pi^* + (\pi^* - \pi) \frac{b}{Z_t} \tag{11.12}$$

where

$$b = \frac{u e^{-\gamma \alpha / \beta} - l}{1 - e^{-\gamma \alpha / \beta}}$$

Remark 1: Observe that the portfolio strategy $f^*(z)$ is a state dependent policy that is inversely modulated by the level of the ratio process Z. The representation in (11.12) shows that the policy is composed of two parts: first it just uses the optimal growth policy π^*, and then multiplies the difference between the optimal growth policy π^* and the tracking portfolio π by the correction term b/z. The sign of the correction factor is determined by the sign of b. Some direct manipulations shows that the sign of b is the sign of

$$\frac{1}{\gamma} \ln \left(\frac{u}{l} \right) - \frac{\alpha}{\beta}$$

We can write this quantity as $G^*(l) - \alpha/\beta$, where $G^*(l)$ is the minimal possible expected time to get from the shortfall level l to the surplus goal u. Thus b is positive (negative) if the ratio α/β is less (more) than this minimal expected time.

Observe further that if $b > 0$, then the active manager invests more heavily in the stock than does π^* so long as the benchmark is underinvested in that stock relative to the optimal growth policy, i.e. so long as $\pi^* > \pi$. Finally, note that we must always have $b \geq -l$.

Remark 2: Observe that the optimal policy of (11.12) depends on the benchmark through $\gamma = \sigma^2(\pi^* - \pi)^2/2$. Furthermore, under this policy, the probability of reaching the goal before the shortfall is given by

$$\frac{(z - l)(u + b)}{(z + b)(u - l)} \tag{11.13}$$

This follows from the fact that the optimal ratio in this case, Z^*, satisfies

$$Z_t^* = \left(1 + \frac{b}{Z_0}\right) Z_t(\pi^*, \pi) - b$$

Remark 3: A quick check with Merton (1990, Section 5.6, p. 137) reveals that there is a one-to-one relation between this probabilistic based objective and optimizing a utility based objective with a particular objective function. In particular, if the investor wants to maximize the terminal utility of the wealth to benchmark ratio, i.e.

$$\sup_f E(U(Z_T))$$

for the special case of a HARA class utility function given by

$$U(z) = \alpha \ln\left(\frac{z + b}{l + b}\right) / \ln\left(\frac{u + b}{l + b}\right)$$

where b is as above, then the optimal investment policy according to Merton (1990, 5.49) is given by (11.12). This extends the class of equivalences between probabilistic based objectives and terminal utility of wealth based objectives as given in the earlier works of Browne (1995, 1997, 1999a).

11.5   RISK-CONSTRAINED MINIMAL TIME

The results of the previous section can now be applied directly to the active portfolio management case where the shortfall probability is prespecified. Specifically, suppose that the shortfall probability is prespecified to the active manager to be no more than $1 - p$, where p is a given number between 0 and 1, i.e. the active manager is told that he must have $P_z(Z_{\tau_f}^f = l) \leq 1 - p$, or equivalently, that he must have $P_z(Z_{\tau_f}^f = u) \geq p$. The risk-constrained active portfolio management problem is now to minimize the expected time to beat the benchmark subject to a constraint on the shortfall probability, specifically, to find the strat-egy $\{f_t^*, t \geq 0\}$ that minimizes $E(\tau^f)$ subject to $P(Z_{\tau^f}^f = u) \geq p$, where p is a given number in $(0, 1)$. This is now related to the gambling problem first solved in Gottlieb (1985). Following Gottlieb, we observe first that the dual of the risk-constrained active portfolio management problem is to maximize the probability that $P(Z_{\tau^f}^f = u)$ subject to a constraint on $E(\tau^f)$. Moreover, observe that should a solution exist, then the constraint will be met at equality, and so we would have $P(Z_{\tau^f}^f = u) = p$.

The dual of this problem is

$$\sup_f [P_z(Z_{\tau^f}^f = u) - \beta E_z \tau^f] \tag{11.14}$$

where now β is Lagrangian multiplier.

From the risk-constraint (met at equality), we can determine β, or equiva-lently b.

When we perform the computations, we find that the optimal strategy is again given by $f^*(z)$ of (11.12), but now with a different b, namely now with $b = \tilde{b}$, where

$$\tilde{b} = \frac{pZ_0(u - l) - u(Z_0 - l)}{Z_0 - l - p(u - l)} \tag{11.15}$$

where Z_0 is the initial value of the ratio.

Remark 4: The risk-constrained problem is feasible only for an initial prob-ability level p that satisfies

$$p > \frac{Z_0 - l}{u - l}$$

Observe that for $p = 1, \tilde{b}$ reduces to $\tilde{b} = -l$, which makes the lower bar-rier l unattainable as in many 'portfolio insurance' models (see Black and Perold, 1992 and Browne, 1997). The insurance level $\tilde{b}$ is positive for values of p satisfying

$$\frac{Z_0 - l}{u - l} < p < \frac{u}{Z_0}\left(\frac{Z_0 - l}{u - l}\right)$$

and $\tilde{b}$ is negative for larger values in the region

$$p > \frac{u}{Z_0}\left(\frac{Z_0 - l}{u - l}\right) \equiv \theta(Z_0)$$

where $\theta(Z_0)$ is the initial probability that the optimal growth wealth/ratio hits u before l. Thus, as intuition suggests, to have a higher 'success' probability than the optimal growth strategy, the active portfolio manager must take less risk and invest less (since $\tilde{b} < 0$) than the ordinary optimal growth investor.

REFERENCES

Black, F. and Perold, A.F. (1992) Theory of constant proportion portfolio insurance, *Journal of Economic Dynamics and Control*, **16**, 403–26.

Browne, S. (1995) Optimal Investment Policies for a Firm with a Random Risk Process: Exponential Utility and Minimizing the Probability of Ruin, *Mathematics of Operations Research*, **20**, 937–58.

Browne, S. (1997) Survival and Growth with a Fixed Liability: Optimal Portfolios in Continuous Time, *Mathematics of Operations Research*, **22**, 468–93.

Browne, S. (1998) The Return on Investment from Proportional Portfolio Strategies. *Advances in Applied Probability*, **30**, 1, 216–38.

Browne, S. (1999a) Beating a Moving Target: Optimal Portfolio Strategies for Outperforming a Stochastic Benchmark, *Finance and Stochastics*, **3**, 275–94.

Browne, S. (1999b) Reaching Goals by a Deadline: Digital options and Continuous-Time Active Portfolio Management, *Advances in Applied Probability*, **31**, 551–77.

Browne, S. (1999c) The Risk and Reward of Minimizing Shortfall Probability, *Journal of Portfolio Management*, Summer 1999.

Browne, S. (2000a) Stochastic Differential Portfolio Games, *Journal of Applied Probability*, **37**, 1, 126–47.

Browne, S. (2000b) Risk Constrained Dynamic Active Portfolio Management, *Management Science*, **46**, 9, 1188–99.

Dubins, L.E. and Savage, L.J. (1975) *How to Gamble If You Must: Inequalities for Stochastic Processes*, Dover, NY.

Duffie, D. (1996) *Dynamic Asset Pricing Theory*, second edition, Princeton University Press.

Gottlieb, G. (1985) An Optimal Betting Strategy for Repeated Games, *Journal Applied Probability*, **22**, 787–95.

Grinold, R.C. and Kahn, R.N. (1995) *Active Portfolio Management*, Probus, IL.

Heath, D., Orey, S., Pestien, V. and Sudderth, W. (1987) Minimizing or Maximizing the Expected Time to Reach Zero, *SIAM Journal of Control and Optimization*, **25**, 1, 195–205.

Merton, R. (1990) *Continuous Time Finance*, Blackwell, MA.

Perold, A.F. and Sharpe, W.F. (1988) Dynamic Strategies for Asset Allocation, *Financial Analyst Journal*, Jan/Feb, 16–27.

Pestien, V.C. and Sudderth, W.D. (1985) Continuous-Time Red and Black: How to control a diffusion to a goal, *Mathematics of Operations Research*, **10**, 4, 599–611.

Chapter 12

Assessing the merits of rank-based optimization for portfolio construction

SOOSUNG HWANG, STEPHEN E SATCHELL AND STEPHEN
M WRIGHT

ABSTRACT

The purpose of this chapter is to assess the merits of portfolio construction based on optimizations using rank information on asset
returns. We carry out simulations and some historical calculations
based on UK FTSE100 stocks. We find conclusive evidence of
enhanced portfolio construction using these methods, in particular, in
terms of reducing turnover and avoiding extreme short positions.

12.1 INTRODUCTION

Practitioners have used rank information to construct robust measures of
expected asset returns for some time. These methods have recently been
advocated in a formal setting (see Chapter 2). There are a number of advantages
of this method. For example, it is possible to construct more stable portfolios due
to reduced sensitivity to a small number of outliers as well as the well-known
robustness of rank statistics. Similar results are well-known in the statistics
literature. Gideon and Hollister (1987) showed how a rank correlation coefficient
is resistant to outliers relative to the Pearson, Spearman, and Kendall correlation
coefficients. Readers interested in statistics research should look for such notions
as quintile regression; for example, Koenker and Bassett (1978, 1982) and
Taylor (1999).

The purpose of our study is to assess the benefits of using ranks instead
of returns using both simulation and historical studies. In the next Section, we

present our model of analysis. We show how to obtain the optimal rank portfolio and calculate the investment weights for the portfolio. Then in Section 12.3 the empirical results are shown and discussed. We find some interesting properties of the rank optimal portfolio. First, as expected, for a given portfolio return, the optimal rank portfolio is less efficient in the return mean-variance space than the optimal mean-variance (MV) return portfolio. This is a disadvantage of using ranks instead of returns. However, we find that the optimal rank portfolio is more stable than the optimal return portfolio. The gearing ratio, defined as the sum of absolute weights of the portfolio, and the changes of weights over time of the optimal rank portfolio are both far less than those of the optimal MV return portfolio. For example, if we try to maintain the optimal portfolio's expected return at the average return of the FTSE All-share index over the last 10 years, we find that the optimal rank portfolio's gearing ratio is less than 200% and the changes in the investment weights are less than 100%. These numbers are far less than those of the optimal return portfolio which shows amounts of 400%–1000% and 100%–800%, respectively. The unstable movement in the gearing ratio and the changes in weights for the optimal return portfolio are another disadvantage of conventional techniques. When we impose non-negativity constraints on the weights (i.e. short positions are not allowed), numerically optimized results show that the optimal rank portfolio is still more stable, despite the fact that the difference between the optimal return and rank portfolios is not so high. We also find that when we increase the number of M-tiles, the optimized rank portfolio performs better in all ways; increased expected returns with smaller standard deviation, smaller but more stable changes in the weights over time.

In Section 12.4, we conclude our study by noting that there exists a tradeoff between portfolio stability and robustness versus MV efficiency. If efficiency in the traditional MV world is preferred, then using ranks may not be a good procedure because the optimal rank portfolio is not efficient. However, we still have to consider that efficiency cannot be attained in practice due to the restriction on short positions, not to mention the large number of other restrictions that institutional investors face. Our study shows that the optimal rank portfolio may be a good alternative for institutional investors who have (a) constrained weights and (b) clients who will not tolerate high turnover.

12.2   OPTIMAL PORTFOLIO WITH RANKS

Suppose that there are N assets available to make a portfolio. The conventional method is to use historical returns to obtain the optimal portfolio; that is, to calculate the optimal portfolio that minimizes variance for a given portfolio return. However, the investment weights of the optimal portfolio are very sensitive to changes in returns and thus the weight vector changes over time significantly.

In addition, in the conventional MV analysis there is no restriction on short and long positions and thus some assets can be several hundred per cent short-positioned whilst some others can be several hundred per cent long-positioned. These highly geared positions and dramatic changes in investment proportion have been important reasons why practitioners frequently avoid MV analysis.

In this Section we shall show how to construct the optimal portfolio using ranks which, we believe, is less noisy. We expect that any portfolio calculated with ranks is less geared than the equivalent portfolio calculated with returns.

12.2.1   Mean and variance–covariance matrix of ranks

Suppose that we are going to rank the N assets according to their returns and assign those assets to M rank-portfolios. That is, we rank the assets and assign 1 to M according to the size of returns at each time. M is a natural number, and $2 \leq M \leq N$. Since we rank asset returns in descending order, the stocks ranked in the first represents higher returns than the other stocks. Thus each asset belongs to jth rank-portfolios, $j = 1, 2, \ldots, M$. Let the $(N \times 1)$ rank vector at time t be denoted by R_t. Then the $(N \times 1)$ expected rank and the $(N \times N)$ variance–covariance matrix of ranks can be denoted by μ_R and Ω_R, respectively. The mean vector and the variance–covariance matrix can be calculated by the usual method once $R_t, t = 1, 2, \ldots, T$, is obtained. That is, the sample mean vector of assets' ranks is

$$\hat{\mu}_R = \frac{1}{T} \sum_{t=1}^{T} R_t \tag{12.1}$$

and the sample variance–covariance matrix of assets' ranks $\hat{\Omega}_R$, is estimated by

$$\tilde{\Omega}_R = \frac{1}{T-1} \sum_{t=1}^{T} (R_t - \hat{\mu}_R)(R_t - \hat{\mu}_R)' \tag{12.2}$$

We can also calculate the rank probability matrix that the ith asset is ranked to the jth rank-portfolio. Let the $(N \times M)$ rank probability matrix denoted by P_R. Then the ijth element of the matrix shows the probability that asset i is in M-tile j. The sample rank probability matrix, $\hat{P}_R$, can be computed by

$$\hat{P}_R = \frac{1}{T} \sum_{t=1}^{T} I_{Rt} \tag{12.3}$$

where I_{Rt} is the $(N \times M)$ indicator matrix whose ijth element is one when the ith element of the vector R_t is j, and zero otherwise.

12.2.2   The optimal rank portfolio

One important property of the rank variance–covariance matrix Ω_R is that the matrix is singular. This is because once we know ranks of any $N - 1$ assets, the last asset's rank will be known automatically. Thus the dimension of the null space is 1. Since any matrix that is singular cannot be inverted, Ω_R cannot be used to derive the optimal portfolio in the usual way.

There are a few methods to solve this problem. In this study we simply use randomly selected $N - 1$ assets. By omitting one asset, the optimal rank portfolio we calculate cannot be the efficient frontier. However, when N becomes large, the difference becomes trivial.

Let $\Omega_{R,N-1}$ be the $(N - 1) \times (N - 1)$ rank variance–covariance matrix for the randomly selected $N - 1$ assets and the $(N - 1)$ weight vector be denoted by $w_{R,N-1}$. Then the problem for the investor reduces to solving the following quadratic program:

$$\min_{w} \frac{1}{2} w'_{R,N-1} \Omega_{R,N-1} w_{R,N-1}$$

$$\text{s.t.} \mu_R^p = w'_{R,N-1} \mu_{R,N-1}$$

$$1 = w'_{R,N-1} e \tag{12.4}$$

where μ_R^p is the expected rank of the optimal portfolio, $\mu_{R,N-1}$ is the $(N - 1) \times 1$ vector of the expected ranks of the $N - 1$ assets, and e is an $(N - 1) \times 1$ vector of ones. We allow negative elements in vector $w_{R,N-1}$ (short sales are allowed) and thus the range of expected ranks on feasible portfolios is unbounded.

Using the Lagrangian multiplier, we obtain

$$W_{R,N-1}^p = \lambda \Omega_{R,N-1}^{-1} e + v \Omega_{R,N-1}^{-1} \mu_{R,N-1} \tag{12.5}$$

where

$$v = \frac{A\mu_R^p - B}{AC - B^2}$$

$$\lambda = \frac{C - B\mu_R^p}{AC - B^2} \tag{12.6}$$

and

$$A = e' \Omega_{R,N-1}^1 e$$

$$B = e' \Omega_{R,N-1}^1 \mu$$

$$C = \mu' \Omega_{R,N-1}^1 \mu \tag{12.7}$$

Note that the optimal weight vector (12.5) provides only $N - 1$ weights, although N assets are used to calculate the $N \times N$ rank variance–covariance matrix. If we want to obtain the weight vector for the optimal rank portfolio using a specific set of N^* assets, one additional asset should be included as the last $(N^* + 1)$ element and then calculate the vector of expected rank and $(N^* + 1) \times (N^* + 1)$ rank variance–covariance matrix for the $N^* + 1$ assets. Finally, the optimization problem in (12.4) can be solved with the first N^* assets as in (12.5). For the MV analysis for returns, since the variance–covariance matrix of returns can be assumed non-singular, we can use all N asset returns and our problem can be represented as the following quadratic programe:

$$\min_w \frac{1}{2} w' \Omega w$$

$$\text{s.t.} \mu_R = w' \mu$$

$$w'e = 1 \tag{12.8}$$

where μ and Ω are the expected return vector and variance–covariance matrix for returns, respectively. Using the same method as in the above, we have

$$w^p = \lambda \Omega^{-1} e + v \Omega^{-1} \mu \tag{12.9}$$

where

$$v = \frac{A \mu_p - B}{AC - B^2}$$

$$\lambda = \frac{C - B \mu_p}{AC - B^2} \tag{12.10}$$

and

$$A = e' \Omega^{-1} e$$

$$B = e' \Omega^{-1} \mu$$

$$C = \mu' \Omega^{-1} \mu \tag{12.11}$$

12.3 EMPIRICAL TESTS

To investigate the difference between the portfolio based on returns and our rank-based portfolio, we use simulations. We first randomly select 50 stocks from FTSE100 constituents; $N = 50$. The sample period is from August 1991 to July 2001.

12.3.1 Properties of ranks

For the selected 50 stocks, the mean and variance–covariance for the returns are calculated. These estimates are assumed to be the true values in the simulations.

The first two columns of Table 12.1 show the mean and standard deviation of the selected stocks.[1] We then generate 10 000 returns for each stocks from the sample (true) mean and variance–covariance matrix calculated in the previous step; $T = 10\,000$. Columns 3 and 4 of Table 12.1 report the estimated mean and standard deviation of 10 000 returns. Note that the estimates are pretty close to the true values in the first two columns.

We note that there are two major differences between the true and sample returns. The first is that the sample returns generated as described are now normally distributed. The true returns may not be normal, but the generated returns are normal. Using the same method, we can also make the sample returns with some other choice of probability density function (pdf). By controlling the pdf of returns, we can investigate the performance of using ranks instead of returns. The second difference between the true and sample returns is that in the sample returns there is no serial autocorrelation, whilst in the true returns there may exist some significant autocorrelation. Any possible serial autocorrelation structure is disregarded in the sample returns.

The next step is to calculate the rank probability, P_R. In the simulations, we assume 10 possible states, i.e. $M = 10$, and for all 50 stocks we have 50×10 vector of states. The numbers of times that each stock belongs to the states are then counted for the generated 10 000 returns, and the numbers are divided by 10 000 to obtain the probabilities. See Equation (12.3). For each stock we have a 1×10 rank probability row vector and thus for all 50 stocks, a 50×10 matrix. Columns 5 to 14 of Table 12.1 report the results. Each row represents each stock and each column (rank) represents probabilities that the stock belongs to the rank on the top of the column. Note that the 50 stocks are listed in ascending order in their true mean returns.

When standard deviations of the stock returns are equal, we expect the probability that a stock, whose expected return is small, belonging to the 10th rank to be smaller than the probability that a stock, whose expected return is large, belonging to the 10th rank, and vice versa. However, in many cases, this is not what we find in the Table 12.1 and the results in the table show that standard deviations are important. For example, when standard deviations are large as in the 1st and 42nd stocks, we can see that the last and first and last rank probabilities become large, suggesting that large swings in the stock returns tend to make the rank of these stocks take the first or the last.

With the returns calculated in the previous step, we ranked the equities and assigned 1 to 10 according to the size of returns at each time. Since we rank stock returns in ascending order, higher ranks represent higher returns. Using Equations (12.1) and (12.2), we calculate the mean vector of stocks' ranks and the variance–covariance matrix of stocks' ranks; see the last two columns of Table 12.1 for the mean and standard deviation of the ranks. The mean ranks

Table 12.1 *Simulation results on rank*

| Stock | Selected stock | | 10000 simulation results | | Rank statistics | | | | | | | | | | | |
| | True mean | True STD | Sample mean | Sample STD | Probability | | | | | | | | | | Rank mean | Rank STD |
					1	2	3	4	5	6	7	8	9	10		
1	-1.66%	18.55%	-1.65%	18.79%	0.28	0.10	0.07	0.06	0.05	0.05	0.06	0.07	0.08	0.17	4.95	3.50
2	-1.33%	15.00%	-1.37%	15.07%	0.22	0.12	0.09	0.07	0.07	0.07	0.07	0.08	0.08	0.12	4.90	3.23
3	-0.46%	10.68%	-0.40%	10.63%	0.13	0.12	0.11	0.10	0.10	0.09	0.10	0.09	0.08	0.08	5.07	2.89
4	-0.44%	10.91%	-0.44%	10.91%	0.12	0.12	0.11	0.11	0.10	0.10	0.09	0.09	0.08	0.07	5.03	2.78
5	-0.34%	11.66%	-0.38%	11.62%	0.13	0.12	0.11	0.10	0.10	0.10	0.09	0.09	0.08	0.08	5.08	2.87
6	-0.22%	10.39%	-0.10%	10.39%	0.09	0.12	0.12	0.11	0.11	0.11	0.10	0.10	0.09	0.05	5.13	2.68
7	0.21%	10.58%	0.38%	10.49%	0.07	0.12	0.13	0.11	0.11	0.11	0.11	0.11	0.09	0.05	5.27	2.65
8	0.33%	8.83%	0.19%	8.72%	0.08	0.11	0.12	0.12	0.12	0.11	0.11	0.09	0.08	0.06	5.21	2.65
9	0.35%	13.08%	0.25%	13.08%	0.16	0.11	0.10	0.09	0.08	0.07	0.08	0.09	0.10	0.13	5.29	3.12
10	0.38%	9.06%	0.43%	9.11%	0.11	0.11	0.10	0.11	0.11	0.10	0.10	0.09	0.09	0.09	5.29	2.84
11	0.49%	8.83%	0.43%	8.83%	0.12	0.11	0.10	0.10	0.10	0.09	0.09	0.09	0.10	0.09	5.34	2.93
12	0.52%	10.68%	0.50%	10.58%	0.12	0.11	0.10	0.09	0.10	0.09	0.10	0.10	0.09	0.10	5.35	2.96
13	0.58%	13.27%	0.58%	13.23%	0.15	0.12	0.09	0.09	0.08	0.08	0.08	0.09	0.11	0.12	5.35	3.12
14	0.58%	13.23%	0.36%	13.19%	0.13	0.12	0.10	0.09	0.09	0.09	0.09	0.09	0.10	0.10	5.30	3.00
15	0.64%	7.07%	0.68%	7.14%	0.07	0.11	0.11	0.12	0.11	0.11	0.11	0.10	0.09	0.06	5.34	2.64
16	0.65%	10.15%	0.65%	10.05%	0.11	0.11	0.10	0.10	0.10	0.10	0.10	0.10	0.09	0.10	5.37	2.88
17	0.73%	9.49%	0.73%	9.38%	0.07	0.10	0.11	0.11	0.12	0.11	0.12	0.10	0.09	0.06	5.39	2.62
18	0.84%	9.54%	0.87%	9.54%	0.08	0.11	0.11	0.10	0.11	0.11	0.11	0.11	0.10	0.07	5.44	2.75
19	0.88%	14.14%	0.87%	14.21%	0.16	0.11	0.09	0.07	0.07	0.07	0.08	0.09	0.11	0.15	5.43	3.22
20	0.97%	10.20%	0.93%	10.20%	0.08	0.10	0.11	0.11	0.11	0.11	0.11	0.10	0.10	0.08	5.46	2.76
21	1.03%	6.86%	0.92%	6.86%	0.03	0.08	0.12	0.14	0.14	0.15	0.13	0.11	0.07	0.03	5.43	2.27
22	1.05%	9.06%	1.17%	9.17%	0.09	0.10	0.10	0.10	0.10	0.10	0.10	0.10	0.10	0.10	5.52	2.85
23	1.07%	9.54%	1.06%	9.49%	0.08	0.10	0.10	0.10	0.11	0.10	0.10	0.10	0.10	0.09	5.48	2.80
24	1.12%	10.10%	1.21%	10.15%	0.09	0.10	0.10	0.10	0.11	0.10	0.11	0.10	0.10	0.09	5.53	2.82
25	1.14%	8.25%	1.04%	8.19%	0.08	0.10	0.11	0.11	0.12	0.12	0.10	0.10	0.10	0.08	5.48	2.71

(continued overleaf)

Table 12.1 *(continued)*

Stock	Selected stock True mean	Selected stock True STD	10000 simulation results Sample mean	10000 simulation results Sample STD	Rank statistics Probability 1	2	3	4	5	6	7	8	9	10	Rank mean	Rank STD
26	1.17%	8.49%	1.08%	8.54%	0.07	0.10	0.11	0.11	0.12	0.11	0.11	0.11	0.10	0.07	5.50	2.67
27	1.18%	10.86%	1.14%	10.86%	0.11	0.11	0.10	0.10	0.09	0.09	0.09	0.10	0.11	0.10	5.50	2.93
28	1.23%	15.81%	1.30%	15.87%	0.20	0.10	0.07	0.06	0.06	0.06	0.06	0.07	0.10	0.21	5.55	3.46
29	1.23%	8.31%	1.25%	8.25%	0.10	0.10	0.10	0.10	0.10	0.09	0.10	0.11	0.11	0.10	5.54	2.87
30	1.29%	6.56%	1.34%	6.48%	0.05	0.08	0.11	0.13	0.12	0.14	0.12	0.11	0.09	0.05	5.58	2.48
31	1.34%	9.06%	1.35%	9.17%	0.04	0.10	0.12	0.11	0.11	0.11	0.11	0.11	0.12	0.05	5.57	2.57
32	1.39%	7.62%	1.32%	7.62%	0.03	0.08	0.11	0.13	0.14	0.14	0.13	0.12	0.09	0.04	5.58	2.34
33	1.60%	6.24%	1.56%	6.16%	0.03	0.07	0.10	0.13	0.14	0.15	0.14	0.11	0.09	0.04	5.64	2.31
34	1.61%	15.46%	1.69%	15.59%	0.17	0.11	0.08	0.07	0.06	0.06	0.07	0.08	0.11	0.19	5.64	3.35
35	1.63%	10.44%	1.60%	10.30%	0.11	0.10	0.09	0.09	0.09	0.09	0.09	0.10	0.11	0.13	5.63	3.00
36	1.68%	7.07%	1.59%	7.07%	0.04	0.08	0.10	0.12	0.13	0.14	0.13	0.12	0.09	0.05	5.67	2.39
37	1.75%	7.87%	1.68%	7.87%	0.07	0.09	0.10	0.10	0.11	0.11	0.11	0.11	0.11	0.10	5.69	2.77
38	1.81%	7.28%	1.66%	7.28%	0.04	0.08	0.10	0.12	0.12	0.13	0.13	0.11	0.10	0.06	5.69	2.49
39	1.83%	7.48%	1.67%	7.55%	0.07	0.10	0.10	0.11	0.10	0.11	0.11	0.11	0.11	0.09	5.67	2.75
40	1.84%	10.15%	1.70%	10.05%	0.08	0.09	0.10	0.10	0.10	0.11	0.11	0.11	0.10	0.10	5.68	2.75
41	1.99%	6.40%	1.94%	6.48%	0.02	0.07	0.10	0.12	0.14	0.14	0.15	0.13	0.10	0.04	5.78	2.29
42	2.05%	17.23%	2.13%	17.32%	0.20	0.09	0.07	0.06	0.06	0.06	0.06	0.07	0.10	0.24	5.68	3.52
43	2.10%	9.75%	2.14%	9.70%	0.07	0.09	0.10	0.09	0.10	0.10	0.11	0.11	0.12	0.10	5.79	2.81
44	2.19%	11.09%	2.13%	11.18%	0.06	0.10	0.11	0.10	0.09	0.10	0.10	0.12	0.14	0.09	5.80	2.79
45	2.25%	8.06%	2.30%	8.12%	0.06	0.08	0.10	0.10	0.11	0.11	0.11	0.11	0.12	0.10	5.87	2.73
46	2.39%	9.11%	2.23%	9.11%	0.06	0.08	0.09	0.10	0.11	0.11	0.11	0.12	0.12	0.09	5.86	2.67
47	2.65%	10.91%	2.55%	10.86%	0.10	0.09	0.08	0.09	0.08	0.09	0.09	0.10	0.12	0.15	5.89	3.02
48	2.85%	14.49%	2.83%	14.53%	0.13	0.10	0.08	0.07	0.07	0.07	0.07	0.09	0.12	0.20	5.92	3.26
49	2.89%	14.07%	2.89%	14.21%	0.10	0.09	0.09	0.08	0.08	0.08	0.09	0.10	0.13	0.16	5.98	3.07
50	2.99%	16.09%	2.95%	16.12%	0.16	0.10	0.07	0.06	0.06	0.06	0.07	0.08	0.11	0.23	5.89	3.40

	Average correlation	Average rank correlation
	0.98668	0.923985
	0.986316	0.923253

are highly correlated with the mean returns in the first and third columns. For both cases, the estimated correlation coefficients are around 0.98. We find that the correlation coefficient between the standard deviations of returns and the ranks is high as well, i.e. 0.92. Therefore, the rank variables are not exactly the same as returns, but retain very similar information to returns. Figure 12.1(a) shows the relationships between return and return standard deviation as well as the relationship between rank and rank standard deviation. The mean returns are not always explained by total risk (standard deviation) except in several cases. We can also see a similar pattern in the mean-standard deviation of ranks in Figure 12.1(b).

12.3.2   The optimal rank portfolio: short sale allowed

We next calculate the optimal weight vectors for given expected ranks as explained in Equation (12.5). As explained in the previous section, once we obtain ranks of N stocks from the returns of N stocks, the first $N - 1$, stocks' ranks are used to calculate the $(N - 1) \times 1$ mean rank vector and the $(N - 1) \times (N - 1)$ rank variance–covariance matrix.

In order to compare the rank optimal portfolio with the return optimal portfolio, we calculate the weight vector for the rank and return portfolios for given expected returns. That is, the optimal rank weight vector is also used to calculate expected returns which in turn are used to calculate the optimal return

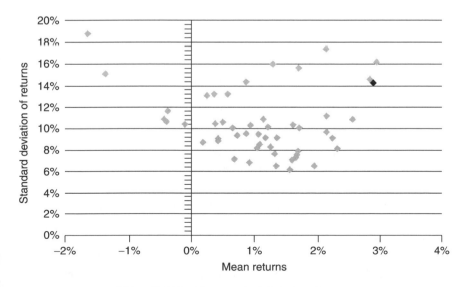

Figure 12.1(a)   *Mean-standard deviation of returns*

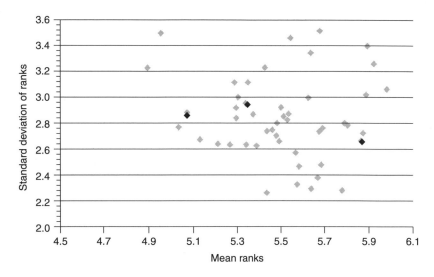

Figure 12.1(b)   *Mean-standard deviation of ranks*

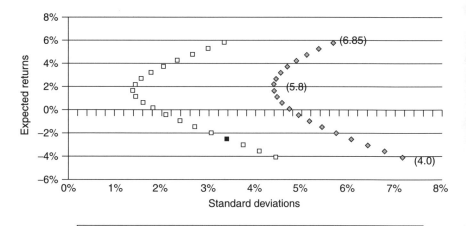

Figure 12.2   *Mean-variance frontiers with returns and ranks*
Notes: The mean-standard deviation XY plots above are obtained with the numbers in Table 12.1

portfolio weight as described in Equation (12.9). Thus, the optimal return port-folios are comparable with the optimal rank portfolios if they show the same expected returns.

Figure 12.2 shows that the frontier portfolios calculated with ranks are not optimal since they are located to the right of the Markowitz efficient frontier. The difference between them does not seem to be trivial. This means that when we use the optimal rank portfolio for investment, we expect that the portfolio is far from the optimal portfolio in the conventional Markowitz MV world, and if all our decisions were for one period. The investor would need to weigh the disadvantages of reduced theoretical efficiency against the wider diversification and potentially more intuitive tilts of a rank optimized portfolio.

Figures 12.3(a) and 12.3(b) show the investment proportions for the 50 stocks for three given portfolio returns. The investment proportions calculated with ranks are much smaller than those calculated with returns for all three cases. Other investment weight vectors for different portfolio returns also show the same pattern. Figure 12.4 summarizes the results. In Figure 12.4, we calculate the sum of the absolute weights for different expected returns (ranks). The figure shows that the gearing ratios of the optimal return portfolios are always larger than those of the optimal rank portfolios. In addition, the gearing ratios are smallest when the expected return of the portfolios is close to the monthly average market return of the sample period; during the sample period, i.e. August 1991 to July 2001, the average monthly return of the FTSE All-share Index was 0.93%.

We further investigate the gearing ratios over time using the rolling windows method. For the above 50 stocks from the constituents of the FTSE100 index we have 120 monthly returns from August 1991 to July 2001 for each of them. Then using the first 60 monthly returns and ranks from August 1991 to July 1996, the optimal weights are calculated as in (12.5) and (12.9) for ranks and returns, respectively. Note that the first 49 stocks are used for the calculation of the weights of the rank optimal portfolio. We then repeat the same procedure

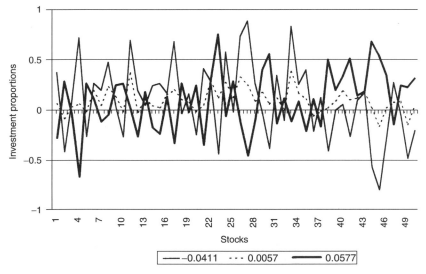

Figure 12.3(a) *Investment proportions for given portfolio returns calculated with mean return and return variance–covariance matrix*

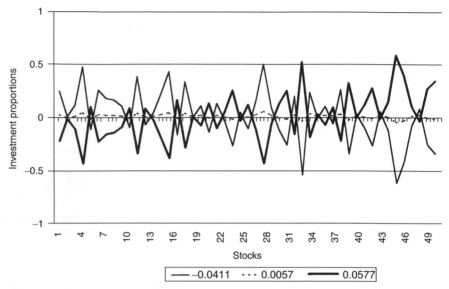

Figure 12.3(b)   *Invesment proportions for given portfolio returns calculated with mean rank and rank variance–covariance matrix*

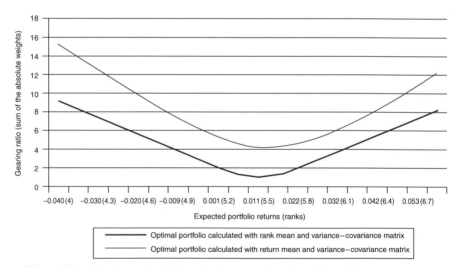

Figure 12.4   *Gearing ratios of the optimal return and rank portfolios without non-negative constrains on investment weights*

again using the next 60 observations from September 1991 to August 1996, and so on. Every month we calculate the gearing ratio by taking sum of the absolute values of the weights. Figures 12.5(a) and (b) report the gearing ratios from July 1996 to July 2001 of the optimal return and rank portfolios for given portfolio returns. As expected in Figure 12.4, for all five portfolio returns from −0.4 to

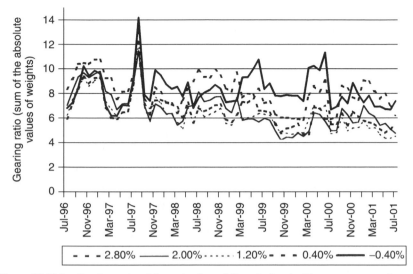

Figure 12.5(a) *Gearing ratio of the optimal portfolio calculated with mean return and return variance–covariance matrix without non-negative constraints on investment weights*

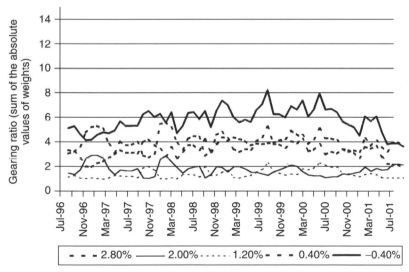

Figure 12.5(b) *Gearing ratio of the optimal portfolio calculated with mean rank and rank variance–covariance matrix without non-negative constraints on investment weights*

2.8%, the gearing ratios in the optimal portfolio weights are far less in the rank portfolios than in the return portfolios. If we try to maintain the return based optimal portfolio with 1.2% a month for example, our gearing ratio ranges from 400% to 1000% of our investment amount, which is unattainable in practice. On the other hand, the gearing ratios of the optimal rank portfolio with 1.2% a month are less than 200%. These gearing ratios are relatively small. If we were to make the portfolio implementation more realistic by imposing sector and stock constraints, we would expect reduction in both cases. For a long–short fund, a gearing ratio of about 200% would be consistent with 150% long and 50% short.

Finally, we further investigate changes in the investment weights over time using the rolling windows method. Even though the gearing ratios of the rank portfolio above are relatively small, if the changes in the weights are large over time, a fund manager cannot maintain the optimal rank portfolio because of large trading costs. Clients will believe, possibly unfairly, that the portfolio is being 'churned'. Using the same procedure we calculate changes in the investment weights and take sum of the absolute value of the changes.

Figures 12.6(a) and (b) report the changes from July 1996 to July 2001 of the optimal return and rank portfolios for given portfolio returns. As expected in Figures 12.4 and 12.5, for all five portfolio returns from -0.4% to 2%, the changes in the optimal portfolio weights are far less in the rank portfolios than in the return portfolios. If we try to maintain the return based optimal portfolio with 1.2% a month for example, we should change 50% to 1000% of our investment amount every month, most of which would be impossible in practice. On the other hand, the optimal rank portfolio with 1.2% a month requires less than 100% of changes every month. These changes are relatively small, but still seem to be too large to be used in practice. However, the interest of the results rests in their relative, not absolute, magnitude.

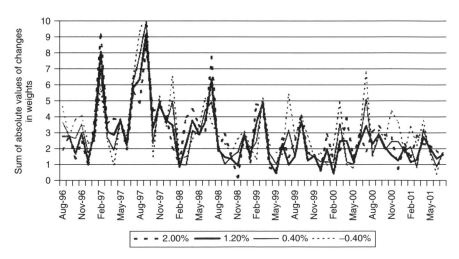

Figure 12.6(a)   *Changes in weights of the optimal portfolio calculated with mean return and return variance–covariance matrix without non-negative constraints on investment weights*

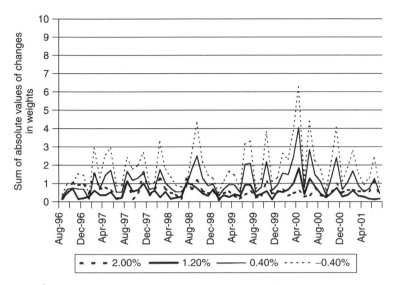

Figure 12.6(b)   *Changes in weights of the optimal portfolio calculated with mean rank and rank variance–covariance matrix without non-negative constraints on investment weights*

Another property we find in the changes in weights is that the changes in the optimal rank portfolio are relatively stable to those in the optimal return portfolio. This may provide useful information for a fund manager who wants to avoid large changes in trading activity if the fund manager is also asked to reduce tracking error. See Hwang and Satchell (2001) for the effects of dynamic trading activity on the ex post tracking error. The results in this section show that using ranks instead of returns can reduce the amount of short sales and thus the gearing ratio. Also the optimal rank portfolio requires that the optimal weights need to be changed less often than those required by the optimal return portfolio. However, we note that the results are possible by increasing risk measured by variance of return but reduced risk measured by degree of diversification. That is, in Figure 12.2 the optimal rank portfolios are not MV efficient measured by returns.

12.3.3   The optimal rank portfolio: short sale not allowed

Another interesting question is what happens when short sales are not allowed. In this case we do not have analytic results as we have in Section 12.2. The optimization needs to be carried out numerically. The calculation is not simple because we need all weights to be non-negative and also the sum of the weights to be one.

We have the following maximization problem for the optimal rank portfolio:

$$\max_{w_R} w'_R \mu_R - \lambda_R w'_R \Omega_R w_R$$

$$\text{s.t.} 1 = w'_R e$$

$$w^i_R \geq 0, \forall i \tag{12.12}$$

where w^i_R is the ith element in the weight vector w_R and λ_R is a positive parameter. On the other hand, for the optimal return portfolio, we have

$$\max_{w} w'\mu - \lambda w'\Omega w$$

$$\text{s.t.} 1 = w'e$$

$$w^i \geq 0, \forall i \tag{12.13}$$

where w^i is the ith element in the weight vector w and λ is a positive parameter.

The choice of λ and λ_R is important. For plausible values of λ, Grinold (1996) suggested 120 to 220 for the US market; see Damant et al. (2000) for the UK market. However, there is no research on the values of λ_R so far. In this study we use various values of λ and λ_R, e.g. from 1 to 1000.

Figure 12.7 plots the mean and standard deviation of the optimal return and rank portfolios for given values of λ and λ_R. The figure is obtained with the same data we used for Figure 12.2; that is mean and variance–covariance matrix of the sample returns and rank generated in Section 12.3.1. For the values of λ for the optimal return portfolio, the figure shows that unless λ is very small, e.g. 10

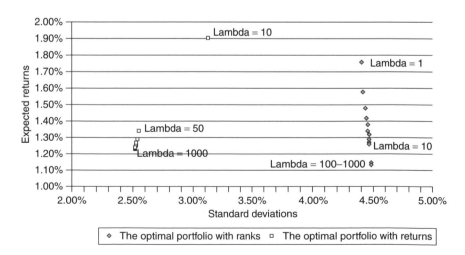

Figure 12.7   *Mean-variance frontiers with returns and ranks with non-negative constraints*

or 50, the choice of λ does not affect the MV relationship; see for the cases that λ > 50. On the other hand, the figure also shows that when λ_R > 100, there is little difference in MV space. Only when λ_R is small, e.g. less than 10, we find that there are some changes. Note that during the sample period, the FTSE All-share index returns show 0.93%, suggesting the values of λ and λ_R should be much larger than 1000.

Another relevant finding is that when λ and λ_R are large, the optimal invest-ment weights show little difference for different values of λ and λ_R e.g. 100 and 1000. Therefore, in this study we arbitrarily select λ = 200 and λ_R = 10, both of which give the same portfolio return 1.26%. Finally Figure 12.7 shows that the optimal return portfolios are always more efficient than the optimal rank portfolio.

Since there are now non-negativity constraints on the weights, we don't need to calculate the gearing ratio; the ratio is always one. Instead, in Figure 12.8(a) and (b) we show the weights of the optimal return and rank portfolios for given portfolio return, i.e. 1.26%. Figure 12.8 obtained with non-negativity constraints can be compared with Figure 12.3 without such constraints. The figure suggests that the optimal rank portfolio consists of all 50 stocks and weights are around 0.02. However, the optimal return portfolio consist of far less than 50 stocks and weights are also very different for different stocks. The wide variety of weights is expected to reduce the portfolio variance for the given return, but at

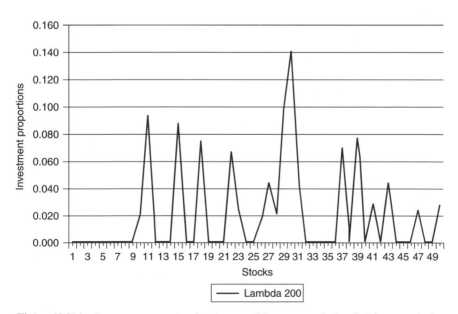

Figure 12.8(a) *Invesment proportion for given portfolio returns calculated with returns in the presence of non-negativity constraints*

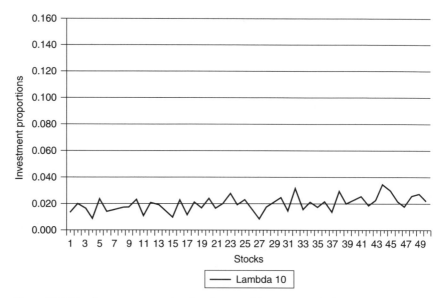

Figure 12.8(b) *Invesment proportion for given portfolio returns calculated with ranks in the presence of non-negativity constraints*

Note: λ = 10 for the rank portfolio and λ = 200 for the return portfolio provide the same.

the same time it also implies that the optimal weights may change dramatically over time.

For Figures 12.9(a) and (b), we use the rolling windows method for the same data we used in the previous section. The comparable figure without the non-negativity constraints can be found in Figure 12.6. Figure 12.9 suggests that the weights of the optimal portfolios calculated with returns and ranks show far less changes in weights over time than those without non-negativity constraints in Figure 12.6, especially in the weights of the optimal portfolio calculated with returns. All of the changes are less than 60%. However, the optimal rank portfolio requires fewer changes than the optimal return portfolio. The mean of the changes over the 61 months is 16.3% for the rank portfolio, whilst the same for the return portfolio is 19.7%. In addition, the changes of the weights of the return portfolio are more volatile than those of the rank portfolio.

12.3.4 The effects of the number of the rank portfolio

Although the detailed results are not reported, we also used two different values of M, the number of rank portfolios, i.e. $M = 5$ and 50, and repeated all the calculations in the previous section. What we found is that as M increases, we have the better optimal rank portfolio in various aspects both with and without the non-negativity constraints. The results suggest that we should use $M = N$ for best results.

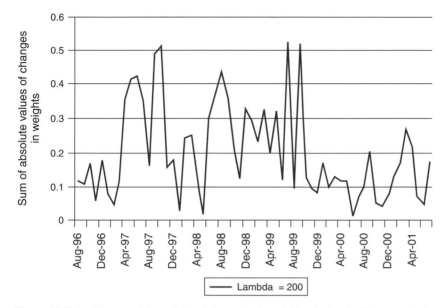

Figure 12.9(a) *Changes of the weights of the optimal portfolio calculated with returns in the presence of non-negativity constraints*

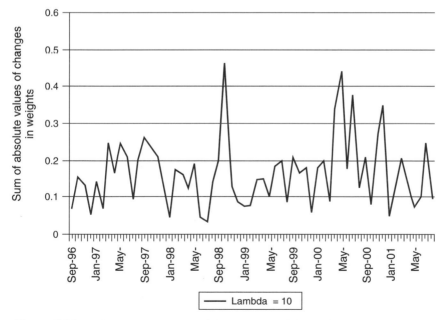

Figure 12.9(b) *Changes of the weights of the optimal portfolio calculated with ranks in the presence of non-negativity constraints*
Note: The average values of the changes over 61 months for the optimal return and rank portfolios.

Table 12.2   *The effects of different numbers of rank portfolios (M) in the presence of non-negativity constraints*

	Optimal Return Portfolio (lambda = 200)	Optimal Rank Portfolio (lambda = 10) when $M = 5$	Optimal Rank Portfolio (lambda = 10) when $M = 10$	Optimal Rank Portfolio (lambda = 10) when $M = 50$
Average Value of the Optimal Portfolio Returns	1.276%	1.044%	1.145%	1.306%
Standard Deviation of the Optimal Portfolio Returns	2.515%	3.740%	3.696%	3.688%
Changes in Weights of the Optimal Portfolio	19.663%	17.934%	16.319%	8.408%
Standard deviation of the Changes in Weights of the Optimal Portfolio	13.904%	11.424%	9.325%	6.453%

Notes: The numbers above are average and standard deviation of 61 monthly results.

Some of the interesting findings with the non-negativity constraints are summarized in Table 12.2. Note that the first column of Table 12.2 serves as the benchmark calculated with returns and $\lambda = 200$. When the number of rank portfolios are increased, i.e. as $M \rightarrow N$, the effects on the return MV space become better slowly in the sense that the optimal rank portfolio with a large M has larger average means but less standard deviation than the optimal rank portfolio with a small M; see the first two rows of Table 12.2. However, any change in M does not give similar average returns and standard deviation to those of the optimal return portfolio in the first column. In addition, as we saw in the above, any different choice of λ_R does not allow the optimal rank portfolio to attain the level of the optimal return portfolio.

The second point is that for given values of λ_R, when M is large, changes in weights of the optimal rank portfolio decrease dramatically, whilst the standard deviation of the changes becomes smaller. Note that the changes in weights over time decrease from 17.9% ($M = 5$) to 8.4% ($M = 50$). The smaller value of the standard deviation of the changes may be another benefit as explained above. Actually, as M increases, the optimal rank portfolio becomes closer to an equally weighted portfolio, suggesting that the optimal rank portfolio is less sensitive to big changes of a small number of stock returns.

12.4   CONCLUSIONS

In this study, we evaluated the merits of using ranks instead of returns using real data. We found that the portfolios based on ranks had decreased MV efficiency taken in a one period context. However, the rank based risk measures were found to be far more reliable out of sample, resulting in far lower turnover than that for the return based portfolio optimization. In addition, they exhibited fewer short positions and lower turnover than the portfolios based on returns. We conclude that such portfolios have a useful role in implementation as their multi-period running costs will be low. We did not investigate non-normality in this study. We expect further gains to be made if some of our assets are derivatives.

REFERENCES

Damant, D.C., Hwang, S. and Satchell, S.E. (2000) An Exponential Risk Measure with Application to UK Asset Allocation, *Applied Mathematical Finance*, 7, 1–26.

Gideon, R.A. and Hollister, R.A. (1987) A Rank Correlation Coefficient Resistant to Outliers, *Journal of American Statistical Association*, 82, 398, 656–966.

Grinold, R.C. (1996) Domestic Grapes from Imported Wine, *Journal of Portfolio Management*, 22, 5, 29–40.

Hwang, S. and Satchell, S.E. (2001) Tracking Error: Ex-Ante versus Ex-Post Measures, Forthcoming in *Journal of Asset Management*.

Koenker, R.W. and Bassett, G.W. (1978) Regression Quantiles, *Econometrics*, 46, 33–50.

Koenker, R.W. and Bassett, G.W. (1982) Robust Tests for Heteroscedasticity Based on Regression Quantiles, *Econometrica*, 50, 43–62.

Taylor, J.W. (1999) A Quintile Regression Approach to Estimating the Distribution of Multiperiod Returns, *Journal of Derivatives*, (Fall) 64–78.

NOTES

1. Other off-diagonal elements are not shown because of shortage of space.

Chapter 13

The mean-downside risk portfolio frontier: a non-parametric approach

GUSTAVO M de ATHAYDE

ABSTRACT

In contrast to the classical Markowitz portfolio frontier, downside risk optimization deals with a positive definite matrix that is endogenous to portfolio weights. This aspect makes the problem far more difficult to handle. For this purpose, a simple algorithm was developed by Athayde (2001) that ensures the convergence to the solution is presented. However, due to some properties of this frontier, when we have a finite number of observations, the portfolio frontier presents some discontinuity on its convexity. In order to overcome that, kernel estimations of the returns were used, creating a smoother portfolio frontier. In this sense, the former algorithm is generalized, and the properties of this improved portfolio frontier carefully analysed. Finally, a new version of the Lower Partial Moment CAPM is presented to deal with kernel estimates.

13.1 INTRODUCTION

The main criticism to variance and volatility as measures of risk is, in essence, that they make no distinction between gains and losses. In fact, in Markowitz's original work (1955) he argues for other measures of risk. Two ways were suggested. The first would be to include higher moments. This has been approached by a few authors like Ingersoll (1975), and Kraus and Litzenberger (1976), among others. However the complete formal characterization of the portfolio frontier with higher moments has not been done since Athayde and Flôres

(2002). In that paper the portfolio set with higher moments and all of its features were presented.

The second way that Markowitz proposed was to use what he called semivariance. That is the sum of the squares of negative deviations from the mean, divided by the total number of observations:

$$\text{Semivariance} \Rightarrow \frac{1}{n} \sum_{i=1}^{n} [\text{Min}(r_i - \mu, 0)]^2$$

The great advantage of the use of semivariance over variance is that it does not include positive gains, so what is considered as risk takes into account only negative deviations.

However one may be led to the wrong conclusion that minimizing semivariance necessarily means minimizing only negative deviations. This common mistake becomes even clearer if the distributions we are dealing with are symmetric, like the normal curve. In this case minimizing variance and semivariance will lead to the same problem.

Nonetheless, normality on assets returns have been widely rejected in practice, see Eftekhari and Satchell (1996). The only case that justifies the use of semivariance is when the presence of skewness or any other measure of asymmetry is observed.

Semivariance was generalized to a broader definition, called Downside Risk (DSR):

$$\text{Downside Risk (DSR)} \Rightarrow \frac{1}{n} \sum_{i=1}^{n} [\text{Min}(r_i - \mu, 0)]^k$$

where μ is a given benchmark, and k is a positive number, chosen to penalize the losses with respect to the benchmark. When k is an odd number, these deviations should be treated in absolute values. When μ is the mean and $k = 2$, we are driven back to semivariance.

Although the approach to use higher moments is far more complete than the use of semivariance, the popularity of the latter is larger, maybe because it measures risk in one number, while the use of variance, skewness and possibly kurtosis would give us three different values to capture risk. In terms of portfolio frontier, we will be dealing only with two dimensions, rather than three or four, and make the analysis simpler (although not so efficient if compared to the multi-dimensioned three or four moment portfolio frontier).

Finding the portfolios with minimum semivariance is not an easy task. This is due to the fact that we do not have a fixed number to represent the downside risk of an asset. For instance, if we have acquired a single asset, its semivariance will be given by negative deviations, while if we short sell this asset, then we will have to deal with positive deviations (because now the risk is for the asset to go up). Thus what will be used to construct its semivariance depends on whether we are short or long.

The problem becomes even more complex when we deal with more than one asset. Suppose we have a given portfolio P_0. To compute the semivariance of this portfolio we have to take into consideration only the observations that were negative deviations. If we change the weights of this portfolio a little, creating a new portfolio P_1, some observations in which the former portfolio was negative might become positive, and vice versa. Thus they will have to be included or excluded from the semivariance of portfolio P_1. Therefore the set of observations that will be taken into account when building the semivariance of this portfolio will be function of the portfolio weights, making the problem more difficult to handle than in the case of minimizing variance per se.

For instance, suppose we have two assets, with zero mean. On one day, one could have a return of 1%, and on another day of -1%. If the weight of the first asset is more (less) than 1/2, the portfolio's return will be positive (negative), and therefore excluded (included) in the semivariance of the portfolio.

In this sense the set of observations that will be used to construct a portfolio's DSR is necessarily a function of the weights of the portfolio per se. It should be clear that there is no such thing as a fixed well-behaved positive definite semivariance matrix, independent of the portfolio weights, which we can pre- and post-multiply by the vector of weights of any portfolio and get its respective semivariance. Therefore the minimization problem becomes much more complicated, because the set of observations that will be taken into account is endogenous to the weights of the portfolio in question.

Athayde (2001) has shown an algorithm to construct a mean-DSR portfolio frontier, along with some properties this frontier will have. Although it is continuous, its convexity is not, in contrast to the Markowitz case. The number of kinks in the convexity will increase with the number of observations, getting closer and closer to each other, until when we reach the asymptotic limit, they will not be qualified as kinks anymore, and the whole portfolio frontier will have a smooth shape.

In practice, we only have a finite number of observations, and although we can always have an enormous number of data, the assumptions of asset returns being identically distributed during the whole period of the sample may not be a very realistic assumption. Thus, when computing a DSR portfolio frontier we will always be facing these kinks on the convexity, which would only disappear if we had a continuous number of observations.

The idea behind this chapter is to make use of nonparametric techniques to estimate smooth continuous distributions of the portfolios in question, and from these estimations, optimize their DSR, constructing with this, a new portfolio frontier.

It will be shown that, instead of these kinks, we will see smoother transitions between optimal portfolios, when we make use of this technique. The analogy is similar to the case in which we move from a histogram to a smooth estimated continuous curve. The properties of the traditional frontier, and also the algorithm presented in Athayde (2001) to build it, can be seen as a particular case of the nonparametric approach, in which the bandwidth (also called the smoothness parameter) goes to zero.

13.2 THE MEAN-DSR PORTFOLIO FRONTIER: THE TRADITIONAL APPROACH

In this Section, we will show the characteristics of the mean-DSR portfolio frontier. For more details, see Athayde (2001).

Let us assume that we have two risky assets a and b. The return of a portfolio p that has w units of a and $(1 - w)$ units of b, at time i can be expressed as:

$$r_p^i(w) = wr_a^i + (1 - w)r_b^i$$

where r_j^i stands for the return of asset j at time i.

Let us consider the case where $k = 2$, and that we have observations that start at time 0 and end at time n.

$$DSR = \frac{1}{n+1} \sum_{i=0}^{n} [\text{Min}(r_p^i(w) - \mu, 0)]^2$$

The value of w at time i that makes the portfolio's return equal to the benchmark μ is given by:

$$w_i = \frac{\mu - r_b^i}{r_a^i - r_b^i}$$

If we had only this observation, assuming that $r_a^i > r_b^i$, the DSR of this portfolio would be given by:

$$DSR(w) = [w(r_a^i - r_b^i) - (\mu - r_b^i)]^2, \text{ if } w < w_i; \text{ and 0 otherwise}$$

$$DSR'(w) = 2\lfloor w(r_a^i - r_b^i) - (\mu - r_b^i)\rfloor$$
$$\times (r_a^i - r_b^i) < 0, \text{ if } w < w_i; \text{ and 0 otherwise}$$

$$DSR''(w) = 2(r_a^i - r_b^i)^2 > 0, \text{ if } w < w_i; \text{ and 0 otherwise}$$

The function is illustrated in Figure 13.1.

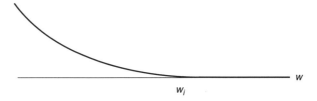

Figure 13.1 *DSR portfolio function (1)*

In case $r_a^i < r_b^i$, the DSR would be described by the curve in Figure 13.2.

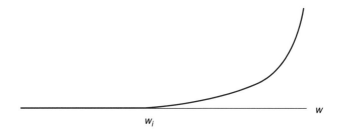

Figure 13.2 *DSR portfolio function (2)*

It is not hard to see that when we are computing DSR as a function of the weight w, we will be adding these piecewise quadratic functions. Every time we cross points like w_i, there will be a change in the convexity of the curve. When we include all observations the whole DSR will be a curve as shown in Figure 13.3.

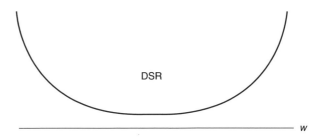

Figure 13.3 *DSR portfolio function (3)*

The expected return of the portfolio will be given by:

$$E(r_p) = wE(r_a) + (1 - w)E(r_b) \Leftrightarrow w = \frac{E(r_p) - E(r_b)}{E(r_a) - E(r_b)}$$

Thus, since we have a linear relation between w and $E(r_p)$, we may conclude that the shape of the set DSR $\times E(r_p)$ will be as shown in Figure 13.4.

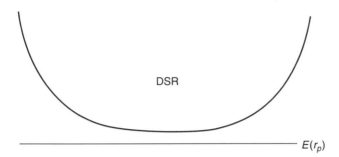

Figure 13.4   *DSR portfolio function (4)*

As it has been shown, this curve is a sum of segments of quadratic functions. The curve will become steeper and steeper as we move toward the extremes, in either direction. The more observations we have, the more quadratic functions will be added and smaller the segment of each will become. The changes in the convexity, when we move from one quadratic function to another will become more frequent and smoother. In the limit case, where we will have an infinite number of observations, each of these quadratic functions will degenerate to a single point, creating a continuous smooth changing in the convexity of the curve. Thus we may conclude that, in the bivariate case, the portfolio set and consequently the portfolio frontier will have a convex shape.

How do we find the vertex of the curve above? Which value of w gives us the minimum DSR? The answer is given in the algorithm presented below.

We start with a given portfolio $w^{(0)}$, and calculate its downside risk. We select only the set of observations S_0 that contains negative deviations of this portfolio $w^{(0)}$.

$$S_0 = \{i \,|\, 1 < i < n \ \& \ r_i(w^{(0)}) < \mu\}$$

Consider the following curve given by:

$$\sigma_0^2(w) = \frac{1}{n} \sum_{i \in S_0} (r_p^i(w) - \mu)^2, \text{ where } r_p^i(w) = w r_a^i + (1-w) r_b^i \qquad (13.1)$$

It should be clear from the last section that for a small neighbourhood of $w^{(0)}$, the set of observations with negative deviations remains the same as S_0, without adding or excluding any observation, remaining on the same quadratic function. When w becomes very different from $w^{(0)}$, some days will enter and some will go away when we compute the downside risk of w (because we have moved to another segment of a different quadratic function in the DSR curve). In this case the curve that describes the downside risk and σ_0^2 will become more and more different. Nevertheless, for small changes on w, if the set of negative deviations is still given by S_0, the two curves will coincide.

The second step is to find a portfolio $w^{(1)}$ that minimizes $\sigma_0^2(w)$. This is an ordinary well-behaved quadratic problem, whose minimum is easily obtained. This optimal portfolio will be given by:

$$w^{(1)} = \frac{\displaystyle\sum_{i \in S_0} (r_a^i - r_b^i)(\mu - r_b^i)}{\displaystyle\sum_{i \in S_0} (r_a^i - r_b^i)^2}$$

Once we find $w^{(1)}$, we compute its DSR, creating a new set of observations S_1, which has only negative deviations of $w^{(1)}$ with respect to the benchmark μ:

$$S_1 = \{i | \ 1 < i < n \ \& \ r_i(w^{(1)}) < \mu\}$$

In the neighbourhood of $w^{(1)}$, the DSR will coincide with the following quadratic function:

$$\sigma_1^2(w) = \frac{1}{n} \sum_{i \in S_1} (r_p^i(w) - \mu)^2, \quad \text{where } r_p^i(w) = wr_a^i + (1 - w)r_b^i \qquad (13.2)$$

We then minimize (13.2) with respect to w. The solution is given by:

$$w^{(2)} = \frac{\displaystyle\sum_{i \in S_1} (r_a^i - r_b^i)(\mu - r_b^i)}{\displaystyle\sum_{i \in S_1} (r_a^i - r_b^i)^2} \qquad (13.3)$$

From $w^{(2)}$ we separate the new set of observations with negative deviations S_2, construct a new quadratic function that takes into consideration only the observations in S_2, minimize it with respect to w, finding $w^{(3)}$, that will give us a new set S_3, and so on. The algorithm will stop when $S_t = S_{t+1}$, which will be the unique minimum DSR.

In order to extend the last example – consider Figure 13.5 in which we have three quadratic functions, each one representing a segment of the DSR function, which is given by the thick black line. It is easy to see that no matter which quadratic function we pick from the start, if we follow the proposed algorithm, we will end up in P_3. The minimum of this quadratic function is also the minimum of DSR, guaranteeing the convergence.

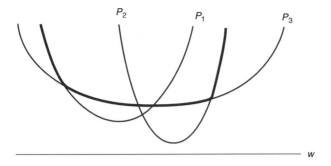

Figure 13.5 *DSR portfolio function (5)*

For instance, if our initial guess of w is very low, we will select the observations in such a way that we will start at P_1. Once we find w that minimizes this quadratic function, we will select a new set of returns that were below the benchmark, ending up with a new quadratic function P_3. Again, we will find the portfolio w that minimizes this quadratic function. However, after this portfolio is found, the new set of observations whose deviations are negative is the same as before, so we will remain at P_3, and the minimum DSR (which coincides with the minimum of P_3) is achieved.

The same goes for the case in which our initial guess of w is high. In this situation, we would have started at P_2 and on the next iteration, be driven back to P_3. In case we have stared on P_3, only one iteration would be necessary to achieve the minimum.

13.3 THE MULTIVARIATE CASE

The procedure for the multivariate case is analogous to the previous procedure. Let us say we have m assets. We will start with a given portfolio $w^{(0)}$. Then we select the set S_0 of observations in which this portfolio $w^{(0)}$ had negative deviations. Then we construct the following positive semidefinite matrix:

$$M^{(0)} = \sum_{i \in S_0} \begin{bmatrix} R_1^i \\ R_2^i \\ \vdots \\ R_M^i \end{bmatrix} [R_1^i \quad R_2^i \quad \cdots \quad R_M^i]$$

where R_m^i means the excess return (actual return minus the benchmark) of asset m on date i.

The next step is to find the portfolio w_1 that solves the following problem:

$$\underset{w}{\text{Min}} \ w^t M^{(0)} w \ \text{s.t.} \ w^t 1 = 1$$

where 1 is a vector of 1s.

The solution to the problem will be given by:

$$w^{(1)} = \frac{M^{(0)^{-1}}1}{1^t M^{(0)^{-1}}1}$$

If $M^{(0)}$ is non-invertible, this means that we will have few observations, and that it will be possible to find a portfolio that will give us a null DSR. This is not an interesting case, it does not mean there is no DSR, it only means that the sample in question is poor, leaving us with few degrees of freedom.

With the new portfolio $w^{(1)}$ we collect the set of observations S_1 that contains only negative excess returns of portfolio $w^{(1)}$. We now form a new positive semidefinite matrix $M^{(1)}$:

$$M^{(1)} = \sum_{i \in S_1} \begin{bmatrix} R_1^i \\ R_2^i \\ \vdots \\ R_M^i \end{bmatrix} [\, R_1^i \quad R_2^i \quad \cdots \quad R_M^i \,]$$

The next step is to find the portfolio $w^{(2)}$ that solves the following problem:

$$\underset{w}{\text{Min}} \ w^t M^{(1)} w \ \text{s.t.} \ w^t 1 = 1$$

The solution to the problem will be given by:

$$w^{(2)} = \frac{M^{(1)^{-1}}1}{1^t M^{(1)^{-1}}1}$$

From then on, we form a new matrix $M^{(2)}$ collecting only the negative observations of portfolio $w^{(2)}$, and so on. The iterations will stop when the matrix $M^{(T)}$ will be the same as $M^{(T+1)}$. The solution will be given by:

$$w^{(T)} = \frac{M^{(T)^{-1}}1}{1^t M^{(T)^{-1}}1} \tag{13.4}$$

This portfolio will give us the minimum DSR. In terms of the portfolio frontier, this will represent the vertex of the curve. In order to build the portfolio frontier, we will have to find some other points on the efficient set. Since we are interested in points with a higher expected return than the vertex, we shall fix an expected return a bit higher than the minimum downside risk portfolio above. So the new recursive minimization procedure will take the following form:

$$\underset{w}{\text{Min}} \ w^t M^{(t)} w \ \text{s.t.} \ w^t 1 = 1 \ \text{and} \ w^t e = E(r)$$

where e is the vector of expected returns, and w^t is the transpose of w.

After we have achieved the convergence, after T iterations, the minimum downside risk portfolio with expected excess return given by $E(r)$ will be given by:

$$w^{(T)} = \frac{\alpha E(r) - \gamma}{\alpha \theta - \gamma^2} M^{(T)^{-1}} e + \frac{\theta - \gamma E(r)}{\alpha \theta - \gamma^2} M^{(T)^{-1}} 1 \tag{13.5}$$

where $\alpha = 1^t M^{(T)^{-1}} 1, \gamma = e^t M^{(T)^{-1}} 1, \theta = e^t M^{(T)^{-1}} e$.

It should be noted that for small changes in the expected return, the matrix we will end up with remains unchanged. Pre-multiplying (13.5) by $w^t M^{(T)}$:

$$DSR(w) = \frac{\alpha (E(r))^2 - 2\gamma E(r) + \theta}{\alpha \theta - \gamma^2}$$

The equation above shows us that while the final matrix $M^{(T)}$ does not change, downside risk will be a quadratic function on the expected return. However, if we change considerably the expected return, we will end up with a new matrix, and therefore a new quadratic function, because we will have new values for α, γ and θ. Thus, as in the bivariate case, the portfolio frontier will be described as a sequence of segments of different quadratic functions.

This result is expected because the portfolio frontier is a convex combination of several bivariate cases, each one like Figure 13.4. One interesting aspect is that the more assets are used, the smoother will be the portfolio frontier in question, creating a similar effect as if we were adding more observations.

The aim of next section is to provide a non-parametric technique, using kernel estimations of asset returns, to create an effect similar to as if we had continuous observations, and therefore build a new portfolio frontier with a smoother shape, and avoid huge changes in the convexity.

13.4   A KERNEL APPROACH

In this section we will make use of a more sophisticated estimation of DSR, in which we estimate the density of the returns using kernels. A kernel estimation of one point can be seen as a weighted average of the observations, in which the weight given to each observation decreases with its distance from the point in question. A kernel estimation of some return $\hat{r}_j$ of a given asset or portfolio is given by:

$$\hat{r}_j = \frac{\sum\limits_i r_i K \left(\frac{r_i - r_j}{h} \right)}{\sum\limits_i K \left(\frac{r_i - r_j}{h} \right)} \tag{13.6}$$

where $K(x)$ is a function that decreases with x. The term h is chosen in order to penalize the distance between r_t and r, it is also called the bandwidth, or smoothness parameter.

It is straightforward to see that

$$\text{if } h \to \infty, \quad K\left(\frac{r_i - r_t}{h}\right) \to K(0), \quad \hat{r}_t = \frac{\sum\limits_i r_i}{n}, \quad \forall \hat{r}_t$$

In this case we would have smoothed our series to the extreme. On the other hand:

$$\text{if } h \to 0, \quad K\left(\frac{r_i - r_t}{h}\right) \to 0, \text{ if } r_j \neq r_i$$

$$\text{and } K\left(\frac{r_i - r_t}{h}\right) \to K(1), \text{ if } r_j = r_i$$

$$\hat{r}_j = 0, \text{ if } r_j \neq r_i, \text{ and } \hat{r}_j = r_i, \text{ if } \hat{r}_j = \hat{r}_i \qquad (13.7)$$

The new estimation of the DSR, called DSR(K) is given by:

$$DSR(K) \Rightarrow \frac{1}{n} \sum_{i=1}^{n} [\text{Min}(\hat{r}_i - \mu, \ 0)]^2 \qquad (13.8)$$

It can be seen by using (13.7) that when $h \to 0$, $DSR(K) \Rightarrow DSR$. The higher h becomes, the more different these two estimations will be. In fact, DSR(K) will always be smaller than DSR. This difference will become smaller as h tends to zero. For details on the optimal choice of kernels and of h (which is far more relevant), see Silverman (1986) and Pagan and Ullah (1999).

We will now present the algorithm for constructing the portfolio frontier with DSR(K). We will begin in the bivariate case, just like in the last section. There, the DSR curve had some segments in which there was a constant convexity, because they belonged to the same quadratic function. In our new case, this will not occur. Even if we set a new portfolio that is very close to another, although the set of observations that will be included might remain the same, there will be a slight change in the convexity, due to the changes in the kernel weights, as will be shown. In other words, the kernel estimation will make the convexity of the curve change continuously and provide us with a smoother estimate of the portfolio frontier, instead of those abrupt changes followed by regions of constant convexities.

Figure 13.6 illustrates this aspect. DSR is the curve constructed with the method proposed in Athayde (2001) (demonstrated in the last section), while DSR(K) is the kernel estimation. It can be seen that the kernel estimation

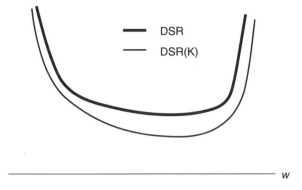

Figure 13.6   *DSR portfolio function (6)*

resembles what would be the curve when we have an infinite number of observations. It would also be expected that the kernel estimation curve would tend to be a little below the first one, because we are dealing with smoother estimation of returns, and consequently offsetting some extreme effects.

There is one aspect that should be emphasized. When we move toward the vertex of the curves above, everytime facing portfolios with lower DSR, they tend to have little extreme values (especially on the losses). If we keep using the same bandwidth h as in the former iterations (portfolios with higher risk), we will tend to underestimate the DSR(K). An ideal bandwidth that was used for a very risky portfolio, when applied to a 'conservative' portfolio (whose losses are small), will tend to penalize little the distance between the observations, making our estimations smoother than desired, and consequently bringing underestimated values for DSR(K).

Thus, when moving towards portfolios with smaller risk, one should diminish the bandwidth used. Therefore one should redefine the bandwidth used for every iteration of the algorithm described below. One simple procedure that has worked reasonably well in our simulations is to define the bandwidth as proportional to the volatility of the portfolio. In this sense we only have to estimate the optimal bandwidth once, and get this constant of proportionality.

How does the algorithm work in this case? As in the previous sections, we start with some portfolio $w^{(0)}$. Then we make n kernel estimations of all the n returns $\hat{r}_0^j$ of this new portfolio:

$$\hat{r}_0^j = \frac{\sum_i r_0^i K\left(\frac{r_0^i - r_0^j}{h}\right)}{\sum_{t=1}^{T} K\left(\frac{r_0^i - r_0^j}{h}\right)}, \quad i, j = 1, \ldots, n \tag{13.9}$$

For the estimation of the n returns of each single asset, we shall follow the same procedure, but we will use the same (kernel) weights of the portfolio w_0:

$$\hat{r}_a^j = \frac{\sum_i r_a^i K \left(\frac{r_0^i - r_0^j}{h} \right)}{\sum_{t=1}^T K \left(\frac{r_0^i - r_0^j}{h} \right)}, \hat{r}_b^j = \frac{\sum_i r_b^i K \left(\frac{r_0^i - r_0^j}{h} \right)}{\sum_{t=1}^T K \left(\frac{r_0^i - r_0^j}{h} \right)} \tag{13.10}$$

Consider S_0 to be the set of the estimated excess returns of $w^{(0)}$ that were negative:

$$S_0 = \{i \mid 1 < i < n \ \& \ \hat{r}_0^i < \mu\}$$

The first minimization will be given by:

$$\text{Min} \sum_{i \in S_0} (\hat{r}_i - \mu)^2, \hat{r}_i = w\hat{r}_a^i + (1 - w)\hat{r}_b^i$$

Let us call the portfolio that solves this problem $w^{(1)}$. The next step will be the kernel estimation of the returns of this portfolio:

$$\hat{r}_1^j = \frac{\sum_i r_1^i K \left(\frac{r_1^i - r_1^j}{h} \right)}{\sum_{t=1}^T K \left(\frac{r_1^i - r_1^j}{h} \right)}$$

And then, the new estimations of the returns of each single asset:

$$\hat{r}_a^j = \frac{\sum_i r_a^i K \left(\frac{r_1^i - r_1^j}{h} \right)}{\sum_{t=1}^T K \left(\frac{r_1^i - r_1^j}{h} \right)}, \hat{r}_b^j = \frac{\sum_i r_b^i K \left(\frac{r_1^i - r_1^j}{h} \right)}{\sum_{t=1}^T K \left(\frac{r_1^i - r_1^j}{h} \right)} \tag{13.11}$$

Consider S_1 to be the set of the estimated excess returns of w_1 that were negative. The second minimization will be given by:

$$\text{Min} \sum_{i \in S_1} (\hat{r}_i - \mu)^2, \quad \hat{r}_i = w\hat{r}_a^i + (1 - w)\hat{r}_b^i$$

where $\hat{r}_a^i$ and $\hat{r}_b^i$ given by (13.11).

From here on, we will follow the same procedure, in contrast to the previous case, in which we would stop the algorithm when $S_T = S_{T+1}$. In this case, we should continue the iterations because even with the same set of observations selected, the kernel estimations will differ for every new portfolio found. Nevertheless, it should be noted that the changes in the portfolio, and consequently on DSR, will be smaller for each iteration. Thus, we should set a convergence limit in which, if the changes in the portfolio are smaller than the limit, we will stop the iterations.

13.5   THE KERNEL APPROACH TO THE MULTIVARIATE CASE

For the multivariate case, we start with some portfolio w_0, then we make a kernel estimation of the returns $\hat{r}_0^j$ of this new portfolio, as in the previous case:

$$\hat{r}_0^j = \frac{\displaystyle\sum_i r_0^i K\left(\frac{r_0^i - r_0^j}{h}\right)}{\displaystyle\sum_{t=1}^{T} K\left(\frac{r_0^i - r_0^j}{h}\right)}$$

Following that, we make estimations of the returns of each single asset m on date j:

$$\hat{r}_m^j = \frac{\displaystyle\sum_i r_m^i K\left(\frac{r_0^i - r_0^j}{h}\right)}{\displaystyle\sum_{t=1}^{T} K\left(\frac{r_0^i - r_0^j}{h}\right)}$$

From that, we select the dates when the estimated returns of portfolio $w^{(0)}$ had negative excess returns. Let us call this set of observations S_0. Then we construct the following positive semidefinite matrix:

$$\hat{M}^{(0)} = \sum_{i \in S_0} \begin{bmatrix} R_1^i \\ R_2^i \\ \vdots \\ R_M^i \end{bmatrix} [\, R_1^i \quad R_2^i \quad \cdots \quad R_M^i \,]$$

where $\hat{R}_m^i$ means the excess return $(\hat{r}_m^i - \mu)$ of asset m on date i.

The first task will be to find a portfolio w_1 that solves the following problem:

$$\underset{w}{\text{Min}} \quad w^t \hat{M}^{(0)} w \text{ s.t. } w^t 1 = 1$$

The solution will be given by:

$$w^{(1)} = \frac{\hat{M}^{(0)^{-1}} 1}{1^t \hat{M}^{(0)^{-1}} 1}$$

Then, we shall collect all the returns r_1^i of this portfolio, and make a kernel estimation of the returns $\hat{r}_1^j$ of this new portfolio $w^{(1)}$:

$$\hat{r}_1^j = \frac{\sum_i r_1^i K \left(\frac{r_1^i - r_1^j}{h} \right)}{\sum_{t=1}^{T} K \left(\frac{r_1^i - r_1^j}{h} \right)}$$

Following that, the new estimations of the returns of each single asset m on date j will be given by:

$$\hat{r}_m^j = \frac{\sum_i r_m^i K \left(\frac{r_1^i - r_1^j}{h} \right)}{\sum_{t=1}^{T} K \left(\frac{r_1^i - r_1^j}{h} \right)}$$

From that, we can construct a new positive definite matrix, taking into consideration only the elements in which $\hat{r}_1^i < \mu$. As in the former cases we will call this set of observations S_1:

$$S_1 = \{i \mid 1 < i < n \ \& \ \hat{r}_1^i < \mu\}$$

$$\hat{M}^{(1)} = \sum_{i \in S_1} \begin{bmatrix} R_1^i \\ R_2^i \\ \vdots \\ R_M^i \end{bmatrix} [\, R_1^i, \quad R_2^i \quad \cdots \quad R_M^i \,]$$

The second task will be to find a portfolio $w^{(2)}$ that solves the following problem:

$$\underset{w}{\text{Min}} \ w^t \hat{M}^{(1)} w \ \text{s.t.} \ w^t 1 = 1$$

The solution will be given by:

$$w^{(2)} = \frac{\hat{M}^{(1)^{-1}} 1}{1^t \hat{M}^{(1)^{-1}} 1}$$

Then we make a kernel estimation of the returns $\hat{r}_2^i$ of this new portfolio, and follow the same procedure as before. The iterations should stop when the changes in the portfolio become negligible, or simply smaller than a pre-established limit.

In order to construct a portfolio frontier, we shall use the same procedure as in Section 13.3, but making use of estimated returns of the assets. The problem becomes computationally more complex, since for every iteration, we have new estimations of returns for every asset, due to the changes in the kernel weights, for every time we alter the portfolio. As already mentioned, the portfolio frontier will be a smoother curve than the former case.

One may ask why we should not make a non-parametric estimation of the whole joint, multivariate distribution of all the assets and construct the portfolios from there, instead of all this series of univariate nonparametric estimations?

A possible answer is given by the so-called 'curse of dimensionality'. This shows that the more dimensions we add to a multivariate nonparametric esti-mation, the less efficient our estimators will become. Therefore, it is better to choose a portfolio, and then to make univariate kernel estimations, rather than estimate the whole joint distribution of all the assets returns first, and then choose the portfolio.

13.6 THE MEAN-DSR PORTFOLIO FRONTIER USING KERNEL ESTIMATES

In order to construct a portfolio frontier, we shall use the same procedure as in Section 13.3, but making use of estimated returns of the assets. The problem becomes computationally more complex, since for every iteration, we will have new estimations of returns for every asset, due to the changes in the kernel weights, for every time we alter the portfolio. As already mentioned, the portfolio frontier will be a smoother curve than the former case.

The algorithm remains the same, and each step can be defined by:

$$\min_{w} \; w^t \hat{M} \, w \quad \text{s.t.} \quad w^t 1 = 1 \text{ and } w^t e = E(r)$$

where e is the vector of expected returns, and this time it will change on every iteration. This is due to the fact that the estimation of the returns of each single asset $\hat{r}_m^i$ will differ due to the change in kernel weights on each iteration.

$$e^{(t)} = \begin{bmatrix} \dfrac{\sum_i \hat{r}_1^i}{n} \\ \vdots \\ \dfrac{\sum_i \hat{r}_M^i}{n} \end{bmatrix}$$

After we have achieved the convergence, after T iterations, the minimum downside risk portfolio with expected excess return given by $E(r)$ will be given by:

$$w^{(T)} = \frac{\hat{\alpha} E(r) - \hat{\gamma}}{\hat{\alpha}\hat{\theta} - \hat{\gamma}^2} \hat{M}^{(T)^{-1}} e^{(T)} + \frac{\hat{\theta} - \hat{\gamma} E(r)}{\hat{\alpha}\hat{\theta} - \hat{\gamma}^2} \hat{M}^{(T)^{-1}} 1 \tag{13.12}$$

where $\hat{\alpha} = 1^t \hat{M}^{(T)^{-1}} 1$, $\hat{\gamma} = 1^t \hat{M}^{(T)^{-1}} e^{(T)}$, $\hat{\theta} = (e^{(T)})^t \hat{M}^{(T)^{-1}} e^{(T)}$.

Pre-multiplying (13.12) by $M^{(T)}$, and then by the transposition of $w^{(T)}$, we will have:

$$DSR(K) = \frac{\hat{\alpha} (E(r))^2 - 2\hat{\gamma} E(r) + \hat{\theta}}{\hat{\alpha}\hat{\theta} - \hat{\gamma}^2} \tag{13.13}$$

In contrast to Section 13.3, where we had a local quadratic function, this time we aim for small changes in $E(r)$, the coefficients $\hat{\alpha}$, $\hat{\gamma}$ and $\hat{\theta}$ will also change, due to the change in kernel weights (they might be negligible changes, but they exist). In this situation, instead of moving from one segment of quadratic function to another, we have a smooth continuous transition as we change $E(r)$.

13.7   ASSET PRICING

In this Section, we will provide a kernel version of the Lower Partial Moment CAPM, derived by Bawa and Lindenberg (1977) other approaches can be seen in Hogan and Warren (1974), and Harlow and Rao (1989). For the original CAPM, see Sharpe (1964), Lintner (1965) and Mossin (1969).

Consider a portfolio z that has the following zero cross-DSR with a frontier portfolio p:

$$\frac{1}{n} \sum_{i=1}^{n} [\text{Min}(r_p^i - \mu, \ 0)](r_z^i - \mu) = 0$$

If we pre-multiply (13.12) by $z' M^{(T)}$, we have:

$$0 = \frac{\hat{\alpha} E(r_p) - \hat{\gamma}}{\hat{\alpha}\hat{\theta} - \hat{\gamma}^2} E(r_z) + \frac{\hat{\theta} - \hat{\gamma} E(r_p)}{\hat{\alpha}\hat{\theta} - \hat{\gamma}^2}$$

Substituting in (13.13) it becomes:

$$p = \frac{\hat{\alpha} E(r_p) - \hat{\gamma}}{\hat{\alpha}\hat{\theta} - \hat{\gamma}^2} M^{(T)^{-1}} (e^{(T)} - E(r_z)1) \tag{13.14}$$

If we pre-multiply the equation above by $p^t M^{(T)}$, we have:

$$DSR(K)_p = \frac{\hat{\alpha} E(r_p) - \hat{\gamma}}{\hat{\alpha}\hat{\theta} - \hat{\gamma}^2} (E(r_p) - E(r_z))$$

Consider now a given portfolio k. If we pre-multiply (13.14) by $i^t M^{(T)}$, we have:

$$\sigma_{kp}* = \frac{\hat{\alpha} E(r_p) - \hat{\gamma}}{\hat{\alpha}\hat{\theta} - \hat{\gamma}^2} (E(r_k) - E(r_z)), \quad \text{where } \sigma_{kp}* = \sum_{i \in S_T} (r_k^i - \mu)(r_p^i - \mu)$$

Comparing the two equations above, we can see that:

$$E(r_k) - E(r_z) = \beta_k * (E(r_p) - E(r_z)), \quad \text{where } \beta_k* = \frac{\sigma_{kp}*}{DSR(K)_p} \qquad (13.15)$$

This means that any asset or portfolio k can be expressed as this version of the CAPM for any portfolio p of the portfolio frontier. The only difficulty in transforming it into a CAPM is that we do not have the two-fund separation property to guarantee that the market portfolio is an efficient portfolio.

Let us consider now the case where we also have a riskless asset, with a given fixed return r_f. Our problem now becomes:

$$\text{Min } w^t M \, w \text{ s.t. } E(r) - (w^t e + (1 - w^t 1) r_f)$$

Let us call this optimal portfolio by portfolio p. After all the iterations, p will be given by:

$$p = \frac{M^{(T)^{-1}} d}{d^t M^{(T)^{-1}} d} (E(r_p) - r_f), \quad \text{where } d = e^{(T)} - r_f 1 \qquad (13.16)$$

If we pre-multiply the equation above by $p^t M^{(T)}$, we have:

$$DSR(K)_p = \frac{(E(R_p) - r_f)^2}{d^t M^{(T)^{-1}} d}$$

Consider now a given portfolio k. If we pre-multiply (13.16) by $k^t M^{(T)}$, we have:

$$\sigma_{kp}* = \frac{(E(r_k) - r_f)(E(r_p) - r_f)}{d^t M^{(T)^{-1}} d}$$

Comparing these two equations above, we can see that:

$$E(r_k) - r_f = \beta_k * (E(r_p) - r_f) \qquad (13.17)$$

Therefore, as regards asset pricing, the results are virtually the same as the traditional Lower Partial Moment CAPM. The only difference is that in the kernel methodology, we shall be replacing DSR by DSR(K), and the semicovariance by $\sigma_{kp}*$.

13.8 CONCLUSION

In this chapter a generalized version of the algorithm developed by Athayde (2001) to construct a mean-DSR portfolio frontier is presented. This generalization allows one to make use of kernel estimations. The great advantage of this technique is that it provides an effect similar to the case in which we had continuous observations. As a consequence, some inconveniences of the traditional portfolio frontier (like 'kinks' in its convexity) are therefore bypassed. The new portfolio frontier has a smoother shape than the traditional one. Finally, a new version of the Lower Partial Moment CAPM, is also derived to deal with these kernel estimates.

REFERENCES

Athayde, G. (2001) Building a Mean-Downside Risk Portfolio Frontier, *Developments in Forecast Combination and Portfolio Choice*, John Wiley and Sons.

Athayde, G. and Flôres, R. (2002) Finding a Maximum Skewness Portfolio, *Journal of Economic Dynamics and Control, Forthcoming*.

Bawa, V. and Lindenberg, E. (1977) Capital Market Equilibrium in a Mean-Lower Partial Moment Framework, *Journal of Financial Economics*, **5**, 189–200.

Eftekhari, B. and Satchell, S. (1996) Non-Normality of Returns in Emerging Markets, *Research in International Business and Finance*, Supplement 1, 267–77.

Harlow, W. and Rao, R. (1989) Asset Pricing in a Generalised Mean-Lower Partial Moment Framework: Theory and Evidence, *Journal of Financial and Quantitative Analysis*, **24**(3), 285–311

Hogan, W. and Warren, J. (1974) Toward the development of an equilibrium capital market model based on semivariance, *Journal of Financial and Quantitative Analysis*, **9**, 1–12.

Ingersoll, J. (1975) Multidimensional Security Pricing, *Journal of Financial and Quantitative Analysis*, **10**, 785–98.

Kraus, A. and Litzenberger, R.H. (1976) Skewness Preference and the Valuation of Risky Assets, *Journal of Finance*, **31**, 1085–100.

Lintner, J. (1965) The Valuation of Risk Assets and The Selection of Risky Investments in Stock Portfolios and Capital Budgets, *Review of Economics and Statistics*, **47**, 13–37.

Markowitz, H. (1952) Portfolio Selection, *Journal of Finance*, **7**, 77–91.

Mossin, J. (1969) Security Pricing and Investment Criteria in Competitive Markets, *American Economic Review*, **59**, 749–56.

Pagan, A.R. and Ullah (1999) *Nonparametric Econometrics*, Cambridge University Press.

Price K., Price, B. and Nantell, T. (1982) Variance and Lower Partial Moment Measures of Systematic Risk: Some Analytical and Empirical Results, *Journal of Finance*, **37**, 843–55.

Sharpe, W. (1964) Capital Asset Prices: A Theory of Market Equilibrium under Conditions of Risk, *Journal of Finance*, **19**, 425–42.

Silverman, B.W. (1986) *Density Estimation for Statistics and Data Analysis*, Chapman and Hall, New York.

Chapter 14

Some exact results for efficient portfolios with given returns

G H HILLIER AND S E SATCHELL

ABSTRACT

We consider the problem of the derivation of the finite sample distributions of a portfolio estimator based on normally distributed data where we are given the proportions of the current holdings. Our portfolio estimator is designed to be efficient and with the same expected return as our current portfolio. We derive the distribution of the risk estimator and the (conditional) distribution of the estimated weights. We also derive the (unconditional) expected value of the estimated weights.

14.1 INTRODUCTION

It is now widely recognized that portfolio optimization suffers greatly from sample fluctuations due to estimation error and that investment decisions based solely on mean-variance calculations are likely to lead to ridiculous portfolios and excessive turnover. The defects of simplistic optimization are detailed in Michaud (1998). Some authors, notably Jobson and Korkie (1980, 1982) have worked on these problems, but their results are approximate rather than exact and they have concentrated on the riskless asset case, rather than the more general zero-beta case. For the zero-beta capital asset pricing model (CAPM), testing and estimation have occurred largely in mean-beta space rather than in portfolio space. Roll's critique that testing the validity of the implied market portfolio has been taken to heart by financial economists, but strangely his original suggestion in Roll (1979) of working directly with the portfolio itself has not been followed up. It is curious that the study of the statistical properties of the sample portfolios has not been a topic of greater interest, since it should be of central importance in the CAPM literature.

The purpose of this chapter is to examine the properties of the estimators of the optimal portfolio, its return and risk, given some ex ante proportions. As such the problem has close similarities to the technique of reverse optimization, and our results could, perhaps, be applied to such a situation. We derive the exact distributions in each case, and find the moments of each of the estimators. The properties of these distributions, although very complex, shed light on some of the commonly used test statistics. In fact, this is a situation where finite sample theory leads to conclusions and conditions that have some economic content, thus justifying a labour intensive approach to the problem. For example, the key parameter in the distribution of the portfolio risk estimator is essentially the population analogue of Shanken's CSR test statistic (Shanken, 1985); under the null of market portfolio mean-variance efficiency, it takes the value of zero. Secondly, the expected value of the estimated market portfolio is a convex combination of the global population minimum variance portfolio and the ex ante market portfolio; we prove that the expected value is ex ante mean-variance efficient if and only if the ex ante market portfolio is ex ante mean-variance efficient. This conclusion is a positive result for applied financial economics and can be contrasted with the pessimism of Roll's conclusions in Roll (1977). We also show that, on average, under certain assumptions, sample portfolios have fewer short and long positions than their population counterparts. Finally, for the expected return and risk of the sample portfolio, we show that on average the sample efficient frontier should be to the left of the ex ante efficient frontier. This implies that as the risk of our current holdings increases, the underestimation of risk increases with it.

We assume that the vector, $x(n \times 1)$, of rates of return on the assets of interest is normally distributed with mean $\overline{\mu}$ and covariance matrix $\sum$. The investor is assumed to know $\overline{\mu}$ and $\sum$, and his problem is to calculate an optimal portfolio, characterized by a vector of proportions a_0, given a vector of 'market' proportions, $\overline{a}$, i.e. an efficient portfolio with the same mean as the market. Other interpretations are possible, for example $\overline{a}$ could be the vector of current holdings of the investor, in which case we wish to estimate the efficient portfolio with the same mean. In what follows, we shall use the term market to mean $\overline{a}$; practitioners may prefer to think of this as their current portfolio weights. Roll (1977) shows that, for a portfolio with return $\pi_0 = \overline{a}'\overline{\mu}$, a_0 is given by

$$a_0 = \sum\nolimits^{-1}(\overline{\mu}, e)\left[(\overline{\mu}, e)'\sum\nolimits^{-1}(\overline{\mu}, e)\right]^{-1}(\overline{\mu}, e)'\overline{a} \qquad (14.1)$$

and that its risk is

$$\sigma_a^2 = \bar{a}'(\bar{\mu}, e)\left[(\bar{\mu}, e)'\sum{}^{-1}(\bar{\mu}, e)\right]^{-1}(\bar{\mu}, e)'\bar{a} \tag{14.2}$$

where e is an $n \times 1$ vector of ones.

Let $a = \sum^{\frac{1}{2}}\bar{a}$, $\mu = \sum^{-\frac{1}{2}}\bar{\mu}$, $c = \sum^{-\frac{1}{2}}e$, and for any matrix A of full column rank, let $P_A = A(A'A)^{-1}A'$ and $\overline{P}_A = I - P_A$. We shall make frequent use of the fact that, if $A = (A_1, A_2)$

$$P_{A_1, A_2} = P_{A_1} + \overline{P}_{A_1}A_2(A_2'\overline{P}_{A_1}A_2)^{-1}A_2'\overline{P}_{A_1} \tag{14.3}$$

Now,

$$\begin{aligned}
\sigma_a^2 &= a'P_{\mu,c}a = a'a - a'\overline{P}_{\mu,c}a \\
&= a'P_c a + a'\overline{P}_c\mu(\mu'\overline{P}_c\mu)^{-1}\mu'\overline{P}_c a \\
&= \lambda a'P_c a + (1-\lambda)a'a
\end{aligned} \tag{14.4}$$

where

$$\lambda = \mu'\overline{P}_{a,c}\mu/\mu'\overline{P}_c\mu \tag{14.5}$$

satisfies $0 \le \lambda \le 1$. Let $a'a = \bar{a}'\sum\bar{a} = \sigma_0^2$, say, and $a'P_c a = 1/e'\sum^{-1}e = 1/\gamma$, say. Note that σ_0^2 is the variance of a portfolio characterized by weights $\bar{a}$, and $1/\gamma$ is the variance of the globally minimum variance portfolio. It follows from (14.4) that

$$1/\gamma \le \sigma_a^2 \le \sigma_0^2 \tag{14.6}$$

with equality on the left just if $\bar{a} = \sum^{-1}e/\gamma$ (so that $a'\overline{P}_c\mu$ in the second line of (14.4) vanishes), and equality on the right just if $\bar{a}$ is a linear combination of the vectors $\sum^{-1}\mu$ and $\sum^{-1}e$ (so that $a'\overline{P}_{\mu,c}a$ in the first line of (14.4) vanishes). The latter is the condition for the market portfolio $\bar{a}$ to be mean-variance efficient: for then, and only then, does $a_0 = \bar{a}$ in (14.1).

Given T independent observations on x, the natural (maximum likelihood) estimators for $\bar{\mu}$ and $\sum$ are $\bar{x}$, the sample mean, and $T^{-1}S$, where

$$S = \sum_{i=1}^{T}(x_i - \bar{x})(x_i - \bar{x})'$$

is the matrix of second moments about the mean.[1] Hence, natural estimators for a_0, π_0, and σ_a^2 are obtained by replacing $\bar{\mu}$ and $\sum$ in the above expressions by their sample estimates. The properties of $\hat{x}_0 = \hat{a}_0'\bar{x}$ are straightforward and are discussed in Satchell (1986), who also shows that the moments of both $\widehat{a}_0$ and $\widehat{\sigma}_a^2$ exist. Our purpose here is to examine in more detail the properties of the estimators for a_0 and σ_a^2. Section 14.2 contains the results for the portfolio risk estimator, and Section 14.3 the results for the portfolio itself. Section 14.4 discusses the riskless case, extending previous work by Satchell (1986) where the properties were derived assuming that $\sum$ is known. The final section contains some discussion and conclusions.

14.2   PROPERTIES OF THE RISK ESTIMATOR

The sample mean, $\bar{x}$, and S are independent, $\bar{x} \sim N(\bar{\mu}, T^{-1}\sum)$, and S has the central Wishart distribution $W_n(T-1, \sum)$. Let

$$q = \bar{a}'(\bar{x}, e)[(\bar{x}, e)'S^{-1}(\bar{x}, e)]^{-1}(\bar{x}, e)'\bar{a} \qquad (14.7)$$

To avoid degeneracy we assume that $n \geq 3$. If $n = 2$ the 2×2 matrix $(\bar{x}, e)$ is almost surely non-singular and q in (14.7) reduces to $q = \bar{a}'S\bar{a} = q_0$, say, see (14.11) below.

First note that, by Theorem 3.2.11 of Muirhead (1982), conditional on $\bar{x}$, $[(\bar{x}, e)'S^{-1}(\bar{x}, e)]^{-1}$ has a central Wishart distribution $W_2(T-n+1, [(\bar{x}, e)' \sum^{-1}(\bar{x}, e)]^{-1})$. Therefore, by Theorem 3.2.5 of Muirhead (1982), given $\bar{x}$, $q|\bar{x} \sim W_1(v, \bar{a}'(\bar{x}, e)[(\bar{x}, e)' \sum^{-1}(\bar{x}, e)]^{-1}(\bar{x}, e)'\bar{a})$. That is, given $\bar{x}$, $q/Q \sim \chi^2(v)$:

$$\text{pdf}(q|\bar{x}) = \frac{\exp\{-\tfrac{1}{2}q/Q\}\, q^{\frac{1}{2}v-1}}{2^{v/2}\Gamma(v/2)Q^{v/2}} \qquad (14.8)$$

where $v = T - n + 1$, and

$$Q = \bar{a}'(\bar{x}, e)\left[(\bar{x}, e)' \sum^{-1}(\bar{x}, e)\right]^{-1}(\bar{x}, e)'\bar{a} \qquad (14.9)$$

Note here that if the market portfolio $\bar{a}$ is globally efficient, so that $\bar{a} = \sum^{-1}e/\gamma$, $Q = 1/\gamma$, and does not depend on $\bar{x}$, so that, unconditionally, $\gamma q \sim \chi^2(v)$. Also, using the same two theorems we see at once that the sample quantities corresponding to $(e'\sum^{-1}e)^{-1}$ and $\bar{a}'\sum\bar{a}$, viz. $q_1 = (e'S^{-1}e)^{-1}$ and $q_0 = \bar{a}'S\bar{a}$ have the following distributions:

$$\left(e'\sum^{-1}e\right)q_1 \sim \chi^2(v) \qquad (14.10)$$

$$q_0/\left(\bar{a}'\sum\bar{a}\right) \sim \chi^2(v) \qquad (14.11)$$

Since $E[\chi^2(v)] = v$ it follows at once that q_1/v and q_0/v are unbiased estimators for $1/\gamma$ and σ_0^2 respectively.

In the case of q itself it follows from (14.8) that, given $\bar{x}$, the conditional moments of q are given by

$$E[q^r|\bar{x}] = (2Q)^r \Gamma(r + v/2)/\Gamma(v/2) \tag{14.12}$$

In particular,

$$E(q|\bar{x}) = vQ \tag{14.13}$$

The unconditional moments of q and the density of q itself may be obtained from (14.12) and (14.8) by averaging with respect to the density of $\bar{x}$.

Let $\tilde{x} = \sum^{-\frac{1}{2}} \bar{x} \sim N(\mu, T^{-1}I_n)$. Since Q in (14.9) is identical to σ_a^2 in (14.1) with μ replaced by $\bar{x}$, we see from (14.4) that

$$Q = \tilde{\lambda}(1/\gamma) + (1 - \tilde{\lambda})\sigma_0^2 \tag{14.14}$$

with

$$\tilde{\lambda} = \tilde{x}' \overline{P}_{a,c} \tilde{x} / \tilde{x}' \overline{P}_c \tilde{x}$$
$$= 1/(1 + u) \tag{14.15}$$

where $u = F/(n-2)$ and

$$F = (n-2)\tilde{x}' \overline{P}_c a (a' \overline{P}_c a)^{-1} a' \overline{P}_c \tilde{x} / \tilde{x}' \overline{P}_{a,c} \tilde{x} \tag{14.16}$$

has a doubly non-central F distribution with 1 and $n-2$ degrees of freedom and non-centrality parameters.

$$\lambda_1 = T(\mu' \overline{P}_c \mu - \mu' \overline{P}_{a,c} \mu) = T\mu' \overline{P}_c \mu(1 - \lambda) \tag{14.17}$$
$$\lambda_2 = T\mu' \overline{P}_{a,c} \mu - T\mu' \overline{P}_c \mu\lambda \tag{14.18}$$

Under market mean-variance efficiency $\lambda = \lambda_2 = 0$.

Let $\delta = T\mu' \overline{P}_c \mu$. From Kendall and Stuart (1969 p. 252), the density of u is

$$\text{pdf}(u) = \exp\{-\delta/2\}\Gamma\left(\frac{1}{2}(n-1)\right) \bigg/ \pi^{\frac{1}{2}}\Gamma\left(\frac{1}{2}(n-2)\right)$$

$$\times \sum_{j,k=0}^{\infty} \frac{\left(\frac{1}{2}\delta\right)^{j+k} \lambda^k (1-\lambda)^j u^{j+\frac{1}{2}-1} \left(\frac{1}{2}(n-1)\right)_{j+k}}{j!k!(1+u)^{j+k+\frac{1}{2}(n-1)} \left(\frac{1}{2}\right)_j \left(\frac{1}{2}(n-1)\right)_k} \tag{14.19}$$

reducing to

$$\text{pdf}(u) = \exp\left(\frac{1}{2}\delta\right) \Gamma\left(\frac{1}{2}(n-1)\right) \bigg/ \pi^{\frac{1}{2}} \Gamma\left(\frac{1}{2}(n-2)\right)$$

$$\times \sum_{j=0}^{\infty} \frac{\left(\frac{1}{2}\delta\right)^j u^{j+\frac{1}{2}-1} \left(\frac{1}{2}(n-1)\right)_j}{j!(1+u)^{j+\frac{1}{2}(n-1)} \left(\frac{1}{2}\right)_j} \tag{14.20}$$

when $\lambda = 0$. Let

$$\Delta = \sigma_0^2 - [1/\gamma]/\sigma_0^2, \qquad 0 \le \Delta \le 1 \tag{14.21}$$

so that Δ measures the proportional discrepancy between the risk of the market portfolio and that of the globally efficient portfolio, and note that Q in (14.14) can be written as

$$Q = \sigma_0^2[1 - \Delta/(1 + u)] \tag{14.22}$$

Using (14.22), (14.8) may be expressed as a multiple series in powers of $(1 + u)^{-1}$:

$$\text{pdf}(q|u) = \frac{\exp\left(-\frac{1}{2}q/\sigma_0^2\right) q^{\frac{1}{2}v-1}}{2^{v/2}\Gamma(v/2)(\sigma_0^2)^{v/2}} \cdot \sum_{i,\ell=0}^{\infty} \frac{(-q/2\sigma_0^2)^i \Delta^{i+\ell}(i+v/2)\ell}{i!\ell!(1+u)^{i+\ell}} \tag{14.23}$$

The expectations $E[(1+u)^{-r}]$ may be evaluated directly from (14.19):

$$E[(1+u)^{-r}] = e^{-\frac{1}{2}\delta} \cdot \sum_{j,k=0}^{\infty} \frac{\left(\frac{1}{2}\delta\right)^{j+k} \lambda^k (1-\lambda)^j \left(\frac{1}{2}(n-1)\right)_{j+k} \left(\frac{1}{2}(n-2)\right)_{k+r}}{j!k! \left(\frac{1}{2}(n-1)\right)_{j+k+r} \left(\frac{1}{2}(n-2)\right)_k} \tag{14.24}$$

Hence, multiplying (14.23) by (14.19) and integrating out u we obtain, for the density of q:

$$\text{pdf}(q) = \frac{\exp\left(-\frac{1}{2}q/\sigma_0^2\right) q^{\frac{1}{2}v-1}}{2^{v/2}\Gamma(v/2)(\sigma_0^2)^{v/2}} \exp\{-\delta/2\}$$

$$\times \sum_{i,j,k,\ell=0}^{\infty} \frac{(-q/2\sigma_0^2)^i \Delta^{i+\ell} \left(\frac{1}{2}\delta\right)^{j+k} \lambda^k (1-\lambda)^j \left(i+\frac{1}{2}v\right)_\ell}{i!j!k!\ell! \left(\frac{1}{2}(n-1)\right)_{j+k+i+\ell}}$$

$$\times \frac{\left(\frac{1}{2}(n-1)\right)_{j+k} \left(\frac{1}{2}(n-2)\right)_{k+i+\ell}}{\left(\frac{1}{2}(n-2)\right)_k} \tag{14.25}$$

Likewise, the moments of q may be obtained by using (14.22) in (14.12) and then using (14.24). In particular, for $r = 1$,

$$E(q) = v\sigma_0^2(1 - \Delta\phi(\delta, \lambda)) = v[\phi(1/\gamma) + (1 - \phi)\sigma_0^2] \qquad (14.26)$$

where $\phi = \phi(\delta, \lambda) = E[(1 + u)^{-1}], \ 0 < \phi < 1$, is given by

$$\phi(\delta, \lambda) = \frac{(n - 2)\exp\{-\delta/2\}}{(n - 1)} \sum_{j,k=0}^{\infty} \frac{\left(\tfrac{1}{2}\delta\right)^{j+k} \lambda^k (1 - \lambda)^j \left(\tfrac{1}{2}n\right)_k \left(\tfrac{1}{2}(n - 1)\right)_{j+k}}{j!k! \left(\tfrac{1}{2}(n + 1)\right)_{j+k} \left(\tfrac{1}{2}(n - 2)\right)_k}$$

$$(14.27)$$

Thus, like the true value σ_a^2 itself (see (14.4) above), $\tfrac{1}{v}E[q]$ is a convex combination of the globally minimum variance, $1/\gamma$, and the variance of the market portfolio, σ_0^2. Evidently the estimator $\widehat{\sigma}_a^2 = q/v$ is biased to the extent that $\phi(\delta, \lambda)$ in (14.27) differs from λ itself, and this depends on $\delta = T\mu'P_c\mu$ and $\lambda = \mu'P_{a,c}\mu/\mu'P_c\mu$, as well as on T and n. Numerical studies of (14.27) are needed to assess the extent of the bias, and we hope to report some results for these in a subsequent paper.

From (14.26), and results in Satchell (1986), we can construct a mean-variance diagram where, for the sample portfolio $\bar{a}$, we plot the expected value of $\widehat{a}_o'\bar{x}$ on the mean axis and the expected value of q/v on the variance axis. This seems the natural locus to compare with the efficient frontier relating $a_o'\overline{\mu}$ and σ_a^2. In finance there has been a regrettable tendency to try and place both sample and population frontiers on the same diagram, leading to an unnecessary confusion of ideas.

Using $E(\widehat{a}_o'\bar{x}) = \widehat{a}_o'\overline{\mu}$ and rewriting (14.26) as $\tfrac{1}{v}E(q) = \sigma_0^2 - \phi(\sigma_0^2 - \tfrac{1}{\gamma})$, we can examine the discrepancies between the two frontiers as we vary $\bar{a}$, the proportions of the market portfolio, in such a way that $\bar{a}'\sum\bar{a}(= \sigma_0^2)$ is increasing. We see that as we move across from the efficient frontier, for any σ_0^2, $\tfrac{1}{v}E(q)$ will lie $\phi(\sigma_0^2 - \tfrac{1}{\gamma})$ to the left of σ_0^2. In relative terms, the bias will be $\phi\left(1 - \tfrac{1/v}{\sigma_0^2}\right)$ so the more volatile is our actual portfolio ($\bar{a}$), relative to global minimum variance, assuming ϕ constant which it will not be.

However, under market mean-variance efficiency, when $\lambda = 0$, (14.25) and (14.27) reduce to

$$\text{pdf}(q) = \frac{\exp\left(-\tfrac{1}{2}q/\sigma_0^2\right)}{2^{v/2}\Gamma(v/2)(\sigma_0^2)^{v/2}} q^{\tfrac{1}{2}v-1} \exp\{-\delta/2\}$$

$$\times \sum_{i,j,\ell=0}^{\infty} \frac{(-q/2\sigma_0^2)^i \Delta^{i+\ell} \left(\tfrac{1}{2}\delta\right)^j \left(i + \tfrac{1}{2}v\right)_\ell \left(\tfrac{1}{2}(n - 1)\right)_j \left(\tfrac{1}{2}(n - 2)\right)_{i+\ell}}{i!j!\ell! \left(\tfrac{1}{2}(n - 1)\right)_{j+i+\ell} \left(\tfrac{1}{2}(n - 2)\right)_k}$$

$$(14.28)$$

and

$$\phi(\delta, \ 0) = \frac{(n-2)}{(n-1)} \exp\{-\delta/2\} \sum_{j=0}^{\infty} \frac{\left(\frac{1}{2}\delta\right)^j \left(\frac{1}{2}(n-1)\right)_j}{j! \left(\frac{1}{2}(n+1)\right)_j} \tag{14.29}$$

Since $\phi(\delta, \ 0) > 0$, and, in this efficient market case, $\lambda = 0$, $\phi(\delta, \ 0) > \lambda$, so that, in the efficient market case, $\hat{\sigma}_a^2 = q/v$ is biased towards the globally efficient risk $1/\gamma$, i.e., biased downwards.[2]

Further analysis of $\phi(\delta, \ 0)$ under market efficiency implies that a lies in the linear space of μ and c from the formula for efficient portfolios; this in turn implies that $\delta = 0$ and $\phi(0, \ 0) = \frac{n-2}{n+1}$.

In expressions (14.25) and (14.27) the key parameters are $\delta\lambda = T\mu'\overline{P}_{a,c}\mu$ and $\delta(1 - \lambda) = T(\mu'\overline{P}_{a,c}\mu)$. The first of these is the population analogue of Shanken's (Shanken, 1985) CSR test statistic (c.f. Roll, 1979) of which $\hat{\sigma}_a^2$ is an ingredient.

Hence, although we shall defer a detailed discussion of testing to a companion paper, the above results do evidently give some support to Shanken's suggestions.

14.3 PROPERTIES OF THE ESTIMATED PORTFOLIO WEIGHTS

The sample analogue of equation (14.1) is

$$\hat{a}_0 = S^{-1}(\overline{x}, e) \ [(\overline{x}, e)'S^{-1}(\overline{x}, e)]^{-1}(\overline{x}, e)'\overline{a} \tag{14.30}$$

We shall consider a fixed linear combination $\alpha = \overline{h}'\hat{a}_0$ of the elements of $\hat{a}_0$:

$$\alpha = \overline{h}'S^{-1}(x, e) \ [(x, e)'S^{-1}(x, e)]^{-1}(x, e)'a$$
$$= g'f, \text{ say} \tag{14.31}$$

with

$$g = [(\overline{x}, e)'S^{-1}(\overline{x}, e)]^{-1}(\overline{x}, e)'S^{-1}\overline{h}$$

and

$$f = (\overline{x}, e)'\overline{a}$$

Defining $\tilde{x}$, c, and a as above, and putting $h = \sum^{-\frac{1}{2}}\overline{h}$ and $\tilde{S} = \sum^{-\frac{1}{2}} S \sum^{-\frac{1}{2}} \sim W_n(T - 1, I_n)$, we have

$$g = [(\tilde{x}, c)'\tilde{S}^{-1}(\tilde{x}, c)]^{-1}(\tilde{x}, c)'S^{-1}h \tag{14.32}$$

Let

$$\overline{W} = [(h, \tilde{x}, c)' \tilde{S}^{-1} (h, \tilde{x}, c)]^{-1} \quad (3 \times 3) \tag{14.33}$$

By Theorem 3.2.11 of Muirhead (1982), given $\tilde{x}$,

$$\overline{W} | \tilde{x} \sim W_3(T - n + 2, [(h, \tilde{x}, c)'(h, \tilde{x}, c)]^{-1})$$

We now transform variables from $\overline{W}$ to $W = \overline{W}^{-1}$ (Jacobian $|W|^{-4}$), and note that $g = W_{22}^{-1} w_{21}$, where W is partitioned as

$$W = \begin{bmatrix} w_{11} & w'_{21} \\ w_{21} & W_{22} \end{bmatrix}$$

with W_{22} 2×2. Transforming next to $s^2 = w_{11} - w'_{21} W_{22}^{-1} w_{21}$, $g = W_{22}^{-1} w_{21}$ and $W_{22} = W_{22}$ (Jacobian $|W_{22}|$) we have

$$\text{pdf}(g, s^2, W_{22} | \tilde{x}) = C_1 \exp \left\{ -\frac{1}{2}(h - Mg)'(h - Mg)/s^2 \right\}$$

$$\times \text{etr} \left\{ -\frac{1}{2} M'M W_{22}^{-1} \right\} \, [s^2 | W_{22}|]^{-\frac{1}{2}(v+1)-2}$$

$$\times |(h, \tilde{x}, c)'(h, \tilde{x}, c)|^{\frac{1}{2}(v+1)} \tag{14.34}$$

where $C_1 = [2^{3(v+1)/2} \Gamma_3(\frac{1}{2}(v + 1))]^{-1}$ and we have put $M = (\tilde{x}, c)$. $\Gamma_n(t)$ here denotes the multivariate Gamma function, Muirhead (1982, pp. 61–62). Transforming to $z = 1/s^2$ (Jacobian z^{-2}) and to $B = W_{22}^{-1}$ (Jacobian $|B|^{-3}$) it is straightforward to integrate out z and B, leaving

$$\text{pdf}(g | \tilde{x}) = \frac{\Gamma\left(\frac{1}{2}(v + 3)\right)}{\pi \Gamma\left(\frac{1}{2}(v + 1)\right)} |M'M|^{-\frac{1}{2}v} |(h, M)'(h, M)|^{\frac{1}{2}(v+1)}$$

$$\times [(h - Mg)'(h - Mg)]^{-\frac{1}{2}(v+3)}$$

$$= \frac{\Gamma\left(\frac{1}{2}(v + 3)\right)}{\pi \Gamma\left(\frac{1}{2}(v + 1)\right)} |(h' \overline{P}_M h)(M'M)^{-1}|^{-\frac{1}{2}}$$

$$\times \left(1 + \frac{(g - (M'M)^{-1} M'h)' M'M (g - (M'M)^{-1} M'h)}{h' \overline{P}_M h} \right)^{-\frac{1}{2}(v+3)} \tag{14.35}$$

That is, conditional on $\tilde{x}$, g has a multivariate t-distribution with $v + 1$ degrees of freedom, conditional mean $(M'M)^{-1} M'h$, and conditional covariance matrix proportional to $(h' \overline{P}_M h)(M'M)^{-1}$.

It follows at once from (14.35) that the conditional distribution of $\alpha = f'g$ given $\tilde{x}$ is

$$
\text{pdf}(\alpha|\tilde{x}) = \left[\Gamma\left(\frac{1}{2}(v+2)\right) \Big/ \pi^{1/2}\Gamma\left(\frac{1}{2}(v+1)\right) \right] (h'\overline{P}_M h f'(M'M)^{-1}f)^{-\frac{1}{2}}
$$

$$
\times \left(1 + \frac{(\alpha - f'(M'M)^{-1}M'h)^2}{h'\overline{P}_M h f'(M'M)^{-1}f} \right)^{-\frac{1}{2}(v+2)} \tag{14.36}
$$

i.e. a t-distribution with conditional mean

$$
E(\alpha|\overline{x}) = a'(\tilde{x}, c)[(\tilde{x}, c)'(\tilde{x}, c)]^{-1}(\tilde{x}, c)'h \tag{14.37}
$$

and conditional variance proportional to $v = h'\overline{P}_M h a' P_M a$. The conditional density of α may be obtained from (14.36) by averaging with respect to the density of $\tilde{x}$. However, the result is so complex as to be of little value in assessing the properties of α. Hence we shall confine attention here to the mean, which may also be obtained from (14.37) by averaging with respect to the density of $\tilde{x}$.

First note that, since

$$
E(\alpha|\tilde{x}) = a'h - a'\overline{P}_{\tilde{x},c}h \tag{14.38}
$$

if $a \propto c$, i.e. $\bar{a} = \sum^{-1} e/\gamma$, then $\overline{P}_{\tilde{x},c}a = 0$ and $E(\alpha|\tilde{x}) = \bar{h}'\sum^{-1} e/\gamma$ does not depend on $\tilde{x}$, and hence is the unconditional mean. Thus, if the market is globally efficient the estimator $\hat{a}_0$ is unbiased. Also note that when $n = 2$ the 2×2 matrix $(\tilde{x}, c)$ in (14.37) is almost surely non-singular and we see that $E(\alpha|\tilde{x}) = h'a - \bar{h}'a_0$, so that α is also unbiased when $n = 2$. In what follows we shall therefore assume that $n \geq 3$.

The following result is proved in the Appendix:

Theorem 14.3.1. *For any fixed $\bar{h}$, and $n \geq 3$,*

$$
E(\alpha) = \psi(\delta)\bar{h}'\bar{a} + (1 - \psi(\delta)) \left(\bar{h}' \sum^{-1} e/\gamma \right) \tag{14.39}
$$

where

$$
\psi(\delta) = \exp\{-\delta/2\}\,{}_1F_1\left(\frac{1}{2}(n-1), \frac{1}{2}(n+1), \frac{1}{2}\delta\right) \Big/ (n-1) \tag{14.40}
$$

satisfies $0 < \psi(\delta) < 1$.

Since (14.39) holds for all $\bar{h}$ we have

$$E(\widehat{a}_0) = \psi(\delta)\bar{a} + (1 - \psi(\delta)) \left(\sum^{-1} e/\gamma \right) \tag{14.41}$$

That is, $E(\widehat{a}_0)$ is a convex combination of the market portfolio $\bar{a}$ and the globally efficient portfolio $(\sum^{-1} e/\gamma)$.

For large n (i.e. many assets) $\psi(\delta)$ in (14.41) will be close to zero, so that $\widehat{a}_0$ is biased towards the globally efficient portfolio. Also, as $T \to \infty$ (so that $\delta \to \infty$) $\psi(\delta) \to 0$, so that $\widehat{a}_0$ is biased towards the globally efficient portfolio in large samples.

Theorem 14.3.1 has some interesting consequences. First note that $E(\widehat{a}_0)$ is itself a portfolio since $e'E(\widehat{a}_0) = 1$. We have

Theorem 14.3.2. $\tilde{a} = E(\widehat{a}_0)$ *is mean-variance efficient if and only if* $\bar{a}$ *is mean-variance efficient.*

Proof: $\tilde{a}$ is mean-variance efficient if and only if $\sum^{1/2} \tilde{a}$ is a linear combination of μ and c. From (14.41), this is so if and only if $\bar{a}$ has this property.

Roll (1977) makes the point that a sample portfolio $\widehat{a}_0$ need not reflect the properties of the market portfolio, whether the latter is mean-variance efficient or otherwise. Theorem 14.3.2 shows that, while this is true, the sample portfolio $\widehat{a}_0$ does reflect the mean-variance efficiency property of $\bar{a}$ on average.

Write $\bar{a}_m = \sum^{-1} e/\gamma$, and write (14.41) as (element by element)

$$E(\widehat{a}_{0i} - \bar{a}_i) = (1 - \psi(\delta))(\bar{a}_{mi} - \bar{a}_i) \tag{14.42}$$

Clearly, $E(\widehat{a}_{0i} - \bar{a}_i)$ has the same sign as $(\bar{a}_{mi} - \bar{a}_i)$. If $\bar{a}$ is mean-variance efficient $(\bar{a} = a_0)$, $\widehat{a}_{0i}$ is biased upwards if $\bar{a}_{mi} > \bar{a}_i$, and biased downwards if $\bar{a}_{mi} < \bar{a}_i$. Hence, for a mean-variance efficient portfolio the element by element biases reflect the relationships of the components of the portfolio to those of the globally efficient portfolio. If the components of $\sum^{-1} e$ are all positive (which is true for certain choices of $\sum$) $\widehat{a}_{0i}$ will be biased upwards if there is a short position on the i-th asset $(\bar{a}_i < 0)$, while if $\bar{a}_i > 0$, so that there is a long position on the i-th asset, $\widehat{a}_{0i}$ will be biased downwards (since the i-th element of $\sum^{-1} e$ is necessarily less than one if all elements of $\sum^{-1} e$ are positive). Hence, under the above assumptions, and on average, the sample value of a mean-variance efficient portfolio will contain fewer long and short positions than its population counterpart. It would be interesting to study the robustness of this result to the assumption of normality.

14.4 THE RISKLESS ASSET CASE

Results for the case in which there is a riskless asset can be obtained by a straight-forward extension of the arguments used above, although the results are somewhat more complicated. If ρ is the rate of return on the riskless asset, let $\bar{x}_2 = \bar{x} - \rho e$ be the sample vector of excess rates of return, $\tilde{x}_2 \, N(\bar{\mu}_2, T^{-1}\sum)$, with $\bar{\mu}_2 = \bar{\mu} - \rho e$. The quantities corresponding to q in (14.7), α in (14.31) and $\hat{\pi}$, are

$$q_2 = [e'S^{-1}\bar{x}_2(\bar{x}_2'S^{-1}\bar{x}_2)^{-1}\bar{x}_2'S^{-1}e]^{-1} \tag{14.43}$$

$$\alpha_2 = \bar{h}'S^{-1}\bar{x}_2/e'S^{-1}\bar{x}_2 \tag{14.44}$$

$$\hat{\pi}_2 - \rho = \bar{x}_2'S^{-1}\bar{x}_2/e'S^{-1}\bar{x}_2 \tag{14.45}$$

Define h and c as in Section 14.2, and $\tilde{S} = \sum^{-1/2} S \sum^{-1/2}$ as in Section 14.3, and put $x_2 = \sum^{-1/2}\bar{x}_2 = \sum^{-1/2}(\bar{x} - \rho e) \sim N(\mu_2, T^{-1}I)$ independently of $\tilde{S}$, where $\mu_2 = \sum^{-1/2}\bar{\mu}_2 = \sum^{-1/2}(\bar{\mu} - \rho e)$. Let

$$W_2 = (x_2, c, h)'S^{-1}(x_2, c, h) \tag{14.46}$$

Then, conditional on x_2, $W_2^{-1}|x_2 \sim W_3(v + 1), (M'M)^{-1})$, i.e. a Wishart distribution, where, now $M = (x_2, c, h)$, and, in terms of the elements of W_2,

$$q_2 = w_{11}/w_{12}^2 \tag{14.47}$$

$$\alpha_2 = w_{13}/w_{12} \tag{14.48}$$

$$\hat{\pi}_2 - \rho = w_{11}/w_{12} \tag{14.49}$$

Thus, q_2, α_2, and $\hat{\pi}_2 - \rho$ are functions only of the elements in the first row of W_2. Transforming from $W_2^{-1} \to W_2$ gives the conditional density:

$$\text{pdf}(W_2|x_2) = C_1 \text{etr}\left\{-\frac{1}{2}M'MW_2^{-1}\right\}|M'M|^{(v+1)/2}|W_2|^{-\frac{1}{2}(v+5)} \tag{14.50}$$

Then, transforming from

$$W_2 = \begin{pmatrix} w_{11} & w_2' \\ w_2 & W_{22} \end{pmatrix}$$

where $w_2' = (w_{12}, w_{13})$, to w_{11}, w_2, and $W_{22\cdot1} = W_{22} - w_2 w_2'/w_{11}$ (the Jacobian is unity), and then to $B = W_{22\cdot1}^{-1}$ (Jacobian $|B|^{-3}$), and integrating over $B > 0$, we find the joint conditional density of w_{11}, w_{12}, and w_{13}:

$$\text{pdf}(w_{11}, w_{12}, w_{13}|x_2) = C_3 \exp\left\{-\frac{1}{2}\gamma_{11}/w_{11}\right\} \gamma_{11}^{(\nu+1)/2} w_{11}^{-\frac{1}{2}(\nu+5)}$$

$$\times |\Gamma_{22\cdot 1}|^{-\frac{1}{2}} (1 + \gamma_{11}(w_{11}^{-1}w_2 - \gamma_{11}^{-1}\gamma_2)'\Gamma_{22\cdot 1}^{-1}(w_{11}^{-1}w_2 - \gamma_{11}^{-1}\gamma_2))^{-\frac{1}{2}(\nu+2)}$$

$$(14.51)$$

where

$$C_3 = \left[\Gamma\left(\frac{1}{2}(\nu + 2)\right) \middle/ 2^{\frac{1}{2}(\nu-1)}\pi\Gamma\left(\frac{\nu}{2}\right)\Gamma\left(\frac{1}{2}(\nu + 1)\right)\right]$$

we have partitioned $M'M$ as

$$M'M = \begin{pmatrix} \gamma_{11} & \gamma_2' \\ \gamma_2 & \Gamma_{22} \end{pmatrix}$$

and $\Gamma_{22\cdot 1} = (\Gamma_{22} - \gamma_2\gamma_2'/\gamma_{11})$.

Next, transforming to

$$u = \begin{pmatrix} u_1 \\ u_2 \end{pmatrix} = w_{11}^{-1}w_2$$

and $q_2 = w_{11}^{-1}$, the Jacobian is q_2^{-4} and we have

$$\text{pdf}(q_2, u|x_2) = C_3 \exp\left(-\frac{1}{2}q_2\gamma_{11}\right) \gamma_{11}^{\frac{1}{2}(\nu-1)-1} q_2^{\frac{1}{2}(\nu-1)-1}$$

$$\times |\Gamma_{22\cdot 1}|^{-\frac{1}{2}} (1 + \gamma_{11}(u - \gamma_{11}^{-1}\gamma_2)'\Gamma_{22\cdot 1}^{-1}(u - \gamma_{11}^{-1}\gamma_2))^{-\frac{1}{2}(\nu+2)}$$

$$(14.52)$$

Thus, conditionally upon x_2, u and q_2 are independent $\gamma_{11}q_2 \sim x^2(\nu - 1)$, and u has a multivariate t-distribution with $\nu + 2$ degrees of freedom, mean $\gamma_{11}^{-1}\gamma_2$, and covariance matrix proportional to $\gamma_{11}^{-1}\Gamma_{22\cdot 1}$. Note that $\hat{\pi}_2 - \rho = u_2^{-1}$, $\alpha_2 = u_2^{-1}u_3$, and $\hat{\sigma}_2^2 = u_2^{-2}q_2$. From these results it is easy to see that none of these statistics possess moments of any order (see also Satchell 1986). It is therefore more difficult to summarize the properties of these sample quantities in the riskless asset case.

The conditional densities of $(\hat{\pi}_2 - \rho)$, α_2, and σ_2^2 can clearly be obtained in a straightforward but tedious manner from (14.52), and can then be converted to unconditional densities by multiplying by $\text{pdf}(x_2)$ and integrating out x_2. The results are extremely complex and seem to shed little light on the properties of the statistics, so we omit these details.

14.5   CONCLUSIONS

In conclusion, our analysis may seem difficult but two clear messages come through. Firstly, there is some linkage between sample and population properties; a sample portfolio is efficient on average if and only if its population counterpart is efficient; this is the good news. The bad news is that any measure of risk seems underestimated by sample data: things are worse than they seem.

14.6   APPENDIX: THE UNCONDITIONAL MEAN OF α

Write (14.37) in the form

$$E(\alpha|\tilde{x}) = a'P_ch + a'\overline{P}_c\tilde{x}(\tilde{x}'\overline{P}_c\tilde{x})^{-1}\tilde{x})^{-1}\tilde{x}'P_ch \tag{14.53}$$

Now let $C(n \times n - 1)$ be such that $\overline{P}_c = CC'$ and $C'C = I_{n-1}$, and define $a_1 = C'a$, $h_1 = C'h$, $x_1 = C'\tilde{x} \sim N(\mu_1, T^{-1}I_{n-1})$, with $\mu_1 = C'\mu$. Then

$$d = E(\alpha|\tilde{x}) - a'P_ch = a_1'x_1h_1'/x_1'x_1'x_1$$

$$= \frac{1}{2}x_1'[a_1h_1' + h_1a_1']x_1/x_1'x_1 \tag{14.54}$$

Next define $z = \sqrt{TA}(a_1, h_1)'x_1$, where

$$A = \begin{pmatrix} a_{11} & a_{12} \\ 0 & a_{22} \end{pmatrix}$$

is such that

$$[(a_1, h_1)'(a_1, h_1)]^{-1} = [(a, h)'\overline{P}_c(a, h)'\overline{P}_c(a, h)]^{-1} = A'A$$

and $r_1^2 = Tx_1'\overline{P}_{a_1}, h_1x_1$. Then z and r_1^2 are independent,

$$z \sim N(\sqrt{TA}(a_1, h_1)'\mu_1, I_2)$$

and for $n > 3$, $r_1^2 \sim \chi'^2(n - 3, T\mu_1'\overline{P}_{a_1}, h_1\mu_1$. If $n = 3$, $r_1^2 = 0$ and we have $d = z'Pz/z'z$, where

$$P = \frac{1}{2}\left[A\begin{pmatrix} 0 & 1 \\ 1 & 0 \end{pmatrix}A'\right]^{-1} \quad (2 \times 2) \tag{14.55}$$

Otherwise we have

$$d = z'Pz/(z'z + r_1^2) \qquad (14.56)$$

Setting $\delta_1 = T\mu_1'\overline{P}_{a_1,h_1}\mu_1$ and $m = \sqrt{TA}(a_1, h_1)'\mu_1$, the joint density of z and r_1^2 is given by

$$\mathrm{pdf}(z, r_1^2) = c_2 \exp\left[-\frac{1}{2}(z'z + r_1^2)\right] \exp(z'm)(r_1^2)^{\frac{1}{2}(n-3)-1}$$

$$\times {}_0F_1\left(\frac{1}{2}(n-3); \frac{1}{4}\delta_1 r_1^2\right) \qquad (14.57)$$

where

$$C_2 = \left[\exp\left(-\frac{1}{2}\delta\right) \middle/ \pi 2^{\frac{1}{2}(n-1)}\Gamma\left(\frac{1}{2}(n-3)\right)\right]$$

We now transform z to polar co-ordinates: $z_1 = r\cos\theta$, $z_2 = r\sin\theta$, where θ is the angle between z and m ($r > 0$, $-\pi < \theta < \pi$). The differential element transforms as $dz_1 dz_2 = \frac{1}{2}dr^2 d\theta$, and $\exp(z'm) = \exp\{r(m'm)^{1/2}\cos\theta)\}$. Also,

$$d = \{r^2/(r^2 + r_1^2)\}[p_{22}\sin^2\theta + 2p_{12}\cos\theta\sin\theta]$$

because, as is easily checked, $p_{11} = 0$. Expanding $\exp\{r(m'm)^{1/2}\cos\theta\}$, multiplying by d, and integrating out θ gives

$$E(d) = \frac{\pi}{2}C_2 \underset{r>0}{\int_2} \underset{r_1>0}{\int_2} \exp\left[-\frac{1}{2}(r^2 + r_1^2)\right] (r_1^2)^{\frac{1}{2}(n-3)-1}[r^2/(r^2 + r_1^2)]$$

$$\times (a_1'h_1){}_0F_1\left(\frac{1}{2}(n-3)\frac{1}{4}\delta_1 r_1^2\right){}_0F_1\left(2, \frac{1}{4}r^2 M'M\right) dr^2 dr_1^2$$

Transforming $(r^2, r_1^2) \to (b = r^2/(r^2 + r_1^2), r_1^2 = r_1^2)$ (Jacobian $r_1^2(1-b)^{-2}$), $0 < b < 1$, $r_1^2 > 0$ and integrating out r_1^2 and b then gives

$$E(d) = \frac{a_1'h_1 \exp\left(-\frac{1}{2}\delta\right)}{n-1} \sum_{j,k=0}^{\infty} \frac{\left(\frac{1}{2}m'm\right)^j \left(\frac{1}{2}\delta_1\right)^k \left(\frac{1}{2}(n-1)\right)_{j+k}}{j!k! \left(\frac{1}{2}(n+1)\right)_{j+k}} \qquad (14.58)$$

$$\frac{a_1'h_1 \exp\left(-\frac{1}{2}\delta\right)}{n-1} {}_1F_1\left(\frac{1}{2}(n-1), \frac{1}{2}(n+1); \frac{1}{4}\delta\right)$$

on summing by diagonals and noting that $m'm + \delta_1 = \delta$.

Substituting (14.58) into (14.53) we have

$$E(\alpha) = \psi(\delta)\overline{h}'\overline{a} + (1 - \psi(\delta)) \sum^{-1} e/\gamma \tag{14.59}$$

where

$$\psi(\delta) = \exp\left(-\frac{1}{2}\delta\right) {}_1F_1\left(\frac{1}{2}(n-1), \frac{1}{2}(n+1); \frac{1}{2}\delta\right) \bigg/ (n-1)$$

satisfies $0 \le \psi(\delta) \le 1$. Hence, in general

$$E(\widehat{a}_0) = \psi(\delta)\overline{a} + (1 - \psi(\delta)) \sum^{-1} e/\gamma \tag{14.60}$$

and we see that the mean of $\widehat{a}_0$ is a convex combination of the market portfolio $\overline{a}$ and the globally efficient portfolio $\sum^{-1} e/\gamma$.

REFERENCES

Frankfurter, G.M. and Phillips, H.E. (1979) Measuring Risk and Expectations Bias in Well Diversified Portfolios, *TIMS Studies in the Management Sciences*, **11**, 73–7, North Holland Publishing Company.

Jobson, J.D. and Korkie, B. (1980) Estimation for Markovitz Efficient Portfolios, *Journal of the American Statistical Association*, **75**, 544–54.

Jobson, J.D. and Korkie, B. (1982) Potential Performance and Tests of Portfolio Efficiency, *Journal of Financial Economics*, **13**, 575–92.

Kendall, M.G. and Stuart, A. (1969) *The Advanced Theory of Statistics*, vol. II., Griffin, London.

Michaud, R.O. (1998) *Efficient Asset Management*, Harvard Business School Press, Boston.

Muirhead, R.J. (1982) *Aspects of Multivariate Statistical Theory*, Wiley, New York.

Roll, R. (1977) A Critique of the Asset Pricing Theory's Tests, *Journal of Financial Economics*, **4**, 129–76.

Roll, R. (1979) Testing a Portfolio for Ex Ante Mean/Variance Efficiency, in *TIMS Studies in the Management Sciences*, 11, 135–49, North Holland Publishing Company.

Satchell, S. (1986) The Finite Sample Distributions of Portfolio Estimators, unpublished.

Shanken, J. (1985) Multivariate Tests of the Zero-Beta CAPM, *Journal of the Financial Economics*, **14**, 331–48.

NOTES

1. The divisor T used in the estimator for $\sum$ can be replaced by any constant with only trivial modification to the results that follow.
2. This result agrees with the Monte Carlo findings in Frankfurter and Phillips (1979).

Chapter 15

Optimal asset allocation for endowments: A large deviations approach

MICHAEL STUTZER

ABSTRACT

This Chapter provides a simple quantitative asset allocation method for an endowment that regularly withdraws a fixed percentage of the fund, yet still wants it to grow in excess of some (possibly zero) rate. The method uses historical asset returns, to estimate portfolio weights that maximize the estimated long-run probability that this growth rate objective will be exceeded. Large deviations theory is used to estimate this probability. An illustrative example is used to quantify the tradeoff between the fund's withdrawal rate and the probability of exceeding its growth rate objective.

15.1 INTRODUCTION

Unlike a mutual fund, an endowment fund is intended to pay for ongoing activities desired by the donors. Hence an ongoing fraction of the invested endowment is withdrawn for those purposes, as well as the fund's own expenses. Recent statistics indicate that a typical university endowment fund currently withdraws funds at an annual rate close to 5%.

Funds generally also want the nominal value of the principal to be maintained, and may also want it to grow faster than some positive growth rate. It will rarely be possible to ensure that this can always be done with certainty. There will be a probability that the fund will not be able to meet both its withdrawal percentage and its minimal growth rate objective. Even if the growth rate objective is zero, i.e. the fund just wants to maintain the initial principal, there will always be a probability of violating it (assuming the withdrawal percentage exceeds the riskless rate of interest).

Hence it is useful to quantify the tradeoffs between the withdrawal rate, the (possibly zero) growth rate objective, and the probability of exceeding the latter. Of course, this probability will be lower when the withdrawal rate and/or the growth rate objectives are higher. Fortunately, this decrease in the probability can be partially mitigated by adjusting the fund's asset allocation weights. This Chapter shows how a fund should adjust its portfolio allocation weights, in order to maximize the long-run probability that its growth rate objective (possibly zero) will be exceeded while it maintains its withdrawal rate.

Finding the optimal allocation weights is complicated by two practical problems: one can never know the form of the joint distribution of portfolio returns, and even if one did, exact calculation of the required probability is generally impossible. But it is possible to approximate this probability well enough to rank portfolios in order of their respective long-run probabilities of exceeding the fund's growth rate objective. Section 15.2 of this paper shows how to do this. An illustrative example is developed in Section 15.3, using historical data from the two biggest and most popular asset classes: domestic equities and fixed income securities. Section 15.4 concludes with useful ideas for future research.

15.2   THE ASSET ALLOCATION MODEL

Consider the simplest conceivable problem of endowment management. A gift of size W_0 is received by the fund, which desires to withdraw a fraction d of the invested fund annually, e.g. $d = 5\%$ of the invested funds will be withdrawn annually. The rest will be invested in a portfolio that earns an uncertain gross return (i.e. one plus a net return) denoted $R_p(t)$, that will generate a total return over T years equal to $\Pi_{t=1}^T R_p(t)$. The fund's size after T periods will then be:

$$W_T = W_0 \prod_{t=1}^T (1-d) R_p(t) = W_0 [e^{\overline{\log(1-d)R_p}}]^T \tag{15.1}$$

where

$$\overline{\log[(1-d)R_p]} \equiv \frac{1}{T} \sum_{t=1}^T \log[(1-d)R_p(t)] \tag{15.2}$$

In light of (15.1), the fund's realized (continuously compounded) growth rate to year T will be the random variable (15.2), i.e. the time average of the portfolio's log gross returns after netting out the withdrawal rate d. Now suppose the management also wants its realized growth rate to meet or exceed a (continuously compounded) growth rate objective, denoted $\log r$, per period. Because (15.2) is a random variable, there will always be some probability that this will not happen for any finite value of T. In order to help minimize this risk, the fund should certainly restrict attention to those portfolios that make this underperformance probability decay to zero asymptotically with T. To ensure this, the law of large numbers implies that attention should be restricted to portfolios with a net-of-withdrawal expected growth rate that exceeds the growth rate objective, i.e. $E[\log[(1-d)R_p] > \log r$. But how should a specific portfolio be chosen, among the infinitely many portfolios p that meet this expected growth rate restriction, i.e. that have their respective probabilities of underperformance decay to zero as the investment horizon $T \to \infty$?

Stutzer (2002) used large deviations theory to calculate the portfolio-dependent exponential rate at which this probability decays to zero, i.e.

$$\text{Prob}[\overline{\log(1-d)R_{pT}} \le \log r] \approx \frac{c}{\sqrt{T}} e^{-D_p T} \tag{15.3}$$

where the underperformance probability decay rate D_p in (15.3) is:

$$D_p \equiv \max_\theta \theta \log r - \log E[e^{\theta \log[(1-d)R_p]}] \tag{15.4}$$

Because of the exponential decay of the underperformance probability (15.3), a portfolio with a high decay rate (15.4) will eventually have a lower underperformance probability – and hence a desirably higher probability of exceeding the growth rate objective – than a portfolio with a lower decay rate. So to rank portfolios in the order of their respective probabilities of exceeding the fund's growth rate objective, the fund should rank the portfolios in the same order as D_p in (15.4). The optimal portfolio for a desired withdrawal rate (d) and growth rate objective ($\log r$) is the portfolio p_{max} that maximizes (15.4). Some algebraic rearrangement of (15.4) shows that this portfolio also maximizes the following specific expected power utility:

$$p_{max} \equiv \arg\max_p[D_p \equiv \max_\theta \theta \log r - \log E[e^{\theta \log[(1-d)R_p]}]] \tag{15.5}$$

$$= \arg\max_p \max_\theta E\left[-\left(\frac{R_p}{\left(\frac{r}{1-d}\right)}\right)^\theta\right]$$

where the maximizing $\theta < 0$ determines the power utility's coefficient of relative risk aversion $1 - \theta > 0$. Moreover, (15.5) shows that the optimal portfolio depends only on the ratio $r/1 - d$, i.e. on the ratio of the fund's *gross effective* annual growth rate objective to the annual fraction of funds that are invested (not withdrawn).

Additional characterizations of the portfolio choice rule (15.5) when $d = 0$, relationships of it to other similarly motivated approaches to portfolio choice, and statistical evidence of its efficacy over finite horizon lengths are provided in Stutzer (2002).

The following section provides a practical way to estimate D_p from (15.4) and the optimal portfolio p_{max} from (15.5) that maximizes it.

15.3   AN ILLUSTRATIVE EXAMPLE

The method is illustrated by examining the asset allocation decision at the broadest level: what weights should be given to domestic equities and domestic fixed income securities in a fund with given withdrawal and growth rate objectives? Letting p represent the market value weight of equities in our portfolio, the gross portfolio return R_p in (15.4) is $R_p = pR_1 + (1 - p)R_2$, where R_1 is the gross return from equity and R_2 is the gross return from fixed income securities. The historical gross return to this portfolio in prior year t is denoted $R_{pt} = pR_{1t} + (1 - p)R_{2t}$; $t = 1, \ldots, T$. In order to estimate the required index of outperformance probability (15.4) of a portfolio with a specific (not necessarily the optimal) value of the equity weight p, I follow Kroll et al. (1984) (and virtually everyone else in academia) in replacing the expected value in (15.4) by a historical time average, yielding the following estimate $\hat{D}_p$ of (15.4):

$$\hat{D}_p = \max_{\theta} \left(\theta \log r - \log \frac{1}{T} \sum_{t=1}^{T} e^{\theta \log[(1-d)(pR_{1t}+(1-p)R_{2t})]} \right) \qquad (15.6)$$

The number (15.6) is used to rank the portfolio's performance relative to other portfolios, analogous to the use of estimated Sharpe Ratios. So in order to find the optimal portfolio, one just finds the value of the portfolio equity weight p that maximizes (15.6), i.e.

$$\hat{p}_{\text{max}} = \arg\max_{p} \hat{D}_p = \max_{p} \max_{\theta} \left(\theta \log r - \log \frac{1}{T} \sum_{t=1}^{T} e^{\theta \log[(1-d)(pR_{1t}+(1-p)R_{2t})]} \right) \qquad (15.7)$$

The maximization problems (15.6) and (15.7) are both easily solved using the 'solver' tool in the standard personal computer spreadsheets. To begin our example, let us first proxy the domestic equities class by use of the Ibbotson Associates large cap stock total return index, and the domestic fixed income securities class by their intermediate term government bond total return index.

The results are shown in the following Tables 15.1 and 15.2, using annual historical returns between 1926 and 1996.

Table 15.1   *Optimal equity weight and invested fund's expected growth rate*

Withdrawal %	Growth objective log $r\%$			
d	0	1	2	3
4	**28**	**50**	**76**	**99**
	2.8	4.0	5.2	6.1
5	**51**	**77**	**100**	**119**
	3.1	4.2	5.0	5.5
6	**79**	**101**	**120**	**136**
	3.2	4.0	4.5	4.8

For each combination of the fund's withdrawal rate and growth rate objective, the optimal portfolio's equity weight and this portfolio's expected growth rate are tabled. Equity returns are proxied by the Ibbotson large cap total return index, while fixed income returns are proxied by the Ibbotson intermediate government bond total return index, using annual data from 1926–1996. The equity weight increases when the fund adopts more ambitious fund objectives. Equity weights in excess of 100% are financed by short selling the other asset (bonds), and hence are unlikely to be adopted.

The top, bold faced numbers in the cells of Table 15.1 show that the optimal portfolio equity weight solving (15.7) must increase in order to achieve higher withdrawal and/or growth rate objectives. Not surprisingly, more ambitious fund objectives require more aggressive portfolios. The second number in any cell of Table 15.1 shows the corresponding invested fund's expected growth rate, which always exceeds the fund's growth rate objective. The higher expected growth rate is needed in order to maximize the probability that the fund's realized growth rate will not fall below the fund's growth rate objective. Table 15.1 shows that a total (i.e. 100%) equity portfolio is needed when the withdrawal rate is 5% and the growth rate objective is 2%, or when the former is 6% while the latter is 1%. Further computations with the spreadsheet indicate that if the fund only cared about preserving the nominal value of the initial endowment, i.e. it adopts a growth rate objective of $\log r = 0\%$, it can still withdraw $d = 6.9\%$ by investing 100% in equities. But as described below, while this aggressive portfolio will maximize the outperformance probability, the probability itself may still be relatively small, i.e. the probability of underperforming the 0% growth objective ('dipping into the principal') may persist for a very, very long time! Less risky policies would be a 51% equity weight, which is optimal when the fund adopts a 5% withdrawal rate, or a 79% equity weight, appropriate when the fund adopts a withdrawal rate of 6%.

Because Table 15.1 showed that higher withdrawal and/or growth rate objectives necessitate higher equity weights and their associated higher expected portfolio returns, it should not be surprising to find out that the risk of not exceeding the growth rate objective also increases accordingly – no risk, no return. This risk is determined by the estimated underperformance probability decay rate (15.6) associated with each optimal portfolio estimated in (15.7). The following Table 15.2 describes the results.

Table 15.2 *Risk of underperforming growth rate objectives*

Withdrawal %	Growth objective $\log r\%$			
d	0	1	2	3
4	**8.2**	**4.2**	**2.3**	**1.2**
	9	17	33	60
5	**4.1**	**2.2**	**1.2**	**0.6**
	18	33	60	120
6	**2.1**	**1.1**	**0.6**	**0.2**
	34	65	120	360

The top number in each cell is the underperformance probability decay rate (D_p) estimated from (15.6), while the bottom number is this probability's half-life ($72/D_p$ in years), associated with Table 15.1's optimal portfolio (15.7) for each combination of withdrawal and growth rate objectives. The risk of not meeting a growth rate objective increases with the magnitude of both objectives.

To read Table 15.2, suppose the fund adopts a growth rate objective of $\log r = 1\%$. Reading down the bold faced numbers in the second column of Table 15.2, note that the decay rate D_p steadily falls, as the fund adopts more aggressive portfolios p_{max} (listed in Table 15.1) in order to meet more ambitious withdrawal rates. To assess the meaning of each decay rate, the second number in each cell is $72/D_p$ years, which approximates the number of years required for the asymptotic probability (of failing to exceed the 1% growth rate objective) to halve. For example, the first cell in the second column of Table 15.2 indicates that a 50% equity portfolio (from the corresponding cell in Table 15.1) results in a probability that decays at a 4.2% rate. Hence, this risk eventually halves about every $72/4.2 \approx 17$ years. In contrast, the second cell in the second column shows that a fund with a more ambitious withdrawal rate of 5%, accordingly placing more weight on equities (77% listed in Table 15.1), has only a 2.2% decay rate, which eventually halves only every 33 years or so. Hence, a significant risk of failing to meet the 1% growth objective will remain for roughly twice as long when the fund adopts the more ambitious withdrawal objective of 5% instead of 4%.

15.4   CONCLUSIONS

Endowment management necessarily strikes a tradeoff between the fraction of funds that users may withdraw, and the growth rate of the remaining funds invested. Of course, the tradeoff is influenced by the fund's asset allocation. This Chapter provides a method of determining the asset allocation that maximizes the probability of achieving a desired (possibly zero) growth rate objective for the invested funds, after fixing the fund's withdrawal rate. In doing so, the paper quantifies the risk vs. return tradeoff associated with increases in the fund's withdrawal and growth rate objectives.

Future research will focus on three areas. First, it is important to determine the influence of other asset classes, other historical periods, and other return measurement frequencies on the estimation results. Second, it is important to develop alternative estimators that continue to perform well when portfolio returns have time-varying and/or dependent distributions. Third, it would be useful to obtain historical endowment fund returns, to rank them according to the outperformance probability indicator developed herein.

REFERENCES

Kroll, Y., Levy, H. and Markowitz, H. (1984) Mean-variance versus direct utility maximization, *Journal of Finance*, **39**, 47–61.

Stutzer, M. (2000) A Portfolio Performance Index, *Financial Analysis Journal*, **56**, (3), 52–61.

Stutzer, M. (2002) Portfolio Choice with Endogenous Utility: A Large Deviations Approach, *Journal of Econometrics*, **106**, (forthcoming).

NOTES

1.   When returns are multivariate normally distributed, an arithmetic average version of this idea provides the same portfolio choice rule as the familiar maximum Sharpe Ratio rule. For details see Stutzer (2000).

ACKNOWLEDGEMENTS

I acknowledge helpful comments and references from John Lorentz, Director of Operations for the University of Minnesota Foundation Investment Advisors.

Chapter 16

Methods of relative portfolio optimization

NIKLAS WAGNER

ABSTRACT

The application of the Markowitz portfolio optimization framework faces the problem of noise in the input parameters. Methods of relative portfolio optimization, commonly also denoted as 'tracking models', can be thought of as simple approaches reducing the impact of noise by combining estimation input with information provided by a given benchmark portfolio. This chapter provides an overview of recent developments.

16.1 INTRODUCTION

Portfolio optimization as pioneered by Harry Markowitz aims at achieving an optimal ex ante tradeoff between risk and return for a portfolio of risky assets. Unfortunately, the practical application of the Markowitz portfolio optimization framework faces the problem of forming an assessment about the unknown joint distribution of asset returns. In a typical application, noisy historical estimates are used. This makes Bayesian methods of portfolio selection a natural choice. Apart from sample information, some prior information on the joint distribution enters the optimization algorithm. This approach was followed for example by Bawa et al. (1979) and subsequent authors. In case a decision maker forms a subjective assessment about the joint return distribution which will circumvent the problem of noise in historical estimates, there is still reason to believe that noise is present in the assessment of his or her input parameters. This is due to inevitable errors in private information processing which naturally precedes the more technical exercise of portfolio optimization.

Models of relative portfolio optimization, frequently also denoted as 'tracking models', can be thought of as simple approaches to estimation noise by combining standard estimation input with information provided by a given benchmark portfolio. Treynor and Black (1973) as well as Brealey (1986) follow this approach. The only assumption made is that benchmark portfolio weights contain useful prior information to the optimization process. Traditional capital market theory suggests this to be the case for broad capitalization weighted market indices. Even when judged from a more critical perspective as in Grossman (1995), there is generally no doubt about the usefulness of such information. Based on the assumption that benchmarks provide useful information, stutzer (2002) derives a behavioral factor model of equilibrium asset prices.

This chapter provides an overview of recent developments in the area. Section 16.2 gives a brief review on the development of the models and points out to literature considering implementation issues. A presentation of the different recent model variants is given in Section 16.3. The chapter continues with a discussion of the models in Section 16.4 and ends with a brief conclusion.

16.2   SOME BACKGROUND ON RELATIVE PORTFOLIO OPTIMIZATION

Relative portfolio optimization emerged from practitioners' experience with the implementation of various portfolio optimization algorithms. Instead of implementing the classical mean-variance or expectation variance (EV) approach, managers started to optimize portfolios focusing on 'tracking error'. The latter can be defined as the difference in a managed portfolios' return and the return of a chosen benchmark portfolio (the approach also followed here) or, alternatively, as the standard deviation of this difference.

16.2.1   Models

In the literature, models of relative portfolio optimization gained growing interest about a decade ago, whilst early work dates back to the 1970s. Without offering a complete list, work by Hodges (1976), Rudd and Rosenberg (1979), Markowitz (1987), Rice and Au (1988), Roll (1992) and Sharpe (1992) led to the foundation of the quadratic tracking approach. Referring to Roll, the procedure can be labelled as tracking error-variance (TEV) optimization. Hodges (1976) and Clarke et al. (1994) point out that the underlying decision theoretic concept must fundamentally differ from that of EV theory.

In subsequent work, Chow (1995) proposed a target function, which includes both an EV and a TEV component. Zhang (1998) extends the target function of EV optimization to include an arbitrary number of risk components. Hence, Chow's and Zhang's models can be denoted as multirisk models. Wagner (1998) suggests a model with 'moment restricted' weights which puts a restriction on the overall set of weights and thereby implicitly restricts tracking error variance. An analytical analysis of TEV-constrained EV optimization is given in Jorion (2002).

A mean-variance-covariance (EVC) model which contains both, the EV and the TEV model, is analysed in Wagner (2002).

16.2.2 Statistical issues

Apart from the developments in modelling, statistical issues play an important role especially in the implementation of the methods. Of course, noise also plays a role for tracking applications. Michaud (1998) points out the problem referring to standard as well as tracking applications and considers various improved estimation approaches to be applied in management practice. In a recent paper, Chan et al. (1999) study ex ante parameter estimation quality for standard and tracking optimization applications. The authors find empirically that, as compared to the standard application, the tracking criterion is less sensitive with respect to errors in forecasting the risk structure of asset returns. Clearly, this is consistent with the hypothesis that relative optimization is a simple way to reduce the impact of noise in the portfolio optimization process. Taking the time dimension into account, Adcock (2002) also points out that optimization relative to a given benchmark is a source of stability in portfolio optimization through time, since benchmark weights usually change slowly, once again reducing the impact of noise in the estimates.

Another important statistical issue is measuring tracking risk given the stylized fact that financial returns over weekly or shorter intervals are not i.i.d. (Independent identically distributed) draws from a normal distribution. Pope and Yadav (1994) were among the first to point out that estimating the variance of tracking error therefore is a non-trivial task. Particularly, when measuring tracking risk, differences in liquidity between the benchmark and the managed portfolio may induce dependence in tracking errors which in turn may cause severe mis-estimation when conventional estimation methods are used. Recently, the effect of volatility clustering was considered in detail by Lawton-Browne (2001), who derives a modified estimator taking autocorrelation and volatility clustering into account. The effects of stochastic portfolio weights and their impact on estimation of the variance of tracking error are considered in Satchell and Hwang (2001). Another issue is the non-normality of returns and tracking errors which reduces efficiency of conventional variance estimators. Bamberg and Wagner (2000) therefore suggest the use of a robust estimator of the variance of tracking error once outliers are present in the sample of returns.

16.3 MODEL APPROACHES FOR RELATIVE PORTFOLIO OPTIMIZATION

This section classifies recent models of relative portfolio optimization.[1] The single period portfolio selection model assumes a decision maker which possesses information about the distribution of returns of N risky assets, $i = 1, \ldots, N$. A portfolio allocation is characterized by the vector of portfolio weights, denoted by $\mathbf{x} = (x_i)_{N \times 1}$. The set of feasible decisions is given as $C = \{\mathbf{x} \in \mathrm{R}^N : \mathbf{x}^T \mathbf{1} = 1, \mathbf{x} \geq \mathbf{0}\}$, where $\mathbf{1} \equiv (1)_{N \times 1}$ and $\mathbf{0} \equiv (0)_{N \times 1}$. The vector of portfolio weights is called admissible if $\mathbf{x} \in C$. Alternatively, short sales may be allowed, i.e. $S = \{\mathbf{x} \in \mathrm{R}^N : \mathbf{x}^T \mathbf{1} = 1\}$ and $\mathbf{x} \in S$.

Assuming a quadratically approximable utility function or normally distributed returns $\mathbf{r} = (R_i)_{N \times 1}$ with expectation $\boldsymbol{\mu} = [E(R_i)]_{N \times 1}$ and positive definite covariance matrix $\boldsymbol{\Omega} = (\sigma_{i,j})_{N \times N}$, the classical mean-variance (or EV) portfolio selection model can be set up as a minimization problem of the form:

$$\text{EV} \qquad \mathbf{x}^T \boldsymbol{\Omega} \mathbf{x} \to \min \qquad (16.1)$$

$$\text{s.t.:} \mathbf{x}^T \boldsymbol{\mu} = E(R_P) \qquad (16.2)$$

$$\mathbf{x} \in C \qquad (16.3)$$

The term $E(R_P)$ is the constant expected return of the managed portfolio P, which results for a given weights vector $\mathbf{x}$. An analytical solution to the problem can be derived when (16.3) is replaced by $\mathbf{x} \in S$, i.e. when short sales are allowed.

For the EV portfolio optimization problem, the information input consists of a risk component $\boldsymbol{\Omega}$ and an expected return component $\boldsymbol{\mu}$. Models of relative portfolio optimization additionally use the weights of a benchmark portfolio $\mathbf{b} = (b_i)_{N \times 1}$, where $b_i > 0$, as an input to optimization. We outline five different variants in the following.

16.3.1 The Markowitz/Roll model

The Markowitz/Roll quadratic tracking model is based on the tracking error, $R_E \equiv R_P - R_B$, defined as the difference between the returns of the managed portfolio (P) and benchmark portfolio (B). The optimization approach is to minimize the variance of tracking error given a constant tracking error expectation:

$$\text{TEV} \qquad (\mathbf{x} - \mathbf{b})^T \boldsymbol{\Omega} (\mathbf{x} - \mathbf{b}) \to \min \qquad (16.4)$$

$$\text{s.t.:} (\mathbf{x} - \mathbf{b})^T \boldsymbol{\mu} = E(R_E) \qquad (16.5)$$

$$\mathbf{x} \in D \qquad (16.6)$$

The portfolio constraint excluding short sales now translates to $\mathbf{x} \in D$ with $D = \{\mathbf{x} \in R_i^N : \mathbf{x}^T \mathbf{1} = 1, \mathbf{x} \geq -\mathbf{b}\}$. Clearly, if the constant tracking error expectation in (16.5) equals zero, $\mathbf{x} = \mathbf{b}$ follows as a trivial solution. Roll (1992) derives the analytical solution of the problem for $\mathbf{x} \in S$. He points out that, for a given EV inefficient benchmark portfolio, TEV optimization yields EV inefficient solutions.

16.3.2 The Rudd/Rosenberg/Roll model

The optimization approach taken by Rudd/Rosenberg and Roll proposes a quadratic tracking model with a constraint that contains portfolio beta. Hence, it may be denoted as a TEV model with beta restriction (TEVBR). Defining the vector of asset betas as $\boldsymbol{\beta} = (\beta_i)_{N \times 1}$ and letting β_P denote the chosen portfolio beta, this model corresponds to the minimization problem:

$$\text{TEVBR} \qquad (\mathbf{x} - \mathbf{b})^{\mathrm{T}} \Omega (\mathbf{x} - \mathbf{b}) \to \min \qquad (16.7)$$

$$\text{s.t.:} (\mathbf{x} - \mathbf{b})^{\mathrm{T}} \boldsymbol{\mu} = \mathrm{E}(R_E) \qquad (16.8)$$

$$\mathbf{x}^{\mathrm{T}} \boldsymbol{\beta} = \beta_P \qquad (16.9)$$

$$\mathbf{x} \in D \qquad (16.10)$$

Roll (1992) discusses the analytical solution of the problem when (16.10) is replaced by $\mathbf{x} \in S$. He points out that, for a given EV inefficient benchmark portfolio and a target beta $\beta_P < 1$, the TEVBR optimization yields portfolios which dominate the benchmark in the EV dimension.

16.3.3 The multirisk model

The multirisk model adds the variance of the tracking error to the standard Markowitz EV model. Having multiple variances in the target function, it may be denoted as a mean-multiple-variance (EMV) model. Introducing a risk aversion parameter $\kappa \geq 0$, one can set up the following minimization problem:

$$\text{EMV} \qquad \mathbf{x}^{\mathrm{T}} \Omega \mathbf{x} + \kappa (\mathbf{x} - \mathbf{b})^{\mathrm{T}} \Omega (\mathbf{x} - \mathbf{b}) \to \min \qquad (16.11)$$

$$\text{s.t.:} \mathbf{x}^{\mathrm{T}} \boldsymbol{\mu} = E(R_P) \qquad (16.12)$$

$$\mathbf{x} \in C \qquad (16.13)$$

16.3.4 The moment restricted model

Basically, the moment restricted model is a generalization of traditional approaches in EV portfolio optimization which set constraints on single portfolio weights.

However, instead of imposing lower and upper bounds on single portfolio weights, the EV moment restricted (EVMR) model restricts the whole set of portfolio weights. This allows for a tradeoff between individual deviations and circumvents the problem of many optimized weights hitting the admissible boundaries. Interpreting the optimal decision variable $\mathbf{x}$ as random due to noise in the estimates, the approach takes the given benchmark portfolio weights $\mathbf{b}$

as the expectation of portfolio weights $\mathbf{x}$. Then, the model sets a constraint on the second centred moment of the portfolio weights:

$$\text{EVMR} \qquad \mathbf{x}^T \Omega \mathbf{x} \to \min \tag{16.14}$$

$$\text{s.t.:} \mathbf{x}^T \boldsymbol{\mu} = E(R_P) \tag{16.15}$$

$$(\mathbf{x} - \mathbf{b})^T (\mathbf{x} - \mathbf{b}) = d \tag{16.16}$$

$$\mathbf{x} \in C \tag{16.17}$$

The parameter $d \geq 0$ in the moment constraint (16.16) is a constant which controls overall squared weights deviations from the benchmark weights. The smaller d, the closer the portfolio weights will replicate the benchmark weights.

16.3.5   The mean-variance-covariance model

The mean-variance-covariance (EVC) model derives its target function from a multi-attribute utility framework imposing standard EV model assumptions and regret aversion. The latter states that the decision maker is worse off once he or she fails to achieve the benchmark realized return. Introducing a regret aversion parameter $\lambda \geq 0$, one can set up the minimization problem:

$$\text{EVC} \qquad \mathbf{x}^T \Omega \mathbf{x} - \lambda \mathbf{x}^T \Omega \mathbf{b} \to \min \tag{16.18}$$

$$\text{s.t.:} \mathbf{x}^T \boldsymbol{\mu} = E(R_P) \tag{16.19}$$

$$\mathbf{x} \in C \tag{16.20}$$

An analytical solution to the problem can be derived allowing for short sales where restriction (16.20) is replaced by $\mathbf{x} \in S$. For $\lambda > 0$, the optimal portfolio weights vector $\mathbf{x}$ is composed of two EV efficient weights vectors as well as the benchmark portfolio weights vector $\mathbf{b}$ (see Wagner (2002)). Given estimates of $\boldsymbol{\mu}$ and Ω, regret averse investors will choose EV *in*efficient *optimal* portfolios whenever the benchmark portfolio is EV inefficient. This generalization of Roll's result is quite obvious: since the portfolios are optimized to be EVC efficient, they cannot be EV efficient with the only exception that the benchmark happens to be EV efficient for given $\boldsymbol{\mu}$ and Ω.

16.3.6   An overview of the optimization models

Table 16.1 gives an overview of the standard EV and the outlined models of relative portfolio optimization.

All models in Table 16.1 were formulated as quadratic minimization problems imposing a constant return expectation. The table entries for each model indicate which variables are optimized in the target function or set constant in one of

Table 16.1 *EV-model and models of relative portfolio optimization*

Model	Authors	Return variance	Return covariance	Tracking error variance
EV	Markowitz	min !	————	————
TEV	Markowitz/Roll	————	————	min !
TEVBR	Rudd/Rosenberg/Roll	————	constant	min !
EMV	Chow/Zhang	min !	————	min !
EVMR	Jorion/Wagner	min !	————	constant
EVC	Wagner	min !	max !	————

Which decision variables are optimized in the target function, which are set constant in a constraint?

the constraints. While the EV and the TEV models focus solely on variance of returns and tracking error respectively, the other models either explicitly consider both variances or explicitly take covariance with the benchmark returns into account. The table also indicates that the list of models is not complete and there may be model variants not yet covered here.

16.4   DISCUSSION OF THE MODELS

The discussion of the models of the preceding section concentrates on the target functions of the minimization problems. This allows for the following statements.

- **The TEV model**: The target function (16.4) is given as the variance of tracking error, which – since Ω is symmetric – can be written as $\sigma_E^2 = \mathbf{x}^T\Omega\mathbf{x} - 2\mathbf{x}^T\Omega\mathbf{b} + \mathbf{b}^T\Omega\mathbf{b}$. Since the variance of benchmark portfolio returns $\mathbf{b}^T\Omega\mathbf{b}$ is a given constant, variance and covariance are relevant to the choice of $\mathbf{x}$ in this model.
- **The TEVBR model**: Since $\beta_P = \mathbf{x}^T\Omega\mathbf{b}/\mathbf{b}^T\Omega\mathbf{b}$ is set constant in (16.9), the model is equivalent to minimizing variance of portfolio returns for a given covariance between the returns of the portfolio and the benchmark. It must therefore yield EV efficient, covariance constrained, portfolios.
- **The EMV model**: One may rewrite the target function (16.11) as $f(\mathbf{x}) = \mathbf{x}^T\Omega\mathbf{x} + \kappa\mathbf{x}^T\Omega\mathbf{x} - 2\kappa\mathbf{x}^T\Omega\mathbf{b} + \kappa\mathbf{b}^T\Omega\mathbf{b}$. Minimization of $f(\mathbf{x})$ is then equivalent to minimizing $g(\mathbf{x}) = \mathbf{x}^T\Omega\mathbf{x} - 2\kappa/(1+\kappa)\mathbf{x}^T\Omega\mathbf{b}$. Hence, the problem contains redundant terms in the target function and is equivalent to an EVC optimization problem with target function (16.18) and $\lambda = 2\kappa/(1+\kappa)$.
- **The EVMR model**: Since $(\mathbf{x} - \mathbf{b})^T(\mathbf{x} - \mathbf{b})$ is constant in (16.16), it follows that the variance of tracking error is constant as well. In particular, $\sigma_E^2 = (\mathbf{x} - \mathbf{b})^T P\Omega(\mathbf{x} - \mathbf{b})$. Therefore, the model minimizes variance of portfolio returns for a given variance of tracking error, i.e. it will yield EV efficient tracking error variance constrained portfolios.

- **The EVC model**: Considering the target function (16.18) for $\lambda = 0$, the EV model follows immediately. For $\lambda = 2$, a target function which is equivalent to the TEV problem follows. Since $(\mathbf{x} - \mathbf{b})^T \boldsymbol{\mu} = \mathbf{x}^T \boldsymbol{\mu} - \mathbf{b}^T \boldsymbol{\mu}$, where the expected benchmark portfolio return $\mathbf{b}^T \boldsymbol{\mu}$ is constant, the only difference between the models (16.4–6) and (16.18–20) is the definition of the set of admissible solutions. Hence, the TEV model is an EVC model with the regret aversion parameter restricted to equal a value of two

16.5   CONCLUSION

Previous theoretical literature, empirical findings and the large popularity in the investment community, indicate that relative portfolio optimization is relevant to questions of quantitative portfolio selection.

This chapter gave a survey of related methods for portfolio construction. Closer inspection of the models reveals that there are more similarities than frequently assumed. The methods discussed here can either be characterized as EV models with covariance or tracking error variance constraint or they can be characterized as EVC models simultaneously minimizing variance of return and maximizing covariance of benchmark and portfolio returns. While the first group of models yields covariance constrained EV efficient optimal portfolios, the second group yields EVC efficient optimal portfolios.

REFERENCES

Adcock, C.J. (2002) Portfolio Optimization. In Taylor, J. and Shadbolt, J. (eds.), *Neural Networks and Beyond: Predicting the Financial Markets*, Springer, New York.

Bamberg, G. and Wagner, N. (2000) Equity Index Replication with Standard and Robust Regression Estimators, *OR Spektrum*, **22**, 525–43.

Bawa, V., Brown, S.J. and Klein, R. (eds.) (1979) Estimation Risk and Optimal Portfolio Choice, *Studies in Bayesian Econometrics*, **3**, North-Holland, Amsterdam.

Beasley, J.E., Meade, N. and Chang, T.-J. (2001) An Evolutionary Heuristic for the Index Tracking Problem, Working Paper, Imperial College, London.

Brealey, R.A. (1986) How to Combine Active Management with Index Funds, *Journal of Portfolio Management,* Winter, 4–10.

Chan, L.K., Karceski, J.J. and Lakonishok, J. (1999) On Portfolio Optimization: Forecasting Covariances and Choosing the Risk Model, *Review of Financial Studies*, **12**, 937–74.

Chow, G. (1995) Portfolio Selection Based on Return, Risk, and Relative Performance, *Financial Analysts Journal*, March–April, 54–60.

Clarke, R.C., Krase, S. and Statman, M. (1994) Tracking Errors, Regret and Tactical Asset Allocation, *Journal of Portfolio Management*, Spring, 16–24.

Grossman, S.J. (1995) Dynamic Asset Allocation and the Informational Efficiency of Markets, *Journal of Finance*, **50**, 773–87.

Hodges, S.D. (1976) Problems in the Application of Portfolio Selection Models, *Omega*, **6**, 699–709.

Jorion, P. (2002) Portfolio Optimization with Constraints on Tracking Error, Working Paper, U.C. Irvine.

Lawton-Browne, C. (2001) An Alternative Calculation of Tracking Error, *Journal of Asset Management*, **2**, 223–34.

Markowitz, H.M. (1987) *Mean-Variance Analysis in Portfolio Choice and Capital Markets*, Blackwell, New York.

Michaud, R.O. (1998) *Efficient Asset Management: A Practical Guide to Stock Portfolio Optimization and Asset Allocation*, Oxford University Press, Oxford.

Pope, P.F. and Yadav, P.K. (1994) Discovering Errors in Tracking Error, *Journal of Portfolio Management*, Winter, S. 27–32.

Rice, R.K. and Au, K.L. (1988) Tracking Error: A Tool for the Active Fund Manager as well as the Index Fund, *Journal of International Securities Markets*, Summer, 89–95.

Roll, R. (1992) A Mean/Variance Analysis of Tracking Error, *Journal of Portfolio Management*, Summer, 13–22.

Rudd, A. and Rosenberg, B. (1979) Realistic Portfolio Optimization. In Elton, E.J. and Gruber, M.J. (eds.) *Portfolio Theory, 25 Years after, Studies in the Management Sciences*, **11**, North-Holland, Amsterdam, 21–46.

Rudolf, M., Wolter, H.-J. and Zimmermann, H. (1999) A Linear Model for Tracking Error Minimization, *Journal of Banking and Finance*, **23**, 85–103.

Satchell, S.E. and Hwang, S. (2001) Tracking Error: Ex Ante versus Ex Post Measures, *Journal of Asset Management*, **2**, 241–46.

Sharpe, W.F. (1992) Asset Allocation: Management Style and Performance Measurement, *Journal of Portfolio Management*, Winter, 7–19.

Stutzer, M. (2002) A Behavioral Theory of Linear Multi-Factor Models, Working Paper, University of Colorado.

Treynor, J.L. and Black, F. (1973) How to Use Security Analysis to Improve Portfolio Selection, *Journal of Business*, **46**, 66–86.

Wagner, N. (1998) Portfolio Optimization with Cap Weight Restrictions. In Refenes, A.P.N., Moody, J. and Burgess, N. (eds.) *Decision Technologies for Computational Finance*, Kluwer, Dordrecht, 403–16.

Wagner, N. (2002) On a Model of Portfolio Selection with Benchmark, *Journal of Asset Management*, **3**.

Zhang, L.H. (1998) Global Asset Allocation with Multirisk Considerations, *Journal of Investing*, Fall, 7–14.

NOTES

1. The section is restricted to portfolio selection models. Alternative applications based on regression approaches can be found in Rudolf, Wolter, and Zimmermann (1999) and in Bamberg and Wagner (2000), for example. Beasley et al. (2001) propose an optimization heuristic for the index tracking problem under optimal subset selection and transaction costs.

Chapter 17

Predicting portfolio returns using the distributions of efficient set portfolios

C J ADCOCK

ABSTRACT

Forecast and actual asset returns may often be modelled by multivariate elliptically symmetrical distributions. In such cases, the returns of an efficient set portfolio are distributed as quadratic forms in such variables. This chapter describes a practical methodology based on this property that allows builders of efficient portfolios to make improved predictions of future actual portfolio returns. The method is illustrated using an international asset allocation portfolio.

17.1   INTRODUCTION

It is widely accepted that the realized or ex post performance of optimized portfolios is often very different from that expected ex ante. Furthermore, the performance is usually inferior. Either the realized returns will be significantly less than expected ex ante, or the volatility will be greater, or both. This topic has been widely discussed in the portfolio selection literature. It is well known that the portfolios produced by formal optimization methods are sensitive to the inputs – see the well-known papers by Best and Grauer (1991) and Chopra and Ziemba (1993), for example. This means that, even in the situation where the user is equipped with good estimates of the input parameters, the outputs are likely to produce results that are different from those expected. In circumstances where the estimates of the inputs are poor, it is inevitable that ex post performance will be inferior. This veracity of the strong statement in the preceding sentence is borne out by empirical evidence, as well as in the writing of leading exponents of portfolio selection methods, notably Richard Michaud. It is also confirmed by a theoretical portfolio selection model reported in Adcock (2000), henceforth CA.

Portfolio selection, regardless of the methodology of portfolio construction, is a complex process. As Michaud (1998) makes clear, many factors are involved. From the perspective of a quantitative construction methodology, however, there are two issues which are of paramount importance. First, given a process that generates the inputs to portfolio selection, how should users compute the best estimates of what ex post performance will actually be? Second, how should users improve the quality of their inputs so that ex post performance is close to that predicted ex ante?

The aim of this short article is to describe a methodology that provides an answer to the first of the two questions above. It is shown that it is possible to construct a systematic process that will generate better predictive information about realized returns. This does not provide higher quality inputs per se, but it does create a framework of more realistic expectations for portfolio returns. It may also implicitly provide information about specific weaknesses in current parameter estimates.

The methodology described in this paper requires that a discrete reconstruction of the efficient frontier is computed at each time period. This reconstruction uses the current inputs, normally forecasts of future expected returns and an estimate of the variance–covariance (*VC*) matrix. The actual returns on this set of portfolios over the following time period are then calculated ex post. This data forms the input to an algorithm that constructs an ex post efficient frontier. This frontier, which differs in definition from the Markowitz quadratic function, may be used to generate more realistic predictions of ex post returns. It is shown that, when the vector of expected returns and the corresponding *VC* matrix are assumed, portfolio expected return is a piecewise linear function of risk appetite. This function is approximated by a continuous quadratic function of risk, which may be estimated from ex post returns. The effect of estimation error on the optimal portfolio weights and hence on ex post return is also discussed. The quadratic model may also be used in these circumstances.

Estimation of the ex post frontier may be done in several ways. The methodology used in this paper is ordinary least squares regression. However, as noted in the conclusions, it would be straightforward to implement a more sophisticated estimation method.

The methods described are based on the standard mean-variance portfolio selection objective function. In the usual notation,[1] this is:

$$\min_w \phi = \theta w^T \mu - \tfrac{1}{2} w^T V w \text{ such that } A^T w \geq b \tag{17.1}$$

where μ is the vector of expected returns on a set of assets over a single time period. V is the *VC* matrix, assumed to be non-singular. The scalar $\theta \geq 0$

represents an investor's degree of risk appetite, with small values corresponding to a cautious or low risk investor. The vector w contains the portfolio weights. The matrix A contains the constraint normals and b the corresponding values. The inequality sign above applies elementwise to the vector $A^T w$ and to b. For basic portfolio selection with N assets, the constraints are the budget constraint and the non-negativity restrictions on each asset's weight. A is then an N by $(N + 1)$ matrix:

$$A = [1, I]$$

where I is an N by N unit matrix and 1 is an N vector of ones. The vector b contains the corresponding $(N + 1)$ constraint values:

$$b = \begin{bmatrix} 1 \\ 0 \\ . \\ . \\ 0 \end{bmatrix}$$

More general constraints, including upper bounds,[2] may be added to (A, b).

The structure of this chapter is as follows. Section 17.2 describes the efficient set mathematics for the general portfolio selection problem defined at (17.1) for the case when μ and V are given. Section 17.3 extends the ideas for the case when V is assumed, but the uncertainty in μ is recognized. Section 17.4 describes the resulting model and process. An empirical study based on an asset allocation portfolio is in Section 17.5 and Section 17.6 concludes. Notation is that in common use. The use of 1 to represent a vector of ones is clear from the context. An Appendix provides some additional detail to support the material in Section 17.3.

17.2   EFFICIENT SET MATHEMATICS FOR GIVEN μ AND V

When the non-negativity restrictions and any other constraints are ignored, there is an analytic solution to the simplified portfolio selection problem:

$$\min_w \phi = \theta w^T \mu - \tfrac{1}{2} w^T V w \text{ such that } 1^T w = 1.$$

The portfolio weights are given by:

$$w^* = \frac{1}{1^T V^{-1} 1} V^{-1} 1 + \theta \left\{ V^{-1} - \frac{1}{1^T V^{-1} 1} V^{-1} 1 1^T V^{-1} \right\} \mu$$

For the more general portfolio selection problem stated at Equation (17.1), w^* will depend on the constraints that are active at the solution. Suppose that the constraints are given, as stated above, by $A^T w \geq b$; where A is an N by M matrix and b is an M vector. Define A_S as the N by P matrix of constraint normals that are active at the solution, with $P \leq N$, and b_S as the corresponding P vector of constraint values. The weights that solve the portfolio selection problem in Equation (17.1) are given by:

$$w^* = V^{-1} A_S (A_S^T V^{-1} A_S)^{-1} b_S + \theta\{V^{-1} - V^{-1} A_S (A_S^T V^{-1} A_S)^{-1} A_S^T V^{-1}\}\mu$$

$$(17.2)$$

The solution vector w^* varies with S, the set (A_S, b_S) that is active at the solution. However, when μ and V are given, w^* is deterministic even though it depends on the parameter set $(\mu, V; \theta)$. Consequently, there are analytic expressions for the mean and variance of return on the optimal portfolio, R_p^* say. These are:

$$E[R_p^*] = \alpha_{0,S} + \theta\alpha_{1,S} = E^*, \text{ say}$$

$$(17.3)$$

$$V[R_p^*] = \alpha_{2,S} + \theta^2\alpha_{1,S} = V^*, \text{ say}$$

The three α constants are defined in terms of μ and V as follows:

$$\alpha_{0,S} = \mu^T V^{-1} A_S (A_S^T V^{-1} A_S)^{-1} b_S$$

$$\alpha_{1,S} = \mu^T \{V^{-1} - V^{-1} A_S (A_S^T V^{-1} A_S)^{-1} A_S^T V^{-1}\}\mu$$

$$(17.4)$$

$$\alpha_{2,S} = b_S^T (A_S^T V^{-1} A_S)^{-1} b_S$$

It should be noted that whereas $\alpha_{1,S}$ and $\alpha_{2,S}$ are always non-negative, it is possible for $\alpha_{0,S}$ to take negative as well as positive values. For portfolio selection based only on the budget constraint, these reduce to the usual efficient set constants:

$$\alpha_0 = \frac{\mu^T V^{-1} 1}{1^T V^{-1} 1}$$

$$\alpha_1 = \mu^T \left\{V^{-1} - \frac{1}{1^T V^{-1} 1} V^{-1} 1 1^T V^{-1}\right\}\mu$$

$$\alpha_2 = \frac{1}{1^T V^{-1} 1}$$

These appear in various papers concerned with efficient set mathematics; for example Roll (1977) or Best and Grauer (1991).

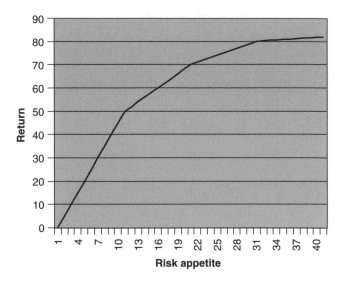

Figure 17.1   *A sketch of expected return v risk appetite*

As indicated by equations (17.3) and (17.4), for general portfolio selection the relationship between expected portfolio return E^* and risk appetite θ is piecewise linear. The slope changes when the active set S changes. In general, as risk increases from zero, the number of active constraints increases.[3] The relationship between E^* and θ resembles the sketch shown in Figure 17.1.

The methodology described in this article is motivated by the sketch. This suggests that a piecewise linear function of θ may be approximated by a low order polynomial. Specifically, it is proposed to model E^* by:

$$E^* = \gamma_0 + \gamma_1\theta + \gamma_2\theta^2$$

The coefficients $\gamma_{0,1,2}$ are estimated by regression based on the model:

$$R_{p,\theta,t} = \gamma_0 + \gamma_1\theta + \gamma_2\theta^2 + \varepsilon_{p,\theta,t}$$

where $R_{p,\theta,t}$ is the return on a portfolio at time t constructed using the methodology above at risk level θ.[4] As noted in the Introduction, the details of these models and the estimation process are described in Section 17.4.

A detailed general discussion of the geometry of the efficient set and in particular the relationship between (A_S, b_S) and $(\mu, V; \theta)$ is beyond the scope of this article. However, it is straightforward to show for basic portfolio selection that as the number of active constraints increases, $\alpha_{1,S}$ the slope of E^* decreases but remains non-negative. For more complex constraints, the expected return may be a higher order polynomial in θ.

17.3 THE EFFECT OF FORECASTS

Efficient set mathematics assumes that the vector of expected returns μ and the *VC* matrix are both given. In practice, these are both estimated quantities. Furthermore, the estimates will generally be revised each time period as new observations on returns become available. As noted in Adcock (2002), 'analytical investigation of the effects of estimates is in general an open question, although the effect of estimates on the maximum Sharpe ratio portfolio has been reported in some detail by Jobson and Korkie (1981)'. Other authors who have considered aspects of the effect of estimation error include Bawa et al. (1979), Hillier and Satchell (Chapter 14) and Britten Jones (1999).

In this section it is assumed that the distribution R and the vector of forecasts F have a joint multivariate normal distribution. The mean vector is:

$$\begin{bmatrix} \mu_R \\ \mu_F \end{bmatrix}$$

and the *VC* matrix is:

$$\begin{bmatrix} V_{RR} & V_{RF} \\ V_{FR} & V_{FF} \end{bmatrix}$$

It is assumed that both V_{RR} and V_{FF} are non-singular. For the general portfolio selection problem with inequality constraints, the optimal weights may be written as:

$$w^* = V_{RR}^{-1} A_S (A_S^T V_{RR}^{-1} A_S)^{-1} b_S$$
$$+ \theta \{ V_{RR}^{-1} - V_{RR}^{-1} A_S (A_S^T V_{RR}^{-1} A_S)^{-1} A_S^T V_{RR}^{-1} \} F \tag{17.5}$$

The active set now depends on $(F, V; \theta)$. Actual portfolio return is given by:

$$R_p^* = R^T V_{RR}^{-1} A_S (A_S^T V_{RR}^{-1} A_S)^{-1} b_S$$
$$+ \theta R^T \{ V_{RR}^{-1} - V_{RR}^{-1} A_S (A_S^T V_{RR}^{-1} A_S)^{-1} A_S^T V_{RR}^{-1} \} F$$

In most circumstances, there will be single value of the vector of forecasts. In this case, the proper approach to inference for the portfolio w^* and its subsequent performance is to use the conditional distribution R given F. This is multivariate normal with mean vector and *VC* matrix:

$$\mu_R + V_{RF} V_{FF}^{-1} (F - \mu_F) \text{ and } V_{RR} - V_{RF} V_{FF}^{-1} V_{FR}$$

respectively. Hence:

$$E[R_p^*|F] = \{\mu_R + V_{RF} V_{FF}^{-1}(F - \mu_F)\}^T V_{RR}^{-1} A_S (A_S^T V_{RR}^{-1} A_S)^{-1} b_S$$
$$+ \theta \{\mu_R + V_{RF} V_{FF}^{-1}(F - \mu_F)\}^T \{V_{RR}^{-1} - V_{RR}^{-1} A_S$$
$$\times (A_S^T V_{RR}^{-1} A_S)^{-1} A_S^T V_{RR}^{-1}\} F$$

This function is, like that in equation (17.4), piecewise linear in risk appetite θ. However, it is no longer necessarily true that the slope of the conditional expected value[5] is always non-negative, even though the matrix

$$V_{RR}^{-1} - V_{RR}^{-1} A_S (A_S^T V_{RR}^{-1} A_S)^{-1} A_S^T V_{RR}^{-1}$$

is positive semi-definite. This suggests that a quadratic model in θ, of the form proposed in Section 17.2, may sometimes have a negative γ_2 coefficient.

Computation of unconditional expected values, that is expectations taken over the marginal distributions of returns, is more complicated. In CA it is shown that, when uncertainty in estimation of the mean μ is taken into account, the expected return and variance of a standard efficient set portfolio are respectively:

$$E[R_{port}^*] = \alpha_0 + \theta \alpha_1 + \beta_0 \theta, \quad V[R_{port}^*] = \alpha_2 + \theta^2 \alpha_1 + 2\theta \beta_1 + \theta^2 \beta_2$$

where $\alpha_{0,1,2}$ are as defined above. The beta terms are functions of the parameters of the assumed multivariate normal joint probability distribution of asset returns and of the estimates used in portfolio construction. The coefficients $\beta_{0,1,2}$ are defined in CA, where it is shown that β_0 and β_1 may take both positive and negative values. The equations above indicate therefore that, depending on the beta values, expected return and variance may be less or more than that predicted by standard theory.

If the constraints are equalities and the active set S holds for all values of $(F, V; \theta)$, expected value and variance may be computed using the methods in CA. For general portfolio selection with inequality constraints, it is impractical to compute exact expressions for the unconditional expected values. However, the discussion in the Appendix indicates that the relationship between $E[R_p^*]$ and θ is non-linear. The quadratic model is therefore proposed for this case as an approximation.

17.4   MODEL AND PROCESS

The model and estimation/prediction process is as follows. It is assumed that one-period ahead forecasts of the inputs and the corresponding returns are available for times 1 through T. At each time period, t say, the efficient frontier is reconstructed at a set of specified values of risk appetite, θ_i say, $i = 1(1)M$. The actual return of the portfolio, $R_{p,i,t}$ say, corresponding to risk θ_i is computed using the actual returns. The cross-sectional regression model:

$$R_{p,i,t} = \gamma_0 + \gamma_1\theta_i + \gamma_2\theta_i^2 + \varepsilon_{p,i,t}$$

is estimated using OLS. If the estimated coefficients in this model are denoted by g_0, g_1 and g_2 respectively, the portfolio return at risk level θ_i at time $(t + 1)$ is predicted as:

$$\hat{R}_{p,i,t} = g_0 + g_1\theta_i + g_2\theta_i^2$$

Cross-sectional regression based on OLS is used on pragmatic grounds. In Section 17.4, the reported regression diagnostics suggests that there is scope for a more refined estimation methodology. There are some grounds a priori for expecting the model coefficients $\{\gamma_j\}$ to be time varying. Investigation of this and implementation of a more sophisticated method is a possible future development.

17.5   DATA AND EMPIRICAL RESULTS

The model described above is exemplified by an asset allocation portfolio. This is based on six asset classes, as follows:

1. US   equity index;
2. US   bond index;
3. Japan   equity index;
4. Japan   bond index;
5. Europe   equity index;
6. Europe   bond index.

All returns are measured in Japanese yen. The data is monthly and runs from September 1989 to October 1997 inclusive, giving 98 months of forecasts. Forecasts of future expected returns are produced each month according to the convention above. Also estimated each month is the *VC* matrix of returns. The basic performance statistics for actual returns and for the corresponding forecasts are shown in Table 17.1 of Adcock (2002). Optimization is carried

Table 17.1   *Risk levels used in model*

0	0.001	0.0025	0.005	0.0075	0.01
0.025	0.05	0.075	0.1		
0.25	0.5	0.75	1		
2.5	5	7.5	10		

out relative to a benchmark portfolio, for which the percentage weights for the above six assets are 9, 6, 40, 30, 9 and 6 respectively.

The procedure described in Section 17.3 was implemented using 18 levels of risk appetite. These are as listed in Table 17.1.

Figure 17.2 shows the average forecast expected return at each level of risk. The average was computed over all 98 months. Also shown are the corresponding actual returns at the same level of risk. As the diagram shows, on average actual returns are markedly less than those forecast at the start of each period. This chart corresponds to Table 25.3 of Adcock (2002).

The shape of the forecast expected return curve is, as expected, non-decreasing in θ. The changing slope reflects the different constraints that are active at different levels of risk. The behaviour of the actual return curve is not unusual. The portions of the curve that are decreasing in θ reflect both the fact that the 98 months is a sample and the complex relationship between risk, constraints and the joint probability distribution of forecasts and returns.

The regressions were carried out for all 98 months as described in the Section above. Detailed regression diagnostics are omitted. These are available on request, but need to be interpreted with some care because of the small number of observations,[6] 18, in each cross-section. The key points from the diagnostics are: (1) the F ratio test was significant at the 5% point on 61 out of 98 months; (2) a Bera–Jarque test of normality of the fitted residuals was significant at the 5% in only two months; but (3) the Durbin–Watson statistic

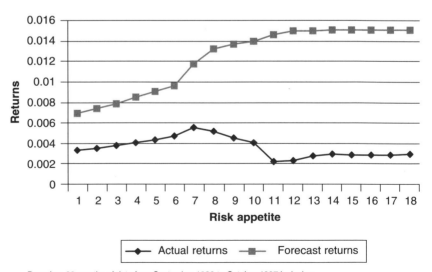

Based on 98 months of data from September 1989 to October 1997 inclusive.
All returns and forecasts measured in Japanese yen.

Figure 17.2 *Forecast and actual returns along the efficient frontier*

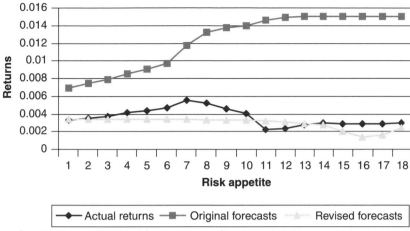

Based on 98 months of data from September 1989 to October 1997 inclusive.
All returns and forecasts measured in Japanese yen.

Figure 17.3 *Forecast actual returns and revised forecasts along the efficient frontier*

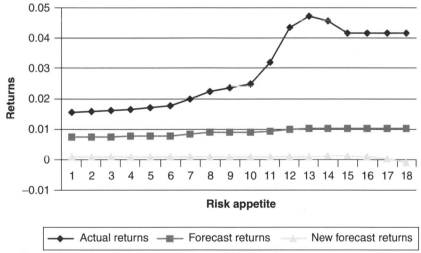

Based on 98 months of data from September 1989 to October 1997 inclusive.
All returns and forecasts measured in Japanese yen.

Figure 17.4 *Example of actual returns forecasts and revised forecasts for a single month*

provided evidence of cross-sectional correlation in the residuals. The 37 non-significant F ratios suggest that for 37 out of 98 months the forecasts had no signal capable of exploitation by the optimization process.

Figure 17.3 shows forecasts and actual returns, together with the revised forecasts produced by the quadratic model.

As the figure shows, on average over the 98 months, the forecasts generated by the model predict actual returns more accurately than the original forecasts. This should not be taken to imply that predictions for a single month will always be as accurate. Indeed Figure 17.4 gives an example of a month where they are not. However, it does suggest that the quadratic model has the capability to predict actual average returns of portfolios along the efficient frontier.

17.6   CONCLUSIONS

This chapter presents a cross-sectional model that may be used to compute more accurate predictions of actual portfolio return. A similar approach could be employed to make revised predictions of portfolio volatility.

The modelling methodology used in this chapter is OLS. Although OLS is effective, at least for the data in the study reported here, the regression diagnostics suggest that it may be a sub-optimal estimation methodology. Another potential development recognizes that the shape of the efficient frontier changes as time progresses. There is some scope for considering a methodology, such as the Kalman filter, which would allow the dynamics to be modelled.

As noted in the introduction, this methodology does not lead explicitly to improved forecasts. It does, however, give information about the performance of forecasts. This is one of the inputs to the process of forecast improvement.

17.7   APPENDIX: EFFECT OF ESTIMATION ERROR IN μ

It is assumed that the return vector R and the vector of forecasts F have a joint multivariate normal distribution with mean vector and VC matrix as defined in Section 17.3. For the general portfolio selection problem at Equation (17.1), the optimal weights are:

$$
\begin{aligned}
w^* &= V_{RR}^{-1} A_S (A_S^T V_{RR}^{-1} A_S)^{-1} b_S \\
&\quad + \theta \{ V_{RR}^{-1} - V_{RR}^{-1} A_S (A_S^T V_{RR}^{-1} A_S)^{-1} A_S^T V_{RR}^{-1} \} F \\
&= w^* (F; \theta, S)
\end{aligned}
$$

Actual portfolio return is given by:

$$
\begin{aligned}
R_p^* &= R^T V_{RR}^{-1} A_S (A_S^T V_{RR}^{-1} A_S)^{-1} b_S \\
&\quad + \theta R^T \{ V_{RR}^{-1} - V_{RR}^{-1} A_S (A_S^T V_{RR}^{-1} A_S)^{-1} A_S^T V_{RR}^{-1} \} F
\end{aligned}
$$

Computation of expected return and variance is done in two stages. First, expectations are computed over the conditional distribution of R given F. Second, expectations are computed of the distribution of F.

1. Expectations over the distribution of R given F

The conditional distribution of R given F is multivariate normal with mean vector and VC matrix given in Section 17.3. As already noted:

$$E[R_p^*|F] = \{\mu_R + V_{RF}V_{FF}^{-1}(F - \mu_F)\}^T V^{-1}A_S(A_S^T V^{-1}A_S)^{-1}b_S$$
$$+ \theta\{\mu_R + V_{RF}V_{FF}^{-1}(F - \mu_F)\}^T \{V^{-1} - V^{-1}A_S$$
$$\times (A_S^T V^{-1}A_S)^{-1}A_S^T V^{-1}\}F$$

Assuming that forecasts are unbiased, i.e.

$$\mu_F = \mu_R = \mu, \text{ say;}$$

this may expressed as:

$$E[R_p^*|F] = \alpha_{0,S} + \theta\alpha_{1,S} + (F - \mu)^T h_S + \theta(F - \mu)^T K_S(F - \mu)$$

where, using the definition of $w^*()$ above:

$$h_S = V_{RF}V_{FF}^{-1}w^*(\mu; \theta, S) + \theta\{V_{RR}^{-1} - V_{RR}^{-1}A_S$$
$$\times (A_S^T V_{RR}^{-1}A_S)^{-1}A_S^T V_{RR}^{-1}\}\mu$$
$$K_S = V_{RF}V_{FF}^{-1}\{V_{RR}^{-1} - V_{RR}^{-1}A_S(A_S^T V_{RR}^{-1}A_S)^{-1}A_S^T V_{RR}^{-1}\}$$

2. Expectations over the distribution of F

The active set (A_S, b_S) at the solution will be determined by the values of F, θ and V. If the inactive constraints are denoted by the set $\overline{S},$[7] the optimal weights satisfy:

$$A_{\overline{S}}^T w^* > b_{\overline{S}}$$

This may be written as:

$$\theta A_{\overline{S}}^T\{V_{RR}^{-1} - V_{RR}^{-1}A_S(A_S^T V_{RR}^{-1}A_S)^{-1}A_S^T V_{RR}^{-1}\}F > b_{\overline{S}}$$
$$- A_{\overline{S}}^T V_{RR}^{-1}A_S(A_S^T V_{RR}^{-1}A_S)^{-1}b_S$$

In principle, the probability of this inequality in F may be computed. It is a function, inter alia, of θ. The subspace of R^N defined by the above inequality will be denoted Ξ_S. With this notation, the expected value of R_p^* is:

$$E[R_p^*] = \sum_S \int_{\Xi_S} \{\alpha_{0,S} + \theta\alpha_{1,S} + (f - \mu)^T h_S$$
$$+ \theta(f - \mu)^T K_S(f - \mu)\}p(f)\,df$$

where $p()$ is the density function of the multivariate probability distribution of forecasts and integration is over the N variables in F. This is a non-linear function of θ in general.

REFERENCES

Adcock, C.J. (2000a) The Dynamic Control of Risk in Optimised Portfolios, *IMA Journal of Mathematics Applied in Business and Industry*, **11**, 127–138.

Adcock, C.J. (2002b) Portfolio Optimisation in *Neural Networks and the Financial Markets* (Taylor, J. and Shadbolt, J. eds), Springer Verlag.

Bawa, V., Brown, S.J. and Klein, R. (1979) Estimation Risk and Optimal Portfolio Choice, *Studies in Bayesian Econometrics*, **3**, North Holland, Amsterdam.

Best, M.J. and Grauer, R.R. (1991) On The Sensitivity of Mean-Variance-Efficient Portfolios to Changes in Asset Means: Some Analytical and Computational Results, *Review of Financial Studies*, **4**, 315–42.

Britten-Jones, M. (1999) The Sampling Error in Estimates of Mean-Variance Efficient Portfolio Weights, *Journal of Finance*, **54**, 655–72.

Chopra, V. and Ziemba, W.T. (1993) The Effect of Errors in Means, Variances and Covariances on Optimal portfolio Choice, *Journal of Portfolio Management*, Winter, 6–11.

Hillier, G. and Satchell, S.E. (2002) Some Exact Results for Efficient Portfolios with Given Returns. In *Advances in Portfolio Construction and Implementation* (Satchell, S.E. ed), Butterworth Heinemann, London.

Jobson, J.D. and Korkie, B. (1981) Estimation for Markowitz Efficient Portfolios, *Journal of the American Statistical Association*, **75**, 544–54.

Michaud, R.O. (1998) *Efficient Asset Management*, Harvard Business School Press, Boston.

Roll, R. (1977) A critique of the Asset Pricing Theory's Tests, *Journal of Financial Economics*, **4**, 349–57.

NOTES

1. This notation is in common use. Further details are in Adcock (2002), for example.
2. Multiplication by -1 turns an upper bound into a lower bound.
3. This is not necessarily true when the constraints are more complex. For example, an active constraint can be replaced by another as risk increases, or it can sometime be removed from the active set.
4. A similar analysis leads to a model for portfolio variance V^* which includes terms up to θ^4. Elimination of θ between the equations for expected return and variance gives the ex post efficient frontier.
5. This is the coefficient of θ.
6. The choice of 18 values is arbitrary. More observations along the discretized frontier could be obtained by using more values of θ.

7. From an operational perspective, these would be reduced to a set of $P < N$ linearly independent constraints.

ACKNOWLEDGEMENTS

I should like to thank Jimmy Shadbolt for allowing me to use the asset allocation portfolio data.

Index